William Harris

A Complete Collection of All the Marine Treaties Subsisting

between Great-Britain and France, Spain, Portugal. Commencing in the year 1546,

and including the definitive treaty of 1763.

William Harris

A Complete Collection of All the Marine Treaties Subsisting
between Great-Britain and France, Spain, Portugal. Commencing in the year 1546, and including the definitive treaty of 1763.

ISBN/EAN: 9783337245238

Printed in Europe, USA, Canada, Australia, Japan

Cover: Foto ©ninafisch / pixelio.de

More available books at **www.hansebooks.com**

A COMPLETE COLLECTION

OF ALL THE

MARINE TREATIES

SUBSISTING BETWEEN

GREAT-BRITAIN

AND

FRANCE,	DENMARK,	MOROCCO,
SPAIN,	SWEDEN,	ALGIERS,
PORTUGAL,	SAVOY,	TRIPOLI,
AUSTRIA,	HOLLAND.	TUNIS, &c.
RUSSIA,		

Commencing in the Year 1546, and including the Definitive Treaty of 1763.

WITH AN

INTRODUCTORY DISCOURSE, explaining the Force and Meaning of the principal Articles.

The Whole forming

A copious Body of Instruction, for Commanders of Privateers, Letters of Marque, &c. in making legal Captures:

And exhibiting,

To the Merchant, a satisfactory Enumeration of those naval Stores and warlike Instruments, the Commerce of which, in Times of Hostility, is allowed or prohibited.

LONDON:

PRINTED FOR
D. STEEL, N°. 1, UNION-ROW, LITTLE TOWER-HILL;
And
J. MILLAN, CHARING-CROSS.
M.DCC.LXXIX.

PREFACE,

OR

Introductory Discourse.

SEVERAL very interesting Events in the present maritime War, have brought clearly before our Eyes the Importance of the following Extracts from the marine Treaties, and must needs have convinced every Person concerned in Commerce and Navigation, of the Necessity incumbent on him, to be acquainted with the Force and Extent of the Articles contained therein. The Use of them to the Commanders in the Royal Navy has been long observed; so that the Lords of the Admiralty have taken Care to print them for that Purpose, from Time to Time, with such Alterations and Additions as were made by succeeding Treaties. But these Copies in Quarto are reserved solely for the Use of such Commanders, and distributed to them alone, exclusive of all other Persons whatever. It was presumed, therefore, that an Edition of them, reduced, as this is, to an easy Price, would be no unacceptable present to the Publick, especially as it comes attended with some Remarks, which are conceived to be necessary for the right understanding of them, and which are not to be found in the Quarto Book.

The Want of some such Kind of Comment, as it may be fitly called, has been very sensibly felt of late, in regard to one of these Treaties with the *Dutch:* this shall be considered in it's proper Place. The Method of the present Collection directs us to begin with those between *England* and *France.* At the Head of which, the famous Treaty of Commerce, concluded at *Utrecht* in 1713, stands as still subsisting, since it has not been made void by any subsequent Treaty. Yet it imports to know, that as some Articles, particularly the IXth, could not, by the express Tenor of them, take Place without an Act of Parliament, and no such Act being ever passed; the *French,* notwithstanding these Articles as well as the rest were signed by the Plenipotentiaries on both Sides, shew little or no Regard to any of them, making this Defect in some, a Pretence, as it suits their Interest, to reject the whole. It is not our Business at present to enter into the Merits of this Affair: By turning to the Remark at the End of the Supplement to this Treaty *, the Reader will find, that it was not confirmed by that of *Aix la Chapelle;* whence it follows, that by the Treaty of *Utrecht* in 1713, which is confirmed in the IIId Article of the Treaty at *Aix la Chapelle,* can only be meant the Treaty of Peace and Friendship.

It may well be thought not a little astonishing, how it should come to pass, that a solemn Treaty, signed in due Form by all the *British* Plenipotentiaries, under the Direction of the Ministry, should escape a Ratification, in such

* In p. 246.

Articles

Articles as required it, by a *British* Parliament, while the same Miniſtry continued. This Miſcarriage was entirely owing to the mal-Formation of the Treaty itſelf, which happened to be ſo unluckily tempered, as to pleaſe neither of the contracting Parties; and on our Side, the Cry againſt it grew ſo loud, that the Miniſtry found their utmoſt Efforts, to ſway the Parliament in it's Favour, utterly baffled. Lord *Bolingbroke*, who, 'tis well known, had the Direction and Management of this whole Affair, ingenuouſly owns, that this Peace, in general, was leſs anſwerable to the Succeſs of the War, than it might, and ought to have been; that it was driven forward by the Zeal of particular Men, in their ſeveral Provinces, though they were not backed by the concurrent Force of the whole Adminiſtration, nor had the common Helps of Advice 'till it was too late, 'till the very End of the Negotiations; even in Matters, ſuch as that of *Commerce*, which they could not be ſuppoſed to underſtand; that when it was laid before the Parliament, ſome even of the Miniſtry grew nice about the Conſtruction of the Articles, and could come up to no direct Approbation: ſo that " the very Work, ſays he, which ought " to have been the Baſis of our Strength, was " in Part demoliſhed before our Eyes, and we " were ſtoned with the Ruins of it *." The weak and unſettled Condition of the Duke of *Orleans*, who had uſurped the ſole Regency of *France*, contrary to the Eſtabliſhment made by *Lewis* XIV. juſt before his Death, opened an Opportunity of mending this Matter by a

* Lord *Bolingbroke*'s Letter to Sir *W. Wyndham*.

new Treaty; but that was neglected by our succeeding Ministry: And having thus once passed the Season, when it was in our Power, we never found another to repair the Fault. This, in the Course of Events, became out of our Power, and the unhappy State of our Affairs at the Treaty of *Aix la Chapelle*, turned up the Reverse of that Face which had been seen at *Utrecht*. In 1748, the Treaty of Commerce was never mentioned, as if grown obsolete; a Sort of tacit Acknowledgment of that Right which the *French* had assumed of rejecting it. All that we then aimed at was, to obtain a Confirmation of the Treaty of Peace; and as this was a Concomitant of the other, we shall now proceed to take it under our Consideration.

This, indeed, is of greater Importance than it's Companion, relating purely to Commerce; of such Importance, as to be made a Basis for all our Treaties since, not only with *France*, but with other Kingdoms and States. And yet some of the most interesting Stipulations in this Treaty are so loosely worded, that they gave Rise to those Disputes and Animosities, which proved the Fuel of the present War with *France*.

By the XIIth Article of this Treaty,* His Most Christian Majesty stipulated to yield and make over to our Nation all *Nova-Scotia* or *Acadie*, comprehended within it's ancient Boundaries. This is the Expression, and there needs no Comment to shew it's Ambiguity, without some further Description to ascertain these Boundaries. Hence a Door was left open for the Disputes which followed, and which remain

* Pag. 31.

undecided

undecided to this Hour. The *English*, on one Hand, extending these Boundaries northward to the River of *St Lawrence*, westward as far as their own Settlements, and to the Sea on every other Side; while the same Boundaries are confined by the *French* within the narrow Limits of the *Peninsula*, as being particularly called *Acadie*. 'Tis well worth While, on Account of future Negotiations, to mark some of the unhappy Consequences, which flowed from this fatal Neglect, in drawing so momentous a Stipulation: A Neglect which was but ill salved, by the Expedient of referring these ancient Boundaries to be settled and determined by Commissaries, forthwith to be named on each Side; which, in reality, was no better than a Piece of After-Wit, as was found too late on our Side; whilst our Enemies thereby got Time to breathe, to repair the broken State of their Affairs, and revive that all-grasping Spirit, which had been long curbed and kept under by the superior Force of *Marlborough*'s Arms.

Whether any Commissaries were appointed, or ever met, is not worth the Trouble of an Enquiry; since it is but too certain, that nothing effectual was done towards a Determination of the Point. On the contrary, four Years afterwards, in 1717, we saw a triple Alliance concluded between *Great-Britain*, *France*, and *Holland*, without the least Mention, much less a Regulation, of this Dispute. We had, indeed, been suffered to keep what we had acquired in the preceding War, *viz.* Possession of the *Peninsula*, or *Acadie* properly so called. Accordingly, a Governor was appointed, and sent

sent thither with a Regiment, who obliged the *French* Inhabitants there to submit to our Government, and take the Oaths to his present Majesty after his Accession. Yet, being allowed to continue under Magistrates of their own chusing, they kept a much closer Correspondence with the Governor of *Cape-Breton* than they did with ours; called themselves, and were called by our People, the *Neutral French*; and, as soon as the War broke out with *France*, they took every Opportunity to shew, that they were true and loyal *Frenchmen*; who looked upon the forced Oath they had taken to our King as no way binding the Conscience. However, the continental Part of *Nova-Scotia*, which was the only Part in Dispute, continued in a State of Neutrality 'till the Treaty of *Aix la Chapelle* in 1748: But our Affairs then were so far from being mended, that they grew worse, and even soon became desperate. The same Things were repeated as had passed at *Utrecht*. The Treaty of Peace concluded there, and consequently the XIIth Article of it, was confirmed without any Revision; and all Disputes with *France* left again to be settled in a subsequent Negotiation.

'Tis foreign to our Design, nor indeed have we any Inclination, to set forth the unlucky Turn in our Affairs, which obliged our Ministers to accept of these Terms, though they had sufficient Reason to expect no good Effect from such a Negotiation; and the Behaviour of *France* very soon furnished a convincing Proof, that nothing was to be expected from any Negotiation. 'Tis true, they were actually

set

set on Foot, and the Commissaries on both Sides met, according to the Agreement, at *Paris*. *Great-Britain* likewise soon after sent a Colony, which had been hitherto neglected, to the Peninsula of *Acadie*; a Garrison was built, and the Town of *Hallifax* planned, which presently began to shew itself on the Bay of *Chebucto*. But in the mean Time, we had no sooner restored the Island of *Cape Breton* to the *French*, than their Governors in that Island made it their Business to encourage the *Indians* of *Nova-Scotia* to attack our infant Colony, and to murder or captivate such of our People as they met with straggling at any Distance from the Garrison; they were likewise furnished with Arms and Ammunition, and even with *French* Leaders and Directors. This, however, was done privately, in a covert Manner; and when Complaints were made upon this Head, instead of Redress there came evasive Answers, under such Pretences as were every one of them known to be false.

They went more openly to work the next Year, 1749, when a large Body of regular Troops and *Canada* Militia were dispatched by that Governor, to take Post on the Mouth of the River *Chignecto*, where it opens into the Bay of the same Name, and to erect a Fort there; though, when the Commissaries were appointed, it had been expresly agreed, that, during their Negotiation, neither Side should make any new Settlement, or erect any new Fortification, in any of those Parts of *America*, the Right to which was controverted between the two Nations. This Fortification was no sooner finished, on the North Side of *Chignecto* River,

River, than the Design of raising it came into View. The *French* Inhabitants, who were very numerous, and had a large Village upon the South Side of that River, notwithstanding their Oaths of Allegiance, immediately broke out in open Rebellion; inclosed themselves within strong Intrenchments; nor could they be reduced by such of our Troops, as were sent under the Command of Major *Lawrence* for that Purpose; for, being driven from their Intrenchments, they set Fire to their Houses, and, with every Thing that belonged to them, passed over to the other Side of the River, where they were received by their Countryman M. *Corne*, who declared that he would, and did actually, protect them, having drawn up his Troops there for that Purpose. Whereupon, Major *Lawrence* being restrained by his Orders from pursuing them over the River, or attacking their insolent Protectors, was obliged to content himself with raising a Fort at the Bottom of the Bay, upon the South Side of *Chignecto* River, which from him was called *St Lawrence-*Fort.

All this while, the Commissaries continued negotiating at *Paris*, without any proper Notice taken, either of the notorious Infraction of the Neutrality by one Side, or of the religious Observance of it by the other. The Consequence of this profound Silence was, a Resolution of the *French*, to take it for a tacit Acknowledgment of their Right to the whole continental Part of *Nova-Scotia*, lying North of the Bay of *Fundy* and *Chignecto* River. Upon this Principle, besides the last-mentioned Fort at the Mouth of that River, which they called

Beau-

Beau-sejour, they proceeded presently after to erect another upon the East End of the *Isthmus*, at the Bottom of a Bay, called by them *Baie Verte*, or *Green Bay*; by which Means, they made themselves entirely Masters of the *Isthmus*, and thereby kept a Passage open for the *Indians* to pour in from the *Continent* against our Colony in the *Peninsula*. Nor did they rest here, but about the same Time began to erect another Fort at the Mouth of *St John*'s River, upon the Bay of *Fundy*; by which they opened a Communication and a Water-Carriage from that Bay, almost quite to the River *St Lawrence*, and very near to *Quebec*.

These bitter Fruits were the direct Produce of suffering the Stipulation, whereby *Nova-Scotia* was ceded to us, to pass in general Terms only, leaving the Boundaries of that Country to be settled by Commissaries afterwards. But the Mischief was not confined within any Boundaries of that Country; the pernicious Consequences of it were presently felt on the *North-West* Borders of *Virginia*, where the same Cause had indeed long before produced the same Effect. By the XVth Article of the same Treaty of *Utrecht*, the *French* had obliged themselves not to give any Hindrance or Molestation to any of the *Indian* Nations, who were then subject to the Dominion of *Great-Britain*, or Friends to the same, without expresly enumerating or describing what Nations these were; which again was left to be done by Commissaries. This Neglect was the more dangerous, as *Lewis* XIV. had made a Grant of the *Missisipi* River to one of his Ministers, Mr *Crouzat*, the preceding Year, 1712; in which

which it was expresly declared, that the Intention of making a Settlement in that Country was, to establish, by Means of the great Lakes of *Canada*, an inland Communication between the Rivers *Miſſiſipi* and *St Lawrence*. And though, upon the Death of *Lewis* XIV. their Affairs were too much embroiled at Home to suffer them to look Abroad for a While; yet, after the Concluſion of the Triple Alliance in 1717, already mentioned, a *Miſſiſipi* Company was established the same Year, and a Colony sent either that or the next Year; by whom the Town of *New Orleans* was planned, and begun to be erected upon the East Side of the *Miſſiſipi*; between which and the River *St Lawrence* they resolved to carry their designed inland Communication, by the Way of the River *Ilianois*; from one of the Heads of which there is but a short Land-Carriage, to a River that runs into the great Lake *Michigan*.

But, for the Safety of Paſſengers by this Route, it was neceſſary to have a Fort at the great Cataract of *Niagara*, the Country round which was poſſeſſed by the *Iroquois*, who would never conſent to the erecting such a Fort; and, to compel them to submit, would be a direct Violation of the said XVth Article of the Treaty of *Utrecht*.

However, both these Difficulties were got over, by watching proper Opportunities. After a fruitleſs Attempt in 1720 or 1721, which was defeated by the *Iroquois*, they compleated their Deſign in 1725; having, by fair Words and fine Promises, cajoled many of the *Indians* not to oppose them: And so calling them their Friends

Friends and not ours, by this Means the Stipulation of the Treaty with us was evaded; and, at the same Time, they sent so strong a Party upon that Service, as the refractory *Indians* not daring to encounter, a Fort of such Strength was erected, and so well provided with Artillery, that the *Indians* of themselves alone could never think of reducing it; and none of our Governors in *America* were ever impowered to assist them.

This Philosophic Patience on our Part, probably encouraged them to proceed further; and, having first attempted in vain to make a Settlement in 1726 upon the East Side of the Head of the Lake *Corlaer*, or *Champlain*, as they call it, within the Territory of *Massachuset*'s Bay in *New England* *; they began another on the West Side of the said Lake, within the Province of *New York*. This succeeded to their Wish; and, in 1730 or 1731, their Settlement was executed at *Crown-Point*, and the Fort built, which they called Fort *Frederick*; and which they afterwards made one of the strongest Forts in *America*. This was the bad State of our Affairs in these Parts, when the Treaty commenced at *Aix la Chapelle*. But after we had submitted to that dishonourable Peace, they soon became much worse.

It was well known to the *French*, that the easiest and shortest Way of establishing their designed inland Communication, between the Rivers *Mississipi* and *St Lawrence*, was by the

---

* They desisted, upon receiving a Message from this Colony, threatning otherwise immediately to attack them.

River *Ohio*, as it is one of the moſt navigable Rivers in *North-America*, and as the head Branches of it paſs very near the Lake *Erie*; but, as almoſt the whole Country through which this River holds it's Courſe, being poſſeſſed by the Five Nations called *Iroquois*, or elſe by the *Cherokees*, both of whom were Friends to the *Engliſh* long after the Peace of *Utrecht*, the *French* durſt not at firſt think of taking that Route, how much ſoever they could wiſh for it; but after this Treaty, and our Submiſſion to the Encroachments in *Nova-Scotia* conſequent upon it, they might well begin to think, as they did, that the long wiſhed for Opportunity was come, to make themſelves Maſters of the River *Ohio*, and thereby eſtabliſh that juſt-mentioned ſhort and eaſy Communication by Water, almoſt the whole Way from the Mouth of the *Miſſiſipi* to that of *St Lawrence*. For this Purpoſe they built a Fort upon the South Side of Lake *Erie*, and about fifteen Miles South from thence they built another, upon a navigable River called *Beef* River, one of the Branches of the *Ohio*; by which two Forts, and their Fort at *Niagara*, which they had very much improved, together with a new Fort they had erected at the Conflux of the Rivers *Ohio* and *Wabache*, they compleated their Deſign; for they might now travel and tranſport Goods by Water from *Quebec* to *New Orleans*, and back again, without any Land-Carriage, except about ten or fifteen Miles at *Niagara*, in order to avoid the great Cataract in that River; and fifteen Miles from their Fort, upon the South Side of Lake *Erie*, to their Fort upon

Beef

Beef River; and two or three Portages, of a few Yards only, in order to avoid the Falls or ripling Streams in the two great Rivers *St Lawrence* and *Ohio*.

In the mean Time, on our Side, a Company consisting of some Gentlemen in *Virginia*, and some Merchants in *London*, was established in 1749, by Charter, under the Name of the *Ohio* Company; to which was granted 600000 Acres of Land upon that River. And, in 1751, a Surveyor was sent to lay out these Acres in the best Lands there, and such as were most convenient for the *Indian* Trade. We had been for many Years before possessed of some Settlements in this Country, by the Consent of the *Iroquois Indians*, to whom it belonged; but these *Indians* presently grew jealous of this Company, as likely to become dangerous Rivals in their Trade, and from Friends, as they were at the Time of concluding the Treaty of *Utrecht*, and had continued so ever since, they now sided against us, and went over to the *French*, who failed not to make the most of this Advantage; and being provided with a sufficient Number of regular Troops to drive us out of this Country, the Governor of *Canada* now acquainted our Governors of *New York* and *Pensylvania*, that our *Indian* Traders had encroached on their Territories, by trading with their *Indians*, and that if they did not forbear, he should be obliged to seize them wherever they were found.

This was the first Time, that either Side had pretended to an exclusive Trade with any *Indians*, even those that were declared Friends

or

or Allies of the other: It being expressly stipulated by the XVth Article of the Treaty of *Utrecht*, now under Consideration, "That, on both Sides, the two Nations should enjoy the full Liberty of going and coming among the *Indians* of either Side, on Account of Trade: And that the Natives of the *Indian* Countries should, with the same Liberty, resort as they pleased to the *British* and *French* Colonies, for promoting Trade on the one Side and the other, without any Molestation or Hinderance, either on the *British* Subjects or the *French*." These, however, in 1751, put the Menace in Execution, and seized three of our *Indian* Traders, whom they found trading among the *Twigtees*, a numerous Nation, inhabiting the Country westward of the *Ohio*, and next beyond the Country of the *Iroquois*. Notwithstanding these last had again changed Sides, and joined in Friendship with us, when they saw the *French* began to build their two Forts beforementioned, on the Side of the Lake *Erie*, and upon *Beef* River, in Hopes of having those Forts demolished by us; yet no effectual Notice being taken of this Encroachment on our Side, the *French* after this began to seize and plunder every *British* Trader they found upon any Part of the River *Ohio*; and a Messenger being sent, in 1753, from the Governor of *Virginia*, to the Commander of these two Forts, to summon him to retire, and demand a Reason for his hostile Proceedings, he returned for Answer, "That he knew of no Hostilities that had been committed; That he could receive

"receive no Orders, nor would obey any, but those of His Most Christian Majesty, or his Governor of *Canada*: That as the Country belonged to the King of *France*, no *Englishman* had a Right to trade upon any of it's Rivers, and therefore that he would, according to his Orders, seize and send Prisoners to *Canada* every *Englishman* that should attempt to trade upon the *Ohio*, or any of it's Branches." Nor were these vain or empty Threats; for all our People were soon after driven from their Settlements upon that River, and the *French*, early the next Year, built another Fort upon it, called Fort *du Quesne*; and, before the Expiration of the Year, were joined by the *Indian* Inhabitants on the Banks of that River, who actually declared War against us *.

All this While, the Negotiations were still carried on for settling all Disputes amicably, though Mr Shirley, the chief of our Commissaries, had retired from *Paris*, the preceding Year, 1753; yet the Ambassadors continued at the respective Courts, and by their Means we continued to negotiate 'till the Death of the Earl of *Albemarle*, our Ambassador at *Paris*, which happend there on the twenty-second of *December*, 1754. This was followed the next Year by an open Rupture between the Nations, the Events of which produced a Declaration of the present War on our Side, *May* 17, 1756.

Thus the Lion was roused at last, and, by exerting his natural Strength, he has made his

* This was done in Resentment of a Treaty concluded this Year, between our Colonies and the other *Iroquois Indians* who had no lands there, to purchase the Estates of them on the Banks of that River, without their Consent.

a Aggressors

Aggressors sufficiently sensible of their Imprudence in rouzing him.

Next to *France* follow the Treaties with *Spain*; among which, the principal are those of 1667 and 1670, both confirmed by the Treaty of Commerce at *Utrecht* in 1713. By the Xth Article of the former it is stipulated, that *British* Ships, sailing towards, or entring into, the Dominions or Ports of the King of *Spain*, shall not be subject to any Visitation or Search *; and the like Favour is granted on both Sides, by the Xth Article of the latter, to Ships forced by Distress, into any of the Places, Harbours, &c. in *America*, which are allowed free Ingress and Egress, without any Molestation or Impediment †. But after the Treaty of *Utrecht*, our *West-India* Traders, especially at *Jamaica*, carrying on an illicit Trade to the *Spanish* Main, for Gold, Silver, and other Commodities, whose Exportation thence was prohibited by the *Spaniard*; this Infraction of the Treaties, after several Years Practice, raised the Indignation of that Court to such a Degree, that, not being able to restrain their own Subjects from joining in it by the severest Punishments, they ordered their *Guarda Costas* to visit and search any of our Ships, which they should find in those Parts, though sailing upon the Ocean, and out of the utmost Limits of the Jurisdiction of their Ports or Coast. These Orders were accordingly executed with Severity, and even with Cruelty, several

* See p. 52, 53.
† See p. 65.

of our trading Veſſels being plundered, and ſome of the Maſters barbarouſly and inhumanly treated.

Hereupon, Complaints being made on our Side, a Negotiation was ſet on Foot, in order to ſettle the Matter amicably; but this proving ineffectual, Recourſe was had to the *ultima ratio Regum*, and we declared War againſt *Spain* in 1739. The War terminated in the Treaty of *Aix la Chapelle*, in 1748; where, though we obtained a Confirmation of the Treaty of 1670, which had been omitted in all the preceding Treaties, of 1715, 1721, and 1729; yet we were not able to oblige the *Spaniards* to renounce, in a ſolemn Manner, the Right they claimed to ſearch our Ships in the Seas of *America*, and to ſeize upon and confiſcate them, if they found on Board any *Spaniſh* Money, or any Goods which they were pleaſed to call contraband or prohibited. So that the Treaty of 1670 not being confirmed by that of 1750, this Point is left undecided, and we are ſtill negotiating with *Spain* about it.

Some Diſputes have alſo ariſen about the true Force and Extent of the XXIſt and XXIId Articles of the Treaty in 1667, which declare in general, " That the Subjects of the two
" Crowns reſpectively, ſhall have Liberty to
" traffick throughout all Countries, cultivating
" Peace, Amity, or Neutrality, with either
" of them; and that the ſaid Liberty ſhall in
" no wiſe be interrupted by any Hindrance or
" Diſturbance whatſoever, by Reaſon of any
" Hoſtility, which may be between either of
" the ſaid Crowns, and any other King-
" doms

"doms *." It has been alledged, that the Liberty here stipulated, fairly extends so far, as to grant a Right to carry freely the Effects of an Enemy; but surely this is stretching the Article beyond it's true Intent and Meaning. The Liberty of Traffick to the Countries of the Enemies of *Great-Britain*, as thus in general stipulated, can be explained to grant to the Subjects of the Crown of *Spain*, no other Right but that of carrying on, without any injurious Molestation or Disturbance, the ordinary Means of Traffick, with their own Produce or Property, on their own Account; provided that in Case of War they do not, under this Pretence, attempt to screen the Effects of the Enemy; and on Condition also, that they carry not any Implements of War, or whatever else, according to the Nature of their respective Situations, or the Circumstances of the Case, may be necessary to such Enemies for their Defence. 'Tis true, this Liberty is no more than what is allowed by the Principles of natural Equity, or the Law of Nations, and consequently, at first Sight, may seem not to require a particular Stipulation. But History will inform us †, that amid the Irregularities of War, the Rules of Equity in this Respect were not always enough regarded, and that many Governments, in Time of War, did often most licentiously disturb, and sometimes prohibit totally, the Commerce of neutral Nations with their Enemies. Hence it

* See p. 56.
† Grotii Annales & Historiæ de Rebus Belgicis, lib iii.

became

became neceſſary to fix and determine what was the general Law of Nations, by particular Treaties; and hence it is, that about the middle of the laſt Century, when the commercial Regulations which now ſubſiſt between the *European* Powers firſt began to be formed, we find Articles, to the ſame Purpoſe as thoſe abovementioned in our Treaty with *Spain*, aſſerting in general a Right to trade unmoleſted with the Enemies of each other *. Theſe are uſually placed among thoſe Articles of general Import, which are commonly firſt laid down in Treaties †, as the Baſis on which the ſubſequent Stipulations are founded, eſtabliſhing ſuch Privileges as the Rule alone would not admit. And among the reſt, ſome Nations, we ſhall ſee preſently ‖, granted mutually to each other, by new and expreſs Articles, the Right of carrying freely the Property of their reſpective Enemies. Theſe laſt Articles, therefore, muſt be conſidered, as wholly diſtinct in their Nature from thoſe beforementioned, and in their Meaning totally different. The firſt are in Affirmance of an old Rule; The laſt create a new Privilege. Thoſe only confirm a Right, which was determined by the Law of Nations before; Theſe make an Exception to

---

* So in the Treaty of Commerce between *France* and *Holland*, Art. XXVI, XXVII. Treaty of Commerce between *England* and *Holland*, Feb. 17, 1608, Art I. and II. Idem, between *England* and *Holland*, Dec. 1, 1674. Art. I. and II. Treaty of Commerce between *England* and *France*, Feb. 24, 1677, Art. I and II.

† See the Treaties referred to in the preceding Note.

‖ In conſidering the Treaties between *England* and the *States General*.

that Law. Upon the whole then it follows, that by a general Stipulation in Favour of Trade with the Enemies of another Power, such as is made by the XXIst and XXIId Articles of the Treaty of *Madrid* in 1667, the contracting Parties never intended to imply a Right to carry freely the Effects of that Enemy; and that to establish such a Right, it is necessary to have it expressly mentioned.

By the XVth Article of the Treaty of *Aix la Chapelle* *, it appears, that the Treaty of the *Assiento*, signed at *Madrid*, on the 27th of *March*, 1713, and the Article of the Annual Ship, were confirmed for the four Years, during which the Enjoyment was lost, after the Commencement of the preceding War. But it must be observed, that since the Treaty of *Aix la Chapelle*, the whole *Assiento* Treaty has been made void by that in 1750.

We come now to the Treaties with the *States-General*. Among these it was thought proper to give the first Place to that most important maritime Regulation of 1674, which has lately given Rise, upon Occasion of our present War with *France*, to so warm a Contest between the two most natural Friends in *Europe*, as would apparently have ended in a Rupture, had not some lucky Incidents in the Course of the War hitherto prevented it. By the VIIIth Article of this Treaty it is agreed, we see †, " That all which shall be found on Board the

---

* See p. 47.
† In p. 90.

" Vessels

" Veſſels belonging to the Subjects of either
" of the contracting Parties, ſhall be accounted
" clear and free, although the whole Lading,
" or any Part thereof, ſhall by juſt Title of
" Property belong to the Enemies of the other,
" contraband Goods only excepted." Here, again, as in the Treaty of *Utrecht*, the Diſpute is entirely owing to the general Terms of the Stipulation; one Side taking them in their full Extent, while the other inſiſts upon ſuch Reſtrictions and Limitations to be put upon them, as right Reaſon and the Nature of Things neceſſarily require. Indeed, the Privilege, as it is expreſſed, is of ſuch prodigious Advantage to the *Dutch*, and ſo very little, if any, to *England*, that it is well worth while to enquire, how it came to be admitted by an *Engliſh* Miniſtry into any Treaty. This Enquiry is the more intereſſing, as it will alſo help to lead us into the true Intent and Purport of it.

For the original Springs of this Article, we muſt go as far back as to the Year 1648, when the *United Provinces* erected themſelves into a ſovereign State by the Treaty of *Munſter* *. From this Time the Commercial Provinces obtained the Lead among them; whence the Intereſts of Trade became of courſe the chief Object of their Councils; and the Views of their Miniſters were directed to eſtabliſh, upon a firm footing, that extenſive Traffick, which had ſupported them through all their Diſtreſſes, and to the Effects of which they

---

* See Supplement, p. 263.

principally

principally attributed all their Power and Freedom. Among the several Branches of Trade, that of Freightage, or the Carrying-Trade, demanded their Attention above all others; besides being a profitable Branch of Traffick in itself, it was the principal Basis of their naval Power, upon which the Security of the rest depended. This Trade was first taken up by the *Hanse Towns*, who, in the Time of our *Edward* III. and before, were the greatest Freighters in the western Parts of *Europe* *. But the *Dutch* had now long succeeded these *Hanseatic* Traders, and long Possession had furnished them with great Numbers of Ships and Sailors. This was the Effect of an uncommon Parsimony and Industry, the natural Endowments of their People; whence, being contented with small Profits, they were enabled to carry the Manufactures and other Produce of each Country, even cheaper than the Natives themselves could do.

With a People so happily tempered for this Branch of Trade, every patriot Minister must needs be prompted to study how to perpetuate the Monopoly of it to his Country. Accordingly, a Plan was framed to carry it to it's full Extent, in these two Points: First, that no Nation should grant to it's own Natives any Privilege, in Relation to Freightage, which the People of *Holland* should not equally enjoy: And secondly, That in Case of any other Nation's engaging in War, they should enjoy, as Neutrals, the Right of carrying the Property

* Rymer's Fœdera, Tom. IV. p 361.

of it's Enemies unmolested. I need not observe, that these Points once established, would make them entire Masters of all the Commerce of the World. The Number of their Ships and Sailors would be continually increasing; no other Nation besides had more Shipping than what was equal to the Carriage of it's own Manufactures; and even these would by Degrees dwindle away, as the *Dutch* Carriage was found the cheapest. No Wonder then, that we find the Regency of *Holland* labouring, with unabated Perseverance, through every Difficulty that arose, to obtain these two Points. Their great Minister *de Witte*, filled all his Instructions and Dispatches with every Argument and Motive that his active Mind could invent in Support of them *, and even appears willing to give up any temporary Advantage, to gain that, which, once acquired, would prove for Ages an everflowing Spring of Wealth, and consequently of Power too. I repeat it of Power too. Wealth, indeed, might, perhaps, at first be the only Object in their View; yet they could not be ignorant, that Power is the genuine Offspring of Wealth; and I chose to repeat it, since to this well-known Truth, may be fairly ascribed the ill Success of all their Attempts, to carry the first Point, which required an extreme Indolence and Inattention to this Truth in all other Nations.

To enter into a general Detail of their Negotiations on this Head, would be too tedious; let it suffice to relate the Conduct of *France*

---

* See his Letters printed at the *Hague* in 1722.

and

and *England* on the Occasion. Not many Years after the abovementioned Treaty of *Munster* in 1648, the Tax of fifty Sous per Ton was laid upon all foreign Shipping, by Mr *Fouquet* *, in *France*, with a View of encouraging and augmenting the Freightage of that Country, in Opposition to the *Dutch*. *Colbert*, the succeeding Minister, continued it; nor were the *Dutch* able to get it taken off in their Favour 'till the Peace of *Ryswic*, in 1697, when *France* found it necessary to give a larger Vent, by this Means, to her Manufactures. Every one knows the short Duration of the Peace of *Ryswic*, and since that Time she has regulated her Conduct, in remitting or preserving the Tax, as best suited the Interest of her Trade.

The *Dutch*, however, had better Success in the other Point of their Policy, *viz.* A Right, as Neutrals, of protecting the Effects of an Enemy. One Step towards it was obtained as early as the Year 1646, when, by a temporary Treaty, the neutral Vessel, and all the Effects of a Friend found on Board it, were agreed to be spared. This was confirmed and enlarged by a Declaration of the *French* King in 1651 †, and the Privilege was at length granted in it's full Extent, in the memorable Treaty of Defensive Alliance between the two Nations, in 1662: By the XXXVth Article of which Treaty it is reciprocally agreed, that " All

---

* This Minister was made Superintendant of the Finances in the Beginning of the Year 1653, and was succeeded by *Colbert* in 1661.

† In *De Witt*'s Letters, those from *Boreel*, in p. 77, 78.

" which

"which shall be found on Board the Vessels of either of the contracting Parties, although the whole or any Part thereof shall belong to an Enemy, shall be free." We see the Favour was not obtained 'till near twenty Years after the first Step had been laid towards it; and to obtain it, was one great Part of the *Dutch* Ambassador's, Mr *Boreel*'s, Employment, in his long Embassy at *Paris*; and no Doubt the Point was the more industriously laboured with *France*, in the View of urging it as an Argument to bring *England* to the like Compliance.

Here, indeed, lay the greatest Concern of *Holland*, as she apprehended this Nation to be her chief Rival in Trade. Here, therefore, she most exerted her Policy, in Regard to both her Maxims. As to the first, the Juncture appeared to be favourable enough in 1648, and some few Years afterwards. The Ignorance of the *English* Ministers in Point of Commerce, and the little Attention which they had paid to the Interests of it, had given such Advantages to the *Dutch*, that more Vessels of that Country were seen in the Ports of our Colonies, than even of our own. But in 1651, there happened an Event, which put us upon vindicating the Advantages of our own Industry and Produce to ourselves. *England* being lately become a Republick as well as *Holland*, by such Means, as made it necessary to leave nothing untried for strengthening herself by foreign Connections, it was natural, in these Circumstances, for her to apply first of all to her near Neighbour and Sister Republick. Accordingly,

cordingly, Mr *Oliver St John* was sent, with *Walter Strickland*, in *March* this Year, to negotiate, not a bare Alliance, but an Union, with *Holland*; such as might render them one Commonwealth. But the *Dutch*, comparing the ill-settled State of the *English* usurped Republick, with their own acknowledged Sovereignty, were so far from accepting the Proposal, that they treated it with Disdain; so that the Envoys returned Home in *July*, not only with a Refusal, but with the Sting of some Insults which had been offered to them by the Rabble at the *Hague*. *St John* was not of a Temper to pocket this Affront; and, as he was one of the ablest Lawyers then in *England*, he projected the Act of Navigation, whereby it was prohibited to import any foreign Commodities, except upon *English* Bottoms, or such as were of the Country from whence the Commodities came; and the Act was passed by the Council of State, on *December* 1, this Year. The *Dutch* were so sensible of it's Consequences, that it was the principal Cause of the ensuing War in 1650 *; in which they were made still more sensible of the very respectable Power of the *English*, which they had despised. At the Negotiations for that Peace which put an End to the War, *De Witte* laboured, with his usual Industry and Acuteness, to procure the Abolition of the Act; but all his Efforts proved fruitless. They who made the Law attended with Vigour to

* In a Manifesto published in 1652, they called it A Vile Act and Order.

the

the Execution of it, and our succeeding Princes have approved and confirmed it. This was the Fate of their first political Maxim, to enjoy equal Privileges with ourselves in Relation to Freightage.

In the other Point, with a worse Prospect at setting out, they succeeded to the utmost of their Wishes. By a Treaty made between *Henry* VII. King of *England*, and *Philip* Duke of *Burgundy*, the Sovereign of the *Low Countries*, it was agreed, that the Subjects of either Prince should not carry, or cause to be carried, by Sea, fraudulently, or under any Pretence whatever, any Goods or Merchandises belonging to the Enemies of the other Prince. And it further stipulated, that in Case the Master of a neutral Vessel shall endeavour, by a false Report, to defraud the Captor of any of his Enemies Effects, he shall be obliged to make good the Loss thereby sustained, by the Forfeiture of as much of his own *; and it appears from *de Witte*'s Letters, that the *Dutch* never could obtain the Rule, that free Ships should make free Goods, during the Usurpation and Protectorship of *Cromwell*. On the contrary, upon their Ambassador *Newport*'s so often repeated Sollicitation about the Marine Treaty, the Answer given by *England* was, that the Demand of free Ships making free Goods, and protecting their Enemies Property, was very unjust; for which the Reasons then alledged are as strong as any that have been made Use of since †.

* *Intercursus magnus*, in *Rymer*'s Fœdera, Vol. XII. p. 585.
† *Aitzema* of the State of Affairs and of War, under the year 1656.

After the Restoration, the *Dutch*, in Consequence of the Treaty with *France* in 1662, wherein that Kingdom had ceded this favourite Point to them, entered into a defensive Alliance, and joined *France* in the War against *England* the ensuing Year. That War terminated in a Treaty of Peace at *Bredah*, dated *July* 21, 1667, between the three Powers; in which, general Freedom of Navigation was allowed to the *English*, which seems to have been the great Point contended for by our Ministers. During the Negotiations, Sir *William Temple*, in a Letter of the 21st of *May*, to Lord *Coventry*, then Ambassador to the States, writes thus: Mr *Godolphin* assured me, that all Parts of the Treaty of Commerce are so much to our Desire and Advantage, that he hopes to see many a rich Man in *England* by it. In this good Humour, they suffered seventeen Articles of the Treaty between *France* and *Holland* in 1662 (among which was the XXXVth, in which the *French* consented to grant the Right of Protection to neutral Vessels) to be inserted into the Treaty of Commerce at *Bredah* " to serve for a Rule and Law, and so to " make Way for concluding a more perfect " and compleat Treaty, concerning maritime " Commerce between *England* and *Holland* *." At the Time of treating, there happened an unlucky Event in the War, which apparently helped to dispose our Ministers to make this Concession. On the 15th of *June*, the *Dutch* Fleet sailed up the River *Medway*, as far as

---

* Article III. p. 100, 101.

Chatham,

Chatham, and burnt the *Royal Oak*, the *Royal London*, and the *Great James*, with several Ships of War lying there; by which bold Action, they forwarded, says one of our considerable Merchants *, the Conclusion of such a Treaty of Marine, as they had long desired in vain.

It is not improbable, however, that one, if not the principal, Motive for making this Concession was, to facilitate the compassing of a Project, then formed by our Court, to engage the *Dutch* in a defensive Alliance with *England*, and so take them out of the Hands of *France*. 'Tis certain, that Sir *William Temple* was dispatched to the *Hague* in *January* following, with Propositions for such an Alliance. Hereupon, the *Dutch* turned that Proposal to their own Advantage, and resolved not to join in any Alliance, unless the provisional Concessions at *Bredah* were made perpetual, and formed into a permanent national Treaty. *De Witte* expressly told our Envoy, that " the " Treaty of defensive Alliance must, for a Ba- " sis, have at the same Time an Adjustment " of Matters of Commerce †." And unless this could be obtained, it was the avowed Opinion of that great Pensionary, not to conclude. Influenced by the Sentiments of their Minister, the States persisted in the same Resolution; and though *England* was averse ‖,

* Mr *Magens*, in a Treatise upon Insurances, &c. in two Volumes, 4to. 1753, Vol. II.
† Sir *William Temple*'s Letter to Lord *Arlington*, *January* 24, 1668.
‖ Eadem iidem, *Feb.* 12, 1668.

Sir *William* huddled up the Point by a Sort of Conftraint; being apprehenfive of the leaft Delay, and of the Uncertainties which would follow from it, he ventured to comply with their Defires, though he thereby exceeded his Inftructions: A private Promife paffed firft between him and *De Witte*, and in Confequence of that, a few Weeks after, a Treaty of Commerce was concluded in *February* 1668, of which the XXXVth Article of the *French* Treaty in 1662 was made a Part. This Treaty was confirmed by the Treaty of 1674, which is now the maritime Regulation between the two Powers.

However, as the *Dutch* never happened to be Neutrals in Refpect to *England*, from the Time of making it 'till the Commencement of our prefent War with *France*, the VIIIth Article lay dormant during that whole Interval, and fome Time longer. But in 1758, when the *French* finding themfelves unable to carry on their own Trade in their own Bottoms, refolved to employ the *Dutch*, and not only exempted their Veffels from the Tax of 50 *Sous* per Ton, but opened to them all their Ports in *America*. The Mifchief of fuffering the Rule to pafs in general Terms, became notorioufly manifeft, and *Britain* refolved to make Ufe of thofe Means which God had put into her Hands, to remedy it. Great Numbers of thefe *Dutch* Veffels were taken *, and fome of them adjudged to be lawful Prizes by our Court of Admiralty.

* See a Lift of the Captures in the Magazines.

The

The *States* being extremely vexed to fee the Net, which they had fo cunningly woven, and fpread over us by the Treaty, now prove at length, upon the firft Trial, too weak to hold us, and forcibly broken, did not fpare to make heavy Complaints of the Breach. No lefs than four Memorials were prefented, by large Deputations from their Merchants to the Princefs Gouvernante. In one of which, they threaten to oppofe Force to Force, in Cafe a Deputation, which was propofed to be fent to *England* by their High-Mightineffes, to follicit fpeedy and fatisfactory Redrefs, and to infift ftrongly on it, fhould prove ineffectual. " And, " continues this Memorial, if we might not " feem to anticipate the Deliberations of our " legal Regency, we would at the fame Time " propofe, that a Refolution fhould be taken, " when the Deputation is fent to *England*, to " fend Commiffions to *Ruffia*, *Spain*, *Sweden*, " and *Denmark*, that in Cafe the Court of " *England* fhould give a negative Anfwer, Al- " liances, Succours, and Affiftance, might be " fecured, to oppofe, in Concert with us, the " defpotic Empire of the *Englifh* on the Sea." The Princefs Regent, in her Anfwer to this Memorial, takes Notice, that fhe had received " A Letter from the King her Father, wherein " his Majefty fays, *The Affair of the Dutch is* " *now under Confideration: and* York *will fpee-* " *dily receive the neceffary Inftructions for fet-* " *tling it amicably. Some Methods fhall be* " *thought of to curb the Infolence of the Priva-* " *teers:* That fhe was informed Mr *York* had " afked a Conference to treat of this Matter;

b   " And

" And that she hoped the Negotiation would
" be attended with Success." She had, in Answer to a former Memorial, assured them, that Negotiations were carrying on at *London*, for an Accommodation. But Mr *Hop*, the *Dutch* Minister here, soon afterwards acquainted his Masters, that our Court insisted upon these two Points; namely, That the *Dutch* should relinquish the Trade and Navigation to the *French* Islands, and also forbear supplying the *French* with Materials for Ship-building. These, in the last Memorial, are called Conditions prescribed, to which those Merchants who are the Sufferers could not subscribe, and which could not be accepted for the Merchants in general. We find, notwithstanding, that both these Conditions were peremptorily insisted on in the Memorial, which Mr *Yorke* presented by his Majesty's Command to the *States-General*, on the 22d of *December* that Year, 1758; where having hinted, that the Treaty of 1674 was enervated, by their ill Faith in observing some Stipulations of other Treaties which were connected with it, and taken Notice, that a Trade of the Nature which they now claimed was never permitted by themselves to others, and had been opposed by the *Salus Populi* in all Countries; he requires, in his Master's Name, " That such Naval Stores, as consist
" of Materials for building and repairing the
" *French* Fleets, should be comprehended in
" the Class of contraband Goods;" and then gives them to understand, " That it was his
" Majesty's Intention, that the Subjects of
" their High-Mightinesses should enjoy all the
                                                    " Privileges

" Privileges and Immunities refulting from the
" Treaty of 1674, *so far as the Tenor of it
" was not derogated from by the prefent Ac-
" commodation* *." In the mean Time, an
Equipment of eighteen Ships of War had been
refolved on by the *Dutch*, to take Place as
foon as poffible: And in *April* the next Year,
1759, arrived at *London* the two Deputies,
according to the Intimation given in the abovementioned Memorial of their Merchants. But
feeing the prodigious Succefs of our Arms this
Year, efpecially in taking *Guadaloupe*, *Quebec*,
and, upon the Matter, the whole Country of
Canada, together with the Failure of the *French*
Finances; thefe unfriendly Allies have thought
fit to foften their Animofity, and wait the further, and probably the final, Iffue of the War;
leaving the *French* Trade, as not worth contending for by the Government at the Hazard
of a Rupture, to private Adventurers; and, as
to Captures, acquiefcing in the Sentences of the
Lords of Appeal, who apparently regulate their
Decrees by the Accommodation, prefcribed to
the Treaty of 1674, in Mr *Yorke*'s Memorial.

In the laft War, when the *Dutch* acted in
Conjunction with us againft *France*, we fee a
very different Conduct obferved on both Sides,
in Regard to this Treaty. Among the Inftructions for Commanders of Ships carrying
Letters of Marque and Privateers, given by his
Majefty in *June* 1744, a Copy of which is
annexed to the prefent Collection, we find,
" That no Goods laden in *Dutch* Ships fhall

---

* This is further explained in An Extract, &c. in the *Gentleman's Magazine* for *September* 1758, p. 403, 404.

" be

" be deemed contraband, other than such as
" are declared so to be, by the Marine Treaty
" concluded between *England* and *Holland* in
" the Year 1674." And that " All Captains
" and Commanders of such Ships are required
" and enjoined to observe carefully and reli-
" giously, the Terms of the Treaty marine,
" between his late Majesty King *Charles* II.
" and their High-Mightinesses the States-Ge-
" neral of the *United Netherlands*, concluded
" at *London* the first Day of *December*, 1674,
" old style, and confirmed by subsequent Trea-
" ties: And they are hereby required to give
" Security, pursuant to the Xth Article of the
" aforesaid Treaty Marine, for their due Per-
" formance thereof *."

The *Dutch*, likewise, on their Side, pub-
lished a Placart, *July* 7, 1747, prohibiting
the Exportation " of the following Sorts of
" Arms, Ammunition, and other warlike
" Stores; as also Fodder and Provisions; to
" wit, Salt-Petre, Sulphur refined or unre-
" fined, Gunpowder, Matches, Cannon, Swi-
" vel-Guns, Mortars, Carriages, Balls, Bombs,
" Curcasses, Grenadoes, Muskets, Forkets,
" Fusils, Pistols, Petards, Salsages, Pitch,
" Crantzes, Helmets, Caskets, Curasses,
" Bandeliers, Pouches, whole and half Pikes,
" Halberts, Swords; and further, all Sorts of
" Weapons, serving for the Hand, or firing
" Instruments; among which are comprehen-
" ded Gun-Barrels and Locks, and what fur-
" ther may be requisite to mount the same;
" Boots, Saddles, Pistol-Cases; and all what

* Instruction III. and IV. in p. 221.

" is

" is necessary for the dressing of Horses. *Item*,
" Masts, and all Sorts of round Timber for
" building of Ships sawed or unsawed, Sail-
" Cloth, Hemp, Ropes, Anchors, Pitch, Tar,
" Lead, Pewter, Iron and Steel Filings, all
" Sorts of Copper and Metal, Sea-Coal; as
" also Hay, Oats, Straw, and Horse-Beans;
" all under the Penalty of forfeiting the said
" Species, which shall be endeavoured to be
" exported, and found out; and moreover, of
" twice the Value thereof, one third Part for
" the Informer, one third Part for the Officer
" that shall seize them, and one third Part for
" the Publick."

This Placart * was also followed by another, called Placart of Ampliation, dated *August* 31, the same Year. " Whereby it is declared, First,
" that under the Word Masts, Yards, Tops,
" and all Sorts of round Timber and other,
" fit for the building of Ships, sawed and un-
" sawed, the Exportation whereof is prohibi-
" ted in our Placart of the seventh of *July*,
" are contained and to be understood, green
" Firr, and *Norway* and other Masts, Stumps
" for Bowsprits, Yards, Tops, and all other
" round Timber; there are likewise contained
" among it, Milrods for Oars, and six or eight-
" Square cut Timber, used, or fit to be made
" useful, for any of the said Articles; Knee-
" Timber; crooked Timber, of what Quality
" of Wood soever, without any Distinction of
" Length, Thickness, and Breadth; *Silesia*,
" *Hamburgher*, *Weeselish*, or *Rhenish* Timber;
" Wood, Blocks of Oak, or Beach-Wood,

* P. 204, 205.

" either

"either whole or sawed; as also green Firr,
"and *Norway* Balks, either entire or cut,
"above twenty Feet long, and above one Inch
"and a half thick; all oaken Planks, be it
"*Dantzick* Plank, or the so called, Upper or
"Low-Land, of what Dimension or Thick-
"ness soever; likewise all green Firr or *Nor-*
"*way* Deal-Boards, sawed either abroad, or
"in these Provinces, longer than twenty Feet,
"and thicker than one Inch and a half, with-
"out any further.

"*Secondly*, that under the Words Ropes
"and Cordage, prohibited to be exported by
"the said Placart, are also comprehended
"bending Ropes; as also Cable-Yarn, Rope-
"Yarn, Leach-Yarn, Sail-Twine, and the
"like."

And because some lesser Implements in Iron and Copper are declared not to be comprehended under the general Words Iron and Copper, prohibited in the former Placart; in Order to prevent any Abuse that may be made of this Concession, " Such Shippers and Ma-
"sters of Ships, as shall be found to have
"made their Machinations to send their pro-
"hibited Goods to *France*, shall also be cor-
"porally punished, besides and above the For-
"feiture and Penalty of treble the Value of
"the Forfeiture of the Ship, if, and as far as,
"the same doth belong to the Shipper or Ma-
"ster *."

Agreeable to this Spirit of Fidelity to each other, a Cargo of Brandy and Salt, loaden in a

* P. 199, 200, 202.

Dutch

Dutch Ship, bound from *Nantz* to *Dantzick*, for Account of the Owner of the Ship, was first condemned in our Court of Admiralty, and the Sentence confirmed afterwards by the Lords of Appeal, as contraband Goods; for this Reason, because, though *Dunkirk* was no blockaded Place *, yet Brandy and Salt were of Service to the *French* Army, which lay encamped at no great Distance from it.

In the Treaties with *Portugal*, which follow those with the *States-General*, we find a very different Temper. By the XXIIId Article † of the Treaty in 1654, it appears, that *Cromwell* agreed with the *Portuguese*, in the Rule of free Ships making free Goods, which he would not allow to the *Dutch*. No Body knew better than he did, that the Weight of the *English* lay chiefly in the Superiority of their maritime Strength, of which he had very lately seen a noble Proof in his War with the *Dutch*; and consequently, that he cannot be supposed not to know, that it was bad Policy in general to allow this Rule to any Nation. But he seems to have something further in View at this Time. *Portugal* was then contending for the Possession of it's *East* and *West Indies* with the *Dutch*. The Protector therefore resolved, that the *English* should reap the Benefit of that Trade in the mean while. The *Portuguese*, in their then present Situation, must have found it difficult to have supplied

---

* As was required by Article IV. of the Treaty of 1674, p. 86, 87.
† In p. 119.

the *Indies* themselves, and consequently might well allow the Proviso granted in the XIth Article * of this Treaty, " That the People " and Inhabitants of *Great-Britain*, might " navigate and trade, freely and safely, from " *Portugal* to *Brasil*, and to the *East* and " *West Indies*, paying the Duties and Customs " which others pay who trade with those " Countries, and that they should have the " same Freedom which had been granted by " any former Treaty, or should be granted " hereafter to the Inhabitants of any other " Nation, in Alliance and Friendship with " that Kingdom." However, this Freedom ended, with the End of the Contests about their Possessions. For, as their Friends and Allies monopolized the Trade of those Places, where they had been admitted, and got footing in the *East* and *West Indies*; the *Portuguese*, in Return, excluded them from trading to those Settlements, which they still retained.

It seems a little surprizing at first Sight, to find so few Treaties of Commerce and Navigation with *Portugal*; and none later than 1654. This is the Result of that perfect good Harmony and friendly Disposition, which has long subsisted between the two Nations. Hence it is, that the XIXth Article of the last mentioned Treaty, by which it is stipulated, that " Ships and Goods of one Party, carried by an " Enemy into the Ports of the other, shall be " restored †," is agreed to be annulled by a

* In p. 117.
† In p. 118, 119.

contrary

contrary Practice, without any special Contract, either publick or private, to rescind it; and there are also other Articles in the same Treaty that are become void, as being obsolete, and out of Date now. It is so much the mutual Interest of both Nations, to keep always well together, that there has been no Occasion for any more particular Treaties to preserve them in Amity. There was, indeed, a Circumstance in 1683, which threatened a Rupture between them; when the *Portuguese*, having set up a Manufacture of woollen Cloth, and made some Progress in it, prohibited the Admission of our Cloths, in order to promote their own Manufacture: But the Clouds were dispersed, by a well-judged Piece of Policy, which *England* made use of in forming the Treaty of Alliance with them in 1703, when they joined us in the War against *France* and *Spain*. By that Treaty it was stipulated, that our Cloths should be admitted for ever, granting them an Equivalent in admitting theirs; which answered very well on our Side, having proved the Ruin of their Manufacture.

In proceeding from *Portugal* to the Treaties with the *Emperor*, the Reader will find, by Article V. of the Convention in 1715, that the Parties had then some Intention to agree upon a new Treaty of Commerce. The same is also actually stipulated in the Vth Article of the Treaty of Peace in 1731, and that a new Tariff should be settled for the *Austrian Netherlands*, by Commissioners to meet at *Antwerp* within two Months, and to be concluded
within

within two Years: But that no such Treaty has as yet been concluded *. Nor, indeed, can any Thing be done in it during the Continuance of the present War; the Issue of which, however, may not improbably give our Merchants an Opportunity of repairing their Fault, during the last War, when, though they must needs see how greatly the House of *Austria* was in want of our Assistance, yet they neglected to represent in a proper Manner to the Ministry in what their Wants consisted, and what would redound to the Benefit of Trade. This was the more surprizing, as it might have been presumed, that the Court of *Vienna* would not then have hesitated to have made some more favourable Concessions to us than to other Nations; since, besides defending them with a powerful Army, we assisted them with a Subsidy, from 300,000 *l.* to 500,000 *l.* a Year in ready Money, and so paid dear enough for whatever Privileges we might have obtained.

Among the Treaties with *Russia*, which appear next in Order, the short Duration of four Years, fixed for the Subsistence of the Treaty in 1755, as is seen in this Collection †, seems somewhat extraordinary. To account for it, we must take a View of the Situation of Affairs in *Germany* at that Juncture. The Rupture between *England* and *France* had grown in the Beginning of this Year to such a Height, as must unavoidably bring on a declared

* P. 124, and
† Supplement, p. 268.

War;

War; the Consequence of which, it was obvious to foresee, would be an Invasion by the *French* of our King's *German* Dominions. In order, therefore, to provide a sufficient Defence for their Security, it became necessary to procure as powerful a Confederacy as could be had. For that Purpose, his Majesty set out for *Hanover* on the 28th of *April*, and concluded a Treaty on the 18th of *June* with the Landgrave of *Hesse-Cassel*; by which that Prince engaged to hold in Readiness, during four Years, for his Majesty's Service, a Body of 8000 or 12000 Men, to be employed, if required, upon the Continent, or in *Britain* or *Ireland*, but not on Board the Fleet or beyond the Seas; and, on the other Hand, his Majesty engaged to pay, remount, and recruit, these Troops, whilst in his Service; and besides, to pay the *Landgrave*, during the Term of four Years, an annual Subsidy of 150,000 Crowns Banco, valued at 4 s. 9 d. ¾ Sterling each, together with a large Sum for Levy-Money, to be paid at the Exchange of the Ratifications; which Subsidy was to be at the Rate of 300,000 Crowns yearly, from the Time of requiring the Troops, to the Time of their entering into *British* Pay; and in Case they should be again dismissed, the said Subsidy of 300,000 Crowns was to remain and to continue at that Rate, during the Residue of the Term. Some other of the *German* Princes, particularly *Bavaria* and *Saxony*, were probably applied to on this Occasion, but without Success.

In the mean Time, the War being in some Measure begun, by Admiral *Boscawen*'s attacking and taking the *Lys* and the *Alcide*, two *French* Men of War, off the Coast of *Newfoundland*, his Majesty returned to his *British* Dominions sooner than usual; he arrived at *Kensington* on the 15th of *September*, and on the 30th was concluded the Treaty of Alliance now under Consideration between him and *Russia*. By this Treaty, her *Russian* Majesty engaged to hold in Readiness in *Livonia*, upon the Frontiers of *Lithuania*, a Body of Troops, consisting of 40,000 Infantry and 15,000 Cavalry; and also on the Coasts of the said Province, forty or fifty Gallies, with the necessary Crews, in a Condition to act on the first Order; but neither these Troops nor Gallies to be put in Activity, unless his *Britannick* Majesty or his Allies should be somewhere attacked: In which Case, the *Russian* General should march, as soon as possible, after Requisition, to make a Diversion, with 30,000 Infantry and 15,000 Cavalry, and should embark on Board the Gallies the other 10,000 Infantry, to make a Descent, according to the Exigence of the Case. On the other Side, his *Britannick* Majesty engaged to pay to her *Russian* Majesty, an annual Subsidy of 100,000 *l*. Sterling, from the Day of the Exchange of the Ratifications, to the Day that these Troops should, upon Requisition, leave the *Russian* Dominions; and from that Day, an annual Subsidy of 500,000 *l*. Sterling, until the Troops should return into the *Russian* Dominions, and for three Months after their Return. His *Britannick* Majesty
further

further engaged, that in Cafe her *Ruffian* Majefty fhould be difturbed in this Diverfion, or attacked herfelf, he would furnifh immediately the Succour ftipulated in the Treaty of 1742; and that in Cafe a War fhould break out, he would fend into the *Baltic* a Squadron of his Ships of Force, fuitable to the Circumftances. And both Parties agreed, that this Convention fhould fubfift, as has been said, for four Years, from the Exchange of the Ratifications. The Reafon of which now is clearly feen : Neither did the large Expence on one Side admit, nor the greatnefs of the Force on the other Side require, a longer Term for effectuating the intended Purpofe.

Nay, fo fhifting and changeable were the Politicks at that Time, that this Treaty had never any vital Subfiftence at all, or was never carried into Execution, being counteracted by our Refufal to accede to a defenfive Alliance between the two Courts of *Vienna* and *Ruffia*; in which there was an Article, that if the King of *Pruffia* fhould attack either of the Allies, neither fhould make Peace with him, unlefs he agreed to reftore *Silefia*. That Monarch no fooner got a Copy of our Treaty with *Ruffia*, than he declared by his Minifters, at all the Courts of *Europe*, that he would oppofe, with his utmoft Force, the Entrance of any foreign Troops into the Empire. The Court of *Verfailles* was apparently much difturbed at fo unexpected a Declaration, by a Prince ftill in Alliance with it, and who could not be ignorant, that a numerous *French* Army was already affembled near the *Lower Rhine*, and
Magazines

Magazines provided for their March the whole Way to *Hanover*; so that all they wanted was a Passage through the *Prussian* Dominions, to enable them to swallow up that Electorate, before the *Russian* Auxiliaries could be brought thither, or any Way formed for protecting it. But his *Prussian* Majesty persisted firmly in his Resolution to oppose it; whereupon, a Negotiation being set on Foot by our Court at *Berlin*, a new Treaty of Alliance was concluded in the Beginning of the next Year 1756. On the other Hand, the Court of *Petersburgh* adhering to her Alliance with that of *Vienna*, proceeded presently to perform her Stipulations with Regard to *Silesia*; and what has been the Event of these Changes I need not say. It is more to the Purpose of the present Discourse to take Notice, that the forementioned Treaty with the Prince of *Hesse Cassel* was renewed before the Expiration of the four Years; but it's Partner (if I may call it so) with *Russia* remains extinct, so that the Treaty of 1742 is the last Treaty now subsisting between the two Kingdoms.

We must not dismiss the Treaties with this Court, without considering the Claim that has been lately offered thence, of carrying the Property of an Enemy. This Right is deduced from a general Stipulation, declaring, that *Russia* shall be treated in like Manner as the most favoured Nation. The Stipulation is inserted in several Articles of the Treaty of 1734; but it appears in every one of them, to relate only to the particular Privileges which the Subjects of each were to enjoy, while they were trading

within

within the Dominions of the other. In the IId Article, this Equality of Favour is expressly said to be granted throughout the Dominions of the contracting Parties in *Europe*. In the IIId it relates only to the favourable Reception of the Subjects of each other, in the Ports of their respective Countries *. In the XIVth, it grants only an equal Freedom, to import such Merchandise into each other's Dominions, as is allowed to the Subjects of any other Country. And in the XXVIIIth, it refers only to the Respect and Treatment which is to be given to the Subjects of one Party, who come into the Dominions of the other †. Hence it is manifest, that the Stipulation of equal Favour relates to nothing else, but such Advantages as may be granted to foreign Traders, by the municipal Laws or Ordinances of each Country; such as Equality of Customs, Exemption from the Rigour of ancient Laws, which would affect them as Aliens, and the Privileges of Judges-Conservators and Consuls. But because the whole Detail of these could not easily be specified, for that Reason they are thus comprehended in general Terms.

After *Russia* follows *Sweden*; where, in Pursuance of our Method, the Treaty of *October* 21, 1661, is placed first, as the principal one at present in Force between the two Nations. And it is observable, that the IVth Article of this Treaty ‖ has the same Stipulation, of equal

* P. 132.
† P. 134, 135.
‖ P. 139, 140.

Favour

Favour as that abovementioned with *Ruſſia*; and that it likewiſe refers to ſuch Favours only as may be enjoyed in Matters of Traffick within their reſpective Dominions: The Treatment which the contracting Parties ſhall there give to the Subjects of each other, is the principal Purport of the Article: It ſpecifies many Particulars; and among the reſt ſtipulates, that the People of both Countries ſhall have " Li-" berty to import and export their Goods at " Diſcretion, the due Cuſtoms being always " paid, and the Laws and Ordinances of both " Kingdoms univerſally obſerved:" And then manifeſtly connecting this with what follows it, adds: " Which Things being preſuppoſed, " they ſhould hold ſuch ample Privileges, Ex-" emptions, Liberties, and Immunities, as " any Foreigner whatſoever doth or ſhall en-" joy." The general Equality, therefore, here ſtipulated, plainly relates to thoſe Places alone, where the Cuſtoms of theſe Kingdoms are to be duly paid, and the Laws and Ordinances of them are in Force; and that is only within their reſpective Dominions, as is evident from the Words, " In the Dominions " and Kingdoms of each other," which are twice repeated. 'Tis true, we find the following Stipulation in the XIth Article *, that " It is by no Means to be underſtood, that " the Subjects of one Confederate, who is not " a Party in a War, ſhall be reſtrained in their " Liberty of Trade and Navigation with the " Enemies of the other Confederate, who is

* P. 144.

" involved

" involved in such War." But the Meaning of these Words is clearly explained in the next Article XII. which is so far from supposing, that the Liberty here granted implies any Right to convey the Effects of an Enemy, that the very Attempt to practise it, under Favour of this Liberty, is there called a Fraud, and, as a most heinous Crime, is ordered to be most severely punished *.

The Treaty of Commerce at *Stockholm*, *February* 16, 1666, is said ‖ to be no more than an Extract made *ex parte* by *Charles* II. King of *Sweden*, of several Marine Articles, out of the two Treaties of 1664-5 and 1661, between him and *Great-Britain*, together with his Edict for the due Observance of the same by his own Subjects. The Truth of the Matter seems to be, that the said Treaty of 1666, was communicated at the *Hague*, signed in *Sweden* by *Hederig Eleonora*, *Sered Baat*, *Lorens de Lynde*, *Gustave Steenback*, *Magnus Gabriel de Gardie*, and *Claudius Rolande*. It was therefore probably sent from *Stockholm* to *London* to be exchanged †; but we do not find any where, that it had been respectively signed and sent on the Side of *England*. We were at that Time at War with *Holland*, and the *Swedes* proposed their Ambassadors to act as Mediators, which certainly was a good Opportunity to obtain a Treaty to their own liking. In our Answer to the *Prussian* Exposition, no other Treaty with *Sweden* is mentioned than that of 1661.

* P. 145, 146.   ‖ P. 155.
† *Aitzema*, Tom. XII. p. 407.

IN the Treaties with *Denmark,* that of 1691 appears at the Head, as it contains a diſtinguiſhing Stipulation, whereby that Prince obtained an extraordinary Favour, more than was granted to any other Nation at that Juncture. *England* and *Holland* being then at War with *France,* did not ſuffer any Nation to trade at all with her, agreeable to their Notifications made to all Courts in 1689. Yet *Denmark* being then an Ally of *England,* and keeping a Body of Troops in *Engliſh* Pay, were allowed, in 1691, a direct Trade with *France,* for ſuch Goods as could be of no bad Conſequences. The Liſt of contraband Goods was ſomewhat large, and the King of *Denmark* accepted of the Reſtriction, as he expreſſed it himſelf in his Edict, to avoid all Vexations and Interruptions, for as long as the War with *France* might laſt; whence it followed of Courſe, that as ſoon as Peace was reſtored, this Treaty became void. However, becauſe it is of Uſe to know how far they extended contraband Goods in former Wars, we ſhall inſert a Specification of them, as follows: All Sorts of Fireworks, and Things thereto belonging; as Cannons, Muſkets, Mortars, Petaroes, Bombs, Grenadoes, Puddings, Torches, Carriages for Ordnance, Reſts for Muſkets, Bandeliers, Gunpowder, Lead, Saltpetre, Balls, Pikes, Swords, Murrions, Curaſſes, Halberts, Darts, Horſes, Gorgets, Belts, Sails, Cordage, Maſts, Matches, Pitch, Tar, Hemp, and all what is in Uſe for equipping by Sea and Land, without comprehending therein any other Sorts of Merchandiſe, of what Nature ſoever. Agreeable to this Specification,

fication, we find the fame, with very little Variations, inferted among the Inftructions to Commanders of Ships carrying Letters of Marque, and to Privateers, given by our Court in 1744, No. V. by which any of thefe Goods being laden in *Danifh* or *Swedifh* Ships, or Ships belonging to Neutral Countries, and bound to the Enemy's Country, are accounted contraband *. Here we have a Precedent for the Demand in Mr *Yorke*'s Memorial to the States-General abovementioned, that certain Articles of Naval Stores, fuch as confift of Materials for building and repairing the *French* Fleet, fhould be comprehended in the Clafs of contraband Goods.

In the Treaty of Commerce of 1669, is inferted the fame Stipulation, of equal Favour as that with *Ruffia* and *Sweden*. By the XLth Article it is declared, that " If the *Hollanders*,
" or any other Nation whatever, hath or fhall
" obtain from his Majefty of *Great-Britain*,
" any better Articles, Agreements, Exemp-
" tions, or Privileges, than what are contained
" in this Treaty, the fame and like Privileges
" fhall be granted to the King of *Denmark* and
" his Subjects alfo, in moft full and effectual
Manner.†." A Right of free Trade with the Enemy is alfo granted in the XVIth Article ‖ ; but it is a little worth obferving, what Care was taken to prevent any Liberty conceded in this Treaty, from being interpreted fo as to give a Right of carrying the Property of an Enemy. The Words

* P. 221, 222.
† Supplement, p. 279.
‖ P. 158.

are, "Left such Freedom of Navigation or Paſ-
"ſage for one Ally, his Subjects and People,
"might, during a War which the other may be
"engaged in, by Sea or by Land, with any
"other State, be of Prejudice to ſuch other
"Ally, and the Goods and Merchandiſe be-
"longing to the Enemy be fraudulently con-
"cealed, under the colourable Pretence of
"their being in Amity together: Wherefore,
"in order to prevent all Frauds of that Sort,
"and to remove all Suſpicion, it is thought
"proper, that the Ships, Merchandiſes, and
"Ships-Crew, belonging to the other, be fur-
"niſhed upon their Voyages with Paſſports
"and Certificates, according to the Form and
"Tenor following." Then is inſerted the Form;
whereby it appears, that the King of *Denmark*
bound himſelf to declare, that " the Ship and
"the Goods with which it is laden belong to
"his Subjects, or to others having an Intereſt
"therein, who are the Subjects of Neutral
"Powers;" and that " they do not appertain
"to either of the Parties now engaged in
"War †." This is the more remarkable, as
the *Dutch* had obtained this Right of carrying
the Property of an Enemy in 1668, the Year
before the Stipulation of equal Favour was
granted to *Denmark* in this Treaty of 1669,
and confirmed the following Year.

FROM *Denmark* we proceed to a State next
in Importance to it with Regard to the
Marine, which is that of *Savoy:* With whom it

† Ibid. and p. 275. in the Supplement.

ſeems

seems we have subsisting only one single Treaty; and that made so long ago as the Year 1669. This is plainly owing to that reciprocal Affection, which is stipulated in the first Article of the Treaty, and which is there said to have then continued for many Years uninterrupted *, and which continues to this Day between the two Nations. The Treaty appears to be made, for the Encouragement of Trade to *Nice*, *Villa-Francha*, and *St Hospice*, the three Ports in the Dominions of the Duke of *Savoy*; and it is remarkable, that the *English* are allowed in this Treaty, almost the same Privileges that were allowed in 1749, in Favour of all Nations, when they were made free Ports. It is true, they do not allow us now, as they did then, the Privilege, in Case of Disputes, to chuse our own Delegates. But they allow something better, in Favour of all Nations; that is, in Case of any Disputes concerning Trade and Commerce, all persons shall represent their own Cases before a Court of Commerce, without the Intervention of Lawyers and Atornies, whereby they are determined immediately and absolutely.

AFTER *Savoy*, for the Reason lastmentioned, follows *Turkey*. In Regard to the Treaties with this Nation, it greatly imports to be apprized of the Difference that has been made in Captures, between the *Turkish* Effects and those of all other Countries. In an additional Instruction to all Ships of War, Privateers, and Letter of Marque Ships, given at *St James*'s

* P. 169.

March

March 30, 1747, it is ordered and directed, "That no Effects or Merchandifes, taken on "Board any Enemy's Ship, which fhall be "claimed by any Subjects of the Grand-Seig- "nior's, as being their Property, fhall be pro- "ceeded againft for Condemnation in any other "Court but the High Court of Admiralty of "*England*; nor in that Court, until Notice be "firft given of the faid Proceeding to the *Tur-* "*key* Company, to the End that Care may be "taken, that a proper and legal Defence may "be made on Behalf of the Claimants, Sub- "jects of the Grand-Seignior *." During the laft War, the *Ruby* Merchant-Man, upon a Commiffion granted from our Admiralty to cruize in the *Mediterranean* Sea, took fome *French* Veffels, which were condemned, with their entire Cargoes, by the Judge of the Admiralty. And the Owners of the *Ruby*, not having been cautioned, in taking out the Commiffion, to deal with *Turkifh* Effects, otherwife than with thofe belonging to other Nations (who all know our Treaties with *France* to be, that unfree Ships make unfree Goods, and fo would naturally avoid fhipping any in the fame), thought themfelves quite fafe with their Prizes, but found it otherwife, by the *Turks* having made the *Britifh* Factory at *Aleppo* pay for them; who thereupon fent to *England* fome *Turks*, to prove the Goods on Board to have been their Property. And the Caufe being brought before the Lords of Appeal, they, in Confequence of

* P. 233, 234.

the

the said Proof, ordered the Goods to be restored with Costs, alledging, that the Treaties made with *France* ought not to affect the Concerns of the *Turks*, who were supposed to be unacquainted with the Treaties made by us with other Nations in *Europe*.

THE Treaties with *Morocco*, *Algiers*, *Tripoli*, and *Tunis*, are placed the last, as being of lesser Importance than the rest; neither is any Part of them so liable to be misunderstood, as to require, or even to excuse, a particular Explanation.

WHAT has been said will it is hoped be candidly accepted, in an Attempt not hitherto made, of shewing the true Force, Extent, Design, and Meaning, of the principal Articles in our Marine Treaties. But we must not conclude this Preface, without giving some Account of the present Edition. The unfavourable Aspect of it requires an Apology; and the best that can be made, I am sure, is to declare the Truth without any Disguise, which is as follows: That the Extracts were first collected, in Pursuance of a Request from the Lords of the Admiralty, by the late Dr *Henry Edmonds*, LL.D. an eminent Civilian and Advocate in Doctors-Commons. After whose Death, the Manuscript came into the Hands of a Bookseller, who put it to the Press; but leaving off Business before it was quite finished there, it lay in that Condition, 'till our Disputes with the *Dutch* brought it under the Consideration of the present Proprietor: The Result of which
was,

was, a Refolution to have it revifed by a proper Perfon, that fuch Articles, if any, as were found to be omitted in the Treaties then fubfifting, might be fupplied, and fuch others added, as were found relative to the Marine in the Treaties that had been made fince. To this End, the whole Book, as has been faid, being nearly printed off, a Supplement became neceffary, in which the Method prefcribed by the firft Collector was alfo to be obferved. And thus much at leaft may be truly faid in it's Behalf, that, by placing the principal Treaties with each Nation firft, and ranking the reft in the Order of their Importance, the Reader fees by Infpection which are the moft important Treaties with each Nation; an Advantage that is wanting in the Method of other Collections; which are likewife printed without any fuch Copies of the Inftructions given to the Commanders of either publick or private Men of War, or *Dutch* Placarts, as are to be found in the prefent Edition, the Ufe whereof has fufficiently appeared in the Courfe of this Preface.

A TABLE OF THE CONTENTS.

TREATIES with *FRANCE*.

                                      Page

MARINE Treaty of *Utrecht*, 1713,   1
Free Trade and Navigation in *Europe*, *ib.*
Subjects of either Nation not to act under any Commission against the other,— *ib.*
Free Passage in *Europe*,   2
Free Import and Export of all Goods not prohibited   3
Subjects or Goods of either Party not to be seiz'd or detained,   *ib.*
Privateers of Enemies not to fit or provide themselves, or dispose of Captures in any Port of either Party,   4
Free Intercourse for either Party with an Enemy of the other,   *ib.*
Free Ships make free Goods, except contraband; and free Men, except Soldiers   5
Contraband Goods excepted and specified   *ib.*
Goods not Contraband specified,   6
Ships of both Parties to have Passports and Certificates   7

Merchant

CONTENTS.

	Page
Merchant Ships not obliged to give Account of their Lading, unless suspected,	7
Ships suspected must produce their Passports, &c.	8
Ships of War to keep at Distance from Merchant Ships, and only to send their Boats aboard,	ib.
Merchant Ships, making into an Enemy's Port, must produce their Passports, &c.	ib.
Hatches not to be broke up, on Discovery of contraband Goods on board,	9
Contraband Goods not to be dispos'd of, before they are legally condemn'd,	ib.
The Ship, and other Goods on board, not to be confiscated,	ib.
The Ship to go free, upon giving up the contraband Goods to the Captor,	ib.
All Goods on board an Enemy's Ship, liable to Confiscation, unless laden within certain Times and Limits,	10
Injuries on both Sides to be punished and repair'd	ib.
Ships and Goods rescued from Pirates to be restored,	11
Free Ingress and Egress for all Ships of War and Privateers on both Sides, with their Prizes,	ib.
No Capture of any Ship or Goods of one Party to be suffer'd on the Coast, or in any Port of the other,	12
In Case of Torture committed, the Capture to be releas'd, and the Delinquents punish'd,	ib.
Form of the *French* Passports, &c.	ib.

American TREATY, 1686.

PEACE and Amity in all Parts of *America*,	15
Ships not to be fitted out in the Dominions of either Party, to attack the other,	ib.

Soldiers

	Page
Soldiers or Subjects of either Party not to injure the other, or assist the *Indians* against them,	16
Both Kings to retain all Rights and Dominions in *America*, *uti possident*,	*ib.*
Neither Side to trade or fish on the Coasts, or in the Dominions of the other,	*ib.*
Ships so trading or fishing to be confiscated,	17
Party aggriev'd by Sentence of Confiscation, may apply to the Privy Council,	*ib.*
Liberty of Navigation not to be disturb'd,	*ib.*
All Ships and Subjects of the one, forced into the Ports of the other, to be well used and assisted,	*ib.*
Ships so forced in not to unliver or take in any Goods there,	18
Such Ships to hang out their Colours, and discharge a Musket on coming in,	*ib.*
Ships of one Party stranded, wreck'd, or any Way endanger'd on the Coast of the other to be assisted,	*ib.*
Three or four Ships forced in together, not to stay longer than shall be allow'd,	*ib.*
Slaves or Goods taken from either by the *Indians*, not to be harbour'd,	19
Neither Party to molest the other,	*ib.*
Ships of War of either not to injure the other, and all such Injuries to be punish'd and repair'd.	*ib.*
Pirates not to be assisted or protected,	*ib.*
Subjects of either taking Commissions against the other as Privateers, to be punished as Pirates,	20
The *French* may fish for Turtles in the Isles of *Cayman*,	*ib.*
A War between the Parties in *Europe*, shall occasion no Hostilities in *America*,	*ib.*

TREATY of PEACE, at *Utrecht*, 1713.

S*T. Chriſtopher's, Nova Scotia,* with the Fiſhery there, and *Annapolis Royal* quitted to the *Engliſh,* ⸻ ⸻ 21

Newfoundland quitted to the *Engliſh,* with the Right reſerv'd to the *French,* to take and dry Fiſh, ⸻ ⸻ 22

Cape Breton to remain to the *French,* ⸻ *ib.*

MARINE TREATY of *St. Germains,* 1676-7.

FREE Trade and Navigation with all Neutral Powers, ⸻ ⸻ 23
Same Freedom of Trade in Time of War as Peace, except as to contraband Goods, 24
Contraband Goods ſpecified, ⸻ *ib.*
Goods not contraband, ⸻ *ib.*
Ships of either Nation, on producing their Paſſports, not to be detained, or moleſted, ⸻ 25
Ships paſſing into an Enemy's Country, ſhall be obliged to produce Certificates, as well as Paſſports, ⸻ ⸻ 26
Contraband Goods only to be confiſcated, but other free Goods not to be meddled with, 27
On giving up all contraband Goods on board, the Ship to be diſmiſs'd, ⸻ *ib.*
All Goods in Enemies Ships forfeited. ⸻ *ib.*
Free Ships make free Goods, except contraband, ⸻ ⸻ ⸻ *ib.*
Times and Diſtances as to Forfeiture of Goods in Enemies Ships on the breaking out of a War, ⸻ ⸻ 28
Ships of War of one Party to do no Injury to any Ships of the other, ⸻ ⸻ 29
Tortures on Board Prizes, prohibited and puniſhed, ⸻ ⸻ *ib.*

CONTENTS.

Treaty of *Westminster*, 1655.

	Page
FREE Navigation in all Harbours and Coasts,	30
Free Commerce in *Europe*,	ib.
Sea-Commanders of the one Party not to injure the other, on Pain of Restitution and Punishment,	31
All Books and Papers of a Prize Ship to be delivered to the Judge of the Admiralty,	ib.
Men or Goods not to be taken out but by Authority of that Court,	32
No Officer or Mariner of a Prize to be carried from his Ship, but in order to be examin'd,	ib.
Pirates not to be harbour'd or assisted, but pursued and punished,	ib.
Ships and Goods taken by Pirates, and brought into any Port of either Party, to be restor'd,	ib.
Free Commerce with all Neutral Powers, except as to Places besieg'd, and contraband Goods,	33
Six Months allow'd to Subjects on both Sides to retire in case of a new War,	34

Marine Treaty of *St. Germains*, 1632.

MERCHANT Ships to strike to Ships of War, and present their Commissions and Bills of Lading,	ib.
Such Ships not to be hinder'd, or taken out of their Course,	ib.
Books and Papers of Prizes to be laid before the Judge of the Admiralty,	35
Officers of Prize Ships to be presented to and examined before the Judge of the Admiralty,	ib.

CONTENTS.

                                         Page
Men or Goods not to be taken out without Order, —— —— — 35

Treaty of *London*, 1610.

Goods taken from Pirates to be brought into Port and lodged there, — 36
Such Goods to be restored to the Owners, being Subjects of either Party, —— ib.

Treaty of 1549.

Universal Peace and Amity, 37
    Free Navigation and Commerce, ib.

Treaty of 1546.

Peace and Amity, —— ib.
    Free Navigation and Commerce, ib.

Treaties with *France* renew'd and confirm'd.

Treaty of *Seville*, 1729, confirms all former Treaties of Peace and Commerce. —— —— 39
Commerce settled on the Foot of Treaties preceding the Year 1725, —— ib.
Treaty of *Utrecht*, 1713, settles a free Navigation and Commerce as before the last War, 40
Treaty of *Reswick*, 1697, settles a free Navigation, Passage and Trade, as before used, ib.
American Treaty of Commerce of 1686, confirms the Treaty of *Bredah*, of 1667, 41
Treaty of *St. Germains*, 1676-7, confirms the Freedom and Security of Commerce, ib.
Treaty of *Bredah*, 1667, confirms universal Peace and Amity, —— ib.

                                                Free

CONTENTS.

	Page
Free Navigation and Commerce as before us'd	42
ACT of the Oath in 1644, confirming the Treaties of 1606, 1610, 1625, 1629, and 1632, — — —	ib.
TREATY of *St. Germains* of 1632, confirming the Treaties of 1606, and 1610,	43
TREATY of 1629 for a safe and free Commerce,	ib.
The DECLARATION, being a Sequel to the same, — — —	ib.
TREATY of 1610, confirming all former Treaties, — —	44
TREATY of 1606, confirming all former Treaties, — — —	45
TREATY of 1596, confirming all former Alliances and Treaties, — —	ib.
TREATY of 1572, confirming all former Alliances and Treaties, —	46
TREATY of perpetual Peace and Amity of 1564, — —	ib.
TREATY of 1515, confirming all Commerce and Intercourse as before used, —	47
Definitive Treaty of universal and perpetual Peace, 1748, — —	ib.
The Treaty of the *Assiento* and the Annual Ship confirm'd, — —	ib.
Two Hostages to continue in *France* till the Restitution of *Cape Breton*, —	48

N. B. These not in the Quarto Edition.

TREATIES with *Spain*.

TREATY of Peace at *Utrecht*, 1713, confirming all Commerce and Navigation as before the War, — 49

MARINE TREATY of *Utrecht* of 1713, reciting and confirming the Treaty of 1667, ib.

TREATY

CONTENTS.

	Page
Treaty of 1667, Universal Peace and Amity,	50
Free Access and Traffick where before used or allow'd to any other Nation,	ib.
Both Sides to abstain from all Violence,	51
Free Navigation, Passage and Trade where before used, with a Saving to the Rights, Customs, and Laws of both Nations,	ib. & seq.
All Privileges of the Treaty of *Munster* granted by *Spain* to the Subjects of *Great Britain*, [See fol. 61]	52
Ships of *Great Britain* not to be searched or visited by any Officer of the King of *Spain*,	ib.
Ships of either Nation may cast Anchor in the Roads or Coasts of the other,	53
Ships forced by Enemies or otherwise, may freely come in and go out of any Port,	ib.
Such Ships may not break Bulk, and must produce their Passports and Certificates,	ib.
Ships of War of either Nation meeting with Merchant Ships at Sea, to keep at a Distance, and only to send their Boat to examine the Papers,	ib.
Prohibited Goods bound to be exported out of either Nation, to be confiscated, and no other,	54
If *British* Coin, Wool, or Fullers-Earth, be found exported out of the *British*, or any Gold or Silver out of the *Spanish* Dominions, the Laws of each Country shall take Place,	ib.
All Ships of both Nations may freely enter, abide in, and depart from any Ports of the other,	55
If drove in by Stress of Weather, they may refit, and buy in Provisions, but not to exceed eight Ships of War, nor stay longer than necessary, nor to disturb the Commerce of the Place,	ib.

CONTENTS.

	Page
Ships of War more than usual not to enter into Port, or anchor in any Road without Leave,	ib.
Ships and Subjects of both Nations may carry all Kinds of Arms,	56
Free Navigation and Traffick with Neutral Powers,	ib.
Such Freedom not to be disturb'd by reason of any Hostility with any other State,	ib.
Contraband Goods only to be taken and confiscated,	ib.
Contraband Goods specified,	57
Goods not contraband,	ib.
All Things found in an Enemy's Ship liable to Confiscation,	58
Subjects of both Nations to enjoy all Privileges granted to any other State,	ib.
Subjects on both Sides to observe these Articles,	ib.
Form of the *Spanish* Passport,	59

Sequel of the MARINE TREATY of *Utrecht*, 1713.

AMERICAN Treaty of 1670, confirm'd,	60
Subjects on both Sides to enjoy full Benefit of Peace until Declaration of War,	61

TREATY of *Munster*, 1648, referr'd to fol. 52.

FREE Access and Commerce,	ib.
Subjects of both Parties not to sail or trade in Places possessed by the other in the *West* Indies,	62
Neither Party to enter or stop at any Port or Road of the other with Ships of War, without Leave, unless forced in,	ib.

CONTENTS.

AMERICAN TREATY of 1670.

	Page
TREATY of 1667 confirmed,	62
Universal and perpetual Peace and Amity,	63
All Hostilities and Depredations to cease,	ib.
King of *Great Britain* to hold all Places, &c. in the *West Indies* or *America, uti possidet,*	ib.
Subjects of both to forbear all Commerce and Navigation in Places possessed by the other in the *West-Indies,*	64
Either King may grant Licence to the Subjects of the other to navigate and trade in his Dominions there,	ib.
All Ships forc'd in to be well receiv'd and assisted,	65
Men belonging to Ships stranded or wreck'd to be reliev'd and assisted,	ib.
Ships forced in, if three or four in Number, to stay no longer than allow'd and necessary,	66
All Rights of both Parties in the *American* Seas saved,	ib.
Freedom of Navigation not to be interrupted,	ib.

TREATY of PEACE at *Utrecht,* 1713.

RIGHT of the *Guipuscoans,* in the *Newfoundland* Fishery saved,	67

TREATY of Peace and Alliance, 1630.

FREE Navigation, Passage and Commerce according to antient Treaties,	ib.
Free Access and Departure for all Ships,	68
Number of Ships limited,	ib.
Subjects of one Party not to supply or assist the Enemy of the other,	69
Subjects of both Parties to be treated as Natives,	ib.

Prohi-

CONTENTS.

Prohibited Goods only to be confifcated, and the Offender only to be punifh'd, —— *ib.*
Ships not to be detained for any Service without Confent, —— —— —— *ib.*

TREATY of Peace and Alliance, 1604.

FREE Navigation and Commerce as before ufed, —— —— —— 70
Free accefs and departure for all Ships of both Nations, —— —— 71
Number of Ships limited, —— —— *ib.*
Subjects of the one Party not to fupply or affift the Enemy of the other, —— —— *ib.*
Subjects of both to be ufed as Natives, —— *ib.*
Subjects of the one Party not to affift an Enemy of the other with Money, Arms or Provifions, —— —— —— 72
Prohibited Goods exported to be confifcated and no other, and Delinquents only punifh'd, *ib.*
Ships not to be forc'd into any Service, —— *ib.*
TREATY of 1542, Perpetual Peace and Amity, 73
Free Navigation, Paffage and Commerce, —— *ib.*
Neither Party to attempt any Thing againft the other, or to aid his Enemies, —— —— 74
Peace to continue, though violated by Subjects or Allies, —— —— —— *ib.*
Upon any Injury done, no Commiffions to be granted or War made, but Reparation by the Prince of the Party offending, —— 75
Treaty of 1520, confirm'd, —— —— *ib.*

TREATIES with *Spain* renewed and confirm'd.

TREATY of *Seville* 1729, confirms all former Treaties, —— —— 77
Commerce eftablifhed on the Foot of Treaties preceding the Year, 1725, —— —— *ib.*

CONTENTS.

Treaties of 1667, 1713, 1715, and 1716, confirm'd, — 78
PRELIMINARY ARTICLES of 1727, restore all Privileges of Commerce to the *English*, as before 1725, — 79
TREATY of *Madrid* 1721, confirms all former Privileges of Trade to the *English*, — 79
Treaties of 1667, 1713, 1715 and 1716, confirmed, — 80
TREATY of Commerce of 1715, confirms all Privileges to the *English* as before the War, *ib.*
Marine Treaty of 1713, confirm'd, — 81
TREATY of Peace of 1713, renews and confirms all former Treaties, — *ib.*
TREATY of 1680, confirms the Treaties of 1667, and 1670, — 82
TREATY of 1630, renews and confirms all antient Treaties and Privileges of Merchants, *ib.*
TREATY of 1604, renews the antient Treaties with *Burgundy* and the *Netherlands*, and the Privileges of Merchants, — 83

TREATIES *with the* States General.

EXplanatory Declaration of 1675, settling a free Trade and Navigation to and from Places belonging to an Enemy of either Party, — 84

MARINE TREATY of 1674.

NAvigation and Trade with the Allies of one Party, not to be molested by the other, — 85
Freedom of Trade for all Goods, except contraband, — 86

Contraband

CONTENTS.

	Page
Contraband Goods fepcified,	*ib.*
Goods not contraband	*ib.*
Merchant Ships to fhew their paffports in Port,	87
Merchant Ships, meeting Ships of War at Sea, to pafs freely, on fhewing their Paffports,	88
Merchant Ships going into an Enemy's Port, to produce their Cockets as well as their Paffports,	*ib.*
Ships taken with contraband Goods to be brought into Port,	89
Contraband Goods only to be condemn'd, and the Ship and other Goods to go free,	*ib.*
On delivery of the contraband Goods to the Captor, the Ship to pafs freely,	*ib.*
All Goods in Enemies Ships to be confifcated,	90
Free Ships make free Goods, except Contraband,	*ib.*
Goods laden in Enemies Ships within Times limited not forfeited,	*ib.*
Commanders of Ships of War not to injure the Subjects of the other Party,	91
Torture on Board Prizes prohibited and punifh'd	92
Form of the *Dutch* Paffport,	93

TREATY of 1673-4.

ALL *Dutch* Ships to ftrike to the King of *Great Britain*'s Ships in certain Seas, — 94
Neither Party to furnifh any Supplies to the Enemy of the other, — 94

MARINE TREATY of 1667-8.

FREE Trade with Neutral Powers at War with the other Party, — 95
Free Trade for all Goods, except contraband, *ib.*
Contraband Goods fpecified, — *ib.*

Goods

CONTENTS.

	Page
Goods not contraband may be carried to an Enemy's Country,	96
Merchant Ships of the one going out of any Port of the other to any Place of the Enemy, to shew their Passports,	ib.
Ships in any Port or Road not obliged to unliver or give Account of their Cargo, unless suspected,	97
In Case of Suspicion, to shew their Passports,	ib.
Ships of War to keep at a Distance from Merchant Ships at Sea, and only send their Boats to examine their Papers,	ib.
Contraband Goods only to be confiscated,	98
All Goods in Enemies Ships to be confiscated,	ib.
Free Ships make free Goods,	ib.
The above Rules equal to both Parties,	99
Commanders of the King's Ships or Privateers, not to injure any of the States Subjects; and all Transgressors to be punished, and to make Reparation,	ib.
Captors not to meddle with contraband Goods at Sea, but to bring them in, and land them in Port,	99
On Delivery of the contraband Goods at Sea to the Captor. the Ship to pass freely,	100
PROVISIONAL MARINE TREATY of 1667, reciting the Marine Treaty of 1662, between the *French* and *Dutch*, and confirming the same between the *English* and *Dutch*,	ib.

TREATY of *Bredah*, 1667.

FREE Passage and Commerce in *Europe*,	101
Subjects of the contracting Parties to pay the same Duties with other Nations,	ib.
All *Dutch* Ships to strike to the King's Ships in the *British* Seas,	102
Pirates	

CONTENTS.

	Page
Pirates not to be harbour'd or affifted, and Goods taken by them to be reftor'd,	102
Subjects of one Party not to act under any Commiffion againft the other,	ib.
Perfons acting under other Commiffions againft either Party, not to be affifted by the other, or fuffered to difpofe of their Prizes,	103
Goods taken from either Party, and brought into the Dominions of the other, to be reftor'd,	ib.
Free Paffage and Intercourfe on both Sides in their *European* Dominions,	ib.
Merchant Ships of either Party, if forc'd into any Port of the other, may depart freely,	104
Men or Ships of the one not to be forced into the Service of the other,	ib.
Ufe of Arms allow'd on both Sides,	105
Ships of War of the one to protect the Merchant-Ships of the other Party at Sea,	ib.
Ships of one Party taken out of the Port of the other, to be purfued and reftor'd,	ib.
Free Ingrefs and Egrefs for all Ships of both Parties into and out of all Ports,	106
Number of Ships of War limited, and not to come into any Port of the other Party, without Leave, unlefs forced in,	ib.
TREATY of 1662, comprehended in that of 1667,	107
TREATY of 1654, comprehended in thofe of 1662 and 1667,	ib.

TREATIES with the STATES renewed and confirmed.

TREATY of *Vienna* 1731, confirming all former Treaties,	108
TREATY of *Seville* 1729, confirming all former Treaties,	ib.

Treaty

CONTENTS.

                                        Page

Treaty of 1715-6, confirming the two Treaties of *Bredah* of 1667, the Marine Treaty of 1667-8, the Treaty of 1673-4, the Marine Treaty of 1673-4, the Declaration of 1675, the Article settled in 1674-5, the Treaty of Alliance of 1677-8, the two Treaties of 1689, and the Barrier Treaty of 1612-3 is allowed by the Treaty of 1715, —   —   109

Treaty of Succession and Barrier of 1712-3, confirming all former Treaties, except that of 1709,   —   —   110

All antient Privileges confirm'd to the *English* in the *Netherlands* and Barrier,   ib.

Treaty of 1700, confirming all former Alliances,   —   —   —   111

Treaty of 1689, confirming the Treaties of 1667, 1673-4, 1679, 1674-5, 1677-8, and 1689,   —   —   ib.

Treaty of 1685, confirming the Treaties of 1667, 1673-4, 1674, 1675, 1674-5, and 1677-8,   —   —   113

Treaty of 1677-8, settling universal Peace and Amity,   —   —   114

Treaty of 1673-4, confirming the Treaty of *Bredah* 1667,   —   114

Treaty of 1667-8, confirming the same Treaty of *Bredah*, -   —   —   ib.

Treaty of *Bredah* of 1667, renewing and confirming the Freedom of Trade in *Africa* and *America*, as upon the Conclusion of the Treaty of 1662,   —   —   115

CONTENTS.

TREATIES with *Portugal*.

	Page
TREATY of Peace and Alliance 1664,	115
Free Paſſage and Commerce, —	ib.
Maſters or Mariners of *Britiſh* Ships not to bring Suits for Wages, or deſert their Service in *Portugal*, — —	116
Britiſh Ships, Men or Goods, not to be conſtrain'd or meddled with in *Portugal* without Conſent, — —	ib.
Free Navigation and Trade in all the Dominions of *Portugal*, — —	117
Acceſs, Shelter, and mutual Aſſiſtance for all Ships of both Parties in all Ports, —	118
Ships or Goods of one Party carried into the Dominions of the other, to be reſtor'd,	ib.
Goods of either Party found in Enemies Ships to be confiſcated, — —	119
Free Ships make free Goods, —	ib.
No Treaty with any other Prince to derogate from this Treaty, — —	ib.
Treaty of Peace and Commerce of 1641-2,	120
Perpetual Peace, Amity, and free Commerce,	ib.
Britiſh Mariners not to ſue for Wages in *Portugal* on Pretence of Religion, —	121
Britiſh Ships or Men not to be forced into *Portugueſe* Service, —	ib.
Free Navigation and Commerce for the Subjects of the one with the Enemy of the other, — —	122
Contraveners to be puniſhed, —	123
Former Treaties with other Powers to be obſerved, — —	ib.

CONTENTS.

Treaties with the *Austrian Netherlands*.

	Page
Treaty of *Vienna* of 1731, confirming perpetual Peace and Amity,	123
Treaty of 1715, establishing Commerce with the *Austrian Netherlands* as before used,	124
Marine Treaty of 1667, confirming all antient Privileges of Trade,	125
Treaty of 1630, confirming antient Treaties and free Trade and Intercourse,	125 & *seq.*
Treaty of perpetual Peace and Amity in 1604,	127
Neither Party to assist an Enemy of the other,	*ib.*
Treaty of 1542, confirming the Treaty of 1520,	128
Treaty of 1520, settling a free Trade and Navigation,	*ib.*
Treaty of 1495, for a perpetual Peace and free Trade,	129
Free Liberty of Fishing for both Parties,	*ib.*
Pirates not to be harboured or assisted,	130
Ships of both Parties to enter and moor in any Port,	*ib.*
Neither Side to bring in any Goods of an Enemy, and Frauds to be made good,	131

CONTENTS.

Treaties with *Russia*.

	Page
TREATY of perpetual Peace and Amity of 1734,	131
Free Navigation and Commerce in *Europe*,	132
Free Ingress for trading, victualling or refitting,	ib.
Men or Ships of either Party not to be forced into the Service of the other,	ib.
Mutual Commerce and Traffick with all Goods and in all Cases not prohibited,	133
Free Export of all Goods not prohibited,	ib.
Free Trade for one Party with an Enemy of the other under certain Restrictions,	134
Warlike Ammunition specified and prohibited,	ib.
A Year allowed to Subjects on both Sides to retire in Case of a War,	ib.
Men or Ships on either Side not to be detained or compelled, and Deserters to be delivered up,	ib.
Mutual good Offices; *Russians* to be protected and favoured in *England*, and Peace and Amity for fifteen Years,	135
Treaty of perpetual Peace and Alliance of 1603,	136
Neither Party to assist the Enemy of the other,	ib.
Free Trade and Commerce,	ib.
Free Passage for Ministers and Messengers,	137

Treaties with Sweden.

	Page
Treaty of perpetual Peace and Amity of 1661,	138
Mutual Friendship and Aid against all Enemies,	ib.
Free Navigation and Commerce,	139
Free Passage and all Privileges of Trade,	ib.
Ships or Goods not to be unduly arrested or detain'd,	140
Ships forced in to be harboured and assisted,	141
Mutual Protection and Assistance, in case of Wrecks and other Losses at Sea,	ib.
Free Export of Arms, and Ingress and Egress for Ships,	142
Ships of War coming into any Port of the other, not to exceed five in Number,	ib.
To exhibibit their Letters of safe Conduct,	ib.
Not to come too near the Forts,	ib.
Not more than forty Men to go ashore together,	143
Not to obstruct Merchant Ships, or go in and out, as in their own Ports,	ib.
A greater Number of Ships not to come in without special Leave	ib.
Free Passage and Commerce on both Sides,	144
Free Trade for one Party with an Enemy of the other; except as to contraband Goods,	ib.
Such Traders to carry Passports and Certificates,	145
English Form of the Passports,	146
All Ships of either Party to pass freely on producing such Passports,	148

Ships

CONTENTS. xxiii

	Page
Ships not to be fearch'd, unlefs wanting Paffports, or on juft Sufpicion,	148
Goods of Enemies only to be confifcated,	ib.
Enemies of either or their Captures not to be receiv'd into any Port,	149
The Peace not to be diffolved by private Injuries,	ib.
Offenders to be punifhed, and to make Reftitution,	150
All former Rights of the Sea faved to both Parties,	ib.
Free Navigation and Commerce in all Places to be defended on both Sides,	ib.
No Treaty to be made with any foreign Nation without the previous Confent of the other Confederate,	151
Treaty of 1656, granting to the *Swedes* the Liberty of fifhing in the *Britifh* Seas,	ib.
Treaty of *Upfal* of 1654, comprehended in that of 1661,	152

TREATIES with *Sweden* renewed and confirmed.

TREATY of 1720, confirming thofe of 1700 and 1665,	153
Treaty of 1700, confirming all former Treaties,	154
Treaty of 1674, confirming that of 1664-5.	ib.

Treaties with Denmark.

	Page
PROVISIONAL Treaty of 1691,	155
Danish Ships meeting *British* Ships of War, to be treated according to the 20th Article of the Treaty of *Nimeguen*, 1679, between *Swedes* and the *States*,	156
Ships of War only to send their Boats to examine the Papers of a Merchant Ship,	ib.
Treaty of perpetual Peace and Amity of 1669,	156
Free Intercourse and Commerce,	157
Exceptions to the above Article,	ib.
Ships not to be molested, or obliged to unliver their Cargo,	ib.
Free Trade with Enemies, except as to contraband,	158
Ships to be furnished with Passport and Certificates,	ib.
Form of the *Danish* Passport and Certificate,	159
Ships to be dismissed on producing their Passports, unless upon a strong Suspicion,	161
No Ships or Goods of either to be made Prize, without legal Process,	ib.
Ships or Goods not to be arrested or detained, unless for public Defence, or by legal Arrest,	162
Ships of War of the one to protect all Ships of the other,	ib.
Pirates not to be harbour'd or assisted,	ib.
Ships and Goods piratically taken to be restor'd,	163
Ships forced in, to be well received and assisted,	ib.
Ships of War coming in voluntarily, limited,	ib.
Previous Notice and Leave in such Cases,	ib.

CONTENTS.

	Page
Subjects of either Party not to act under any Commission against the other, —	164
Ships of one Party taken in any Port of the other to be pursued and restored, —	ib.
Subjects of the one taken by an Enemy, and brought into any Port of the other, to be set at Liberty, — — —	165
Prohibited Goods taken to be landed and inventoried,	ib.
Subjects of either doing any Injury to make Restitution,	ib.
All Actions to be tried in the Court of Admiralty, or special Commissaries, —	166
Treaties of 1661, 1654, and 1621, comprehended in the Treaty of 1669, —	167
Treaties of 1669, 1661, and 1639, confirming all former Treaties, — — —	168

Treaty with *Savoy*.

Treaty of Peace and Commerce of 1669,	169
Free Liberty for *British* Subjects to import and land all Goods in certain Ports of *Savoy*,	ib.
British Ships coming from *English* Ports not infected, having Certificates of Health, not oblig'd to perform Quarantine,	ib.
British Ships of War to be well receiv'd and supplied with Necessaries in the three Ports of *Savoy*,	170

CONTENTS.

Treaty with *Turkey*.

                                       Page

TREATY of 1675, reciting and confirming the antient Treaties and Privileges in the Reigns of Queen *Elizabeth*, *James* and *Charles* I. — 171
Free Navigation for all *English* Ships and Goods, — ib.
Free Ingrefs and Egrefs for all *English* Ships, ib.
English Ships in Diftrefs to be fuccoured and fupply'd, — ib.
English Ships to be kindly treated at Sea, — 172
The *English* to enjoy all Privileges granted to any other Chriftian Nation, — ib.
The *English* to trade freely in *Turkey*, and export all Goods except Arms and Ammunition, — ib.
Free Trade for the *English* to and from *Mufcovy* and *Perfia*, paying the ordinary Duties, 173
Free Trade to *Aleppo*, &c. and all Places in the *Turkish* Dominions, paying the antient Cuftoms, — ib.
Pirates of *Tunis* and *Algiers* not to hurt the *English* in Perfons or Goods, — 174
Free Importation of all Goods into *Turkey*, and Exportation of all but prohibited Goods, — ib.
Turkish Ships of War, or thofe of *Algiers*, &c. not to moleft or fearch any *English* Ships at Sea, — 175

Treaty

Treaty with *Morocco*, 1727-8.

MOORS and *Jews*, Subjects of *Morocco*, allowed to traffick at *Gibraltar*, or *Minorca*, for thirty Days, — — 176
British Subjects taken by *Moorish* Cruizers to be set at Liberty, — — *ib.*
Free Liberty to buy all Necessaries for the *British* Fleet, or for the City of *Gibraltar*,— *ib.*

Treaties with *Algiers*.

TREATY of mutual Amity and Forbearance from Injuries, — — 177
Minorca and *Gibraltar*, Part of the *British* Dominions, and the Inhabitants to have the same Privileges, — — — *ib.*
Algerines not to cruize in Sight of either Place, — — — *ib.*
The *English* to defend the Persons and Goods of the *Algerines* on board their Vessels, — *ib.*
Such Goods to be registred before the Consul, before shipped, — — — 178
English Ships, with proper Passes, to go free, *ib.*
Treaty of 1703, that all Prizes and *American* Ships belonging to *England*, shall pass freely with Certificates only, — — *ib.*
Treaty of 1700, confirming the Treaty of 1682, — — 179

CONTENTS.

Algerines not to cruize near any Place belonging to *Great-Britain*,, or in the *British* Channel, — — — 17

Goods in an *English* Ship, without a Pass, to be a lawful Prize; with a saving as to the Men, Ship, and Freight, — — 18

A special Officer to protect all *English* Ships of War in the Mole of *Algiers*, — *ib.*

Treaty of Peace and Commerce in 1686, — *ib.*

Free Navigation and Trade in *Algiers*, paying the usual Customs, — — 18

Free Passage and Commerce for all Ships of both Nations, and Safety for all Persons and Goods on board, — — *ib.*

All Ships on both Sides to pass freely, on producing their Passes and Certificates, — 18

Algerines not to force away any Person found on board an *English* Ship, — — *ib.*

Algerine Ships not to be disposed of for Service against *Great Britain*, — — 18

Algerines not to cruize near any *British* Ports, &c. — — — — *ib.*

English Ships, Men or Goods, brought into *Algiers*, not to be sold there, — *ib.*

English Ships of War may dispose of their Prizes in *Algiers*, and buy all Necessaries without any Custom, — — *ib.*

Christian Captives escaping on board *English* Ships of War, after Notice of Arrival, not to be remanded, — — 18

No *British* Subjects to be made Slaves in *Algiers*, — — — *ib.*

Passengers, being Subjects of either Party, and found on board Enemies Ships, not to be molested in Person or Goods, — *ib.*

Mutual Salutes on *English* Ships of War entering the Port of *Algiers*, — — *ib.*

CONTENTS.

Contraveners to be punished, and to make Restitution; but the Peace to hold and continue, — — — 185
Treaty of 1682, comprehended in that of 1606, — — *ib.*
Form of the *Algerine* Passport, — 186
Treaties of 1672, 1664, and 1662, comprehended in that of 1686, — — *ib.*

TREATIES with *Algiers* renewed and confirmed.

TREATY of 1716, confirming the Treaties of 1686, 1700, and 1703, — 187
Treaty of 1703, confirming the Treaties of 1682, 1686, and 1700, — — 188

TREATIES with *Tripoly.*

TREATY of perpetual Peace and Amity of 1716, — — — 188
Ships on both Sides to pass freely with all Persons and Goods, — 189
All Ships producing Passes, or the major Part of the Crew being Subjects of either, to pass freely, — — *ib.*
Ships of *Tripoly* not to use Violence to any Persons on board *English* Ships, — 190
Ships of *Tripoly* not to be carried or disposed of into any Service against *Great Britain*, — *ib.*
British Ships, Men or Goods, taken by an Enemy, not to be sold in *Tripoly*, — *ib.*
British Subjects, found on board and Enemy of *Tripoly*, not to be molested, — 191

British

British Ships of War may difpofe of their Prizes, and buy all Neceffaries in *Tripoly*, without paying Cuftom, —— 1t
Chriftian Captives efcaping to *Englifh* Ships of War, after Notice of their Arrival, not to be remanded, — — — *i*
Mutual Salutes on *Englifh* Ships of War coming into *Tripoly*, — — *it*
Britifh Merchant-Ships not to be detained in *Tripoly* longer than three Days, — 1
Minorca and *Gibraltar*, Part of the *Britifh* Dominions, and the Inhabitants entitled to the fame Privileges, —— — *il*
Ships of *Tripoly* not to cruize before *Minorca* or *Gibraltar*, —— 1(
All former Treaties confirmed, — *ib*
Treaties of 1676, 1686, and 1662, comprehended in that of 1716, —— *ib*

Treaties with *Tunis*.

TREATY of perpetual Peace and and free Trade 1716, — — 19
Freedom of Trade for all Ships of both Parties, paying the antient Duties, —— 19
All Ships on both Sides to go unmolefted, — *it*
All Paffengers and Goods in *Englifh* Ships to be free, —— —— *ib.*
Englifh Ships to protect all Goods on board them belonging to *Tunis*, — — *ib.*
Goods or Subjects of *Tunis* fhipped on board *Englifh* Ships to be entered before the Conful and certified, —— — *ib.*

Minorca

CONTENTS.

Page

Minorca and *Gibraltar* Part of the *British* Dominions, and the Inhabitants to have the same Privileges, —— — 195
Ships of *Tunis* not to cruize before or near *Minorca* or *Gibraltar*, — — 196
Liberty of repairing, &c. all Ships of War on both Sides in all Ports, ——— *ib.*
British Ships of War or Troops at *Port Mahon*, freely to send for, and buy Provisions at *Tunis*, ——— — *ib.*
Englishmen taken in the Service of an Enemy may be made Slaves, but not Merchants or Passengers, ——— ——— 197
Proper Salutes to be paid, and returned on the Arrival of a *British* Flag Officer, — *ib.*
Due Honour to the *British* Consul, — *ib.*
British Ships importing Stores or Provisions to *Tunis*, not to pay Duty, ——— 197
Treaties of 1686, 1674, and 1662, comprehended in that of 1716, ——— — 198

Note, The Treaties with *Spain* are considered and inserted in this Collection, as they subsisted and were in force before the breaking out of the War in 1739.

A Placard of Ampliation, ——— 199
Another Placart, · ——— ——— 204
A Copy of a Certificate for a private Ship to annoy the Enemy in Time of War, — 207
Instructions for Commanders of such Merchant Ships or other Vessels, as may have Letters of Marque or Commissions for private Men of War against the *French* King, his Vassals, &c. dated the 29th of *March*, 1744. — 211

Further

CONTENTS.

                                                            Page

Further Instructions for such Commanders as in the last Article, extracted from the Regiftry of the High Court of Admiralty of *England*, dated the 18th of *June*, 1744. 220

Additional Instructions to such Commanders as in the two last preceding Articles, (against *France* and *Spain*) dated the 27th of *December*, 1744, ——— — 231

An additional Instruction to the three last preceding Articles, dated the 30th of *March*, 1747, ——— — 233

Form of a Protest from the Capture of a Ship as Prize, ——— —— 235

Interrogatories concerning whose Right or Property (Prizes taken from the Enemy in Time of War belong) to be first administred before any Distribution can be made, — 237

Treaty of Navigation and Commerce between the Crowns of Great-Britain and France; concluded at Utrecht, *March 31, O. S.* 1713.

ARTICLE I.

THAT there shall be a reciprocal and intirely perfect Liberty of Navigation and Commerce between the Subjects on each Part, through all and every the Kingdoms, States, Dominions, and Provinces of their Royal Majesties in *Europe*, concerning all and singular Kinds of Goods in those Places, and on those Conditions, and in such Manner and Form as is settled and adjusted in the following Articles.

Free Navigation and Commerce in Europe.

ARTICLE III.

That the Subjects and Inhabitants of the Kingdoms, Provinces, and Dominions of each of their Royal Majesties, shall exercise no Acts of Hostility and Violence against each other; neither by Sea, nor by Land, nor in Rivers, Streams, Ports or Havens; under any Colour or Pretence whatsoever, so that the Subjects of either Party shall receive no Patent, Commission, or Instruction for arming and acting at Sea as Privateers, nor Letters of Reprisals (as they are called) from any Princes or States, which are Enemies to one Side or the other;

Subjects of either Nation not to act under any Commission against the other.

B nor

nor by Virtue or under Colour of such Patents, Commissions or Reprisals, shall they disturb, infest, or any way prejudice or damage the aforesaid Subjects and Inhabitants of the Queen of *Great-Britain*, or of the most Christian King; neither shall they arm Ships in such manner as is abovesaid, or go out to Sea therewith. To which End, as often as it is required by either Side, strict and express Prohibitions shall be renewed and published in all the Regions, Dominions and Territories of each Party wheresoever, that no one shall in any wise use such Commissions or Letters of Reprisals, under the severest Punishment that can be inflicted on the Transgressors; besides Restitution and full Satisfaction to be given to those to whom they shall have done any Damage.

ARTICLE IV.

Free Passage in Europe. The Subjects and Inhabitants of each of the aforesaid Confederates shall have Liberty, freely and securely, without Licence or Passport, general or special, by Land or by Sea, or any other Way to go into the Kingdoms, Countries, Provinces, Lands, Islands, Cities, Villages, Towns wall'd or unwall'd, fortified or unfortified, Ports, Dominions, or Territories whatsoever of the other Confederate in *Europe*, there to enter and to return from thence, to abide there, or to pass through the same, and in the mean Time to buy and purchase as they please all Things necessary for their Subsistance and Use; and they shall be treated with all mutual Kindness and Favour: Provided however, that in all these Matters they behave and comport themselves conformably to the Laws and Statutes, and live and converse with each other friendly and peaceably, and keep up reciprocal Concord by all manner of good Understanding.

ARTICLE

ARTICLE V.

The Subjects of each of their Royal Majesties may have Leave and Licence to come with their Ships; as also with the Merchandizes and Goods on board the same (the Trade and Importation whereof are not prohibited by the Laws of either Kingdom) to the Lands, Countries, Cities, Ports, Places and Rivers of either Side in *Europe*, to enter into the same, to resort thereto, to remain and reside there without any Limitation of Time; and moreover they shall have free Leave, without any Molestation, to remove themselves; and if they shall happen to be married, their Wives, Children and Servants; together with their Merchandizes, Wares, Goods and Effects, either bought or imported, whensoever and whithersoever they shall think fit, out of the Bounds of each Kingdom, by Land and by Sea, on the Rivers and fresh Waters, discharging the usual Duties, notwithstanding any Law, Privilege, Grant, Immunity, or Custom, in any wise importing the contrary.

Free Ingress and Egress with all Goods not prohibited.

ARTICLE VII.

Merchants, Masters of Ships, Owners, Mariners, and all other Persons; Ships, and all Merchandizes and Effects in general of one of the Confederates, and of his Subjects and Inhabitants, shall, on no public or private Account, by Virtue of any general or special Edict, be seized in any the Lands, Ports, Havens, Shores, or Dominions whatsoever of the other Confederate, for the publick Use, for warlike Expeditions, or for any other Cause; much less for the private use of any one; shall they be detained by Arrests, constrained by any Kind of Violence, or in any wise molested or injured. Moreover, it shall be unlawful for the Subjects of both Parties to take any Thing, or to extort it by Force, except the Person to whom it belongs consent, and it be paid for with ready Money. Which however is not to

Subjects or Goods of either not to be seized or detained.

be understood of that Detention and Seizure which shall be made by the Command and Authority of Justice, and by the ordinary Methods, on account of Debt or Crimes, in respect whereof, the Proceeding must be by way of Law, according to the Form of Justice.

ARTICLE XV.

Privateers of Enemies not to fit themselves, or dispose of Captures in the Ports of either Party.

It shall not be lawful for any foreign Privateers, not being Subjects of one or the other of the Confederates, who have Commissions from any other Prince or State in Enmity with either Nation, to fit their Ships in the Ports of either the one or the other of the aforesaid Parties, to sell what they have taken, or in any other Manner whatsoever, to exchange either Ships, Merchandizes, or any other Lading; neither shall they be allowed even to purchase Victuals, except such as shall be necessary for their going to the next Port of that Prince from whom they have Commissions.

ARTICLE XVII.

Free Navigation and Passage to and from Places at Enmity with either.

It shall be lawful for all and singular the Subjects of the Queen of *Great-Britain*, and of the most Christian King, to sail with their Ships with all manner of Liberty and Security; no Distinction being made who are the Proprietors of the Merchandizes laden thereon from any Port, to the Places of those who are now, or shall be hereafter at Enmity with the Queen of *Great-Britain*, or the most Christian King. It shall likewise be lawful for the Subjects and Inhabitants aforesaid, to sail with the Ships and Merchandizes aforementioned; and to trade with the same Liberty and Security from the Places, Ports and Havens, of those who are Enemies of both, or of either Party, without any Opposition or Disturbance whatsoever, not only directly from the Places of the Enemy aforementioned to neutral Places; but also from one Place belonging to an Enemy, to another Place belonging to an Enemy, whether they be under the Jurifdiction of the fame Prince, or under feveral: And as it is now ftipulated concerning Ships and Goods, that free Ships fhall alfo give a Freedom to Goods, and that every thing fhall be deemed to be free and exempt, which fhall be found on Board the Ships belonging to the Subjects of either of the Confederates; although the whole Lading, or any Part thereof fhould appertain to the Enemies of either of their Majefties, Contraband Goods being always excepted; on the Difcovery whereof, Matters fhall be manged according to the Senfe of the fubfequent Articles: It is alfo agreed in like manner, that the fame Liberty be extended to Perfons who are on board a free Ship, with this Effect, that although they be Enemies to both or either of Party, they are not to be taken out of that free Ship, unlefs they are Soldiers, and in actual Service of the Enemies.

ARTICLE XVIII.

This Liberty of Navigation and Commerce fhall extend to all Kinds of Merchandizes, excepting thofe only which follow in the next Article, and which are diftinguifhed by the Name of Contraband. *Exception of Contraband Goods.*

ARTICLE XIX.

Under this Name of Contraband, or prohibited Goods, fhall be comprehended Arms, Great Guns, Bombs with their Fuzees, and other Things belonging to them; Fire-Balls, Gunpowder, Match, Canon-Ball, Pikes, Swords, Lances, Spears, Halberds, Mortars, Petards, Granadoes, Saltpetre, Mufkets, Mufket-Ball, Helmets, Head-Pieces, Breaft Plates, Coats of Mail, and the like Kinds of Arms proper for arming Soldiers, Mufket-refts, Belts, Horfes with their Furniture, and all other warlike Inftruments whatever. *Contraband Goods fpecified.*

ARTICLE

ARTICLE XX.

What Goods shall not be deem'd Contraband. These Merchandizes which follow, shall not be reckoned among prohibited Goods; that is to say, all Sorts of Cloths and all other Manufactures woven of any Wool, Flax, Silk, Cotton, or any other Materials whatever; all Kinds of Cloths and Wearing-Apparel, together with the Species whereof they are used to be made; Gold and Silver as well coined as uncoined, Tin, Iron, Lead, Copper, Brass, Coals; as also Wheat and Barley, and any other Kind of Corn and Pulse; Tobacco, and likewise all manner of Spices; salted and smoak'd Flesh, salted Fish, Cheese and Butter, Beer, Oils, Wines, Sugars and all Sorts of Salt; and in general, all Provisions which serve for the Nourishment of Mankind, and the Sustenance of Life: Furthermore, all Kinds of Cotton, Hemp, Flax, Tar, Pitch, Ropes, Cables, Sails, Sail-cloths, Anchors, and any Parts of Anchors; also Ships Masts, Planks, Boards, and Beams, of what Trees soever; and all other Things proper either for building or repairing Ships, and all other Goods whatever which have not been work'd into the Form of any Instrument or Thing prepared for War, by Land or by Sea, shall not be reputed Contraband, much less such as have been already wrought and made up for any other Use; all which shall wholly be reckoned among free Goods; as likewise all other Merchandizes and Things which are not comprehended, and particularly mentioned in the preceding Article; so that they may be transported and carried in the freest manner by the Subjects of both Confederates, even to Places belonging to an Enemy, such Towns or Places being only excepted as are at that Time besieged, block'd up or invested.

ARTICLE

ARTICLE XXI.

To the End that all Manner of Diffentions and Quarrels may be avoided and prevented on one Side and t'other, it is agreed, That in cafe either of their Royal Majefties, Parties hereto, fhould be engaged in War, the Ships and Veffels belonging to the Subjects of the other Ally, muft be furnifhed with Sea-Letters or Paffports, expreffing the Name, Property and Bulk of the Ship, as alfo the Name and Place of Habitation of the Mafter or Commander of the faid Ship, that it may appear thereby, that the Ship really and truly belongs to the Subjects of one of the Princes; which Paffports fhall be made out and granted according to the Form annexed to this Treaty; they fhall likewife be recalled every Year, that is, if the Ship happens to return home within the Space of a Year. It is likewife agreed, That fuch Ships being laden, are to be provided, not only with Paffports as abovementioned, but alfo with Certificates containing the feveral Particulars of the Cargo, the Place whence the Ship failed, and whither fhe is bound; that fo it may be known whether any forbidden or contraband Goods, as are enumerated in the 19th Article of this Treaty, be on board the fame; which Certificates fhall be made out by the Officers of the Place whence the Ship fet fail, in the accuftomed Form. And if any one fhall think it fit or advifable to exprefs in the faid Certificates the Perfon to whom the Goods on board belong, he may freely do fo.

All Ships of Subjects on both Sides to be furnifhed with Paffports and Certificates.

ARTICLE XXII.

The Ships of the Subjects and Inhabitants of either of their Moft Serene Royal Majefties coming upon any Coaft belonging to either of the faid Allies, but not willing to enter into Port, or being entred into Port, and not willing to unload their Cargoes, or break Bulk, fhall not be obliged to give an Account of their Lading, unlefs they fhould be fufpected

Ships not obliged to give Account of their Lading, unlefs fufpected.

suspected upon some manifest Tokens of carrying to the Enemy of the other Ally any prohibited Goods called contraband.

ARTICLE XXIII.

If suspected, to produce their Passports and Certificates.

And in such Case of manifest Suspicion, the said Subjects and Inhabitants of the Dominions of either of their Most Serene Majesties shall be obliged to exhibit in the Ports their Passports and Certificates, in the Manner before specified.

ARTICLE XXIV.

Ships of War and Privateers to keep at Distance from Merchantmen at Sea, and only to send their Boat to examine the Passports,

That if the Ships of the said Subjects or Inhabitants of either of their Most Serene Majesties shall be met with, either sailing along the Coasts, or on the high Seas, by any Ship of War of the other, or by any Privateers, the said Ships of War or Privateers, for the avoiding of any Disorder, shall remain out of Cannon-Shot, and may send their Boats aboard the Merchant-Ship, which they shall so meet with, and may enter her to the Number of two or three Men only, to whom the Master or Commander of such Ship or Vessel shall exhibit his Passport, concerning the Property of the Ship, made out according to the Form inserted in this present Treaty; and the Ship, when she shall have shewed such Passport, shall be free and at liberty to pursue her Voyage, so as it shall not be lawful to molest or search her in any Manner, or to give her Chace, or force her to quit her intended Course.

ARTICLE XXV.

Merchant-Ship making into an Enemy's Port, to produce Passport and Certificates.

The Merchant-Ship of either of the Parties, which shall be making into a Port belonging to the Enemy of the other Ally, and concerning whose Voyage and the Species of Goods on board her, there shall be just Grounds of Suspicion, shall be obliged to exhibit, as well upon the High Seas as in the Ports and Havens, not only her Passports, but likewise Certificates, expressly shewing that her
Goods

Goods are not of the Number of those which have been prohibited, and which are specified in the 19th Article of this Treaty.

ARTICLE XXVI.

That if by the Exhibiting of the abovesaid Certificates, the other Party discover there are any of those Sorts of Goods which are prohibited and declared contraband by the 19th Article of this Treaty, and consigned for a Port under the Obedience of his Enemies, it shall not be lawful to break up the Hatches of such Ship, or to open any Chests, Coffers, Packs, Casks, or any other Vessels found therein, or to remove the smallest Parcels of her Goods, whether such Ship belong to the Subjects of *France* or of *Great Britain*, unless the Lading be brought on Shore in the Presence of the Officers of the Court of Admiralty, and an Inventory thereof made; but there shall be no Allowance to sell, exchange, or alienate the same in any manner, until after that due and lawful Process shall have been had against such prohibited Goods, and the Judges of the Admiralty respectively shall, by a Sentence pronounced, have confiscated the same, saving always as well the Ship itself, as any other Goods found therein, which by this Treaty are to be esteemed free; neither may they be detained on pretence of their being as it were infected by the prohibited Goods, much less shall they be confiscated as lawful Prize: But if not the whole Cargo, but only Part thereof shall consist of prohibited or contraband Goods, and the Commander of the Ship shall be ready and willing to deliver them to the Captor who has discovered them, in such Case the Captor having received those Goods, shall forthwith discharge the Ship, and not hinder her by any means freely to prosecute the Voyage on which she was bound.

On Discovery of contraband Goods, not to break up the Hatches.

Contraband Goods not to be alienated before Sentence.

Contraband Goods only to be confiscated, and not the Ship or other free Goods.

On delivering of the contraband Goods to the Captor, the Ship to go free.

ARTICLE

ARTICLE XXVII.

All Goods on board Enemies Ships confiscated, unless put on board before War declared, or within the Times and Distances specified.

On the contrary, it is agreed, That whatever shall be found to be laden by the Subjects and Inhabitants of either Party, on any Ship belonging the Enemy of the other, or to his Subjects, the whole, although it be not of the Sort of prohibited Goods, may be confiscated in the same manner as if it belonged to the Enemy himself, except such Goods and Merchandizes as were put on board such Ship before the Declaration of War, or even after such Declaration, if so be it were done within the Time and Limits following, that is to say, if they were put on board such Ship in any Port and Place within the Space of six Weeks after such Declaration within the Bounds called the *Naze* in *Norway*, and the *Soundings*; of two Months from the *Soundings*, to the City of *Gibraltar*; of ten Weeks in the *Mediterranean Sea*, and of eight Months in any other Country or Place in the World, so that the Goods of the Subjects of either Princes, whether they be of the Nature of such as are prohibited, or otherwise, which, as is aforesaid, were put on board any Ship belonging to an Enemy before the War, or after the Declaration of the same, within the Time and Limits abovesaid, shall noways be liable to Confiscation, but shall well and truly be restored without Delay to the Proprietors demanding the same; but so as that if the said Merchandizes be contraband, it shall not be any ways lawful to carry them afterwards to any Ports belonging to the Enemy.

ARTICLE XXVIII.

All Injury on both Sides to be forbid, punished, and repaired.

And that more effectual Care may be taken for the Security of the Subjects of both their Most Serene Royal Majesties, that they suffer no Injury by the Men of War or Privateers of the other Party, all the Commanders of the Ships of the Queen of *Great Britain*, and of the Most Christian King, and all their Subjects, shall be forbid doing any Injury or

(11)

: to the other Side; and if they act to the
hey shall be punished, and shall more-
und to make Satisfaction for all matter of
ınd the Interest thereof, by Reparation,
Pain and Obligation of their Person and

ARTICLE XXXV.

ps and Merchandizes, of what Nature fo- Ships or Goods
:h shall be rescued out of the Hands of rescued from Pi-
s or Robbers on the High Seas, shall be ed.
nto some Port of either Kingdom, and
elivered to the Custody of the Officers of
in order to be restored entire to the true
r, as soon as due and sufficient Proof shall
:oncerning the Property thereof.

ARTICLE XXXVI.

be lawful for the Ships of War of either Free Ingress and
/lajesties, and Privateers, freely to carry of War and Pri-
ever they please, the Ships and Goods vateers with their
n their Enemies, without being obliged any Duty,
y Duty to the Officers of the Admiralty, Search, or Moles-
her Judges; nor shall such Prizes be ar-
feized, when they come to and enter the
:ither of their Most Serene Majesties; nor
Searchers or other Officers of those Places
:fame, or make Examination concerning the
:fs of such Prizes, but they may hoist Sail
me, and depart and carry their Prizes to
expressed in their Commissions or Patents,
: Commanders of such Ships of War shall
d to shew: On the contrary, no Shelter or
hall be given in their Ports to such as shall Captors of the
de Prize of the Subjects of either of their Party not to be
; but if such should come in, being forced sheltered.
of Weather, or the Danger of the Sea, all
/leans shall be vigorously used, that they go
etire from thence as soon as possible, so far

as

as this shall not be contrary to former Treaties made in this Respect with other Kings and States.

ARTICLE XXXVII.

Capture of Ship or Goods of one Party, not to be suffered on the Coast or in the Port of the other.

Neither of their Most Serene Royal Majesties shall permit that the Ships or Goods of the other be taken upon the Coasts, or in the Ports or Rivers of their Dominions, by Ships of War, or others having Commission from any Prince, Commonwealth, or State whatsoever; and in case such a Thing should happen, both Parties shall use their Authority and united Force that the Damage done be made good.

ARTICLE XXXIX.

In case of Torture committed, the Ship to be released, and the Guilty punished.

But if it shall appear that a Captor made use of any kind of Torture upon the Master of the Ship, the Ship's Crew, or others who shall be on board any Ship belonging to the Subjects of the other Party; in such Case, not only the Ship itself, together with all Persons, Merchandizes, and Goods whatsoever, shall be forthwith released without any further Delay, and set entirely free, but also such as shall be found guilty of so great a Crime, as also the Accessaries thereunto, shall suffer the most severe Punishment suitable to their Crime: This the Queen of *Great Britan* and the Most Christian King do mutually engage shall be done without any Respect of Persons.

Form of the Passports and Letters which are to be given in the Admiralty of France, *to the Ships and Barks, which shall go from thence, according to the* 21*st Article of this present Treaty.*

*L*EWIS Count of *Thoulouse*, Admiral of *France*, to all who shall see these Presents, greeting; We make known, that we have given Leave and Permission to   Master and Commander

mander of the Ship called   of the Town of
       Burthen   Tons or thereabouts, lying
at prefent in the Port and Haven of   and
bound for   and laden with
after that his Ship has been vifited, and before Sailing, he fhall make Oath before the Officers who have the Jurifdiction of maritime Affairs, that the faid Ship belongs to one or more of the Subjects of his Majefty, the Act whereof fhall be put at the End of thefe Prefents; as likewife that he will keep, and caufe to be kept by his Crew on board, the marine Ordinances and Regulations, and enter in the proper Office a Lift figned and witneffed, containing the Names and Sirnames, the Places of Birth and Abode of the Crew of his Ship, and of all who fhall embark on board her, whom he fhall not take on board without the Knowledge and Permiffion of the Officers of the Marine; and in every Port or Haven where he fhall enter with his Ship, he fhall fhew this prefent Leave to the Officers and Judges of the Marine, and fhall give a faithful Account to them of what paffed and was done during his Voyage, and he fhall carry the Colours, Arms, and Enfigns of the King and of us during his Voyage. In witnefs whereof, we have figned thefe Prefents, and put the Seal of our Arms thereunto, and caufed the fame to be counterfigned by our Secretary of the Marine at   the
Day of   17   Signed *Lewis* Count of *Thoulouse*, and underneath by

Form of the Act containing the Oath.

  We   of the Admiralty of
do certify that   Mafter of the Ship named in the above Paffport, hath taken the Oath mentioned therein. Done at   the
Day of   17   .

Form

Form of the Certificates to be required of and to be given by the Magistrate or Officers of the Customs of the Town and Port in their respective Towns and Ports, to the Ships and Vessels which sail from thence, according to the Directions of the 21st Article of this present Treaty.

We *A. B.* Magistrate (or) Officers of the Customs of the Town and Port of *C.* do certify and attest, That on the   Day of the Month of   in the Year of our Lord 17   *D. E.* of *F.* personally appeared before us, and declared by a solemn Oath, That the Ship or Vessel called *G.* of about   Tuns, whereof *H. I.* of *K.* his usual Place of Habitation, is Master or Commander, does rightfully and properly belong to him and others Subjects of Her Most Serene Majesty our most gracious Sovereign, and to them alone: That she is now bound from the Port of *L.* to the Port of *M.* laden with the Goods and Merchandize hereunder particularly described and enumerated, that is to say, as follows.

In witness whereof we have signed this Certificate, and sealed it with the Seal of our Office. Given the   Day of the Month of   in the Year of our Lord 17   .

AMERICAN *Treaty of Peace, good Correspondence, and Neutrality, between the Crowns of* Great Britain *and* France; *concluded at* London, November 16. 1686.

ARTICLE I.

THAT from the Day of this present Treaty, there shall be between the *French* Nation and the *English* Nation, a firm Peace, Union, Agreement, and good Correspondence, as well upon Sea as upon Land, both in the Northern and Southern *America*, and in the Islands, Colonies, Forts, and Towns, (without Exception of Places) belonging to the Dominions of his Most Christian Majesty and of his *Britannick* Majesty, and under the Jurisdiction of the Governors of their said Majesties respectively.

Peace and Amity in all Parts of America.

ARTICLE II.

That no Ships or Vessels, great or small, belonging to the Subjects of his Most Christian Majesty, shall be fitted out or employed in the said Islands, Colonies, Fortresses, Towns and Governments belonging to his Most Christian Majesty, to attack the Subjects of his *Britannick* Majesty, in the Islands, Colonies, Fortresses, Towns and Governments belonging to his said *Britannick* Majesty, or to do them any Injury or Damage: And in like manner, no Ships or Vessels, great or small, belonging to the Subjects of his *Britannick* Majesty, shall be fitted out or employed in the said Islands, Colonies, Fortresses, Towns and Governments of his said Majesty, to attack the Subjects of his Most Christian Majesty in the Islands, Colonies, Fortresses, Towns and Governments of his said Majesty, or to do them any Injury or Damage.

Ships not to be fitted out in the Dominions of either to attack the other.

ARTICLE

(16)

ARTICLE III.

Soldiers or Subjects of the one not to do any Injury to those of the other, or assist the 'Indians' against them.

That no Soldiers, armed Men, or any others whatsoever inhabiting and living in the said *English* Islands, Colonies, Forts, Cities, and Governments, or who shall come out of *Europe* to be in Garrison there, shall commit any Act of Hostility, or do any Injury or Damage, directly or indirectly, to the Most Christian King's Subjects in the said *French* Islands, Colonies, Forts, Cities, and Governments; neither shall they give any Assistance, or Supplies of Men or Victuals to the barbarous or wild *Indians* with whom the Most Christian King shall hereafter be at War.

In like Manner, no Soldiers, arm'd Men, or any other whatsoever inhabiting and living in the said *French* Islands, Colonies, Forts, Cities, and Governments, or who shall come out of *Europe* to be in Garrison there, shall commit any Act of Hostility, or do any Injury or Damage, directly or indirectly, to the King of *Great-Britain*'s Subjects in the said *English* Islands, Colonies, Forts, Cities, and Governments, neither shall they give any Assistance or Supplies of Men or Victuals to the barbarous wild *Indians*, with whom the King of *Great-Britain* shall be at War.

ARTICLE IV.

Both Kings to retain all Rights and Dominions in America, according to their Right and present Possession.

That both Kings shall have and retain to themselves all the Dominions, Rights, and Pre-eminences in the *American* Seas, Roads, and other Waters whatsoever, in as full and ample manner as of Right belongs to them, and in such manner as they now possess the same.

ARTICLE V.

Subjects of either not to trade or fish in the Dominions, or on the Coasts of the other.

And therefore the Subjects, Inhabitants, Merchants, Commanders of Ships, Masters and Mariners of the Kingdoms, Provinces and Dominions of each King respectively, shall abstain and forbear
to

to trade and fish in all the Places possessed, or which shall be possessed by one or the other Party in *America*, viz. The King of *Great-Britain*'s Subjects shall not carry on their Commerce and Trade, nor fish in the Havens, Bays, Creeks, Roads, Coasts or Places, which the most Christian King holds, or shall hereafter hold in *America*: And in like manner, the most Christian King's Subjects shall not carry on their Commerce and Trade, nor fish in the Havens, Bays, Creeks, Roads, Coasts or Places, which the King of *Great-Britain* possesses, or shall hereafter possess in *America*; and if any Ship or Vessel shall be found trading or fishing contrary to the Tenor of this Treaty, the said Ship or Vessel, with its Lading, Proof being made thereof, shall be confiscated; nevertheless, the Party who shall think himself aggrieved by such Sentence or Confiscation, shall have Liberty to apply himself to the Privy-Council of that King, by whose Governors or Judges Sentence was pronounced against him, so as the Execution of the Sentence shall not be stopp'd or hindered on that Account; but it is always to be understood, that the Liberty of Navigation ought in no manner to be disturbed, where nothing is done contrary to the genuine Sense of his Treaty.

Ships found so trading or fishing, to be confiscated.

Party aggrieved may apply to the Privy-Council of either King.

Liberty of Navigation not to be disturbed.

ARTICLE VI.

That in case the Subjects and Inhabitants of either of the Kings, with their Shipping, whether public and of War, or private and of Merchants, be forced through Stress of Weather, Pursuit of Pirates or Enemies, or any other urgent Necessity, for seeking of Shelter and Harbour, to retreat and enter into any of the Rivers, Creeks, Bays, Havens, Roads, Ports, or Shores belonging to the other Party in *America*; they shall be received and treated with all Humanity and Kindness, and enjoy all friendly Protection and Help; and they shall be permitted to refresh and provide themselves at

All Ships and Subjects of either forced into any Ports of the other, to be well received and supplied.

reason-

reasonable and usual Rates with Victuals, and all Things needful for the Sustenance of their Persons, or Reparation of their Ships, and Conveniency of their Voyage; and they shall no ways be detained or hindered from returning out of the said Ports or Roads, but may remove and depart when and whither they please, without any Lett or Hindrance; and they shall be obliged to unliver their Cargo, or to carry out and expose to Sale any of their Goods or Merchandizes; and likewise on their Part, they shall not take in any Merchandizes on board their Vessels, nor employ themselves in fishing, under the Penalty of the Confiscation of their Ships and Goods, as in the foregoing Article is express'd; and it is further agreed, that whensoever the Subjects of either King shall be forced to enter with their Ships into the Ports of the other, they shall be obliged at their coming in to hang out the Flag or Colours of their Nation, and to give Notice of their Arrival by three Discharges of a Musket; in default of which, and of sending their Boat on Shore, they shall be liable to Confiscation.

_{Not to unliver their Cargo, or take in any Merchandize.}

_{To hang out their Colours, and discharge a Musket on their coming in.}

ARTICLE VII.

_{Ships stranded, wreck'd, or in Danger to be assisted.}

If any Ships belonging to either of the Kings, their People or Subjects, shall, within the Coasts or Dominions of the other, stick upon the Sands, or be wreck'd (which God forbid) or suffer any other Damage, all friendly Assistance and Relief shall be given to the Persons ship-wreck'd, or such as shall be in Danger thereof; and Letters of safe Conduct shall likewise be given to them for their free and quiet Passage from thence, and the Return of every one to his own Country.

ARTICLE VIII.

_{Three or four Ships forced in together, not to stay longer than shall be allowed.}

When it shall happen that the Ships of either Party (as abovementioned) through Danger of the Sea, or other urgent Cause, be driven into the Ports of the other; if they be three or four together, and may

(19)

may give juft ground of Sufpicion, they fhall immediately upon their Arrival, acquaint the Governor or chief Magiftrate of the Place, with the Caufe of their coming; and fhall ftay no longer than the faid Governor or chief Magiftrate will allow, and fhall be requifite for fupplying themfelves with Provifions, and repairing their Ships.

ARTICLE X.

The Subjects of either Nation fhall not harbour the barbarous or wild Inhabitants, or the Slaves or Goods which the faid Inhabitants fhall have taken from the Subjects of the other Nation; neither fhall they give them any Affiftance or Protection in their faid Depredations.

Slaves or Goods taken from either Party by the Indians, not to be harboured.

ARTICLE XI.

The Governors, Officers, and Subjects of either King, fhall not in any wife moleft or difturb the Subjects of the other, in fettling their refpective Colonies, or in their Commerce and Navigation.

Neither Party to moleft the other.

ARTICLE XII.

And the more to affure the Subjects of the King of *Great-Britain*, and of the moft Chriftian King, that no Injury fhall be offered them by the Ships of War or Privateers on either Side; all the Captains of the Ships of War of his Majefty of *Great-Britain*, as alfo of the moft Chriftian King, and all their Subjects who fit out Privateers; and likewife their privileged Companies, fhall be enjoined not to do any Injury or Damage whatfoever to the other; and if they do, they fhall be punifhed, and be moreover liable to fatisfy all Cofts and Damages, by way of Reftitution and Reparation, upon Pain and Obligation of Perfon and Goods.

Ships of War and Privateers on both Sides not to injure the other.

Party injuring to be punifhed, and obliged to Reftitution.

ARTICLE XIV.

And whereas feveral Pirates roving up and down in the *American* Seas, as well Nothern as Southern, do much

Pirates not to be affifted or protected.

C 2

much Damage to Trade, and moleſt the Subjects of both Crowns in their Navigation and Commerce in thoſe Parts; it is agreed, that ſtrict Orders ſhall be given to the Governors and Officers of both Kings, that they give no Aſſiſtance or Protection to any Pirates, of whatſoever Nation they be; nor ſuffer them to have any Retreat in the Ports or Roads of their reſpective Governments; and the ſaid Governors and Officers ſhall alſo be expreſsly commanded to puniſh, as Pirates, all ſuch as ſhall fit out any Ship or Ships, without lawful Commiſſion and Authority.

ARTICLE XV.

Subjects of either taking Commiſſions as Privateers againſt the other, to be puniſhed as Pirates.

No Subjects of either King ſhall apply for, or take any Commiſſion or Letters of Marque for arming any Ship or Ships to act as Privateers in *America*, whether Nothern or Southern, from any Prince or State, with which the other ſhall be at War; and if any Perſon ſhall take ſuch Commiſſions or Letters of Marque, he ſhall be puniſhed as a Pirate.

ARTICLE XVII.

Concerning the Turtle Fiſhery.

The moſt Chriſtian King's Subjects ſhall have Liberty to fiſh for Turtles in the Iſland of *Cayman*.

ARTICLE XVIII.

In Caſe of a War in Europe between the Parties, no Hoſtilities to be comitted between their Subjects reſiding in America.

If any Breach ſhould happen (which God forbid) between the ſaid Crowns in *Europe*, no Act of Hoſtility, either by Sea or Land, ſhall however be done by any of the King of *Great-Britain*'s Garriſons, Soldiers or Subjects whatſoever, of the Iſlands, Colonies, Forts, Cities and Governments, which now are, or ſhall hereafter be under the *Engliſh* Dominion in *America*, againſt the moſt Chriſtian King's Subjects inhabiting or reſiding in any of the *American* Colonies: In like manner and reciprocally in the Caſe aforeſaid of a Breach in *Europe*, no Act of Hoſtility, either by Sea or Land, ſhall

shall be committed by any of the most Christian King's Garrisons, Soldiers or Subjects whatsoever, of the Islands, Colonies, Forts, Cities, and Governments, which now are, or hereafter shall be under the *French* Dominion in *America*, against the King of *Great-Britain*'s Subjects inhabiting or residing in any of the *American* Colonies; but a true and firm Peace and Neutrality shall continue in *America* between the said *British* and *French* Nations, in the same Manner as if such Breach in *Europe* had not happened.

Treaty of Peace between Great-Britain *and* France; *concluded at* Utrecht, March 31, 1713.

ARTICLE XII.

THE most Christian King shall take care to have delivered to the Queen of *Great-Britain*, on the same Day that the Ratifications of this Treaty shall be exchanged, solemn and authentic Letters or Instruments, by Virtue whereof it shall appear, that the Island of *St. Christopher's* is to be possessed hereafter by *British* Subjects only; likewise all *Nova Scotia* or *Acadie*, with its ancient Boundaries; as also the City of *Port Royal*, now called *Annapolis Royal*, and all other Things in those Parts which depend on the said Lands and Islands; together with the Dominions, Property, and Possession of the said Islands, Lands and Places, and all Right whatsoever by Treaties, or any other way attained, which the most Christian King, the Crown of *France*, or any the Subjects thereof, have hitherto had to the said Islands, Lands and Places, and to the Inhabitants of the same, are yielded and made over to the Queen of *Great-Britain* and to her Crown for ever; as the most Christian King doth now yield and make over all the said Premisses,

St. Christopher's, Nova Scotia, and the Fishery there, and *Annapolis Royal* quitted to the *English.*

misses, and that in such ample Manner and Form that the Subjects of the most Christian King shall hereafter be excluded from all Kind of fishing in the Seas, Bays and other Places on the Coast of *Nova Scotia*, that is to say, on those Coasts which lye towards the East, within thirty Leagues, beginning from the Island commonly called *Sable* inclusively, and thence stretching along towards the South-West.

ARTICLE XIII.

Newfoundland quitted to the English, with Right reserved to the French to catch and dry Fish there.

The Island called *Newfoundland*, with the adjacent Islands, shall from this Time forward belong of Right wholly to *Great-Britain*, and to that End the Town and Fortress of *Placentia*, and whatever other Places in the said Islands are in the Possession of the *French*, shall be yielded and given up within seven Months from the Exchange of the Ratifications of this Treaty, or sooner, if possible, by the most Christian King, to Persons having a Commission from the Queen of *Great-Britain* for that Purpose: Nor shall the most Christian King, his Heirs and Successors, or any of their Subjects, at any Time hereafter claim any Right to the said Island and Islands, or to any Part of it or them; moreover it shall not be lawful for the Subjects of *France* to fortify any Place in the said Island of *Newfoundland*, or to erect any Buildings there, besides Stages made of Boards, and Huts necessary and usual for drying of fish; or to resort to the said Island beyond the Time necessary for fishing and drying of Fish: But it shall be allowed to the Subjects of *France* to catch Fish and to dry them on Land, in that Part only and no other of the said Island of *Newfoundland*, which extends from the Place called *Cape Bonavista* to the Nothern Point of the said Island; and from thence bearing down along the Western Side, reaches as far as the Place called *Point Riche*. But

Cape Breton to belong to the French.

the Island called *Cape Breton*, as also all others both in the Mouth of the River of *St. Lawrence*, and in the

the *Gulph* of the same Name, shall hereafter belong of Right to the *French*; and the most Christian King shall have full Liberty to fortify any Place or Places there.

Marine Treaty between the Crowns of Great-Britain *and* France; *concluded at* St. Germains, *the* 24th *of* February, 1676-7,

ARTICLE I.

ALL the Subjects of the most Christian King may sail, trade, and use all Kind of Traffick with full Freedom and Security in all the Kingdoms, Countries and Territories that now are, or hereafter shall be at Peace or in Neutrality with the said most Christian King, without being hindred or molested by the Ships of War, or any other Ship belonging to the King of *Great-Britain*, or his Subjects, upon the Account, or under Pretence of any War or Hostility now subsisting, or which may be hereafter between the said King of *Great-Britain*, and any other Princes or States, which now are, or hereafter may be at Peace and Neutrality with the said most Christian King; and reciprocally all the Subjects of the King of *Great-Britain*, may navigate, negociate, and carry on all Manner of Traffick, with full Freedom and Security, in all the Kingdoms, Countries, and States, which now are, or hereafter shall be at Peace and Neutrality with the said King, without being disturbed or molested by any Ships of War, or other Ships whatsoever appertaining to the most Christian King, or his Subjects, upon the Account, or under Pretence of any War and Hostility now subsisting, or which hereafter may be between the most Christian King, and any other Princes or States which now are, or hereafter may be at Peace or Neutrality with the said King of *Great-Britain*.

Free Navigation and Trade with all neutral Powers.

C 4 ARTICLE

ARTICLE II.

The same in Time of War as Peace, Contraband Goods excepted.

They may carry on Trade during a War, with all the same Merchandizes as in time of Peace, but with an Exception of all Contraband Goods, as explained in the following Article.

ARTICLE III.

Contraband Goods specified.

Goods prohibited and Contraband are, Cannon and their Furniture, Fire-Arms, Powder, Match, Bullets, Pikes, Swords, Lances, Halberts, Partizans, Bombs, Mortars, Petards, Granadoes, Musket-Stocks, Bandaliers, Saltpetre, Ball, Head-Pieces, Shields, Cuirasses, and the like Armour: Under the same Name likewise, the transporting of Soldiers, Horses, Harnesses, Pistol-Stocks, Belts, and other Things appertaining to and used in War, is prohibited.

ARTICLE IV.

What Goods are not to be deem'd Contraband.

The following Merchandizes are not to be comprised in the Number of Prohibited and Contraband Goods, *viz.* Woollen, Linen, Silk, Cotton, or any other Stuffs and Manufactures whatsoever; all Sorts of Cloaths and Dresses made of Stuffs, or any other Matter; Gold or Silver, coined or uncoined, Tin, Iron, Lead, Copper, Coal, Corn, Barley, and other Grain, and Pulse; Tobacco, Spices, salted and dry'd Flesh, dry and salt Fish, Cheese, Butter, Beer, Oil, Wine, Sugar, Salt, and every Thing appertaining to the Nourishment and Support of Life; nor Cottons, Hemp, Flax, Pitch, Cordage, Sails, Anchors, Masts, Boards, and Wood wrought of any Sort of Trees, and that may serve for building Ships or the Repair of them; but the said Commodities shall remain free, as well as all others in general, that are not comprehended in the preceding Article, in such Sort, that the Subjects of the most Christian King may not only transport the same from one neutral Place to another neutral Place,

(25)

ı neutral Place or Port to another
Enemy of the King of *Great-Britain*;
ı Place belonging to an Enemy,
is neutral, but alſo from one Port
ging to the Enemy of the ſaid
likewiſe belonging to his Enemy,
orts or other Places be under the
ıe Prince or State, or of ſeveral
es, with one or all of which the
Britain ſhall be at War; the Sub-
; of *Great-Britain* may reciprocally
ſ Merchandizes not only from one
another neutral Place, or from a
Port to any other belonging to an
ıoſt Chriſtian King; or laſtly, from
g to an Enemy, to any other neu-
alſo from a Port or other Place be-
nemy of the ſaid King, to another
ning to his Enemy, whether theſe
be under the Obedience of one
or of ſeveral Princes and States,
of which the ſaid moſt Chriſtian
t War: Nevertheleſs ſuch Things
ied at all to Towns and Places be-
ıp or inveſted.

RTICLE V.

:erminate all Differences that may   Ships of either
Sea or Land, it has been agreed,   Nation producing
                                     Paſſports, not to
or other Veſſels belonging to the   be detained or
moſt Chriſtian King, which ſhall   moleſted.
Havens, or Ports of the King of
nd would proceed elſewhere from
ıt be detained any longer than to
:hibit their Paſſports (the Form
:ed to this Treaty) to the Officers
g; or, if there ſhould be in the
ıvens any Ships of War belonging
Great-Britain, or any Privateers, to
; of the ſaid Ships, ſo as they ſhall
not

not exact or demand any Money or other Thin[g]
whatsoever on that Account: If any Ships or oth[er]
Vessels appertaining to the Subjects of the mo[st]
Christian King, be met with on the open Sea, or [in]
such Places as are not under the Dominion of th[e]
King of *Great-Britain*, by the Ships of War of th[e]
said King, or others fitted out by his Subjects, th[e]
said Ships keeping at a reasonable Distance o[f]
may send their Boat on board such Ships or Vesse[l]
of the Subjects of the most Christian King, and p[ut]
two or three Men only on board, to the end th[at]
the Master or Owner may exhibit to them his Pa[ss]
port; after which they shall freely pass, withou[t]
being any way molested, searched, stopped, [or]
forced to alter their Course. The Subjects of t[he]
King of *Great-Britain* shall enjoy the same Fre[e]
dom and Immunities, upon producing their Pa[ss]
ports according to the Form before mentioned.

ARTICLE VI.

Ships passing into an Enemy's Country, to produce Certificates and Passports.

If any Vessel or Bark belonging to the Subjec[ts]
of the Most Christian King, and passing to a Cou[n]
try at Enmity with the King of *Great Britain*, mee[t]
with a Man of War in her Passage, in like manne[r]
if a Ship appertaining to the *English* or other Sub[jects]
jects of the King of *Great Britain*, is met with goin[g]
towards a Port belonging to an Enemy of the Mo[st]
Christian King, it shall not be sufficient for her [to]
exhibit her Passports, but also Certificates in d[ue]
and authentick Form from the Officers and Searc[h]
ers of the Customs, of such Ships going out of th[e]
Port which she came from, and containing an A[c]
count of all her Cargo, to the End that it may [be]
known whether there are any contraband Goods [on]
board, and such as are particularized in the Thi[rd]
Article of this Treaty.

ARTICLE VII.

If by producing the said Certificates it be fou[nd]
that there are contraband Goods on board consign[ed]

for an Enemy's Port, it shall not be allowed to go under the Deck of such Ship, nor to open or break any Chests, Bales, Casks, or Tuns, or take the least Thing out of her, 'till she is brought into Port, where a just Inventory shall be taken in the Presence of the Customhouse-Officers: And nothing therefore shall be sold or bartered till after a fair Trial before the Judge of the Admiralty-Court, and Sentence be passed for the Confiscation of such Goods: In which Confiscation nevertheless the Hulk of the Vessel, and the lawful Merchandize on board her shall not be comprized, nor may such free Goods be detained, much less be declared good Prize upon the account of the said contraband Goods. If the Vessel be laden but in part with contraband Goods, and the Master thereof offers at the same time, to put them into the Captor's Hands, he shall not then oblige him to go into any Port, but suffer him to continue his Voyage. *[margin: Contraband Goods to be confiscated. Free Goods not to be detained. On Delivery of contraband Goods to the Captor, the Ship to go free.]*

ARTICLE VIII.

Merchandizes appertaining to the Subjects of the Most Christian King, which shall be found on board Ships belonging to the Enemies of the King of *Great Britain* shall be liable to Forfeiture, tho' they are not contraband; and on the contrary, the Goods of the Enemies of the King of *Great Britain* shall not be taken or confiscated; if they be found on board any Ships appertaining to the Subjects of the Most Christian King, altho' the said Goods make up the best Part of the whole Lading of such Ships; but still with an Exception of all Contraband, which when taken shall be disposed of in the Manner directed by the preceding Articles. In like manner, all Merchandizes belonging to the Subjects of the King of *Great Britain*, which are found on board any Ships belonging to the Enemies of the Most Christian King, shall be liable to Confiscation tho' they be not Contraband; and on the contrary, any Merchandizes of the Enemies of the said Most *[margin: All Goods in Enemies Ships forfeited. Free Ships make free Goods, contraband excepted.]*

Christian

(28)

Christian King shall not be taken or confiscated if they are found on board any Ships appertaining to the Subjects of the King of *Great Britain*, tho' the said Merchandizes make up the best Part or the Whole of the Lading of the said Ships; but still with an Exception to contraband Goods; as to which when taken, they may be disposed of in manner as in the preceding Articles mentioned. And in order to prevent any future new War breaking out from proving injurious or prejudicial to the Subjects of either Side, which shall continue in Peace, it is agreed, that the Ships of any new Enemy laden with Effects and Merchandizes belonging to the Subjects of the other Party that shall be at Peace, shall not make them liable to Confiscation, if they have been laden therewith before the End of the Term hereafter specified, which Term shall be six Weeks after the Declaration of the War, between the *Soundings* and the *Naze* in *Norway*; two Months between the *Soundings* and *Tangier*; two Months and a half, in the *Mediterranean*; and eight Months in all other Parts of the World. So that the Effects of the Subjects of the Most Christian King, taken in the Vessels of any new Enemy of the King of *Great Britain*, may not be confiscated upon that Account, but shall forthwith be restored to the Owners, unless they have been put on board the said Ships after the Expiration of the respective Terms abovementioned, however contraband Goods, which likewise in such Case are not liable to Confiscation for the Reasons aforesaid, must not be carried into an Enemy's Port; and reciprocally the Effects of the Subjects of the King of *Great Britain* taken on board the Ships of any new Enemies of the Most Christian King, shall not be confiscated upon that Account, but shall forthwith be restored to the Owners, unless they have been put on board after the End of the respective Terms before specified; nevertheless, contraband Goods, which shall not be liable

Times and Distances, as to Forfeiture of Goods in Enemies Ships on the breaking out of a War.

liable to Confiscation for the aforesaid Reasons, must not be conveyed into an Enemy's Port.

ARTICLE IX.

And for their more perfect Security, and that the Subjects of both Nations may be under no Apprehensions from the Ships of War, their Majesties shall give most strict Orders and Injunctions to all Captains of Ships and all Privateers, that they do no Injury or Damage to the Merchant-Ships, under the most severe Punishments; besides the strongest Obligations to make full Restitution and Reparation of all Damage to those whom they shall have wronged.

Ships of War and Privateers not to injure any Ships of the other.

ARTICLE XIV.

Whereas it sometimes happens, that the Ships which take Prizes in Time of War, treat the Masters, Pilots, and Passengers, taken therein, very inhumanly, in order to extort such Confession and Declaration from them as they have a mind to; it is agreed, that their Majesties shall prohibit such Treatment under the most severe Penalties, and shall cause all such as shall be convicted thereof to be punished according to their Demerit, and in such a Manner as may deter others from doing the like: And all Captains and Officers who shall be found guilty of such Barbarities and violent Doings, whether they have been committed by themselves, or have been caused or suffered to be done by them, shall forthwith be cashier'd; and they shall besides be proceeded against according to the Heinousness of the Crime; and every Vessel that shall be taken whereof the Mariners and Passengers shall have been ill used, shall be released and set at Liberty, (with her Cargo) without any further Examination or proceeding judicially or otherwise.

Tortures on board Prizes prohibited and punished.

Treaty

Treaty of Peace between Great-Britain an[d] France; concluded at Westminster, No[-]vember *the* 3d, 1655.

ARTICLE I.

Free Navigation in Harbours.

THE People and Subjects of both Natio[ns] may safely and freely sail and ride at Ancho[r] in each other's Harbours and Roads, as they sha[ll] think fit, without any Damage or Injury.

ARTICLE IV.

Free Navigation, Passage and Commerce in *Europe*.

Commerce shall be intirely free betwixt the tw[o] Nations of *England* and *France*, and other Peop[le] and Subjects, by Land and by Sea, and on the fre[sh] Waters, through all and singular the Countries, Do[-]minions, Territories, Provinces, Cities, Towns, Vi[l]lages, and all other Places throughout *Europ*[e,] where Commerce and Trade hath been used to b[e] carried on; so that without any Letters of sa[fe] Conduct, or Application for any general or speci[al] Licence whatsoever, the People and Subjects of th[e] said two Nations shall freely pass and repass, b[y] Land, Sea, or on the fresh Waters, to the sai[d] Countries, Kingdoms, and Dominions; and to a[ll] the Cities, Harbours, Shores, Stations, and Streights[,] and may enter all the Places and Harbours of either with their Ships laden or unladen; and with Car[-]riages, and with Beasts of Draught or Burthen, which are usually employed in carrying Merchan[-]dizes, and may there buy and sell what they please[,] paying only the Market-Price in such Places fo[r] such Necessaries as they may want, either for thei[r] Provision or their Voyage; and may likewise, a[s] Occasion shall require, rig their Ships and repai[r] their Carriages; and it shall be equally free fo[r] them to return to their own Country, or to go t[o] any other Places at their own Discretion with thei[r]
Mer[-]

Merchandize, Goods, or any other Effects whatsoever, without Molestation; provided they pay the due Customs and Port Duties to the other Party, and a proper Regard be likewise had to all the Laws and Ordinances of the Country.

ARTICLE XVI.

Both Parties shall strictly command the Admirals and Commanders of the Fleets, and all other their Sea Captains whatsoever, either carrying their Flags, or bearing Commissions from them, or acting in their Service, not to seize, take, or in any Manner to obstruct or damage the Ships, Vessels, Goods, or Merchandize of the People or Subjects of the other; but that they diligently observe this Treaty and Convention; and all Contraveners shall make Satisfaction to the Party concerned, by suffering corporal Punishment, according to the Nature of the Offence, and by making Reparation for the Damage done by them, if they are able; but if they should not be able, then that Confederate to whom the Offenders belong, shall satisfy and repair the Damage within three Months after Knowledge thereof and Satisfaction demanded; and all Ships of War meeting any Merchant Ships of either Party, shall protect them, while they keep the same Course, against all who shall offer them any Violence. *Sea Commanders of either Party not to injure the other, on pain of Restitution and Punishment.*

ARTICLE XVII.

If the Commanders of any Ships belonging to either Party, or to their People, shall take any Prize at Sea, they shall within twenty-four Hours after their coming into Port, deliver all the Books of Accompts, Papers, Cockets, and Bills of Lading, which they shall have found in such Prizes, to the Judges of the Admiralty, to the Intent that any Person interested may take Copies of the same; and where there shall be no Judge of the Admiralty, the said Papers and Books shall be delivered *All Books and Papers of a Prize Ship to be delivered to the Judge of the Admiralty.*

to the Officers of such Places, who shall send the same sealed up to the Judges of the Admiralty during which, the Mariners on board the Prizes shall not be taken out; nor any Part of the Cargo touched, or any of the Goods set a shore, unless by the Authority of the Court of Admiralty; and a Schedule shall be made of all the Goods, in the Presence of those whom it concerns, who shall also have a Copy of the said Schedule from the Judge.

Men or Goods not to be taken out, but by Authority of the Court.

ARTICLE XVIII.

Officer or Mariner of a Prize, not to be carried away, but in order to be examined.

The Commanders and Captains of any Ships, which shall take any Prizes at Sea, shall not take out of her the Captain, Master, or any Mate or Mariner, unless for the Purpose of examining them; and in that Case they shall not take out above two or three, who shall be carried within the Space of twenty-four Hours before the Judge of the Admiralty; or if there be no such Judge in the Place, before the Magistrate or Officers of the Place, who shall examine them; and such Examination being finished within the same Space of Time, the said Judge or Magistrate shall dismiss them freely, every one to their own Business: All Contraveners hereto shall suffer corporal Punishment.

ARTICLE XIX.

Pirates not to be harboured or assisted, but pursued and punished:

Neither of the Confederates shall receive any Pirates or Robbers into any of their Ports, Havens, Cities or Towns; nor shall they permit them to be received by their People or Inhabitants, or to be harboured, assisted, or supplied; but shall use their Endeavours that such Pirates and Robbers, and their piratical Accomplices, Partners and Assistants, shall be pursued, apprehended, and duly punished, for a Terror to others; and all Ships, Goods and Merchandize, piratically taken by any such, and brought into the Ports of either Confederate, as much as can be found thereof, although they have been already sold to others, shall be restored to the right

Ships and Goods piratically taken, to be restored.

(33)

right Owners, or Satisfaction made for the fame to their Owners, or to thofe who fhall lay Claim to the fame, by Virtue of Letters of Attorney; provided the Owners Right appear from due Proofs according to Law in the Court of Admiralty; and whatever Goods fhall be recovered from them, fhall be carried into the Ports of either Confederate, and be delivered to the Cuftody of the Officers of the Port, who fhall be refponfible for the fame; if the faid Goods are not reftored without Delay to their Owners, after Proof firft made of the true Property thereof before the Judges of thofe Places, where the Goods taken by the Pirates were put on board the Ship: Neverthelefs all Perfons accufed fhall be allowed to try their Right by Law, and to make their Defence.

ARTICLE XXII.

The People and Inhabitants of *Great-Britain* may freely and fecurely fail and traffick in all the Kingdoms, Dominions and Territories which cultivate Peace, Friendfhip or Neutrality with them; nor fhall they be any ways molefted by the Ships or Subjects of *France*, although there fhould be Enmity and Hoftility between *France* and the faid Kingdoms, Dominions and Territories, or any of them: And the fame fhall likewife be obferved on the Part of *Great-Britain* towards the Subjects and Inhabitants of *France*; provided that fuch Trade be not carried to any Port or Town which is befieged by either of the Confederates, and that neither Party, nor the People or Subjects of either, fhall import any Prohibited and Contraband Goods to thofe Kingdoms, Dominions or Territories, which are at Enmity or War with the other.

Free Paffage and Commerce in all neutral Places at Enmity with the other; Places befieged and Contraband Goods excepted.

ARTICLE XXVI.

For the better promoting of Commerce on both Sides, it is agreed, that if a War fhould break out between the faid two Nations of *England* and *France*,

D fix

<small>Six Months allowed to Subjects on both Sides in case of a War.</small> six Months after the Proclamation of War, shall be allowed to the Merchants, in the Cities and Towns where they live, for selling and transporting their Goods and Merchandize; and if any thing be taken from them, or any Injury be done them within that Term by either Party, or the People or Subjects of either, full Satisfaction shall be made for the same.

Marine Treaty between Great-Britain *and* France; *concluded at* St. Germains, March 29, 1632.

ARTICLE III.

FOR as much as under the Pretext of Search or Visit that may be made by the Ships of War of the one or the other Prince, or their Subjects a Sea, of Merchant Ships, to know whether they are laden with Merchandizes prohibited, or belonging to the Enemy, there have been several Outrages committed for the Time past, which have, without any lawful Cause, hindered the Course of the said Ships, and occasioned many other great Damage to Merchants; to obviate such Inconveniences, it has been agreed, that such Ships of War happening <small>Merchant Ships to strike to Men of War, and present their Commissions and Bills of Lading.</small> to meet such Merchant Ships at Sea, may order them to strike, which the said Merchant Ships shall be obliged to do, and to present their Licences, Commissions, and Bills of Lading, to the Captains or such as they shall send aboard the said Merchant Ships, into which more than two or three at most may not not. enter, nor exact or take any Duties under Pretext of such Visit; which done, if those of the said Ship of War will not forbear, notwithstanding, to stop the Voyage of the said Ship <small>Not to be hindered or taken out of their Course.</small> whether by carrying them along with them, or obliging them to go aside out of their Course, the said People belonging to the Ship of War shall in that Case be answerable for all the Expences, Damages, and Interests, and besides be punished corporally, according as the Quality and Circumstance of the Fact shall require; for which Expences, Damages, and Interests, not only the Delinquents shall answer, but likewise those who furnished them with Arms and Provisions, and put them to Sea.

ARTICLE V.

The Captains, Lieutenants, and the Masters of Ships that shall take any Prize, shall be obliged within twenty-four Hours after their Arrival, to lay all the Books of Accompts, Papers, Licences, Commissions, and Bills of Lading, which they shall find in the Ships they take, before the Judge of the Admiralty, or his Clerk, that so the Parties interested may take Copies thereof for their Use; and where there is no Judge of the Admiralty, the said Papers and Bills of Lading shall be put into the Hands of the King's Officers, to be sent closed up and sealed to the Judge of the Admiralty.

Books and Papers of Prizes to be laid before the Judges of Admiralty.

ARTICLE VI.

In like Manner the said Captors shall be obliged to bring along with them the Persons whom they found in the said Ships, or at least the Captain and Master, or two or three of the principal Officers, and present them within twenty-four Hours to the Judge of the Admiralty to be examined; and in case there be no Judge of the Admiralty, before the Mayors of the Towns, or the King's Officers: And they may not hold or keep them Prisoners in their Houses beyond that Time, on Pain of being punished, and losing the Prize; and after the said Prisoners shall have been heard and examined, the said Judge shall be obliged to set them at Liberty, to follow their Affairs as they shall think good.

Officers of a Prize Ship to be examined before the Judge of the Admiralty.

ARTICLE VII.

When any Prizes are brought into any Harbours or Ports, the Mariners and Seamen belonging to them shall not be forced away from their said Ships,

Men or Goods not to be taken from on board Prizes without an Order.

D 2   nor

nor any of their Goods put a-fhore, without previous Order from the Judge, and an Invento made by him or his Deputies, in Prefence of t principal Perfons concerned, whereof a Copy fh: be delivered to them from the faid Judge.

Treaty of Alliance between Great-Britain a France; *concluded at* London, Auguft *t* 29*th*, 1610.

ARTICLE XXXIII.

Goods taken from Pirates to be I rought into Port and there lodged.

THAT all the Goods that fhall be taken l the Captains and other Officers of the one the other Prince from Pirates, fhall be brought re pectively to fome Port of the one or the oth Kingdom, and there put under good and fafe Cu tody of the Admiral, Vice-Admiral, or other O ficers of the faid Ports; which Officers fhall l bound to anfwer for the faid Goods in their ov Name.

ARTICLE XXXIV.

Such Goods to be reftored to the Owners, Subjects of either Party.

That all the Goods which fhall be thus tak(and recovered from Pirates, whether they be Gold or Silver Money, or other Merchandiz appertaining to the Subjects of either of the fa: Kings, fhall be rendered and reftored to the tri Owners and Proprietors of the fame, without ar Delay, after having firft made legal Proof of tl Property thereof.

Treaty of Peace between England *and* France *concluded the* 24*th of* March, 1549.

ARTICLE II.

1549.

IT is agreed and concluded, that as long as th Peace and Friendfhip fhall continue, all an fingul:

abitants of both the said Kingdoms, *Universal Peace and Amity.*
ands and Dominions which now
shall be possessed by either of the
vhatsoever Dignity, State, and Con-
:eive and treat each other with all
and mutual good Offices, and may
id securely pass and repass too and
and by Sea, and on Rivers; sail and
ch other, buy and sell, and abide
they think fit, or retire and depart
henever they please, into their own,
Nation or Place whatsoever, and *Free Navigation, Passage and Commerce.*
m what Things they shall have ac-
iased by their Industry and Labour,
rful Arts or Means whatsoever, with-
iment, Molestation, or Restraint,
ticence, or special Commission, in
; they lawfully might by Virtue of
; and Alliances, saving always the
, and Customs of the said King-

---

eace and Alliance between England
ce; *concluded at the Camp, between
nd* Guines, June *the 7th,* 1546.

RTICLE III.

all and singular the Vassals and Sub-   1546.
both the said Princes, and of their
:cessors, whether they be Princes,
Bishops, Dukes, Marquesses, Earls,   *Peace and Amity.*
rchants, or of what State and Con-
hall, during the said Peace, conduct
all Places in the most kind and
r, performing all mutual good Of-
each other; and may freely, safely,   *Free Navigation, Passage and Commerce.*
without the Hindrance of any one,
iduct or Licence, travel in all Places,
        D 3   by

by Land or by Sea, or on fresh Waters, and sai
and come into the Ports, Dominions and District
whatsoever of both the said Princes, their Heirs an
Successors, provided they do not exceed the Num
ber of an hundred arm'd Men together, and ma
abide there as long as they please, trade, buy an
sell all Goods, Merchandizes, and Jewels whatso
ever, if not prohibited by the Laws and Ordinance
of the said Kingdoms respectively; and may freel
depart from thence to their own Countries, or else
where at their Pleasure; and as often as they please
with their own, or hired or borrowed Vessels, Car
riages, Horses, Armour, Merchandize, Baggage
Goods and Things whatsoever, without any Im
pediment, Molestation or Arrest, by Reason of an
Marque, Countermarque, or Reprisals, or othe
Distress whatsoever, as well upon Land as upoi
Sea, and in fresh Waters, in the same Manner a
they lawfully might, by Virtue of ancient Treatie
and Alliances.

> This last recited general Article of Commerc
> and free Intercourse is inserted almost ver
> batim in a preceding Treaty of Peace. an(
> Commerce; concluded at *Moore*, in 1525
> as likewise in the three temporary Treatie:
> of 1514, 1492, and 1478.

Articles

Articles and Clauses of Treaties subsisting between Great-Britain *and* France; *containing the Continuance, Renewal, and Confirmation of former Treaties between the two Crowns.*

Treaty of Peace between Great-Britain *and* France, *and* Spain; *concluded at* Seville, November *the* 19*th*, 1729.

ARTICLE I.

1729.

ALL former Treaties and Conventions of Peace and Friendship, and Commerce, concluded between the contracting Powers respectively, shall be, as they hereby are, effectually renewed and confirmed, in all those Points which are not derogated from by the present Treaty, in as full and ample Manner as if the said Treaties were here inserted Word for Word; their said Majesties promising not to do, or suffer any thing to be done, that may be contrary thereto, directly or indirectly.

All former Treaties confirmed.

ARTICLE IV.

It having been agreed by the preliminary Articles, that the Commerce of the *English* and *French* Nations, as well in *Europe* as in the *Indies*, should be re-established on the foot of the Treaties and Conventions antecedent to the Year 1725; and particularly that the Commerce of the *English* Nation in *America*, should be exercised as heretofore; it is agreed by the present Article, that all necessary Orders shall be dispatched on both Sides, without any Delay, as well for the Execution of the said Treaties of Commerce, as for supplying what may be wanting for the entire Re-establishment of Com-

Commerce settled on the Foot of Treaties preceding the Year 1725.

Commerce on the Foot of the said Treaties and Conventions.

Treaty of Peace between Great-Britain *and* France; *concluded at* Utrecht, March *the* 31*st*, 1713.

ARTICLE VII.

1713.
Free Navigation and Commerce as before the last War.

THAT there be a free Use of Navigation and Commerce between the Subjects of both their Royal Majesties, as it was formerly in Time of Peace, and before the Declaration of the last War; and also as it is agreed and concluded by the Treaty of Commerce, this Day made between the two Nations.

Treaty of Peace between Great-Britain *and* France; *concluded at* Reswick, September *the* 10*th*, 1697.

ARTICLE V.

1697.
Free Navigation, Passage and Trade as before used.

THAT there be a free Use of Navigation and Commerce between the Subjects of both the said Kings, as was formerly in the Time of Peace, and before the Declaration of the late War; so that every one of them may freely come into the Kingdoms, Marts, Ports and Rivers, of either of the said Kings, with their Merchandizes, and may there continue and trade without Molestation, and shall use and enjoy all Liberties, Immunities, and Privileges granted by solemn Treaties and ancient Customs.

American

American *Treaty of Commerce between* Great-Britain *and* France; *concluded at* London, November *the* 16*th*, 1686.

ARTICLE XIX.

THIS prefent Treaty fhall not in any wife derogate from the Treaty concluded between the moft Serene Kings at *Breda, July* 21, 1667: But all and fingular the Articles and Claufes of the faid Treaty fhall remain in Force and be obferved.

1686.
Treaty of *Bredah* 1667, confirmed.

General Treaty of Commerce between Great-Britain *and* France; *concluded at* St. Germains, February *the* 24*th*, 1676-7.

PREAMBLE.

AS the Kings of *France* and *Great-Britain* have no greater Defire than to ftrengthen anew the Friendfhip that is between the faid Kings, and the faithful and fincere Union that is between their Subjects and Kingdoms; their Majefties believed nothing could contribute more thereunto, than a new Treaty about the Freedom and Security of Commerce; and they have to this End named Plenipotentiaries, who have agreed upon the following Articles.

1676-7.
Freedom and Security of Commerce.

Treaty of Peace between Great-Britain *and* France; *concluded at* Bredah, July 21, 1667.

ARTICLE II.

ALL Enmities, Hoftilities, Difcords and Wars, fhall ceafe and be for ever abolifhed between the faid two Kings; fo as they fhall for the future forbear to pillage or injure each other; nor fhall they moleft or incommode one another in any Man-

1667.
Peace and Amity by Sea and Land.

Manner whatsoever, either by Sea or Land, or or Rivers, in any Part of the World whatsoever, and especially within the Extent and Limits of their own Kingdoms, Lands, Dominions, or Places whatever.

ARTICLE IV.

Free Navigation and Commerce as before used.

Navigation and Commerce shall be free between the Subjects of both the Kings, as it was during the Peace, and before the Declaration of the last War; so as they may freely and without Molestation, go with their Goods into each other's Kingdoms, Provinces, Places of Commerce, Ports and Rivers, and there abide and traffick.

Act of the Oath taken by the King of France ana the Queen Regent, whereby they confirm all former Treaties made with Great-Britain.

1644.

WE *Lewis* King of *France* and *Navarre*, do swear and promise, in the Presence of Lord *Goring*, Ambassador extraordinary, specially appointed and sent for this Purpose by the King of *Great-Britain*, that we will observe and fulfil all and singular the Points and Articles which have been agreed to and established by the Treaties, which have been made and concluded by the Kings our Predecessors between our respective Kingdoms,

Treaties of 1606, 1610, 1625, 1629, and 1632, confirmed.

States, Countries, and Subjects; and more especially those made in the Years 1606, 1610, 1625, 1629, and 1632, in such Manner as they have been established and ratified, and according as they shall be found to derogate the one from the other: Which Treaties and Articles we have approved and confirmed, and do now swear and promise in most solemn Manner, that we will observe the same, and never contravene any Points or Articles of the said Treaties, directly or indirectly; nor will we, to the utmost of our Power, suffer the same to be violated in any Manner:

And

And We *Anne*, Queen Regent of *France* and *Navarre*, having likewise on our Part, as far as in us lies, agreed to, approved and ratified the said Treaties, do now, by Virtue of our Oath, confirm and promise a due Observance of the same, and that they shall not be contravened in any Sort.

Treaty of Commerce between Great-Britain *and* France; *concluded at* St. Germains, 1632.

ARTICLE VIII.

BY these present Articles, the said Kings do not mean to derogate from preceding Agreements and Treaties made between them, which shall remain in their Force and Virtue; but only in so far as shall be derogated from them by these Presents, and particularly, that the Treaties of 1606, and 1610, shall be duly and faithfully executed.

1632.
Treaties of 1606, and 1610, confirmed.

Treaty of Peace and Alliance between Great-Britain *and* France; *concluded at* Susa, April *the* 24th, 1629.

ARTICLE I.

THE two Kings shall agree to renew the ancient Alliances between the two Crowns, and to preserve them inviolably, together with opening a safe and free Commerce.

1629.
Safe and free Commerce.

The Declaration of the King of France, *for the Re-establishment of Commerce with* England, *being a Sequel and Part of the said Treaty of* 1629.

LEWIS King of *France* and *Navarre*. To all, &c. Although by the Publication which we have already ordered to be made through our King-

1629.

Kingdom and Dominions of the Peace settled between us and the King of *Great-Britain*, it be expresly signified that Trade and Commerce shall for the future be safe and free between our Subjects and his, by Sea and Land, as it was before the last War; nevertheless, we have thought it proper to dispatch our express Letters of Declaration; and We do say and declare by these Presents, signed with our own Hand, that our Will and Intention is, that for the future there be a sure and free Commerce and Trade, both by Sea and Land, between our Subjects and those of the King of *Great-Britain*; We will, ordain, and it is our Pleasure, that upon this Account they have all safe and free Access to our Ports, Harbours and Towns, and may bring there all Sorts of Merchandizes, sell, truck, and exchange the same; buy and transport other Merchandizes of our Kingdoms, (except such as are prohibited by our Orders) all in the same Manner as they did before the Wars, notwithstanding any Prohibitions formerly made by us to the contrary, which We have and do remove and take away in Favour of the said Treaty of Peace.

<sure and="" free="" commerce="" by="" sea="" and="" land="">

Treaty of Alliance between Great-Britain *and* France; *concluded at* London, August *the* 29*th*, 1610.

ARTICLE I.

1610.

THAT by any of the Compacts, Conventions, Articles or Points contained in this Treaty, it is not meant in any Sort to depart from the preceding Treaties and Alliances made between the said Kings or their Predecessors, either for the Kingdoms of *France* and *England*, or of *France* and *Scotland*; but that notwithstanding, they shall remain in their full Force and Vigour; provided

Preceding Treaties confirmed.

they be not contrary or repugnant to this present Treaty of Union, or any Articles contained therein.

Treaty of Commerce between Great-Britain *and* France; *concluded at* Paris, February *the* 24th, 1605-6.

ARTICLE I.

THAT the preceding Treaties shall not in any wise be thought to be departed from by any Article or Matter contained in this present Treaty, but they shall remain in their full Strength, Force and Vigour, excepting only so far as any thing is derogated from them by this present Treaty.

1606.

Preceding Treaties confirmed.

Treaty of Alliance between England *and* France; *concluded at* Greenwich, May *the* 14th, 1596.

ARTICLE I.

ALL former Alliances and Treaties which have been in Force till this present, between the Queen of *England* and the King of *France*, and their Kingdoms, shall be confirmed, and remain in their former Force and Vigour; and it shall not be thought that they are departed from in any Point, but in so far as is derogated from them by this present Treaty.

1596.

All former Alliances and Treaties confirmed.

Treaty

Treaty of Alliance between England *and* France; *concluded at* Blois, April *the* 23*d*, 1572.

ARTICLE I.

1572.

Preceding Treaties and Alliances confirmed.

NO Articles or Agreement contained in this prefent Treaty, fhall be deemed to intend or imply a Departure from preceding Treaties or Alliances formerly entered into by the faid Confederates, or their Predeceffors; but they fhall, notwithftanding, remain in their full Force, Virtue and Vigour, in fo far as they are not contrary or repugnant to this prefent Treaty, or any Articles therein contained.

Treaty of Peace and Alliance between England *and* France; *concluded at* Trojes, *the* 11*th of* April, 1564.

ARTICLE I.

1564.

Perpetual Peace and Amity.

THERE fhall be a true, firm, folid, fincere, perpetual and inviolable Peace, Friendfhip, Union, Confederacy, League, mutual good Underftanding, and true Concord, by Sea and Land, and in all Places to endure, to all future Ages, between the Queen of *England* and King of *France,* their Heirs and Succeffors, and all their Subjects and Vaffals whatfoever.

Treaty

Treaty of Peace and Commerce between England and France; concluded April *the 5th,* 1515.

ARTICLE V.

AS to what concerns the mutual Dealing, Commerce and Intercourse of Merchandizes between the Subjects of both Kingdoms, the said Subjects shall in all things esteem and treat one another in the same Manner as they were obliged to do at the Time of the last Peace.

1515.

Commerce and Intercourse as before used.

The Definitive Treaty of Christian, universal, and perpetual Peace, Friendship and Union; concluded at AIX-LA-CHAPELLE, *on the* $\frac{7}{18}$*th of* October, 1748.

ARTICLE XVI.

THE Treaty of the *Assiento*, signed at *Madrid* the 27th of *March*, 1713, and the Article of the annual Ship, making Part of the said Treaty, are particularly confirmed by the present Treaty for the four Years during which the Enjoyment was lost since the Commencement of the present War, and shall be executed on the same Footing, and on the same Conditions, they have been, or might be before the said War.

1748.

The Treaty of the *Assiento* and the annual Ship confirmed.

ARTICLE XVII.

Dunkirk shall remain fortified on the Land Side in its present State, and for the Sea Side on the Footing of ancient Treaties.

(48)

ARTICLE IX.
Of the separate ARTICLES.

Two Hostages to continue in France 'till the Restitution of Cape Breton.   His Britannick Majesty engages on his Side to send to the most Christian King, immediately after the Exchange of the Ratifications of the present Treaty, two Persons of Rank and Condition, to continue in *France* as Hostages 'till such Time as they have certain and authentick Advice of the Restitution of the Royal Isle called *Cape Breton*, and of all the Conquests that the Arms or Subjects of his Britannick Majesty may have made before or after the Signature of the Preliminaries, in the *East* and *West-Indies*. Their Britannick and most Christian Majesties oblige themselves likewise to remit, on the Exchange of the Ratifications of the present Treaty, the Duplicates of the Orders addressed to the Commissaries respectively appointed to restore and receive all which may have been conquer'd on each Side in the *East* and *West-Indies*, conformable to the second Article of the Preliminaries, and to the Declarations of the 21st and 31st of *May*, and the 8th of *July* last, in what concerns the said Conquests in the *East* and *West-Indies*.

Be it well understood nevertheless, that the Royal Isle, called *Cape Breton*, shall be restored with all the Artillery and Ammunition found therein on the Day of its Surrender; and as to the other Restitutions, they shall have their Effect conformable to the Tenor of the 11th Article of the Preliminaries, and the Declarations and Conventions of the 21st and 31st of *May*, and the 8th of *July*, in the State wherein Things were found on the 11th of *June*, N. S. in the *West-Indies*, and the 31st of *October*, likewise N. S. in the *East-Indies*. All other Things to be restored on the Footing they were before the present War.

Treaty of Peace between Great-Britain *and* Spain; *concluded at* Utrecht, July 2, 1713.

ARTICLE VIII.

THAT there be a free Use of Navigation and Commerce between the Subjects of both Kingdoms, as it was heretofore in Time of Peace, and before the Declaration of the late War, in the Reign of *Charles* the Second, King of *Spain*, according to the Treaties of Friendship, Alliance and Commerce, which were formerly made between both Nations, and according to ancient Customs, Letters Patent, Schedula's, and other special Acts; and also according to the Treaty or Treaties of Commerce newly made, or forthwith to be made at *Madrid*.

1713.

Free Navigation and Commerce as before the late War.

Treaty of Navigation and Commerce between Great-Britain *and* Spain; *concluded at* Utrecht, November 28, 1713.

ARTICLE I.

THE Treaty of Peace, Commerce, and Alliance concluded at *Madrid* between the Crowns of *Great Britain* and *Spain*, the 13th Day of *May*, 1667, is ratified and confirmed by this present Treaty; and for the greater Coroboration and Confirmation thereof, it has been thought proper to insert the same here verbatim; together with the Royal Schedula's or Ordinances thereto annexed, as follows.

1713.

Treaty of Peace and Commerce of 1667, confirmed.

Treaty of 1667, *between* Great-Britain *and* Spain.

ARTICLE I.

1667.

Univerſal and perpetual Peace and Amity.

IT is agreed and concluded, that there ſhall be an univerſal, good, ſincere, true, firm and perfect Amity, Confederation and Peace, between the Crown of *Great-Britain* on the one Part, and the Crown of *Spain* on the other; and alſo between the Lands, Countries, Kingdoms, Dominions and Territories belonging unto, or under the Obedience of either of the ſaid Kings; which ſhall endure from this Day for ever, and ſhall be inviolably obſerved, as well by Land as by Sea, and on all Waters; and that the Subjects and People of the ſaid Kings, and the Inhabitants of their Dominions, of what Degree or Condition ſoever, ſhall reciprocally help, aſſiſt, and ſhew to each other all kind of Benevolence and mutual good Offices and Friendſhip.

ARTICLE II.

Neither of the ſaid Kings, nor their reſpective People, Subjects or Inhabitants within their Dominions, ſhall, upon any Pretence whatſoever, either openly or ſecretly, attempt, do, or procure to be done, any thing which may be of Damage or Detriment to the other Party, in any Place whatſoever, either by Sea or by Land, or in Ports or Rivers, but they ſhall treat each other with all Love and Friendſhip: Moreover, either Party ſhall have free and

Free Acceſs and Traffick in all Places where before uſed or allowed to any other.

ſafe Acceſs and Admittance, as well by Sea as by Land, into the Countries, Kingdoms, Iſlands, Dominions, Cities, Towns wall'd or not wall'd, fortified or unfortified, of the other Party; and likewiſe into their Harbours and Ports, wherever Trade and Commerce did uſe before Time to be carried on, ſo as every Perſon of the one Party or the other may buy, ſell, and carry on all Manner of Trade, and traffick in what Place ſoever he will belonging

to

to the other Party, with the same Freedom and Security as they trade with their own Fellow-Citizens or Countrymen; or as any other foreign Nation whatever does, which is allowed to frequent the said Places of either Party.

ARTICLE III.

The Kings of *Great-Britain* and *Spain* shall take most special Care, that their respective Subjects and People do from henceforward abstain from all Force, Wrong and Violence to each other. <small>Both Sides to abstain from all Wrong.</small>

ARTICLE IV.

That between the King of *Great-Britain* and King of *Spain*, and their respective Subjects, People and Inhabitants, there shall be allowed on both Sides a free Liberty and Power of trading, and of setting on Foot and carrying on all Manner of Commerce; as well by Sea as by Land, and upon all Waters, throughout all and singular the Kingdoms, Countries, Territories, Provinces, Islands, Colonies, Cities, Towns, Villages, Ports, Rivers, Creeks, Bays, Streights, and Currents, under the Obedience of either King, where Trade or Commerce hath at any time heretofore been used to be carried on; so as, without Letters of safe Conduct, or other Form of general or special Licence, the People and Subjects on both Sides may, as well by Land as by Sea, and upon the fresh Waters, freely navigate and pass into the Countries, Kingdoms, Dominions, Cities, Ports, Currents, Bays, Districts, and other Places whatsoever under the Obedience of either of the Confederates; and may come and enter into any Ports whatsoever as they shall think fit, with their Ships laden or unladen, and with all Kind of Merchant Ships, and Carriages whatsoever; and when they have enter'd into such Ports, they may buy, sell and barter all Kind of Merchandize whatsoever, of what Value, or to what Quantity soever; they may likewise provide themselves at just and usual Rates with Victuals, <small>Free Navigation, Passage and Trade, by Land and Water where before used, without Letters of Licence or safe Conduct.</small>

Victuals, and all Kind of Provisions necessary either for their Subsistance or Voyage; and repair and fit out their Ships and other Vessels of Burthen and Carriages; and likewise remove from thence, and freely depart with their Ships and other Vessels of Burthen, Goods, Merchandizes and Effects, wheresoever they shall think fit, whether they be minded to return to their own Countries, or to proceed elsewhere, without any Molestation or Impediment; saving always on both Sides, the Rights, Customs *Right and Customs, Laws and Ordinances of both Kingdoms saved.* and Duties to be demanded and paid; saving likewise the Laws and Ordinances which have been made and observed throughout the several Dominions and Countries of both the said Kings.

ARTICLE VIII.

All Privileges of the Treaty of Munster 1648, granted to the Subjects of Great-Britain. For what may concern both the *Indies*, and any other Parts whatsoever, the Crown of *Spain* doth grant to the King of *Great-Britain* and his Subjects, all that was granted to the united States of the Low Countries, by the Treaty of *Munster* made in the Year 1648, in as strong and ample Manner, as if the same were here inserted, in every Article and Point thereof, without the least Omission: The same Laws being to be observed, to which the Subjects of the said States are obliged and bound; and mutual Offices of Friendship to be performed on each Side.

ARTICLE X.

Ships of Great-Britain not to be searched or visited by any Officers of the King of Spain. The Ships and all other Vessels belonging to the King of *Great-Britain* or his Subjects, when they sail towards, or enter into the Dominions or Ports of the King of *Spain*, shall in no wise be subject to any Visitation or Search by the Officers and Judges of prohibited Goods, or any others whatsoever, either by Virtue of their own or any other Authority; nor shall any Soldiers, arm'd Men, Officers or private Persons whatsoever, under the Name of a Guard or Watch, or on any other Pretence what-

whatſoever be put on board any of the ſaid Ships or Veſſels.

ARTICLE XIII.

It ſhall be lawful for the Ships of the People and Subjects of either of the Confederates, to caſt Anchor in the Coaſts, Bays, or any Stations or Roads for Ships belonging to the other Confederate, without being in any wiſe conſtrained to enter into any neighbouring Port; and in caſe any Ship being forced by Streſs of Weather, or Danger of Enemies or Pirates, or by any other Accident ſhould be neceſſitated to come into Port, provided it appears that ſhe is not bound to an Enemy's Port with prohibited Goods, commonly called Contraband (concerning which ſhe ſhall not be queſtioned without clear Proofs) ſuch Ship may ſail out of Port whenſoever they think fit, and return to Sea without any Impediment whatſoever; upon that Condition however, that they do not break Bulk, and that no Part of the Cargo be expoſed to Sale, or open'd in Port: But when they have caſt Anchor, and are ſtationed in Port, to prevent all Trouble whatſoever about viſiting or ſearching, it ſhall be ſufficient for them to have in readineſs and to produce their Letters of ſafe Conduct, or other Papers of their intended Voyage, and Certificates of their Cargo; which being exhibited and ſhewn to the Officers of either King, when the Matter requires it, ſuch Ships ſhall be permitted to purſue their intended Voyage without further Moleſtation.

Ships of either Nation may caſt Anchor in the Coaſts or Roads of the other.

Forced by Enemies, or otherwiſe, may freely come in and go out of Port.

Not to break Bulk.

To produce Paſſports and Certificates.

ARTICLE XIV.

The Ships of War, whether they belong to either of the ſaid Kings, or be Privateers belonging to the Subjects of either, when they meet with any Merchant Ships either riding at Anchor, or ſailing in the open Sea, ſhall keep without Cannon Shot of them, and ſhall not approach nearer, in order to prevent

Ships of War and Privateers to keep at Diſtance from Merchantmen, and only to ſend their Boat to examine the Papers.

prevent all Damage and Violence; but they may send their Boat or Pinnace, with two or three Men only on board the Merchant Ship, to whom the Master or Owner shall produce his Passport and Sea Letters, prepared according to the Form annexed to this Treaty; whereby they may be certified not only of the Merchandizes with which the Ship is laden, but also of the Place to which she belongs within either Kings' Dominions, and Name of the Ship, Master and Owners; by which Means it may be sufficiently known what Sort of Goods are on board her, whether any such as are prohibited or Contraband; and who is the Master or Owner; and what Kind of a Ship it is: Moreover, such Passports and Sea Letters shall be of the more undoubted Credit and Authority, that as well on the Part of the King of *Great-Britain*, as of the King of *Spain*, they shall (if the same be found necessary) be corroborated with certain counter-signed Certificates, whereby they may be more authentick, and the Imposition of false ones may be prevented.

ARTICLE XV.

Prohibited Goods exported to be confiscated, and no other.

If any prohibited Merchandizes or Goods are exported out of the Kingdoms, Dominions, or Territories of either King, by the People or Subjects of the other; in such case the prohibited Goods only, and no other, shall be confiscated; nor shall the Delinquent in such case, incur any further Penalty, unless haply he convey away and export out of the Kingdoms or Dominions of *Great-Britain* any Money or proper Coin of that Country, or Wool, or what they call Fullers-Earth; or out of the Dominions of the King of *Spain*, any Gold or Silver, either coined or uncoined: In which Cases the Laws of each Country shall on both Sides have their due Force and Effect.

In case of British Coin, Wool, or Fullers-Earth exported out of the British Dominions, or any Gold or Silver out of the Spanish, the respective Laws to take Place.

ARTICLE

ARTICLE XVI.

The People and Subjects of either King may arrive at, and enter into the Ports of the other, and there abide and remain, and depart from thence with the same Liberty and Freedom on both Sides; and that not only with their Merchant Ships and other Vessels used for Trade and Commerce; but likewise with Ships of War fitted out either to resist or attack the Enemy; and if their Ships are drove in by Stress of Weather, they may both repair their Ships and furnish themselves with Provisions, as they may have Occasion, so as the Number of Ships entering in of their own Accord, give no just Cause of Suspicion, which, if they are Ships of War, are not to exceed the Number of eight; nor shall they continue within the Bays or Roads, or in the Neighbourhood of the Ports, any longer Time than shall be judged necessary for the Repair of their Ships, or the taking in of Provisions, much less shall they be the Cause of any Interruption or Molestation of the Commerce, or hinder the Approach or Entrance of any Ships belonging to any other Nation whatsoever at Peace with the King to whom such Port belongs. But when a greater Number than usual of Ships of War, shall by some Accident approach any Port, it shall not be lawful for them to enter into Port, or cast Anchor in the Road, without having first obtained a Permission to enter from the King himself, or from the Governor of such Port, unless they are forced in by the Violence of a Storm, or to avoid some imminent Danger at Sea; in which Case, they shall signify the Cause of their Arrival, as soon as possible, to the Governor of the Port, or chief Magistrate of the Place; and they shall not continue there any longer than such Governor or Magistrate shall judge proper and expedient, much less shall they commit any Act of Hostility against any others being in the same

Marginal notes: All Ships of both Nations freely to enter, abide in, and depart from any Ports of the other. — Drove in by Stress of Weather may repair and provide themselves. — Not to exceed eight Ships of War. — Not to stay longer than necessary. — Not to disturb the Commerce of the Place. — Ships of War more than usual not to enter into Port, or anchor in the Road without Leave.

same Port, which may prove a Prejudice to either of the said Kings.

ARTICLE XVIII.

Ships and Subjects of both Nations may carry all Kind of Arms. The Merchants and Subjects of both Kings, and their Agents and Servants, as also their Ships, Masters and Mariners, both in going and returning, as well upon Sea and other Waters, as in the Havens and Ports of either Party, may carry and use all Kind of Arms, both offensive and defensive, without being obliged to register the same; they may likewise carry and use any portable Arms upon Land (if they please) for their private Defence, according to the Custom of the Place.

ARTICLE XXI.

Free Navigation and Traffick with all neutral States. The Subjects and Inhabitants of the Kingdoms and Dominions under the Obedience of the Kings of *Great Britain* and *Spain* respectively, may with all Security and Liberty navigate and traffick throughout all the Kingdoms, States and Countries, cultivating Peace, Amity or Neutrality, with either of the said Kings.

ARTICLE XXII.

Not to be disturbed by Reason of Hostility with any other State. The Ships or Subjects of either of the said Kings shall in no wise interrupt the said Liberty by any Hindrance or Disturbance whatsoever, by Reason of any Hostility which now is or may be hereafter between either of the said Kings, and any other Kingdoms, Dominions and States, being in Friendship or Neutrality with the other Party.

ARTICLE XXIII.

Contraband Goods only to be taken and confiscated. And in Case any prohibited Goods, commonly called Contraband, which are here particularly mentioned, shall be discovered by the aforesaid Means to be on board such Ships, they shall be taken out of the Ship, and legally proceeded against and con-

confiscated by the Judges of the Admiralty, or other competent Judges; but so as the Ship itself, and the other free and allowed Goods found in such Ship, shall in no wise be seized or confiscated on that Account.

ARTICLE XXIV.

Moreover, to prevent as far as may be, all Controversy which may arise concerning such Goods as are to be deem'd Prohibited or Contraband, it is declared and agreed, that under that Name are comprehended all Fire-Arms, as warlike Ordnance, Musquets, Mortar-Pieces, Petards, Bombs, Granaloes, Fire-Crancels, Fire Balls, Carriages of Guns, Musket rests, Bandeliers, Gunpowder, Match, Saltpetre, Bullets, and Balls; likewise under the same Name of prohibited Goods are comprehended all other Kind of Arms, as Pikes, Swords, Pots, Helmets, Backs and Breasts, Halberts, Javelins, and such like; under the same Name likewise is prohibited the Transportation of Soldiers and Horses, together with their Harnesses, Cases of Pistols, Holsters, Belts, and all Kind of warlike Furniture whatsoever.

Contraband Goods specified.

ARTICLE XXV.

Likewise for the avoiding of all Matter of Dispute and Contention, it is agreed, that under the Name of Goods prohibited and contraband are not comprehended Corn, Wheat, or any other Grain, or Pulse, Salt, Wine, Oil, or any thing appertaining to the Nourishment and Support of Life; but they shall remain free; as likewise all other Goods not mentioned in the foregoing Article, the Transportation of which shall be allowed even to Places belonging to Enemies, excepting Cities and Places besieged and block'd up.

What Goods are not to be deem'd Contraband.

ARTICLE XXVI.

All Things on board Enemies Ships to be confiscated. Whatsoever shall be found laden by the Subjects and Inhabitants of the Kingdoms and Dominions either of the said Kings on board any Ships belonging to the Enemies of either of the said King though such Goods should not be of the prohibited Kind, they shall be confiscated, together with Things else, which shall be found within any such Ship, without Exception or Reserve.

ARTICLE XXXVIII.

Subjects of both Nations to enjoy all Privileges granted to any other. The People and Subjects of both the said Kings shall have and enjoy in the Lands, Seas, Ports, Havens, Roads and Territories of the other, and in all other Places whatever, all the same Privileges, Securities, Liberties, and Immunities, whether they concern their Persons or Trade, which have been already granted, or hereafter shall be granted by either of the said Kings, either to the Most Christian King, or to the States General of the United Provinces, or to the Hanse Towns, or to any other State whatsoever, by their Treaties or Royal Schedula's, with all the beneficial and favourable Articles and Clauses contained in such Grants, in as ample Manner and Form, and to as full and valid Effect of an Agreement entered into and ratified, as if the same were particularly transcribed and inserted in this present Treaty.

ARTICLE XL.

All the Articles of this Treaty to be observed by all Subjects on both Sides. It is likewise agreed and concluded, that the said Most Serene Kings of *Great-Britain* and *Spain* shall sincerely and faithfully observe, and cause to be observed and kept by their Subjects and Inhabitants respectively, all and singular the Articles agreed on and established by this present Treaty; nor will they contravene the same directly or indirectly,

rectly, nor confent that the fame be contravened ; their Subjects and Inhabitants refpectively.

The Form of the certificatory Letters to be given by the Towns and Sea Ports to the Ships and Veffels fetting fail from thence.

TO all unto whom thefe Prefents fhall come: We the Governors, Confuls, or chief Magiftrate, or Commiffioners of the Cuftoms of the City, Town or Province of *N.* do teftify and make known, that *N. N.* Mafter of the Ship *N.* hath before us under folemn Oath declared, that that the Ship *N.* of   Tons (or thereabouts) of which he is at prefent Mafter, doth belong to the Inhabitants of *N.* in the Dominions of the Moft Serene King of *Spain:* And we being defirous that the faid Mafter may be well ufed and affifted in his Voyage and Bufinefs, do intreat all Perfons who fhall meet him, and thofe of all Places where the faid Mafter fhall come with the faid Ship and her Merchandize, that they would admit him favourably, treat him kindly, and receive the faid Ship into their Ports, Bays, Havens, Rivers, and Dominions, permitting her quietly to fail, pafs, repafs, and trade there, or in any other Places, as fhall feem good to the faid Mafter, he paying all Duties and Cuftoms which of Right fhall be due: which we will acknowledge gratefully upon the like Occafions. In Witnefs whereof we have figned thefe Prefents, and fealed them with the Seal of our Town.

The Form of certificatory Letters.

Articles

Articles of the Marine Treaty of the 28th [f]
November, 1713, *immediately following*
Recital of the Treaty of 1667, *and of*
several Schedula's annexed thereto.

1713.

ARTICLE I.

Mutual Stipulations for the Performance of this Treaty.

THEIR Royal Majesties do mutually p[ro]mise, that they will faithfully perform a[nd] fulfil all and singular the Articles of the foregoi[ng] Treaty, and all Privileges, Concessions, Agreemen[ts] or other Advantages whatsoever arising to the Su[b]jects on either Side, which are contained in the[m] or in the Schedula's annexed; and that they will [at] all Times cause the same to be performed and f[ul]filled by their Ministers, Officers, and other Su[b]jects, so as the Subjects on each Side may enjoy [the] full Effects of all and every of them (those only [ex]cepted, concerning which it is otherwise ordered [by] the following Articles to the mutual Satisfaction [of] each Party;) and of all those likewise which [are]

American Treaty of 1670, confirmed.

contained in the following Articles. Moreover, t[he] Treaty of 1670, made between the Crowns [of] *Great-Britain* and *Spain,* for putting an end to [the] Differences, restraining Depredations, and establi[sh]ing Peace between the said Crown in *America,* is ag[ain] ratified and confirmed, without any Prejudice ho[w]ever to any Contract or other Privilege or Licen[ce] granted by his *Catholick* Majesty to the Queen [of] *Great-Britain* or her Subjects, in the late Treaty [of] Peace, or in the Contract of *Assiento*; as likew[ise] without Prejudice to any Liberty or Licence, whi[ch] the Subjects of *Great-Britain* enjoyed before eith[er] of Right, or by Sufferance or Indulgence.

ARTICL[E]

ARTICLE VI.

And as the Use and Liberty of Navigation and [C]ommerce ought to remain on both Sides entire, [se]cure, and free from all Moleftation, to the Sub[je]cts of both their Royal Majefties, as long as the [Pe]ace and Friendship entered into between their [R]oyal Majefties and their Crowns fhall fubfift; fo [lik]ewife their Royal Majefties have thought fit to [pr]ovide, that their faid Subjects fhall not be deprived of that Security, by Reafon of any Sparks of [D]ifcord which may arife; but on the contrary, [th]ey fhall enjoy the full Benefit of Peace, fo long [as] War fhall not be declared between the two [Cr]owns.

Full Benefit of Peace to be enjoyed till War declared.

Treaty of Munfter, *made between* Spain *and the States General in* 1648, *mentioned and refer'd to in the Eighth Article of the Marine Treaty of* 1667, *between* Great-Britain *and* Spain, *and exprefsly taken into the faid Treaty of* 1667, *by the faid Eighth Article, and made Part of the fame, efpecially as to the* Indies.

ARTICLE IV.

THE Subjects and Inhabitants of the Countries of the faid King and States, fhall hold a good [c]orrefpondence and Friendfhip together, without [an]y Refentment of paft Offences or Injuries, and [m]ay likewife frequent and fojourn in the Countries [of] each other, and carry on their Trade and Com[m]erce therein with all Safety, as well by Sea and [ot]her Waters as by Land.

Free Accefs and Commerce.

(62)

ARTICLE VI.

Neither Party to fail or trade in Places poffeffed by the other in the Weſt-Indies.

And as for the *Weſt-Indies*, the Subjects a[nd] Inhabitants of the Kingdoms, Provinces, and Lar[ds] of the ſaid King and States reſpectively ſhall abſt[ain] from ſailing and trading in all Havens, Towns a[nd] Places where there are any Forts, Lodges or Caſtl[es], and all other Places poſſeſſed by either Party, v[iz.] that the Subjects of the ſaid Kings ſhall not ſ[ail] and trade in the Places held by the ſaid States, [nor] the Subjects of the ſaid States in thoſe held by [the] ſaid King.

ARTICLE XXIII.

Not to enter or ſtop at any Ports or Roads of the other with Ships of War, without Leave, unleſs forced in.

Neither Party ſhall land, or enter into, or ſt[op] at any Havens, Ports, Shores or Roads belongi[ng] to the other Party, with any Ships of War in ſu[ch] Number as may give Suſpicion, without the L[i]cence and Permiſſion of him, under whoſe Obe[di]ence ſuch Havens, Ports, Shores or Roads a[re,] unleſs they ſhould be forced in by Streſs of Weath[er] or ſome other Neceſſity, and to avoid ſome Dang[er] of the Sea.

American *Treaty, between* Great-Britain a[nd] Spain, *for the compoſing of Differenc[es,] reſtraining of Depredations, and all Injuri[es,] and eſtabliſhing a good Correſpondence* America; *concluded at* Madrid, July t[he] 8th, 1670.

ARTICLE I.

Treaty of 1667, confirmed.

THE Treaty of Peace and Friendſhip ma[de] between the Crowns of *Great-Britain* a[nd] *Spain*, on the 13th Day of *May*, 1667; or a[ny] Clauſe thereof, ſhall in no wiſe be deem'd or unde[r]ſtood to be revoked or abrogated by the preſe[nt] Articl[e]

rticles and Conventions, but the same shall for
'er remain in its former Force, Strength and
igour, so far as it is not contrary or repugnant to
is present Treaty, or any Articles thereof.

ARTICLE II.

That there be an universal Peace, and true and   Universal and
\cere Amity, as well in *America*, as in the other perpetual Peace
arts of the World, between the Kings of *Great-*   and Amity.
itain and *Spain*, their Heirs and Successors, and
so between the States, Kingdoms, Colonies, Forts,
ties, Governments and Islands, without any Dif-
\ction of Places under the Dominions of either,
d between their People and Inhabitants respec-
ely; which shall endure from this Day for ever,
d shall be religiously observed, as well by Land
by Sea, and in all Waters; so as the one shall
omote the Welfare and Advantage of the other,
d the People shall assist and favour each other
th all mutual good Will and friendly Affection;
d that good Neighbourhood and true Peace and
nity be cultivated and increase daily on all Sides
those remote Countries, like as in those which
: nearer.

ARTICLE III.

That for the Time to come, all Enmities, Hos- All Hostilities
ities and Discords between the said Kings, their and Depredations
bjects and Inhabitants cease and be abolished;   to cease.
d that both Parties do altogether forbear and
tain from all Plundering, Depredation, Hurt,
uries and all Kind of Violence, as well by Land
by Sea, and in fresh Waters, in all Places what-
er.

ARTICLE VII.

The King of *Great-Britain*, his Heirs and Suc- King of *Great-*
ors, shall have, hold, and possess for ever, with *Britain* to hold all
l Right of Sovereign Dominion, Property and he now possesses
                  I   Posses- in the *West-Indies*
                                                     or *America*.

Poſſeſſion, all Lands, Countries, Iſlands, Colors and Dominions whatſoever ſituate in the *Weſt-dies*, or in any Part of *America*, which the [ ] King of *Great-Britain* and his Subjects do at [ ] preſent hold and poſſeſs; ſo as that in regard the of, or upon any Colour or Pretence whatſoev nothing may or ought ever to be urged, nor Queſtion or Controverſy be ever moved concern the ſame hereafter.

ARTICLE VIII.

Subjects of both to forbear all Commerce and Navigation in Places poſſeſſed by the other Party in the *Weſt-Indies*.

The Subjects and Inhabitants, Merchants, C. tains, Maſters of Ships, and Mariners of the Kii doms, Provinces, and Countries of both Kii doms reſpectively, ſhall abſtain and forbear fr all Commerce and Navigation into the Ports Places which have Forts, Caſtles, or Warehou for Merchandize, and all other Places which poſſeſſed by the other Party in the *Weſt-Indies*; to v the Subjects of the King of *Great-Britain* ſhall ſet on foot or carry on any Traffick, Navigat or Commerce, in the Ports or Places which King of *Spain* holdeth in the ſaid *Indies*; nor, the other Hand, ſhall the Subjects of the King *Spain*, ſet on Foot or carry on any Navigation Commerce to thoſe Places which are there poſſeſ by the King of *Great-Britain*.

ARTICLE IX.

Either King may grant Licence to the Subjects of the other, to navigate and trade there.

But if in Proceſs of Time either King ſhall thi fit to grant to the Subjects of the other, any gene or ſpecial Licence or Privilege of navigating a trading in any Places belonging to the Domini of him who ſhall grant ſuch Licences and Pri leges, the ſaid Navigation and Commerce ſhall exerciſed and maintained according to the For Tenor, and Effect of ſuch Permiſſions and Privileg as ſhall be ſo allowed and granted; and this preſ

Ratification thereof shall serve as a
the same.

ARTICLE X.

ects and Inhabitants of either of the   All Ships forced
with their Ships (whether they be   in shall be well received and af-
and of War or Merchant Ships and   sisted.
rty) shall be drove by Stress of
)rced by Pursuit of Pirates and Ene-
ther Distress, for the Sake of Shelter
to retreat and enter into any of the
s, Bays, Havens, Roads and Shores
onging to the other Confederate in
shall be received and treated there
ianity and Kindness, and enjoy all
:tion; they shall likewise have intire
resh themselves, and provide them-
able and usual Rates with Provisions
necessary for the Sustenance of their
Reparation of their Ships, and faci-
'oyage: They shall likewise, on no
indered on either Side, from depart-
out of such Port or Road, but it
for them to remove and depart from
Pleasure, whensoever and whither-
ll think fit, without any Molestation

ARTICLE XI.

he Ships of either Confederate, or of   Persons belong-
either (which God forbid) shall be   ing to Ships stranded or
vay, or wreck'd, or suffer any Damage   wreck'd shall be relieved and pro-
the Coasts, or within any of the Do-   tected.
other, it shall not be lawful to make
: Persons so cast away, or suffering
carry them into Slavery; but on the
Persons endanger'd or shipwreck'd
endly Assistance and Relief, and be
Letters of safe Conduct, so as they
F   may

may pafs from thence freely and without Moleftation, and every Man return to his own Country.

ARTICLE XII.

Ships forced in, if three or four in Number, to ftay no longer than allowed and neceffary.

But when the Ships of either (as is abovementioned) fhall through the Danger of the Sea, or from any other urgent Caufe, be compell'd and driven into the Ports of the other, if they be three or four in Number, and may give juft Ground of Sufpicion, the Caufe of their Arrival fhall be forthwith fignified to the Governor or chief Magiftrate of the Place; and they fhall not ftay there for any longer Time, than fhall be allowed them by the faid Governor or Magiftrate, and fhall be convenient and reafonable for fupplying themfelves with Provifions, and for repairing and fitting out their Ships; but Care fhall always be taken, that they do not difpofe of their Cargo, or carry out of the Ships and expofe to Sale any of the Goods or Packs; neither fhall they receive any Merchandize on board them from the other Party, or do any thing contrary to this Treaty.

ARTICLE XV.

All Rights of both Parties in the American Seas faved.

The prefent Treaty fhall not in any refpect derogate from any Pre-eminence, Right and Dominion whatfoever of either of the Confederates in the *American* Seas, Streights and Waters whatfoever; but that they have and retain the fame to themfelves, in as full and ample Manner as of Right belongs to them; but be it always underftood

Freedom of Navigation not to be interrupted.

that the Freedom in Navigation ought in no wife to be interrupted, nor any thing done, nor any Offence committed contrary to the genuine Senfe of thefe Articles.

Treaty of Peace at Utrecht, *between* Great-Britain *and* Spain, *of* 1713.

ARTICLE XV.

WHEREAS it is infifted on the Part of *Spain*, that certain Rights of fifhing at the Ifland of *Newfoundland* belong to the *Guipufcoans*, or other Subjects of his Catholick Majefty: Her *Britannick* Majefty confents and agrees, that all Privileges which the *Guipufcoans*, or other People of *Spain*, fhall be able to make Claim to by Right, fhall be preferved to them fafe and intire. *Newfoundland Fifhery.*

Treaty of Peace and Alliance between Great-Britain *and* Spain; *concluded at* Madrid, November *the* 15*th*, 1630.

ARTICLE VII.

IT was and is agreed and concluded, that there be and ought to be a free Commerce between the King of *Spain* and the King of *Great-Britain*, and all their Vaffals, Inhabitants, and Subjects, as well by Land as by Sea, and on frefh Waters, in all and fingular the Kingdoms, Dominions and Iflands, Lands, Cities, Towns, Villages, Ports and Diftricts of the faid Kingdoms and Dominions, where Commerce and Trade was carried on between the faid Kingdoms before the War, between *Philip* II. King of *Spain*, and *Elizabeth* Queen of *England*, as it was fettled in the Treaty of Peace in the Year 1604, Article IX, according to the Ufe and Obfervance of ancient Covenants and Treaties preceding the faid Time; fo that without any Paffport, general or fpecial Licence, either by Land, Sea, or frefh Water, Free Navigation, Paffage and Commerce according to ancient Treaties.

ter, the Subjects and Vaſſals of both Kings may go, enter and ſail to all the foreſaid Places, and all their Cities, Towns and Ports, Shores, Coaſts and Diſtricts, and enter into any Ports in which there was a mutual Commerce before the ſaid Time, and according to the Uſe and Obſervance of the ſaid ancient Covenants and Treaties, may import Merchandizes on Waggons, Horſes, Carriages, and Veſſels loaded or to be loaded, and buy and ſell in ſuch Places, and furniſh themſelves at reaſonable Rates with any Quantity of Proviſions, and Things neceſſary for their Subſiſtance and Voyage, and repair their Veſſels and Carriages, whether they be their own, or hired, or borrowed, and with the ſame Liberty depart, with all their Merchandizes, Goods and Things whatſoever, having firſt paid the Tolls and Duties according to the Laws of ſuch Places, and go from thence to their own or any other Countries, as they pleaſe, without any Impediment.

ARTICLE VIII.

It ſhall be lawful to go to the Ports of the ſaid Kings, and there remain and depart from thence with the ſame Liberty, not only with Merchant Ships, but alſo with all Manner of Ships of War, prepared to repulſe the Attacks of the Enemy, whether they ſhall be driven by the Violence of Storm, or to repair their Ships, or to buy Proviſions; provided that if they come in freely, and of their own Accord, they do not exceed the Number of ſix or eight Ships, and do not remain longer in the Ports than ſhall be neceſſary for refitting, or purchaſing Neceſſaries, leſt they ſhould be a Hindrance to the free Commerce of other friendly Nations; but if there ſhall be a greater Number of Ships of War, then they ſhall not come in without firſt conſulting the King; and they ſhall commit no Hoſtilities in the ſaid Ports, in Prejudice of the ſaid Kings, but live and continue quiet like Friends and Confederates.

Free Acceſs and Departure for all Ships.

Number of Ships reſtrained.

ARTICLE

ARTICLE IX.

Provided always, that under Colour and Pretext of Commerce, no Affiftance, whether of Provifions, Arms or warlike Inftruments, or any other Kind of warlike Affiftance, be carried by any of the Subjects, Vaffals or Inhabitants of the forefaid Kings, for the Ufe and Benefit of the Enemies of either of the faid Kings; but whofoever fhall attempt fuch Things, fhall be moft feverely punifhed, as feditious Perfons, and Breakers of Faith and Peace: And further, the Subjects of either Party fhall not be worfe treated in the Territories of the other, than the Natives themfelves, in felling and bargaining for their Merchandizes, either with regard to the Price or otherwife; but the Condition of Foreigners and Natives in the forefaid Refpects fhall be equal and alike, any Statutes or Cuftoms to the contrary notwithftanding.

Subjects of one Party not to carry Provifions or warlike Affiftance to the Enemy of the other.

Subjects of both Parties to be treated as Natives.

ARTICLE XXII.

That in cafe any prohibited Goods or Merchandize be exported, or carried out of the Kingdoms and Dominions of either of the faid Kings, by the Subjects of either, in that cafe the Delinquent only fhall be punifhed, and the prohibited Goods only fhall be confifcated.

Prohibited Goods only to be confifcated, and the Offender only to be punifhed.

ARTICLE XXVI.

That neither of the faid Kings fhall detain or ftop any Ships belonging to the Subjects of the other, lying in their Ports, to ufe them for carrying on War, or for any other Service, in Prejudice of the Owners, without firft acquainting their King to whom the Ships belong, and having his Confent.

Ships not to be detained for any Service without Confent.

Treaty of Peace and Alliance between Great Britain *and* Spain; *concluded at* London Auguſt *the* 18*th*, 1604.

Free Navigation, Paſſage and Commerce, as before uſed.

IT is agreed and concluded, that there be an[d] ought to be a free Commerce between the Moſt Serene King of *England*, and the Moſt Serene King of *Spain*, and between all their Vaſſals, Inhabitant[s] and Subjects whatſoever, as well by Land as b[y] Sea, and freſh Waters, in all and ſingular the Kingdoms, Dominions and Iſlands, and other Land[s] Cities, Towns, Villages, Ports and Diſtricts of th[e] ſaid Kingdoms and Dominions, in which Commerce was uſed before the breaking out of the War, and according to the Uſe and Obſervance of an[c]tient Covenants and Treaties before the War; ſo a[s] the Subjects and Vaſſals of either King may, without any Paſſport or Licence, general or ſpecial, come and enter into the ſaid Kingdoms and Dominions, either by Sea, Land, or freſh Water, and in[to] to the Cities, Towns, Villages, Ports, Shores Creeks and Diſtricts thereof, and enter into an[y] Ports where Commerce was carried on before th[e] War, and according to the Uſe and Obſervanc[e] of the antient Covenants and Treaties, may impor[t] Merchandizes upon Waggons, Horſes, Carriages and Veſſels loaded, or to be loaded; and buy an[d] ſell in ſuch Places, and furniſh themſelves at [a] reaſonable Rate with any Quantity of Proviſion and Things neceſſary for their Subſiſtence an[d] Voyage; and repair their Veſſels and Carriages whether they be their own, or hired, or borrowed and with the ſame Liberty depart with all thei[r] Merchandizes, Goods and Things whatſoever, having firſt paid the preſent Toll and Duties, only according to the Laws of ſuch Places, and go from thence into their own or any other Countries as they please, without any Impediment.

ARTICLE X.

It is agreed, and in like manner concluded, that it shall be lawful to come to the Ports of the said Princes and remain there, and depart from thence with the same Liberty, not only with Merchant Ships, but also with all other Ships of War, fitted to restrain and resist the Force and Attempts of the Enemy; whether they be forced in by the Violence of Storm, or come in to refit their Ships, or to buy Provisions: Provided, that in case they come without being forced, they exceed not the Number of six or eight Ships, nor remain in, or hover about the Ports any longer than shall be necessary for repairing of them, and providing Necessaries; and that they be not a Hindrance in any wise to the free Intercourse and Commerce of other ally'd Nations; but if there shall be a greater Number of Ships of War, then they must not enter the Ports without consulting the Prince; and they must not act in a hostile Manner in the said Ports in Prejudice of the said Princes, but live and remain as Friends and Confederates; provided always, that under Colour or Pretext of Commerce, no Assistance or Provisions of Victuals, Arms, warlike Instruments, or any other Kind of warlike Assistance be brought for the Use and Service of the Enemies of either of the said Kings, by any of the Subjects, Vassals, or Inhabitants of the said Kings; but whosoever shall attempt it, shall be most severely punished, as seditious Infringers of Faith and Peace.

Free Access and Departure for all Ships of both Nations.

Number of Ships restrained.

Subjects of the one not to supply or assist the Enemy of the other.

ARTICLE XI.

That the Subjects of the one Prince shall not be worse treated in the Territories of the other, than the natural born Subjects, in selling and bargaining about their Merchandizes, as well with respect to the

Subjects of both Nations to be treated as Natives.

F 4

the Price, as otherwise; but in the foresaid Cases, the Condition of Strangers shall be the same with that of the Inhabitants and natural born Subjects, any Statutes or Customs to the contrary notwithstanding.

ARTICLE XX.

Subjects of the one not to assist the Enemy of the other with Money, Provisions or Arms,

And as the said Kings solemnly promise never to give any warlike Assistance to the Enemies of either, it is further provided, that their Subjects or Inhabitants, of whatever Nation or Quality they be, shall not either on Pretence of Trade or Commerce, or under any other Colour, assist the Enemies of the said Princes, or of either of them in any Manner; nor furnish them with Money, Provisions, Arms, Engines, Guns or Instruments fit for War, nor afford any other warlike Furniture; and all Contraveners shall be liable to the severest Punishments, as Covenant-Breakers and seditious Persons.

ARTICLE XXIV.

Prohibited Goods only to be confiscated; and the Offender only to be punished.

That if any prohibited Goods or Merchandizes shall be exported or carried out of the Kingdoms and Dominions of the said most Serene Kings by the Subjects of either, in that Case the Delinquent alone shall incur Punishment, and the prohibited Goods only shall be confiscated.

ARTICLE XXVIII.

Ships not to be detained for any Service without Consent.

That neither of the foresaid Princes shall detain the Ships of the other in their Ports or Waters, to use them for War or any other Service, in Prejudice of their Masters and Owners, without first acquainting the Prince to whom the Ship belongs, and obtaining his Consent.

Treaty

Treaty of Peace and Alliance between Great-Britain *and* Spain, *made in the Year* 1542, *viz. between* Henry VIII. *of* England, *and* Charles V. *Emperor and King of* Spain, *and of the* Indies, *and Lord of the* Netherlands.

ARTICLE II.

IT is agreed and concluded, that from this Day there be a good, sincere, true, intire, perfect and [fir]m Friendship, League, Confederacy, Peace and [U]nion, by Land, Sea, and fresh Waters, to endure [for] all future Times between the said two Princes, [th]eir Heirs and Successors, and their Kingdoms, [Co]untries, Dominions, Lands, Vassals, and Subjects whatsoever, present and to come, of whatever [D]egree or Condition they be, so that the aforesaid [V]assals and Subjects on both Sides shall be bound [m]utually to favour each other with sincere and [ho]nest Affection, and they may safely, freely and [se]curely go as well by Land and Sea as fresh Waters, [an]d enter into the said Kingdoms, Countries, Dominions, Lands, Cities, Towns and Places, fortified [or] unfortified, and all their Ports and Districts [w]hatsoever, or any of them; and there be and [ab]ide as long as they please; and there buy and sell [Pr]ovisions and all other Necessaries whatsoever without Contradiction; and may likewise go, depart and [re]turn from the said Kingdoms, Countries, Lands, [Ci]ties, Towns, Villages, Ports and Districts whatever, or any of them, as often as they please, to [the]ir own Countries, or any other foreign Parts [w]hatsoever, with their hired or borrowed Ships, [W]aggons, Carriages, Horses, Armour, Merchandi[z]es, Packs, Goods, and all other Things whatso[e]ver, in the same Manner as they might do in their

Perpetual Peace and Amity.

Free Navigation, Passage and Commerce.

own

own Countries, or as the native Subjects of the Places and Countries might; so as they shall n need any safe Conduct, or general or special Licenc nor be obliged to ask for such safe Conduct Licence in any of the aforesaid Places

ARTICLE III.

Neither Party to attempt any thing against the other.

Neither of the said Princes, nor any of the Heirs and Successors, shall act, do, treat, or attem any thing against the other, either upon Land or ; Sea, or in the Countries, Ports, or fresh Wate upon any Occasion, nor give any Aid, Counf Countenance or Consent, in case of any Invasi which may be made, intended or attempted by a others whatsoever, to the Injury or Prejudice the other Prince, his Heirs or Successors.

ARTICLE IV.

Neither Party to aid or favour the Enemies of the other.

Neither of the said Parties shall give any Ai Counsel or Countenance to the known Enemies the other Party intending or endeavouring to inva him either by Land, Sea, or fresh Waters in a Lands, Kingdoms, Countries, Cities, and Don nions whatsoever and wheresoever situated; r wittingly suffer such Enemies to enter into, or p: through his Kingdoms, Countries, Lands, Citi(and Dominions; nor in any wise favour any su Designs directly or indirectly.

ARTICLE X.

This Peace to remain, though violated by the Subjects or Allies of either.

That if during the foresaid Peace and Amity a thing be attempted, acted, or done against t Force and Effect of the same, by Land, Sea, fresh Waters, by any of the Vassals, Subjects a Allies of the said Princes, their Heirs and Successo or by the Heirs and Successors, Vassals or Subje of their Allies, who are comprehended in tl Treaty; yet notwithstanding, this Peace and Am

hall remain in their full Force and Effect, and the
Persons only attempting such Things, and doing
he Mischief, shall be punished for such their At-
empts and no others.

ARTICLE XI.

Whenever it shall happen that the Subjects of <small>Upon Injury done, no Commissions to</small>
he King of *England* shall be any ways hurt or in- <small>be granted or War</small>
ured by the Subjects of the said Emperor, or that <small>made, but Reparation by the</small>
he Subjects of the said Lord the Emperor shall be <small>Prince of the</small>
urt or injured by the Subjects of the King of <small>Party offending.</small>
England, those who have not done the Injury shall
ot therefore be liable, by Letters of Reprisals,
Marque or Countermarque, or any other Orders or
ommissions whatsoever, without due and pre-
ious Notice or Summons, either upon the Petition
f the Person injured, or some other way, to be
rested in their Persons or Goods, or to be any
ays obstructed or molested, nor shall any War be
ade or levied on that Account; but the Prince of
he said Party offending shall make due Reparation
or all such Attempts and Injuries, and put Mat-
rs into their former Condition: And such Letters
f Reprisals, Marque and Countermarque, and all
ich like Orders (unless such Notices have first gone
it and been duly intimated to the Parties, and
ublick Summons with respect to the Princes) shall
enceforth intirely cease; and if they be otherwise
ranted, they shall be accounted null and void.

ARTICLE XIII.

It is likewise agreed, for the common Benefit of <small>Increase of mutual Commerce</small>
his Peace and Friendship, and that the Subjects of <small>stipulated.</small>
oth the said Princes may daily increase in their
utual accustom'd Commerce with each other,
at as for the Intercourse of Merchandizes
nd mutual Commerce, which they have usually
rried on with each other, the Treaty of Com-
erce, dated the 11th of *April*, 1520, shall be and <small>Treaty of 1520, confirmed.</small>
remain

remain in the same State and Force in which ought to be, and remain by the Treaty of *Cambra* dated the 5th of *August*, 1529.

N. B. The Marine Treaty of 1520, referred in the last recited Article of the foregoing Treaty, made between the same Princes, contains a mutual Stipulation of a general and unlimited Freedom and Liberty of Navigation and Commerce between them, and the Subjects of each reciprocally; but the Treaty of *Cambray* of 1529, likewise referred to in the said Article as declaratory of the Force and Validity of the said Treaty of 1520, does not now appear to be any where subsisting; but the said Treaty of 1520, limited as to its Duration, by one of the Articles thereof, so as to continue and be in Force from five Years to five Years, until such Time as a new Treaty of Commerce should be made between the said Princes, which having been done as to *Spain* by the two several Treaties of 1667 and 1679, that of 1520 cannot be looked upon as valid and in Force at this Time.

Article.

Articles and Clauses of several Treaties made between Great-Britain *and* Spain; *renewing and confirming former Treaties, and amicable Usage and Intercourse between the said two Crowns.*

Treaty of Seville *between* Great-Britain *and* Spain, *and* France, 1729.

ARTICLE I.

ALL preceding Treaties and Conventions of Peace, Amity and Commerce, concluded between the contracting Powers, shall be, as they hereby are, effectually renewed and confirmed in all Points, which are not derogated from by the present Treaty, in as full and ample Manner as if the said Treaties were here inserted Word for Word; their said Majesties promising neither to do, nor suffer any thing to be done, that may be contrary thereto directly or indirectly.

All preceding Treaties confirmed.

ARTICLE IV.

It having been agreed by the preliminary Articles, that the Commerce of the *English* Nation, as well in *Europe* as in the *Indies*, should be reestablished on the foot of the Treaties and Conventions antecedent to the Year 1725; and particularly that the Commerce of the *English* Nation in *America* should be exercised as heretofore; it is agreed by the present Article, that all necessary Orders shall be dispatched on both Sides, without any Delay, if it has not been done already, as well for the Execution of the said Treaties of Com-

Commerce established on the foot of Treaties preceding 1725.

(78)

Commerce, as for supplying whatsoever may b wanting for the entire Re-establishment of Com merce on the foot of the said Treaties and Con ventions.

·Separate ARTICLE I.

Although conformably to the preliminary A ticles, it has been said by the Fourth Article o the Treaty signed this Day, that the Commerce o the *English* Nation in *America* should be re-est: blished on the Foot of the Treaties and Conver tions antecedent to the Year 1725; however, fo the greater Clearness, it is further declared b the present Article between their *Britannick* an Catholick Majesties, which shall have the sam Force, and be under the same Guaranty as th Treaty signed this Day, that under that gener: Denomination are comprehended the Treaties o Peace and of Commerce concluded at *Utrecht* th 13th of *July*, and 9th of *December*, 28th of *N* *vember* O. S. 1713, in which are comprized th Treaty of 1667, made at *Madrid*, and the Sch dula's therein mentioned; the latter Treaty mac at *Madrid* the 14th of *December*, 1715, as all the particular Contract commonly called the *Assient*, for bringing Negro Slaves into the *Spanish West Indies*, which was made the 26th of *March*, 1713 in Consequence of the Twelfth Article of th Treaty of *Utrecht*, and likewise the Treaty of D claration touching that of the *Assiento*, made th 26th of *May*, 1716; all which Treaties mentione in this Article, with their Declarations, sha from this Day be and remain in their full Forco Virtue and Vigour.

Treaties of 1667, 1713, 1715, and 1716, confirmed.

The Preliminary Articles signed at Paris, July *the* 31*st,* 1717, *and at* Vienna, July *the* 13*th,* 1727.

ARTICLE III.

ALL the Privileges of Commerce which the *English* Nation hath heretofore by Virtue of Treaties enjoyed, as well in *Europe* as in the *Indies,* shall be restored to that Usage and Regulation, which are agreeable to what have been stipulated in the Treaties antecedent to the Year 1725.

All Privileges of Commerce restored to the English, as before the Year 1725.

Treaty of Alliance between Great-Britain *and* Spain, *and* France; *concluded at* Madrid, *the* 13*th of* June, 1721.

ARTICLE VI.

HIS Catholick Majesty being desirous of giving his *Britannick* Majesty a particular Proof of his Friendship, confirms, as far as there may be occasion, all Advantages and Privileges, heretofore granted by the King's Predecessors to the *English* Nation; so as the trading Subjects of the King of *Great-Britain* shall always enjoy in *Spain* the same Rights, Prerogatives, Advantages and Privileges for their Persons, Commerce, Merchandize, Estate and Effects, which they either have or ought to have enjoyed by Virtue of Treaties and Stipulations, or which have or shall be granted in *Spain* to any the most favour'd Nation.

Privileges of Trade confirmed to the English.

Treaty

Treaty of Peace between Great-Britain a[nd]
Spain; *concluded at* Madrid, June t[he]
13*th*, 1721.

ARTICLE II.

Treaties of 1667, 1713, 1715, 1716, confirmed.

THE Treaties of Peace and Commerce concl[u]ded at *Utrecht* on the 13th (2d, O.S.) of *Ju*[ly] and the 9th of *December* (28th of *November*, O.[S.] 1713, (wherein are comprehended the Treaty ma[de] at *Madrid* in 1667, and the Schedula's therein m[en]tioned) shall stand confirmed and ratified by this p[re]sent Treaty, except the 3d, 5th, and 8th Articles [of] the said Treaty of Commerce, which are commo[nly] called Explanatory, and which have been annull[ed] by Virtue of another subsequent Treaty made [at] *Madrid* the 14th of *December*, 1715, which Tre[aty] remains likewise confirmed and ratified; as a[lso] the particular Contract commonly called the *Assi*[en]*to*, for the Importation of Negro Slaves into t[he] *Spanish West-Indies*, made the 26th of *March*, 171[3] and likewise the Declaration concerning the *Assien*[to] made the 26th of *May*, 1716; all which Treat[ies] mentioned in this Article, with their Declaratio[ns] shall remain in their full Force, Virtue and Vigo[ur] in every thing, wherein they are not contrary to th[e] present Treaty.

Treaty of Commerce between Great-Britain a[nd] Spain; *concluded at* Madrid, Decemb[er] *the* 14*th*, 1715.

ARTICLE V.

Privileges confirmed to the *English*, as before the late War.

THE *British* Subjects shall enjoy all the Righ[ts] Privileges, Franchises, Exemptions and I[m]munities whatever, which they enjoyed before t[he] laſt War, by Virtue of the Royal Schedula's or Ordinances, and by the Articles of the Treaty of Peace and Commerce made at *Madrid* in 1667, which is hereby fully confirmed; and the like ſhall be granted, obſerved and permitted to the Subjects of *Spain,* in the Dominions of the King of *Great-Britain.*

ARTICLE VII.

The Treaty of Commerce made at *Utrecht* on the 9th of *December* (28th of *November* O. S.) 1713, ſhall continue in Force, excepting ſuch Articles as ſhall be found contrary to what is this Day concluded and ſigned, which ſhall be aboliſhed and rendered of no Force; and eſpecially the three Articles commonly called Explanatory, *viz.* the 3d, 5th and 8th Articles, as inſerted in the Inſtrument of Ratification.

Treaty of Commerce of 1713, confirmed.

Treaty of Peace between Great-Britain *and* Spain; *concluded at* Utrecht, July *the 2d,* O. S. 1713.

ARTICLE XV.

THEIR Royal Majeſties do on both Sides renew and confirm all Treaties of Peace, Friendſhip, Alliance and Commerce heretofore made and concluded between the Crowns of *Great-Britain* and *Spain,* and the ſaid Treaties are renewed and confirmed by this preſent Treaty, in as full and ample Manner as if they were now particularly inſerted; that is to ſay, ſo far as they are not found contrary to the Treaties of Peace and Commerce which were laſt made and ſigned; but more eſpecially by this Treaty of Peace are confirmed and ratified the Treaties, Alliances and Conventions, as well thoſe which relate to the Uſe of Navigation

All former Treaties renewed and confirmed.

and

(82)

and Commerce in *Europe* and elsewhere, as thos[e] which relate to the Introduction of Negroes int[o] *Spanish America*, and which already are, or ver[y] speedily will be made between the two Nations a[t] *Madrid*.

Treaty of Alliance between Great-Britain an[d] Spain; *concluded at* Windsor, June th[e] 10th, 1680.

ARTICLE XII.

Treaties of 1667, and 1670, confirmed.

THE Treaty of Peace and Friendship mad[e] between the Most Serene Kings at *Madrid*, i[n] the Year 1697; and likewise another Treaty mad[e] also at *Madrid*, in the Year 1670, for establishin[g] Peace, &c. in *America*, between the Kingdoms o[f] *Great-Britain* and *Spain*; and also all other Treatie[s] and Conventions made between the Most Seren[e] Kings, shall be sincerely observed in their severa[l] Articles; and the Most Serene Kings and thei[r] Subjects on both Sides shall freely and effectuall[y] hold and enjoy all Things therein. contained, whether they relate to publick or private Affairs.

Treaty with Spain *of* 1630.

ARTICLE XX.

Ancient Treaties revived and confirmed.

AND as to what concerns the many ancient Intercourses and Treaties of Commerce between the Kingdoms of *England*, *Scotland* and *Ireland*, and the Dukes of *Burgundy*, and Princes of the *Netherlands*, which have been interrupted during these Commotions, and perhaps violated in many Respects; it is provisionally agreed, that they shall retain their former Force and Authority;

and

and that they shall be in the same State they were be-
fore the War between *Philip* II. King of *Spain* and
Elizabeth Queen of *England*, as it is settled by the
Treaty of Peace in the Year 1604.

ARTICLE XXIV.

That the Concessions and Privileges granted by the said Kings to the Merchants of both Kingdoms coming to their Kingdoms, and which have ceased because of the War, shall be revived and have their full Effect. *Privileges of Merchants revived.*

Treaty with Spain *of* 1604.

ARTICLE XXII.

BUT as to what concerns the ancient Intercourse, and various Treaties of Commerce between the Dukes of *Burgundy*, and Princes of the *Netherlands*, and the Kingdoms of *England, Ireland* and *Scotland* also, which during these Troubles and Commotions have been intermitted, and perhaps violated in many Respects; it is provisionally agreed, that they retain their former Force, and be of the same Effect on both Sides, as they were before the War broke out. *Ancient Treatie with Burgundy and the Netherlands revived.*

ARTICLE XXVI.

That the Concessions and Privileges granted by the said Princes to the Merchants of both Kingdoms coming to their Dominions, and which have ceased because of the War, shall be revived and become effectual. *Privileges of Merchants revived.*

An Explanatory Declaration of certain Articles of the Marine Treaties, concluded between Great-Britain *and the States General in the Years* 1667-8, *and* 1674.

Done at the Hague, *the* 30th *of* December, 1675.

1675.

WHEREAS fome Difficulties have aro[i]
touching the Conftruction of certain A[r]
ticles, as well in the Marine Treaty which w[as]
concluded $\frac{11}{21}$ of *December* 1674, as in that whic[h]
was concluded $\frac{27}{17}$ of *February* 1667-8, between th[e]
King of *Great-Britain* on the one Part, and th[e]
States General on the other, touching the Liber[ty]
allowed to their Subjects refpectively of trading [to]
the Ports of the Enemies of either of the Partie[s,]
We do declare by thefe Prefents, that the true Sen[se]
and Intention of the faid Articles, is, and ought [to]
Free Trade and be, that the Ships and Veffels belonging to the Su[b-]
Navigation to and jects of the one or the other of the Parties, may [at]
from Places belonging to an all Times, from the Time of the Conclufion of th[e]
Enemy of the other Party. faid Articles, pafs, trade and traffick, not only fro[m]
a neutral Port or Place, into a Place belonging [to]
an Enemy of the other Party, or from a Place b[e-]
longing to an Enemy into a neutral Place ; b[ut]
likewife from one Port or Place belonging to [an]
Enemy, into any other Port or Place belonging lik[e-]
wife to an Enemy of the other Party; wheth[er]
fuch Places belong to the fame Prince or State, [or]
to divers Princes or States, with whom the oth[er]
Party fhall be at War.

Marine Treaty between Great-Britain *and the* United Provinces, *to be observed by Land and by Sea, throughout all Countries and Parts of the World; concluded at* London, December *the 1st,* 1674.

ARTICLE I.

THAT it shall and may be lawful for all and every the Subjects of the Most Serene and Mighty Prince the King of *Great-Britain*, with all Freedom and Safety, to sail, trade, and exercise all Manner of Traffick, in all other Kingdoms, Countries and Estates, which now are, or at any time hereafter shall be in Peace, Amity or Neutrality with his said Majesty, so as they shall not be any ways hindered or molested in their Navigation or Trade by the Military Forces, Ships of War, or any other Vessels whatsoever belonging either to the High and Mighty Lords the States General of the *United Netherlands*, or to their Subjects, upon Account or under Pretence of any Hostility or Quarrel now subsisting, or which may hereafter happen between the said Lords the States General, and any other Princes or People whatsoever, in Peace, Amity or Neutrality with his said Majesty; and likewise, that it shall and may be lawful for all and every the Subjects of the said High and Mighty Lords the States General of the *United Netherlands*, with all Freedom and Safety to sail, trade and exercise all Manner of Traffick, in all other Kingdoms, Countries and Estates, which now are, or at any Time hereafter shall be at Peace, Amity or Neurality with the aforesaid Lords the States; so as they shall not be any ways hindered or molested in their Navigation or Trade, by the Military Forces, Ships of War, or any other Vessels whatsoever, belonging

1674.

Navigation and Trade with Allies of one Party, not to be molested by the other.

longing

longing either to the said King, or to his Subjects, upon Account or under Pretence of any Hostility or Quarrel now subsisting, or which may hereafter happen between his said Majesty and any other Princes or People whatsoever, which are or shall be in Peace, Amity or Neutrality with the said Lords the States.

ARTICLE II.

Freedom of Trade as to all Goods, except Contraband. Nor shall this Freedom of Navigation and Commerce be violated or interrupted by reason of any War, as to any Kind of Merchandize, but such Freedom shall extend to all Commodities, which might be carried in Time of Peace; those only excepted, which are described under the Name of contraband Goods in the following Article.

ARTICLE III.

Contraband Goods specified. Under this Name of Contraband or prohibited Goods, shall be comprehended only Arms, Pieces of Ordinance, with all Implements belonging to them, Fire-Balls, Powder, Match, Bullets, Pikes, Swords, Lances, Spears, Halberts, Guns, Mortar-pieces, Petard, Granadoes, Musket-Rests, Bandeliers, Saltpetre, Muskets, Musket-Shot, Helmets, Corslets, Breast-Plates, Coats of Mail, and the like Kind of Armature; Soldiers, Horses, and all Things necessary for the Furniture of Horses, Holsters, Belts, and all other warlike Instruments whatsoever.

ARTICLE IV.

What Goods are not to be deem'd Contraband. The following Goods shall not be deem'd Contraband, *viz.* All Kind of Cloth, and all other Manufactures woven of any Kind of Wool, Flax, Silk, Cotton, or any other Material; all Sorts of Cloathing and Garments, together with the Materials whereof they are made; Gold and Silver as well coined as not coined; Tin, Iron, Lead, Copper, and Coals; as also Wheat, Barley, and all other Kind of Corn,

Corn, or Pulfe; Tobacco, and all Kind of Spices; falted and fmoked Flefh, falted and dried Fifh, Butter, Cheefe, Beer, Oil, Wine, Sugar, and all Kind of Salt; and in general, all Provifion which ferve for the Nourifhment and Suftenance of Life; likewife all Kind of Cotton, Hemp, Flax and Pitch, and Ropes, Sails and Anchors; alfo Mafts and Planks, Boards and Beams of any Kind of Wood, and all other Materials requifite for building or repairing Ships; but they fhall be wholly reputed free Goods, as likewife all other Wares and Things which are not comprehended in the next preceding Article; fo that the fame may be freely tranfported and carried by the Subjects of his faid Majefty, even unto Places at Enmity with the faid States; as alfo on the other Side, by the Subjects of the faid States to Places under the Obedience of the Enemies of his faid Majefty, except only to Towns or Places befieged, block'd up, or invefted.

ARTICLE V.

And that all Differences and Contentions on both Sides, by Sea and Land, may from henceforth ceafe and be utterly extinguifhed; it is agreed, that all Kind of Ships and Veffels whatfoever belonging to the Subjects of his faid Majefty, entering or being entered into any Road or Port under the Obedience of the Lords the States, and purpofing to pafs from thence, fhall be only obliged to fhew unto the Officers of fuch Port, or to the Captains of the Guardfhips or Privateers belonging to the States (if any happen there to be) their Paffport according to the Form annexed to this prefent Treaty; nor fhall any Money, or any thing elfe be exacted from them upon that Account: But if any Ship belonging to the Subjects of his Majefty of *Great-Britain*, fhall in the open Sea, or elfewhere out of the Dominions of the faid States, meet any Ships of War of the faid Lords the States, or Privateers

Merchant Ships to fhew their Paffports in Ports.

<small>Merchant Ships at Sea meeting Ships of War, to pass freely on shewing their Passports.</small>

belonging to their Subjects, the said Ships of the Lords the States, or of their Subjects, shall keep at a convenient Distance and only send out their Boat, with two or three Men only, to go on board such Ships and Vessels of the Subjects of his Majesty, in order that the Passport (or Sea Brief) concerning the Property thereof, according to the Form here under annexed, may be produced to them by the Captain or Master of such Ship or Vessel belonging to the Subjects of his Majesty; and the said Ships so producing the same, shall freely pass; and it shall not be lawful to molest, search, detain, or force such Ship from her intended Voyage: And the Subjects of the Lords the States shall enjoy in all things the same Liberty and Immunity, they in like manner shewing their Passport (or Sea Brief) made out according to the Form prescribed at the Foot of this Treaty.

ARTICLE VI.

<small>Merchant Ships going into an Enemy's Port to produce their Cockets as well as Passports.</small>

But if any Ship or Vessel belonging to the *English*, or other Subjects of *Great-Britain*, shall be met making into any Port belonging to an Enemy of the Lords the States; or, on the other Side, if any Ship belonging to the *United Provinces* of the *Netherlands*, or other Subjects of the Lords the States, shall be met in her way making into any Port under the Obedience of the Enemies of his said Majesty, such Ship shall shew not only a Passport (or Sea Brief) according to the Form hereunder subscribed, wherewith she is to be furnished, but also her Certificate or Cocket; containing a Particular of the Goods on board, given in the usual Form, by the Officers of the Customs of that Port from whence she came; whereby it may be known whether she is laden with any of the Goods prohibited by the Third Article of this Treaty.

ARTICLE

ARTICLE VII.

But in case that, upon shewing such Cockets containing a Particular of the Goods on board, given in the usual Form by the Officers of the Customs of that Port from whence the said Ship sailed (concerning the shewing whereof it is above agreed) either Party shall discover any of that Kind of Goods, which by the Third Article of this Treaty are declared to be contraband or prohibited, consigned to any Port under the Obedience of their Enemies, it shall not then be lawful to open the Hatches of such Ship, in which the same shall happen to be found, whether she belongs to the Subjects of his Majesty, or of the Lords the States; or to unlock or break open any Chests, Packs, or Casks in the same; nor to convey away any the least Part of the Merchandizes, before the whole Cargo be first put on Shore in the Presence of the Officers of the Admiralty, and an Inventory made of the same; neither shall it be lawful to sell, exchange, or any way to alienate the same, before such prohibited Goods shall be duly and lawfully proceeded against, and that the Judges of the Admiralty respectively shall by Sentence have declared the same confiscated: Provided always, that as well the Ship itself, as the rest of the Goods found in the same, which by this Treaty are to be reputed free, shall not be detained upon Pretence of their being infected by such prohibited Goods, much less confiscated as lawful Prize; and if a Part only, and not the whole of the Lading, shall consist of contraband or prohibited Goods, and the Master of the Ship shall be willing and ready to deliver them to the Captor who discovered the same, in that case the Captor shall not compel the Ship to go out of her Course to any Port he thinks fit, but shall forthwith dismiss her, and upon no account hinder

Ships taken with contraband Goods on board to be brought into Port.

Contraband Goods only to be condemned, the Ship and other Goods to go free.

On immediate Delivery of contraband Goods to the Captor, the Ship to be dismissed.

hinder her from freely purſuing her intend- Voyage.

ARTICLE VIII.

All Goods found in Enemies Ships, to be confiſcated.
Whatſoever ſhall be found laden by his Majeſty's Subjects upon any Ship whatſoever belonging to the Enemies of the Lords the States, altho' the ſame be not of the Quality of contraband Goods, may be confiſcated: But, on the contrary all that which ſhall be found put on board Ships belonging to the Subjects of the King of *Great-Britain*, ſhall be accounted clear and free, altho' the whole Lading, or any Part thereof by juſt Title of Property ſhould belong to the Enemies of the Lords
Free Ships make free Goods, except contraband.
the States, except always contraband Goods: But in caſe any ſuch are intercepted, all things ſhall be done according to the Meaning and Direction of the foregoing Articles; and ſo likewiſe whatſoever ſhall be found laden by the Subjects of the Lords the States in any Ship whatſoever belonging to the Enemies of his Majeſty, although the ſame be not of the Quality of contraband Goods, may be confiſcated: But on the other Side, all that which ſhall be found put on board Ships belonging to the Subjects of the Lords the States, ſhall be accounted clear and free, although the whole Lading, or any Part thereof, by juſt Title of Property ſhould belong to the Enemies of his Majeſty; except always contraband Goods; but in caſe any ſuch are intercepted, all Things ſhall be done according to the Meaning and Direction of the foregoing Articles; and leaſt any Damage ſhould by Surprize be done to the one Party being at Peace, upon the firſt breaking out of a War with the other Party, it is provided and agreed
Goods taken on board Enemies Ships within times limited not forfeited.
that a Ship belonging to the Enemies of either Party, and laden with Goods of the Subjects of the other, ſhall not by its Infection render the ſaid Goods liable to Confiſcation, in caſe they were

laden

den before the Expiration of the Terms hereafter
entioned, after the Declaration or Publication of
ıy fuch War, *viz*. If the Goods were laden in any
ort or Place between the Places or Limits called
ıe Soundings, and the Naze in *Norway*, within
ıe Space of fix Weeks after fuch Declaration; of
vo Months between the faid Place, the Soundings,
ıd the City of *Tangier*; of ten Weeks in the
lediterranean Sea; or within the Space of eight
lonths in any other Country or Place of the
World; fo that it fhall not be lawful to confifcate
e Goods of the Subjects of his Majefty, taken
· feized in any Ship or Veffel whatfoever of any
nemy of the Lords the States upon that account,
ıt the fame fhall be without Delay reftored to the
:oprietors, unlefs they were laden after the Ex-
ration of the faid Terms refpectively; but fo as
fhall not be lawful for them afterwards to carry
 Enemies Ports any of the faid Merchandizes
hich are called Contraband, and which for the
afon aforefaid fhall not be liable to Confifcation;
ither on the other Side, fhall it be lawful to con-
cate the Goods of the Subjects of the Lords the
:ates, taken or feized in any Ship or Veffel whatever of an Enemy of his Majefty upon that
retence, but the fame fhall be forthwith reftored
ı the Proprietor thereof, unlefs they were laden
ter the Expiration of the faid Terms refpectively;
ıt fo as it fhall not be lawful for them afterwards
ı carry to Enemies Ports any of the faid Merchan-
zes which are called Contraband, and which for
e Reafons aforefaid fhall not be liable to Con-
cation.

ARTICLE IX.

And the more effectually to fecure the Subjects his Majefty and of the faid States, that no In-
ry fhall be offered to them by the Ships of War
 Privateers of either Side, all the Captains of
 Ships

Captains and Commanders on either Side, not to Injure the Subjects of the other.

Ships, as well of his Majesty, as of the said State and of all their Subjects, who shall fit out Privateers, and likewise their privileged Companies, sha strictly be enjoined not to do any Injury or D mage whatsoever to the other; and that if the transgress therein, they shall be punished; ar moreover be liable to satisfy all Costs and Damage by due Restitution and Reparation, upon Pain an Obligation of Person and Goods.

ARTICLE XIV.

<small>All Torture of Persons on board Prizes prohibited.</small> And whereas the Masters of Merchant Ship, and likewise the Mariners and Passengers, do som times suffer many Cruelties and barbarous Trea ment, when they are brought under the Power Ships which take Prizes in Time of War, the Ca tors in an inhuman Manner tormenting them, order to extort from them such Confessions as the would have to be made; it is agreed, that both h Majesty and the Lords the States General, shall t the most strict Proclamations or Placarts, forb all such heinous and inhuman Offences; and as mar as they shall by lawful Proofs find guilty of such Act, they shall take care to punish in a just and prop Manner, so as to be a Terror to others; and the shall command that all Captains and Officers Ships who shall be proved to have been guilty such heinous Practices, either by their own Act, by instigating others to act the same, or by cor niving at such doings, shall (besides other Punish ments to be inflicted proportionably to their O fences) be forthwith deprived of their Posts an Commissions respectively; and every Ship brougl in as a Prize, whose Mariners or Passengers sha have suffered any Torture, shall forthwith be di missed and set free, with all her Lading, withou any further Examination or proceeding against he either judicially or otherwise.

The Form of the Passport (or Sea Brief) to be asked of and given by the Burgo-Master of the Cities and Ports of the United Netherlands, *to the Ships or Vessels sailing from thence, according to the Purport of the Fifth Article of this Treaty.*

TO the Most Serene, Most Illustrious, Most Mighty, Most Noble, Most Honourable, and Most Prudent Emperors, Kings, Governors of Common wealths, Princes, Dukes, Barons, Lords, Burger-Masters, Schepens, Counsellors, Judges, Officers, Justices and Rulers of all Cities and Places as well Ecclesiastical as Secular, to whom these Presents shall be shewn: We the Burger-Masters and Rulers of the City of   do certify, that   Master or Skipper of the Ship   appeared before us, and declared by solemn Oath, that the said Ship called the   containing about   Lasts, of which he is at present Master or Skipper, belongeth to the Inhabitants of the *United Netherlands.* So help him God. And in regard it would be most acceptable to us, that the said Master or Skipper be assisted in his just and lawful Affairs, we do request you, and every of you, wheresoever the said Master or Skipper shall arrive with his Ship, and the Goods laden on board and carried by her, that you will please to receive him courteously, and use him kindly, and admit him, upon paying the lawful and usual Customs and other Duties, to enter into, remain in, and pass from your Ports, Rivers and Dominions, and there to enjoy all kind of Right of Navigation, Traffick, and Commerce, in all Places where he shall think fit; which we shall most willingly and readily acknowledge upon all Occasions: In Testimony and Con-

(94)

Confirmation whereof, we have caused the Sea of our City to be put to these Presents, dated in   the   day of   in the Year of our Lord   .

Treaty of Peace between Great-Britain *and the States General; concluded at* Westminster, February *the* $\frac{9}{19}$, 1673-4.

ARTICLE IV.

1673-4.
All *Dutch* Ships to strike to the King of *Great-Britain*'s Ships in certain Seas.

THE States General of the *United Provinces* duly acknowledging on their Part the Right of his Majesty the King of *Great-Britain*, that Honour be paid to his Flag in the Seas herein after mentioned, shall and do declare and agree, that whatever Ships and Vessels belonging to the said *United Provinces*, whether Ships of War or others, and whether they be single, or joined together in Fleets, shall meet in any Seas from *Cape Finisterre* to the middle Point of the *Land Van Staten* in *Norway*, with any Ships or Vessels whatsoever belonging to his Most Serene Majesty the King of *Great-Britain* whether those Ships be single or in a greater Number, if they carry his *Britannick* Majesty's Flag or Jack, the said Ships or Vessels of the *United Provinces* shall strike their Flag and lower their Topsail, in the same Manner and with like Tokens of Honour, as hath ever been at any Time or in any Place heretofore used towards any Ship of his *Britannick* Majesty, or of his Predecessors, by any Ships of the States General, and of their Predecessors.

Secret Article of the said Treaty.

Neither Party to furnish any Supplies to the Enemy of the other.

. Neither of the said Parties shall give nor consent that any of their Subjects or Inhabitants shall give any Aid, Favour or Counsel, directly or indirectly, by y Land or by Sea, or on the fresh Waters, nor all furnish, nor consent that the Subjects and Inhabitants of their Dominions and Countries shall rnish any Ships, Soldiers, Mariners, Provisions, [M]oney, Instruments of War, Gunpowder, or any [ot]her Things necessary for making War, to the [E]nemies of the other Party, of any Rank or Con[di]tion whatsoever.

Marine Treaty between Great-Britain *and the States General; concluded at the* Hague *the* $\frac{7}{17}$ *of* February, 1667-8.

ARTICLE I.

ALL the Subjects and Inhabitants of *Great-Britain* may with all Safety and Freedom, and traffick in all the Kingdoms, Countries and [St]ates, which are or shall be in Peace, Amity or [Ne]utrality with *Great-Britain*, without any Hin[dra]nce or Molestation from the Ships of War, Gal[leys], Frigates, Barques, or other Vessels belonging to [the] States General, or any of their Subjects, upon [Occ]asion and account of any War which may here[afte]r happen between the said States General and the [afo]resaid Kingdoms, Countries and Estates, or any [of] them which are or shall be in Peace, Amity or [Ne]utrality with *Great-Britain*.

1667-8. Free Trade with neutral Powers at War with the other Party.

ARTICLE II.

This Freedom of Navigation and Commerce [sha]ll extend to all Sorts of Merchandize, excepting C[on]traband Goods.

Free Trade for all Goods, except contraband.

ARTICLE III.

This Term of Contraband Goods is to be under[stoo]d to comprehend only all Sorts of Fire-Arms, an[d] their Appurtenances, as Cannon, Muskets,

Contraband Goods specified.

Mor-

Mortar-Pieces, Petards, Bombs, Granadoes, F
Crancels, pitched Hoops, Carriages, Rests, F
deliers, Powder, Match, Salt-petre, Bullets, Pil
Swords, Morions, Head-Pieces, Coats of M
Halberts, Javelins, Horses, great Saddles, H
ters, Belts, and other Utensils of War; calle(
French, *Assortiments Servans a l'usage de la Guer*1

ARTICLE IV.

What are not to be deemed contraband.
All such may be carried to an Enemy's Country.

Under the Head of Contraband Goods, t]
following shall not be comprehended, Corn, Wh
or other Grain; Pulse, Oils, Wines, Salt, or g(
rally any thing that belongs to the Nourishmen
Sustenance of Life, but they shall remain free:
likewise all other Merchandizes and Commod
not comprehended in the foregoing Article;
the Transportation of them shall be permitted e
unto Places at Enmity with the said States Gene
except such Cities and Places as are besie(
block'd up or invested.

ARTICLE V.

Merchant Ships to shew their Passports in Ports, before their going out.

It is agreed, for the due Execution of wha
abovesaid, that the Ships or Vessels of the *Eng*
laden with Merchandize, being entered into
Port of the said States General, and purposing
pass from thence into Places at Enmity with
said States, shall be only obliged to shew unto
Officers of such Port of the said States, their F
ports, containing a Specification of their Ca
attested and mark'd with the ordinary Seal of
Officers of the Admiralty, of those Places f
whence they first came; together with the P
whither they are bound, all in the usual and
customed Form: And after having exhibited t
Passports, as aforesaid, they shall not be moleste
search'd, detained or retarded in their Voyage, u
any Pretence whatsoever.

ARTIC:

ARTICLE VI.

In like manner, *English* Ships and Vessels which shall come into any Roads upon the Coasts under the Obedience of the said States, not intending to enter into Port, or being entered into Port, and not intending to unlade or break Bulk, shall not be obliged to give account of their Lading, except in Case of Suspicion that they carry unto the Enemies of the said States any contraband Goods, such as are above specified. *[margin: Ships in any Port or Road not obliged to unliver or give account of their Lading, unless suspected.]*

ARTICLE VII.

And in case of such apparent Suspicion, the said Subjects of his Majesty shall be obliged to exhibit in Port their Passports according to the Form above specified. *[margin: In case of Suspicion, to shew their Passports.]*

ARTICLE VIII.

But if they shall come near any of the Coasts of the States, and meet in the open Sea with any of the States Ships, or any Privateers fitted out by their Subjects under public Commissions; for the avoiding all Inconveniences, such Ships of the said States, or of their Subjects, shall not come within Cannon-Shot of the *English*, but may send out their Boat and board such *English* Ships or Vessels with two or three Men only, in order that the Master or Captain of the *English* Ship may exhibit to them his Passports as above mentioned, and likewise his Sea Letters or Certificates concerning the Property of the Ship, according to the Form subjoined to this Treaty; whereby it may appear not only what the Lading consists of, but likewise the Place of the Master or Captain's Abode and Residence, together with the Ship's Name, may be known; to the End, that by those Means it be discovered, whether they carry any contraband Goods for the Enemy; *[margin: Ships of War to keep at Distance from Merchant Ships at Sea, and only to send their Boats to examine their Passports and Cockets.]*

Enemy; and the Quality of the Ship, and of the Captain or Master thereof, may sufficiently appear; unto which Passports and Sea Letters entire Faith and Credit shall be given: and for the better Assurance of their being authentick, and that they may not be falsified or counterfeit, some certain Marks and Countersigns of his said Majesty and of the said States shall therein be made use of.

ARTICLE IX.

Contraband Goods only to be confiscated.
 And in case any of those Goods and Commodities, which are before declared to be contraband and prohibited, shall by the means aforesaid be discovered in the said *English* Ships and Vessels, bound for any Port of the said States Enemies, they shall be unladen and then judicially proceeded against, and declared confiscated before and by the Judges of the Admiralty, or other competent Officers; but so as the Ship or Vessel itself, or other free and allowed Goods, Merchandize and Commodities found in the same Ship, may not for that Cause be in any manner seized or confiscated.

ARTICLE X.

All Goods found in Enemies Ships to be confiscated.
Whatsoever shall be found laden by his Majesty's Subjects upon a Ship of the Enemies of the said States, although the same were not contraband, shall yet be confiscated, with all that shall be found in such Ship, without Exception or Reservation; but on the other Side, all that shall be found in any Ships belonging to any Subjects of the King of *Great-Britain*, shall be free and discharged, although the

Free Ships make free Goods.
Lading or any Part thereof belong to the Enemies of the said States, except contraband Goods, in regard whereof such Rule shall be observed, as hath been laid down in the foregoing Articles.

ARTICLE

ARTICLE XI.

The Subjects and Inhabitants of the *United Pro-* The above Rules to be equal to both Parties. *vinces* shall reciprocally enjoy the same Rights, Liberties and Exemptions, with regard to Navigation and Commerce, in the Coasts, Ports, Roads, Seas and Dominions of the King of *Great-Britain*, in the same manner as it is above agreed, that the Subjects of the said King are to enjoy the same in those Places, which are under the Obedience of the States, as likewise in the open Sea, it being intended and to be understood, that they shall be on an equal foot on both Sides, in all and singular Matters, in case the said States shall hereafter be in Peace and Friendship or Neutrality with any Kings, Princes or States, who shall be at War with the King of *Great-Britain*; so that both Parties are directly to use and observe the same Conditions and Restrictions, which are contained in the Articles herein agreed upon and which regard Commerce.

ARTICLE XII.

And the more effectually to secure the Subjects No Injury to be done to the States Subjects. of the said States, that no Violence shall be offered them by the Ships of War belonging to his Majesty of *Great-Britain*, or his Subjects, all the Captains of the King's Ships, and all his Majesty's Subjects, that fit out Privateers, shall be strictly charged and enjoined not to molest or injure them Transgressors to be punished, and to make Reparation. in any Respect whatsoever, upon pain of being punished and made answerable in their Persons and Goods for all Costs and Damages, and for making full Restitution and Reparation.

ARTICLE XIV.

If any Commander of an *English* Ship shall meet Contraband Goods not to be meddled with at Sea by the Captors, but brought into Port and landed. with and take a Ship laden with any of the said contraband Goods, he may not open or break up any of her Chests, Packs, Bags or Casks, nor sell, bar-

barter, or any ways difpofe of the fame, before they are firſt landed in the Prefence of the Judge or Officers of the Admiralty; and that an Inventory be firſt made by them of the Goods found in the faid Ship; unlefs where the contraband Goods make but a Part of the Cargo, and the Maſter of the Ship is willing to deliver up fuch Goods im-

On delivery of contraband Goods at Sea to the Captor, the Ship to be difmiſſed. mediately, fo as they may be taken from on board and carried away, that he may not be retarded in his intended Voyage; in which cafe he fhall not be further molefted or hindered from purfuing his Courfe and Voyage.

N.B. The Form of the Paffport inferted at the Foot of this Treaty, is the fame verbatim with that annexed to the Marine Treaty of 1674.

A Provifional Marine Treaty between Great Britain *and the States General; concluded a* Bredah, *on the fame Day with the General Treaty of Peace and Alliance,* viz, $\frac{21}{31}$ *o* July, 1667.

ARTICLE III.

1667.
Marine Treaty of 1662, between *France* and the States, confirmed between *England* and the States.

IT is covenanted and agreed, that the Treaty of Navigation and Commerce made between th' Moſt Chriſtian King and the faid States General (beginning from the 26th, unto the 42d Article inclufively) in manner as here inferted in the *French* Language, may provifionally ferve for a Rule and Law, and fo make way for concluding a more perfect and compleat Treaty concerning Maritime Commerce between the above mentioned Parties.

[Then the faid Treaty proceeds to recite the faid Seventeen Articles of the Marine Treaty of 1662 between *France* and the States General, from the 26th to the 42d Article inclufively, with an additiona tional Article, whereby the present contracting Powers accept and confirm the same between themselves respectively: But all the said Articles are transferred to and made Part of the Marine Treaty of *February* $\frac{7}{17}$ 1667-8, and are recited therein Article by Article, and almost Word for Word the same with the said Seventeen Articles which compose the whole of this Marine Treaty of *July*, 1667.

Treaty of Peace and Alliance between Great-Britain *and the States General; concluded at* Bredah, $\frac{21}{31}$ *of* July, 1667.

ARTICLE XIII.

THAT the said King of *Great-Britain* and his Subjects, and all the Inhabitants of his Majesty's Dominions; and also the said *United Provinces*, and their Subjects and Inhabitants, of what rank or Condition soever they be, shall be bound to treat each other in a kind and friendly manner in all Things; so that they may freely and safely pass by Land or by Water into each others Countries, Cities, Towns, walled or unwalled, fortified or unfortified, and likewise their Ports, and all other their Dominions situate in *Europe*; and continue and abide therein as long as they please, and there buy such Provisions as shall be necessary for their Use, without any Hindrance; and likewise trade and traffick in Goods and Commodities of all Sorts, as to them shall seem fit, and export and import them at their pleasure; provided they pay the usual Duties, and saving all the Laws and Ordinances of both Nations; so as the Subjects and Inhabitants of either Party carrying on their Trade in each other's Countries and Dominions, shall not be obliged hereafter to pay any more or other Customs, Imposts, or other Duties, than according

Peace and Amity, free Passage and Commerce in Europe.

To pay the same Duties with other Nations.

to that Proportion which other Foreigners trading in the fame Places do ufually pay.

ARTICLE XIX.

Dutch Ships to ftrike to the King of Great-Britain's Ships in the Britifh Seas.

That the Ships and Veffels of the faid *United Provinces*, as well Ships of War as others, meeting any Ships of War belonging to the faid King of *Great-Britain* in the *Britifh* Seas, fhall ftrike the Flag and lower the Topfail, in fuch manner as the fame hath been formerly obferved in any Time whatfoever.

ARTICLE XX.

Pirates not to be harboured or affifted.

And for the greater Freedom of Commerce and Navigation, it is agreed and concluded, that the faid King of *Great-Britain* and the faid States General fhall not receive into their Ports, Cities and Towns, nor fuffer that any of the Subjects of either Party do receive any Pirates or Sea Rovers or afford them any Entertainment, Affiftance or Provifions, but fhall endeavour that all fuch Pirates and Sea Rovers, and their Partners, Sharers and Abettors, be found out and apprehended, and that they fuffer condign Punifhment for a Terror to others: And all the Ships, Goods and Commodities, piratically taken by them, and brought into the Ports of either Party, which can be found even although they be fold, fhall be reftored to the right Owners, or Satisfaction fhall be given either to their Owners, or to thofe who by Virtue of Letters of Attorney fhall demand the fame; provided their Right and Property therein be made to appear in the Court of Admiralty by due Proofs according to Law.

Goods piratically taken to be reftored.

ARTICLE XXI.

Subjects of either Party not to accept or act under any Commiffion againft the other.

The Subjects of the faid King of *Great-Britain* and the Inhabitants of the Kingdoms and Countries under his Obedience; as likewife the Inhabitants and Subjects of the said *United Provinces*, shall not be permitted to do or offer any Hostility or Violence to each other, either by Land or by Sea, upon any Pretence or Colour whatsoever: And consequently it shall not be lawful for the said Subjects or Inhabitants to procure Commissions or Letters of Reprizals from any Prince or State, with whom either of the Confederates are at Variance or in open War; and much less by Virtue of such Letters to molest or do any Damage to the Subjects of either Party; neither shall it be lawful for any foreign Privateers, who are not Subjects to either Confederate, having Commissions from any other Prince or State, to fit out their Ships in the Ports of either of the aforesaid Parties, or to sell their Prizes, or put the same to Ransom, or any other way to truck either the Ships and Goods, or any other Lading whatsoever; and they shall not even be be allowed to buy any Provisions but what shall be necessary to bring them to the next Port of that Prince from whom they obtained their said Commissions; and if perchance any one of the Subjects of the said King of *Great-Britain*, or of the said States General shall buy or get to himself by Truck, or any other way, any Ship or Goods which have been taken from the Subjects of the one or the other Party, in such case the said Subject shall be bound to restore the said Ship or Goods to the Proprietors without any Delay, and without any Compensation or Reimbursement of any Money which may have been paid or promised for the same; provided that they make it appear before the Council of the said King of *Great-Britain*, or before the said States General, that they are the right Owners or Proprietors of the same. *Persons acting under other Commissions against either Party not to be assisted or suffered to sell their Prizes.*

Goods taken from either Party to be restored.

ARTICLE XXIV.

The Subjects of the said King of *Great-Britain*, and those which are under his Dominions, may freely and securely travel in and through all the *Free Passage and Intercourse on both Sides in all their European Dominions.*

Pro-

Provinces of the *United Netherlands*, and all their Dominions in *Europe*, by Sea or Land, and pafs to any other Places therein or beyond them, and thro' all Quarters of the *United Provinces*, and all Cities, Forts or Garrifons whatfoever, which are in any Places of the *United Provinces*, or which are or fhall be in any other their Dominions in *Europe*, and may trade in all thofe Places, as likewife their Agents, Factors and Servants; and may go armed or unarmed (but if armed not above forty in a Company) as well without their Goods and Merchandizes as with them, wherefoever they pleafe. The People alfo and Inhabitants of the *United Provinces* fhall enjoy the fame Liberty and Freedom in all the Dominions of the faid King in *Europe:* Provided that they and every of them do in their Trade and Merchandizing yield due Obedience to the Laws and Ordinances of either Nation refpectively.

ARTICLE XXV.

Merchant Ships forced in, to depart without Search or Moleftation.

In cafe any Merchant Ships belonging to the Subjects of either Nation fhall by Storm, Pirates, or any other Neceffity whatfoever, be driven into any Port of either Dominion, they may depart fecurely and at their Pleafure with their Ships and Goods, without paying any Cuftoms or other Duties; (provided they do not break Bulk nor fell any thing:) nor fhall they be fubject to any Moleftation or Search, provided they do not take on board any Perfons or Goods, nor do any thing elfe contrary to the Laws, Ordinances or Cuftoms of the Places where they fhall happen to arrive as aforefaid.

ARTICLE XXVI.

Ships of the other Party not to be forced into Service.

Merchants, Mafters and Mariners of either Party, or their Ships, Goods, Wares or Merchandizes, fhall not be arrefted or detained in the Lands, Ports, Roads or Rivers of the other to ferve in

War, or for any other Service, by Virtue of any
general or special Order, unless upon an extraordinary Necessity; and then just Satisfaction shall
be made for the same; but so as this shall be no
Prohibition or Hindrance of any Embargoes or
Arrests duly made, and in the ordinary Course according to the Laws of either Country.

ARTICLE XXVII.

Merchants on both Sides, their Factors and Ser- *Use of Arms al-*
vants, and also the Masters and other Mariners, as *lowed on both*
well going as returning in their Ships by Sea and *Sides.*
other Waters, as also in the Ports of either Party,
or going on Shore, may carry and use for the
Defence of themselves and Goods, all Sorts of
Weapons as well offensive as defensive; but coming
to any Lodgings or Inns, they shall there lay by
and leave their Arms, until they go on board
again.

ARTICLE XXVIII.

Ships of War, or Convoys of either Nation *Ships of War to*
meeting or overtaking at Sea any Merchant Ships, *protect the Mer-*
or Vessels belonging to the Subjects or Inhabitants *chant Ships of*
of the other, holding the same Course, or going *the other Party.*
the same Way, shall be bound, as long they keep
the Course together, to protect and defend them
against all Attacks whatsoever.

ARTICLE XXIX.

If any Ship or Ships belonging to the Subjects *Ships of one Par-*
or Inhabitants of either Party, or of any other Na- *ty taken out of a*
tion in Neutrality with them, shall be taken in the *Port of the other,*
Ports of either Nation by any third Party, not *to be pursued and*
being Subjects or Inhabitants of either Nation; *restored.*
they, in whose Port, or out of whose Port or Dominion whatsoever such Ships shall be taken, shall
be obliged to endeavour jointly with the other Party, that the said Ship or Ships be pursued, brought
back

back and reſtored to the Owners; but this ſhall
done at the Charges of the Owners or Perſo
having an Intereſt therein.

ARTICLE XXXIV.

Free Ingreſs and Egreſs for all Ships into and out of all Ports. The Subjects and Inhabitants of either Par
ſhall always have free Acceſs to each other's
Ports, there to remain, and from thence to dep
with equal Liberty; and not only with their M
chant Ships and Cargo, but alſo with their Ships
War, whether they belong to the ſaid King, or
the ſaid States General, or unto ſuch as have obtain
ſpecial Commiſſions from either; and whether th
put in through Streſs of Weather, or other Ca
alty of the Seas, or in order to repair their Shi
or buy Proviſions; ſo as they exceed not
Number of Ships of War limited. Number of Eight Ships of War, when they co
in voluntarily; but they ſhall not remain or ab
longer in ſuch Ports or Places adjacent, than ſh
be requiſite to repair their ſaid Ships, or to b
Proviſions or other Neceſſaries: And in caſe
greater Number of Ships of War ſhould be willi
upon occaſion to come into ſuch Ports, they ſh
in no caſe enter therein, until they have firſt
tained Leave from thoſe to whom ſuch Ports ſh
Ships of War not to come in without Leave, unleſs forced in. appertain; unleſs they be forced by Storm,
ſome Force or Neceſſity, to avoid the Danger
the Sea; in which caſe alſo they ſhall preſently ma
known the Cauſe of their coming unto the Gov
nor or chief Magiſtrate of the Place, and ſhall ſt
no longer than the ſaid Governor or chief Mag
trate ſhall permit them; and ſhall not attempt a
Acts of Hoſtility, or other prejudicial Act of
aforeſaid Ports, during their Abode there.

Treaty of Peace and Alliance between Great-Britain *and the States General; concluded at* Whitehall, $\frac{4}{14}$ *of* September, 1662.

ARticles the 9th, 10th, 11th, 12th, 16th, 17th, 18th, 19th, 20th, 21st, and 25th of this Treaty, are the same verbatim with the above recited Articles of the Treaty of 1667.

Treaty of Peace and Alliance between Great-Britain *and the States General; concluded at* Westminster, April 5, 1654.

ARticles the 12th, 13th, 14th, 17th, 18th, 19th, 20th, 21st, 22d, and 26th of this Treaty, are the same with the several above recited Articles of the two last mentioned Treaties, excepting the 21st Article of the Treaty of 1667, which answers to the 12th Article of the Treaty of 1662, and is not contained in this Treaty.

Articles

Articles and Clauses of several Treaties between Great-Britain *and the* States General; *containing a Renewal or Confirmation of former Treaties, ancient Usages, and amicable Intercourse between the said two Nations.*

Treaty of Vienna.

ARTICLE I.

1731.
All former Treaties confirmed.

ALL former Treaties or Conventions of Peace Friendship and Alliance shall have their full Effect, and shall preserve in all and every Part their full Force and Virtue, and shall even be looked upon as renewed and confirmed by Virtue of the present Treaty; except only such Articles, Clauses and Conditions from which it has been thought fit to derogate by this present Treaty.

Treaty of Seville.

ARTICLE I.

1729.
All former Treaties confirmed.

ALL former Treaties and Conventions of Peace and Friendship, and of Commerce concluded between the contracting Parties respectively, shall be, as they hereby are, effectually renewed and confirmed in all those Points which are not derogated from by this present Treaty, in a full and ample Manner as if the said Treaties were here inserted; the said Parties promising not to do r suffer any thing to be done, that may be contrary thereto, directly or indirectly.

Treaty of Alliance, concluded at Westminster, *between* Great-Britain *and the States General,* February 6, 1715-6.

ARTICLE II.

'T is agreed, that all and every the Treaties of Peace, Friendship, Alliance, Navigation and Commerce hereunder specified, be approved and confirmed, *viz.* The Treaty of Peace, Friendship and Alliance, concluded at *Bredah*, on the $\frac{21}{31}$ Day of July 1667; the Treaty of Navigation and Commerce made at the same Time and Place; the Treaty of Navigation and Commerce settled at the *Hague*, on the $\frac{7}{17}$ Day of *February*, 1667-8; the Treaty of Peace and Friendship, concluded at *Westminster*, on the $\frac{9}{19}$ Day of *February*, 1673-4; the Treaty of Marine, concluded at *London*, on the $\frac{1}{11}$ Day of *December*, 1674; together with the Declaration, signed at the *Hague* on the $\frac{20}{30}$ Day of *December*, 1675; whereby the Sense of certain Articles, as well in the said Treaty of 1674, as in the other Marine Treaty of 1667-8, is explained; the Article for preventing and accommodating Disputes which may arise between the *English* and the *Dutch East-India* Companies, settled at *London* on the $\frac{8}{18}$ Day of *March*, 1674-5; the defensive Alliance concluded at *Westminster*, on the 3d Day of *March*, 1677-8; the Treaty settling the Proportions between the Fleets of both Nations, concluded at *Whitehall*, on the 29th of *April*, 1689; the Treaty concerning the Ships and Goods which might be recovered from the Enemy during the War, concluded at *Whitehall*, on the 22d of *October*, 1689; the Treaty concerning the Succession to the Crown of

1715-6. Confirmation of the two Treaties of Bredah, 1667. Marine Treaty 1667-8. Treaty of Peace 1673-4. Marine Treaty 1674. Declaration 1675. Article settled 1674-5. Treaty of Alliance 1677-8. Two Treaties 1689. Barrier Treaty 1712-13, altered by the Treaty of 1715.

of *Great-Britain*, and the Barrier of the *Unite* *Provinces*, made at *Utrecht*, on the 1/30 of *Januar* 1712-13; excepting wherein it is altered by th Barrier Treaty of *Antwerp*, made on the 15th o *November* 1715; and the abovementioned Treatie and all and singular the Articles thereof, are b this present Treaty actually approved, and cor firmed, and shall have the same Force and Effect; if they had been inserted here verbatim; that to say, so far as they do not differ or are contrar to one another, or are not contrary to this prese Treaty: Yet so as whatever hath been establishe by any later Treaty, shall be understood and pe formed in the Sense therein expressed, without ar regard had to any former Treaty.

Treaty of Succession and Barrier; concluded Utrecht, *on the* 19/30 *of* January, 1712-13.

ARTICLE I.

1712-3.
All former Treaties confirmed, except that of 1709.

ALL Treaties of Peace, Friendship, Unic and Confederacy (except the Treaty of t 29th of *October*, 1709, which is hereby abrogate concluded between her said Royal Majesty and t Lords the States General, are hereby approved ar confirmed; and shall be of the same Virtue ar Force, as if they had been inserted in this prese Treaty.

ARTICLE XIII.

All ancient Privileges confirmed to the *English* in the *Netherlands* and *Barrier*.

The Subjects of the Queen of *Great-Brita* shall for the future, both in Time of War and Time of Peace, enjoy the same Privileges, I munities, Franchises, and all Manner of Adva tages in relation to Trade, as well for Importati as Exportation, which they ever have or ought have enjoyed heretofore, in all Places of the Pr vinc

...ces of the *Spanish Netherlands*, and of the Barr..r, which is to be yielded to the States General; ..d moreover, they shall enjoy all Privileges, Immunities and Advantages which have already been ..nted, or shall at any time hereafter be granted, .. the Subjects of the States General in the Pro-..ces of the *Spanish Netherlands*, and Places be-..ging to the said Barrier.

Treaty of Alliance.

ARTICLE III.

ALL the Alliances concluded between the said King and the said Lords the States General of *United Netherlands*, shall remain entire and in ..rce, every one according to the Term fixed for .. Duration.

1700.
Former Alliances confirmed.

Treaty of Amity and Alliance.

THERE shall be for the future, a sincere, firm and perpetual Friendship and Correspondence, as well by Sea as by Land, in and ..oughout all Places, as well out of as within ..rope, between the King of *Great-Britain*, and .. Successors Kings of *Great-Britain*, and their ..ngdoms on the one Part, and the States General ..f the *United Provinces* of the *Netherlands* on the ..her Part, and their Dominions, Countries and ..bjects reciprocally.

All Treaties of Peace, Friendship, Alliance, Commerce and Marine hereafter specified, shall be approved and confirmed on both Sides, *viz.*

The Treaty of Peace concluded at *Bredah*, in 167.

1689.
Universal Peace and Amity.

Treaties of 1667, 1673-4, 1679, 1674-5, 1677-8, 1689, confirmed.

The

The Treaty of Navigation and Commerce [at] the same Time and Place.

The Treaty of Peace concluded at *Westmins[ter]* in 1673-4.

The Marine Treaty concluded at *London*, [the] 10th of *October*, 1679, with a Declaration [ex]plaining several Articles of the said Marine Trea[ty] of the 17th of *February*, 1667-8, concluded at [the] *Hague* the $\frac{20}{30}$th of *December*, 1675.

[*N.B.* There seems to be an Error in this [last] Article, which probably proceeds from an [er]roneus Copy inserted in the *Traitez de P[aix]* and *Corps Diplomatique*, there being no su[ch] Marine Treaty made between the *English* a[nd] *Dutch* in 1679, but probably that of 16[74] was intended, and originally inserted.]

An Article for preventing and composing D[is]putes between the *English* and *Dutch East-In[dia]* Companies, settled at *London*, in 1674-5.

The defensive League, concluded at *London*, 1677-8.

The Treaty for prohibiting Commerce wi[th] *France*, concluded *August* 22, 1689.

All the said Treaties, and all and every Artic[le] contained in them, are effectually approved a[nd] confirmed by this present Treaty, and shall rema[in] in their original Force and Vigour, as if they we[re] here inserted Word for Word, so far as they [do] not contradict or derogate from one another, [or] from this present Treaty; so as the Points a[nd] Matters stipulated by a later Treaty, shall be fu[l]filled in the Time agreed on, without any regard [to] any Treaty of more ancient Date.

Treaty for renewing the Alliance between Great-Britain *and the States General;* concluded at Windsor, August *the* 17th, 1685.

IT is agreed and concluded, that all and singular the Treaties hereafter mentioned, *viz.*

The Treaty of Peace concluded at *Bredah*, in *July* 1667.

The Treaty of Navigation and Commerce, of the same Date and Place.

The Treaty of Peace concluded at *Westminster*, in *February* 1673-4.

The Marine Treaty concluded at *London*, in *December* 1674, together with the Declaration concluded at the *Hague*, in *December* 1675, more fully explaining certain Articles of the said Treaty of 1674; as likewise of the Marine Treaty of *February*, 1667-8.

The Article concluded at *London*, in *March* 1674-5, for preventing or accommodating Disputes between the two *East-India* Companies.

The Defensive League concluded at *London*, in *March* 1677-8, and all and singular the Articles contained in the said Treaties, and every one of them shall be for ever hereafter continued, confirmed and established, in the same Sense, and to the same Effect, as they were originally formed and concluded; and shall have and obtain the same Force and Vigour hereafter, as they ought or were esteemed to have heretofore; and that in as ample Manner and Form as they were at first drawn up and concluded, and as if the said Treaties and the several Articles of the same were recited and inserted verbatim in these Presents.

<small>Treaties of 1667, 1673-4, 1674, 1675, 1674-5, 1677-8, confirmed.</small>

I   *Treaty*

Treaty of Alliance concluded at Westminster in 1677-8.

ARTICLE I.

1677-8.
Universal Peace and Amity.

THERE shall be for the future a sincere firm and perpetual Friendship, and good Correspondence between the King of *Great-Britain* and his Successors and Kingdoms, on the one Part, and the States General of the *United Provinces* of the *Netherlands*, on the other Part; and their States, Dominions and Subjects reciprocally, as well by Sea as by Land, in and throughout all Places as well within as out of *Europe*.

Treaty of Peace.

1673-4.
Treaty of 1667, confirmed.

THE Treaty of *Bredah*, concluded in 1667, as likewise all other preceding Treaties confirmed by that Treaty, shall be renewed and remain in full force, in so far as they no ways contradict this present Treaty.

Treaty of Alliance concluded at the Hague January $\frac{13}{23}$, 1667-8.

1667-8.
Treaty of 1667, confirmed.

THE said King and the said States General have agreed to confirm the Treaty concluded at *Bredah*, and the Rules and Articles of Commerce thereto belonging; mutually obliging themselves to a sincere and perpetual Observance of them, and to cause them to be strictly observed by their Subjects on both Sides, according to the genuine Sense and Meaning of the said Treaty and Articles.

Treaty of Peace concluded at Bredah.

ARTICLE IX.

BOTH the said Parties, and their Subjects and Inhabitants, shall have and enjoy the same Liberty of Trade and Navigation, as well in *Africa* as in *America*, as they had and enjoyed, or of Right might have and enjoy at the same time of the Conclusion of the Treaty of 1662.

<small>1667.
Liberty of Trade the same as in 1662.</small>

Treaty of Peace and Alliance between Great-Britain *and* Portugal, *made at* Westminster, July 10, 1654.

ARTICLE II.

THAT there shall be a free Commerce between both Nations and their People, Subjects and Inhabitants, as well by Land as on the Sea, and in Rivers and fresh Waters, in all and singular the Countries, Lands, Dominions, Territories, Provinces, Islands, Colonies, Cities, Towns, Villages, Ports and Borders, where Commerce was heretofore, or is at this time carried on, in such manner, that the People, Subjects and Inhabitants of either, may without any safe Conduct, or other general or special Licence, pass by Land and Sea, by Rivers and fresh Waters, to the aforesaid Dominions and Kingdoms, and all their Cities, Towns, Harbours, Shores, Bays and Places; and sail and enter into the same, and import their Merchandizes, with Carriages, Horses, Packs and Ships, laden or to be laden; and buy and sell Goods there, and supply themselves at a reasonable Price with what Provisions they shall think fit, and with all Things necessary

<small>Free Passage and Commerce.</small>

necessary for their Sustenance and Voyage; and refit their Ships and Carriages, whether their own or such as are hired or lent; and with the sam Liberty depart from thence with their Goods, Merchandize, and all other Things whatsoever, eithe to their own or foreign Countries, as they sha think fit, and without any Hindrance; savin; nevertheless all the Laws and Ordinances of eac Place.

ARTICLE VI.

Masters and Mariners of British Ships not to bring Suits or desert their Service in Portugal, upon any Pretext whatsoever.

That the Captains, Masters, Officers and M: riners of any Ships belonging to the King of Great Britain, or to any of his People or Subjects, sha not bring any Suits against, or in any wise mole the said Ships or People of Great-Britain, withi the Kingdoms or Government of the King of Por tugal, on account of their Stipend or Wages, o Pretence that they profess the Romish Religion nor shall they under this or any other Pretext, er gage in the Service of the King of Portugal, or i any other manner quit the Ships to whose Cre they belong: And if any shall offend in this Poin an Account shall be taken of their Names, an they shall be compelled by the Magistrates an Officers of the Place to return to their Ships; an if they cannot be found, it shall be lawful for t Master of such Ship or Vessel to detain the Cloaths, Goods or Wages, to make Good t Damage sustained thereby.

ARTICLE IX.

British Ships and Goods not to be meddled with in Portugal without his Majesty's Ship. Great. the Se. soever,

That neither the King of Portugal, nor any Ministers, shall detain or arrest any Merchant ters of Ships, Captains or Mariners, or the s, Merchandize, or other Goods belonging Britain, or any Subjects thereof, either f rvice of War, or any other Purpose wha unless the British Government, or those who

(117)

iips and Goods appertain are firſt ap-
, and give their Conſent ; but all ſuch
id Goods, ſhall at their own Pleaſure
erty to depart from the Ports and
˜ the ſaid King, without any Hin-
his ſaid Majeſty, or any of his Mi-
the Sale of the Merchandize and
People of *Great-Britain*, ſhall not be
:lay'd, under Pretence that the King
for them, or for any other Reaſon
or ſhall they be applied to the King's
y other Uſes whatever, without the
Perſons intereſted.

ARTICLE XI.

e and Inhabitants of *Great-Britain* *Free Navigation and Trade in all Dominions of Portugal.*
l traffick freely and ſafely from *Por-*
:il, and the other Conqueſts of the
he *Weſt-Indies*; and from *Brazil* and
Conqueſts to *Portugal*, in all Sorts of
erchandize whatſoever (except Meal,
Oil, and *Brazil* Wood, which are
:he King, in Purſuance of a Contract
il Company) paying the Dues and
h others pay, who trade into thoſe
nd the People and Inhatitants of
ſhall likewiſe have the Liberty of
the Colonies, Iſlands, Countries,
tricts, Towns, Villages and Staples
ie King of *Portugal* in the *Eaſt-Indies*,
and of *St. Thomas*, and elſewhere on
Shores; and may reſide, trade and
by Land or Sea, on the Rivers or
n any Goods or Merchandize what-
nſport all Kind of Merchandize to
'ountry, with the ſame Freedom as
by them, and that was ever granted
Treaty, or ſhall hereafter be granted

I 3   to

to the Inhabitants of any other Nation, in Alliance and Friendship with that Crown.

ARTICLE XVIII.

Mutual Access, Shelter, and Assistance for all Ships of both Parties in all Ports.

It shall be lawful for the People or Subjects of either Party to enter the Ports of the other, there to reside, and thence to depart, with equal Liberty, not only with Merchant Ships and Trading Vessels, but also with Ships of War, Guard Ships, and Convoys, whether drove in by Storm, or come in for refitting or victualling their Ships; provided they do not exceed the number of six Ships of War, in case they come in of their own accord: nor shall they stay or continue longer in the Ports or upon the coasts, than shall be necessary, lest they should give occasion for interrupting the Commerce of other Nations in Friendship and Alliance with the other: And if at any time any unusual number of Ships should come to such Ports by any Chance, it shall not be lawful for them to enter into such Ports without a Power first granted by those to whom such Ports belong, unless they are forcibly drove in by Stress of Weather, or other urgent Necessity, for avoiding the Danger of the Sea and Shipwreck; in which case they shall immediately make known the Cause of their coming thither to the Governor, or chief Magistrate of the Place; nor shall they continue there longer than they shall be allowed by such Governor or chief Magistrate, nor commit any Hostility in those Ports, which may be detrimental to the other Party.

ARTICLE XIX.

Ships and Goods of one Party carried into the Dominions of the other, to be restored.

Neither of the Confederates shall suffer the Ships or Goods of the other, or of the People of either, which shall at any time be taken by the Enemies or Rebels of the one, and carried into any Ports or Places belonging to the Dominion of the other, to be conveyed away from the Owners or Proprietors; but

but the same shall be restored to them, or their Attorneys, provided they lay Claim to such Ships and Goods before they are sold or clear'd, and either prove their Right, or exhibit Testimonies of their Property in them, within three Months after the said Ships and Goods shall have been so carried in; and in the mean time the Proprietors shall pay and discharge the necessary Expences for the Preservation and Custody of the said Ships and Goods.

ARTICLE XXIII.

That all Goods and Merchandize of the said Confederates, or of their People or Subjects, found on board the Ships of the Enemies of either, shall be made Prize, together with the Ships, and confiscated; but all the Goods and Merchandize of the Enemies of either, put on board the Ships of either of them, or of their People or Subjects, shall remain untouched.

<small>Goods of either Party found in Enemies Ships to be confiscated.</small>

<small>Free Ships make free Goods.</small>

ARTICLE XXVI.

It is also agreed and concluded, that no other League or Confederacy whatsoever made, or to be made by either of the Confederates, with any other Princes or Republicks whatsoever, shall derogate from the present Treaty of Peace and Alliance; but that this Peace and Confederacy shall be kept entire and always in full Force.

<small>No Treaty with any other Prince to derogate from this Treaty.</small>

Articles of Peace and Commerce between Great-Britain and Portugal; concluded at London, the 29th of January, 1641-2.

ARTICLE I.

Perpetual Peace and Amity.

THERE shall be for ever a good, true and firm Peace, and Amity between the Kings of *Great-Britain* and *Portugal*, their Heirs and Successors, and their Kingdoms, Countries, States, Lands, People, Vassals and Subjects whatsoever, present and to come, of what Quality and Condition soever they be, as well by Sea as by Land, and fresh Waters; so that the said Vassals and Subjects shall treat one another favourably, and render to each other all manner of good Offices of true Amity and Affection; and that the said Most Renown'd Kings, their Heirs and Successors, shall not do or undertake any thing, either by themselves or by other Persons, against one another; nor against their Kingdoms, by Sea or Land; nor consent or adhere to any War, Counsel or Treaty, that may be to the prejudice of the one or the other.

ARTICLE II.

Free Passage and Commerce.

That there be and shall be between the said Most Renown'd Kings and their Vassals, Inhabitants and Subjects on both Sides, a free Commerce, as well by Sea as by Land, and fresh Waters, in all and every of their Kingdoms, Dominions, Islands, and other Lands, Cities, Towns, Villages, Harbours and Territories of the said Kingdoms and States, wherein Trade has been carried on from the time of the Kings of *Castile*, or has been continued to to this present; so that the Subjects and Vassals of both Kings may go, enter and sail, without any Pass

'assport or other general or special Licence, as well
y Sea as by Land, and in fresh Waters, in the
Kingdoms and Dominions aforesaid, and in the
Cities, Towns, Harbours, Rivers, Roads and Territories thereof; and there carry Merchandizes, and
Loads or Ladings upon Carriages and Horses, or
in Ships, and sell and buy all Kind of Provisions,
and furnish themselves with every thing necessary
for their Subsistance or Voyages; and there repair
their Ships or Carriages, whether they be their own
Property, or hired or borrowed; and they may depart with the same Freedom from thence with their
Goods, Merchandizes and other Effects whatsoever, upon paying only the usual Duties and
Customs, on the Foot that they are established by
the Ordinance of each Place; and go to their own
Countries, or to any other Places whatsoever as
they please, and when they think fit, without any
Molestation or Impediment whatsoever.

ARTICLE VII.

That the Captains, Masters, Officers and Ma- *British* Mariners
ners of the Ships of the King of *Great-Britain* their Wages in
shall not commence or prosecute any Suits or Ac- *Portugal* on Pre-
tions against the said Ships, nor against any of the
Subjects of the said King, within the Extent of the
Kingdoms and Dominions of the King of *Por-*
tugal, for their Wages or Salaries, on Pretence that
they will make Profession of the *Romish* Religion,
or that they will list themselves in the Service of the
King of *Portugal*.

ARTICLE X.

That the King of *Portugal*, or his Ministers, *British* Ships or
within the Extent of his Kingdoms and States, may forced into *Por-*
neither detain the Ships of the Subjects of the King *tugueze* Service.
of *Great-Britain*, nor his Subjects themselves, with-
out his Knowledge or Consent, for warlike Services
or any other Service whatsoever; but the said Ships
and

and Subjects may freely depart when they pleas[e] from the Ports and Dominions of the said King without any Hindrance on the Part of the said King of *Portugal* or his Ministers: And the Goods and Merchandizes of the Subjects of the King of *Great Britain* may not be taken for the Service of th[e] King of *Portugal*, but only at the current and usua[l] Price, to be paid within two Months, unless both Parties agree upon some other Time of Payment.

ARTICLE XI.

That the Subjects of the King of *Great-Britai[n]* may carry in their Ships, all Sorts of Goods, Commodities and Merchandizes whatsoever, Arms Victuals, or any other Provisions, out of the Port and Dominions of the said King, or out of any other Ports or Dominions whatsoever; provided they be not carried directly out of the Ports of *Portugal*, or the Dominions thereupon depending, to be transported into the Ports and Territories of th[e] King of *Castile*; and that neither the King of *Portugal*, nor his Subjects, may by way of Seizure Reprisal, or any other Method whatsoever, hinde[r] any Ships, Goods or Persons of the Subjects o[f] the King of *Great-Britain* from sailing safely into th[e] Ports and Territories of the said King of *Castile*, an[d] carrying on their Trade and Commerce there: An[d] the Subjects of the King of *Great-Britain* and o[f] *Portugal* shall have the same Power on the one Sid[e] and the other, if hereafter it should happen tha[t] either of the said Kings should be at War with an[y] Ally of the other: And the Subjects of the King of *Great-Britain* may bring all Sorts of Merchandizes, or even Arms, Victuals, or any other Provisions whatsoever, and all Things of the like Nature, into the Kingdoms and States of the King o[f] *Portugal*, and may there sell them as they thin[k] good, in open Market, or in a private Way, with[-] ou[t]

Free Navigation and Commerce with the Enemy of either Party.

t any Hindrance from the King of *Portugal* or
Minifters.

ARTICLE XIX.

And if during the prefent Peace and Amity any ng fhould be undertaken, committed or done, itrary to the Force and Effect thereof, either by or Land, or on frefh Waters, by either of the efaid Kings, their Heirs or Succeffors, Vaffals Subjects; neverthelefs the prefent Peace and Aty fhall remain in its Force and Virtue, and the ntraveners and Offenders only fhall be punifhed, l no others. Contraveners to be punifhed.

ARTICLE XX.

That the prefent Peace and Alliance fhall in no e derogate from the Alliances and Confederacies merly made and contracted between the King of *at-Britain* and other Kings, Princes and Comnwealths; but the faid Confederacies and Alices fhall be firmly preferved and remain for the ure in full Force and Virtue, this prefent Treaty Peace notwithftanding. Alliances with other Powers to be maintained.

Treaty of Peace and Alliance between Great-Britain *and the Emperor;* concluded at Vienna, March 16, 1731.

ARTICLE I.

THAT there be and remain between his Sacred Imperial Catholick Majefty, and his red Royal Majefty of *Great-Britain*, and their irs and Succeffors, a firm, fincere and inviolable endfhip, fo eftablifhed for the mutual Advantage he Countries and Subjects belonging to both tracting Powers, that each of them fhall be obliged. Perpetual Peace and Amity.

(124)

obliged to defend the Dominions and Subjects of t
other, and to maintain the Peace, and to promo
the Advantage of the other Party, as much as th
own, and prevent and avert all Damages and Inj
ries whatsoever, according to the Tenor of form
Treaties and Conventions of Peace, Friendship a
Alliance; all and singular which Treaties and Co
ventions shall obtain their full Force and Virtue
all Points, and be renewed and confirmed by t
present Treaty, excepting only those Article
Clauses and Conditions, which it has been thoug
proper to derogate from by this present Treaty.

Note, It is stipulated by the 5th Article of t
present Treaty, that a new Treaty of Co
merce shall be made, and a new Tariff settl
for the *Austrian Netherlands*, by Commission
to be named for that Purpose, to meet at *A
werp* within two Months, and such Treaty
be concluded within two Years from the D
thereof.

Convention between Great-Britain *and the* E.
peror; *made at* London, July *the* 2(
1715.

ARTICLE I.

Commerce with the *Austrian Netherlands* as before.

THE Commerce of the Subjects of his *Brit*
nick Majesty, with the *Austrian Netherlan*
shall remain, continue and subsist wholly on t
same Foot as it does at present, without any Al
ration, Innovation, Diminution, or Augmentati
to be made, till the Parties interested shall agree
on a Treaty of Commerce.

Tre

Treaty of Navigation and Commerce between Great-Britain *and* Spain; *concluded at* Madrid, May *the* 13*th*, 1667.

ARTICLE XX.

ALL *English* Merchants and Traders passing into the Provinces of the *Low Countries*, or the Cities and Towns thereof, for the Business of Trade, and also their Servants, Factors and Agents, shall enjoy from henceforward all Privileges, Exemptions, Immunities and Benefits, which they ever have enjoyed at any time of old, according to the Force and Tenor of Treaties heretofore made between the Kings of *England* and the Dukes of *Burgundy*, and other Governors of the *Low Countries*.

Ancient Privileges of Trade confirmed.

Treaty of Peace and Alliance between Great-Britain *and* Spain; *concluded at* Madrid, November *the* 15*th*, 1630.

ARTICLE XVI.

WHAT is said concerning free Commerce granted to the Subjects of the most Serene Kings, the same is likewise to be understood, and in the same manner between the Subjects of the most Serene King of *England* *Scotland* and *Ireland*; and the Subjects of the Provinces of *Flanders*, viz. That they shall shew all favour to, and treat each other in the most friendly manner, and with all mutual good Offices in all Places; and may on both Sides freely, safely and securely arrive at, and enter into the said Kingdoms, Dominions, Lands, Towns, Cities, Shores, Ports and Creeks whatsoever

Free Passage, Intercourse and Trade.

ever, by Sea, Land, or fresh Water, without Passport or other Licence, general or special; may sail, import and export, buy and sell all M chandizes in all such Places; and abide and trafi there as long as they please, and purchase Pr(sions and all things necessary for their victuall and Voyage, at reasonable Prices, and repair t. Ships and Vessels, whether they be their own hired or borrowed, and freely carry on all Kind Business, and depart from thence with the f Liberty, with all their Goods, Wares and Merch dizes whatsoever, and return into their own or other Country at their Pleasure and Discreti without any Lett or Molestation, paying the I ties and Customs according to the Laws of several Places respectively.

ARTICLE XX.

Ancient Treaties confirmed.   As to what concerns the ancient Treaties of tercourse and Commerce between the Kingdoms *England*, *Scotland* and *Ireland*, and the Dukes *Burgundy*, and Princes of the *Netherlands*, wh have been interrupted during the late Ruptui and perhaps violated in many Respects; it is p visionally agreed, that they shall continue in th former Force and Vigour, and be observed in same manner as they were before the late War tween *Philip* II. King of *Spain*, and *Elizabeth* Qu of *England*.

The Treaty *of* Peace *and* Alliance *between the* King *of* England, *and* Albert *Archduke of* Auſtria, *Duke of* Burgundy, Brabant, &c. *concluded in the Year* 1604.

ARTICLE I.

THERE ſhall be from this Day forward a good, ſincere, true, firm and perfect Amity nd Confederacy, and perpetual Peace, which ſhall be inviolably obſerved between the moſt erene King of *England*, &c. and the moſt Serene Archdukes of *Auſtria*, Dukes of *Burgundy*, &c. nd their Heirs and Succeſſors whatſoever, and their Kingdoms, Countries, Dominions, Lands, eople, Liegemen and Subjects whatſoever, preſent and to come, of whatſoever Condition, State or Degree, as well by Land as by Sea, and freſh Waters; ſo that their Vaſſals and Subjects ſhall behave in a truly friendly manner, and ſhew good Affection, and do all good Offices to each other.

Perpetual Peace and Amity.

ARTICLE XX.

And as the ſaid King and Archduke ſolemnly promiſe never to give any warlike Aſſiſtance to the Enemies of each other, ſo it is likewiſe provided, that their Subjects or Inhabitants, of whatſoever Nation or Quality, ſhall not on Pretence of Trade and Commerce, or under any other Colour, aſſiſt the Enemies of either Prince in any manner; nor furniſh them with Money, Proviſions, Arms, Engines, Guns or Inſtruments fit for War, or any other warlike Furniture: So that whoever ſhall act contrary hereunto, ſhall be liable to the ſevereſt Puniſhments, and be proceeded againſt as Covenant-breakers and ſeditious Perſons.

Neither Side to aſſiſt the Enemies of the other.

The

The 18th and 22d Articles of this Treaty are the same in Subſtance and Effect, and almoſt ſo verbatim with the 16th and 20th Articles of the Treaty of 1630, above recited.

Treaty of League between the Emperor Charles V. *Sovereign of the* Netherlands, *and the King of* England, *made in* 1542.

Article I. is of the ſame Import with the above recited XVI. Article, of the Treaty of 1630.

ARTICLE XIII.

1542.
Treaty of Commerce of 1520 confirmed.

FOR the common Benefit of the preſent Peace, League and Amity, and that the Subjects of both Princes may the better carry on and cultivate a mutual Commerce; it is agreed, that as concerning all Intercourſe of Merchandize and a mutual Commerce between them, the Treaty of Commerce dated the 11th of *April* 1520, ſhall be and remain in the ſame State and Force, as is ſtipulated by the Treaty of the 5th of *Auguſt* 1529.

Treaty of Commerce between the Emperor Charles V. *and the King of* England; *concluded at* London, April 11, 1520.

ARTICLE II.

1520.
Free Paſſage and Trade.

THAT all and ſingular the Subjects of the Kingdoms and Dominions of the ſaid Princes, their Factors, Agent and Servants, with their Ships, Goods, Wares and Merchandize, may ſail and come into all and ſingular the Lands, Countries, Dominions, Cities, Towns, Camps, Forts, Juriſdictions and Diſtricts of either of the ſaid Princes, by Land

Sea or fresh Waters, and abide there, and buy, sell, and barter all Kind of Merchandize with any other Merchants of any Country whatsoever, and freely and lawfully depart from thence with the same, or other Ships, Goods, Wares and Merchandizes, to any other Kingdoms, Ports or Places whatsoever, at their Discretion, and carry on all manner of Trade together, according to the Form, Force and Effect of the Treaty of Commerce dated the 24th of *February*, 1495, and of the following Articles during this present Provision.

Treaty of Peace and Commerce between the King of England *and the Archduke of* Austria, *Duke of* Burgundy, Brabant, &c. *concluded at* London *the 24th of* February, 1495.

THE 1st, 10th and 11th Articles contain a general Stipulation of a perpetual and universal Peace and Amity between the contracting Princes, their Dominions and Subjects, as likewise of an unlimited and reciprocal Freedom of Intercourse, Trade and Passage; by Sea and Land, for all their Subjects in their several Dominions respectively, and as to all Goods and Merchandizes; and are the same in Substance and Effect with the 16th Article of the Treaty of 1630, and the 2d Article of the Treaty of 1520, above recited. *Perpetual Peace and free Trade.*

ARTICLE XIV.

That the Fishers of both Parties (of what Condition soever they be) may freely go and sail every where by Sea, and safely fish without any Impediment, Licence or Passport; and if it shall happen that any of the Fishers of one Party, either by Accident, *Freedom of fishing.*

cident, Storm, Enemies, or otherwife, be force
to enter into any Port or Diſtrict of the other Party
they ſhall be peaceably and amicably received, an
treated there (paying all juſt Duties and Cuſtoms
and may freely depart and return from ſuch Port
and Places, with their Ships and Goods, withou
any Hindrance or Obſtruction whatſoever; pro
vided however that ſuch Fiſhers are not guilty (
any Cheat or Fraud, or that they do not occaſio
Damage to others-

ARTICLE XV.

Pirates not to be harboured or aſſiſted.

That no Pirates or others, making War by Se
without the Authority of their Princes, ſhall b
received into any of the Ports or Shores of the fore
ſaid Princes, or of either of them, whether the
belong to either of the aforeſaid Princes, or to an
other Nation, nor ſhall they or any of them be a
ſiſted in any of the Kingdoms, Countries, Dom
nions, or Lands of the foreſaid Princes, with Mc
ney, Arms, warlike Inſtruments, Victuals, or an
other thing whatever, in any manner; nor ſhall the
be favoured upon any Pretence whatſoever, o
pain of Reſtitution and full Satisfaction for all Da
mages, Expences and Injuries done or to be don
by ſuch Pirates and violent Robbers, to be made t
the foreſaid Subjects, or to any one of them, as we
by the Pirates themſelves, if taken and able to pay
as by their Harbourers, Favourers and Aſſiſtants.

ARTICLE XXII.

Ships freely to enter and moor in any Port.

That the Seamen, Maſters of Ships and Mari
ners, Subjects of the foreſaid Princes, may freel
moor and lay up their Ships, whether laden or un
laden, or Ships of War, which ſhall enter into an
Ports of either of the foreſaid Princes, in the ſam
manner as their own native Subjects may do, pro
vided they have no ways acted or behaved as Pirates

ARTICLE

ARTICLE XXIII.

That the Subjects of either of the foresaid Princes, whether Merchants or Seamen, Masters of Ships or Mariners, shall not bring or cause to be brought by Sea, fraudulently or under any Colour whatsoever, any Goods or Merchandizes of the Enemies of the other of the foresaid Princes; and if they do otherwise, and be called to account thereupon by the Subjects of the other Prince, then lawfully engaged in War, they shall be obliged to mak a true, plain and just Confession and Declaration, which shall be sufficient for that Time; and the said Persons so calling to account, shall make no further Inquiry into the Matter: But if the Person called to account shall afterwards appear to have made a false Answer, then the said Person called to account shall be obliged to give so much out of his own, to the Person who had called him to account, whom he had defrauded by such false Answer, as the Merchandizes of the Enemy by him thus carried and concealed shall appear to be worth. *Goods of Enemies not to be imported.* *Frauds to be made good.*

Treaty of Amity, Commerce and Navigation, between Great-Britain *and* Russia; *concluded at* Petersbourg, December 2, 1734.

ARTICLE I.

THE Peace, Friendship, and good Correspondence which happily subsist between their Russian and Britannick Majesties, shall be confirmed and established by this Treaty, so as from henceforwards there shall be between the Crown of all the Russias on one Side, and the Crown of *Great-Britain* on the other; as likewise between the States, Countries, Realms, Dominions and Territories which are under their Obedience, a true, firm, and perfect Peace, *Perpetual Peace and Amity.*

(132)

Peace, Friendſhip, and good Underſtanding, whic
ſhall endure and be inviolably maintained for eve₁
as well by Sea as by Land, and on all freſh Water₅
and the People, Subjects and Inhabitants on bot
Sides, of whatſoever Condition or Degree, ſhall be
have with intire good Will towards each other, an
give each other all poſſible Aid and Aſſiſtance, with
out doing or offering the leaſt Wrong or Damag
whatſoever.

ARTICLE II.

Free Navigation and Commerce in Europe. There ſhall be an entire Freedom of Navigatio
and Commerce throughout all the Dominions of th
two contracting Parties in *Europe*, where Naviga
tion and Commerce are at this Time permitted, c
ſhall be permitted hereafter by the contracting Pa₁
ties to the Subjects of any other Nation.

ARTICLE III.

Free Ingreſs for trading, victualling, or refitting. The Subjects of both contracting Parties ma
enter at all Times into all the Ports, Places c
Towns of either of the contracting Parties, wit
their Ships, Veſſels and Carriages, laden or unlader
into which the Subjects of any other nation are pe₁
mitted to enter, to trade or abide there; and the Ma
riners, Paſſengers and Veſſels whether *Ruſſian* c
Engliſh, even though there ſhould be any Subjects c
any other ſtrange Nation among the Crew, ſhall b
received and treated in like manner as the moſt fa
The Mariners not to be forced into Service. voured Nation, and the Mariners and Paſſenge₁
ſhall not be forced to enter into the Service of eithe
of the contracting Parties, which may have occaſio
for their Service; and the Subjects of both con
tracting Parties may buy all Kind of Neceſſarie₅
which they ſhall ſtand in Need of, at the curren
Price; and repair and refit their Ships, Veſſels c
Carriages, and furniſh themſelves with all Manne
of Proviſions for their Subſiſtance and Voyage
abide and depart at their Pleaſure, without Moleſ
tatio.

tation or Impediment; provided they conform themselves to the Laws and Ordinances of the respective States of the said contracting Powers, where they shall so arrive or continue.

ARTICLE IV.

The Subjects of *Great-Britain* may bring by Sea or by Land, into all or any of the Dominions of *Russia*, wherein the Subjects of any other Nation are permitted to trade, all Sorts of Goods and Merchandizes, whereof the Importation and Traffick are not prohibited; and in like manner the Subjects of *Russia* may bring into all or any of the Dominions of *Great-Britain*, wherein the Subjects of any other Nation are allowed to traffick, all Sorts of Merchandizes of the Produce or Manufacture of the Dominions of *Russia*, whereof the Importation and Traffick are not prohibited; and likewise all Merchandizes of the Produce and Manufacture of *Asia*; provided that it is not actually prohibited by any Law now in Force in *Great-Britain*; and they may buy and export out of the Dominions of *Great-Britain*, all Manner of Goods and Merchandizes, which the Subjects of any other Nation may buy therein and export from thence, and particularly Gold and Silver, wrought or unwrought; excepting the Silver coined Money of *Great-Britain*.

Mutual Commerce and Traffic with all Goods, and in all Cases not prohibited.

ARTICLE IX.

It shall be permitted to the Subjects of both contracting Parties reciprocally, in all accustomed Places of Export, to load on board their own Ships, Vessels or Carriages, or any other, all Merchandizes bought by them, excepting only such as are prohibited to be exported; and freely to send or carry away the same: Provided they have paid the Duties, and such Ships, Vessels or Carriages have been cleared according to Law,

Free Export of all Goods not prohibited.

ARTICLE

ARTICLE XI.

Free Trade for one Party with an Enemy of the other, under Restrictions.

The Subjects of either Party may freely pass, repass, and trade in all Countries which now are, or hereafter shall be at Enmity with the other of the said Parties, Places actually block'd up or besieged only excepted; provided they do not carry any warlike Stores or Ammunition to the Enemy; as for all other Effects, their Ships, Passengers and Goods shall be free and unmolested.

ARTICLE XII.

Warlike Ammunition specified and prohibited.

Cannons, Mortars, Fire-Arms, Pistols, Bombs, Granadoes, Bullets, Balls, Fuzees, Flints, Matches, Powder, Saltpetre, Sulphur, Cuirasses, Pikes, Swords, Belts, Pouches, Cartouch-Boxes, Saddles and Bridles, in any Quantity, beyond what may be necessary for the Ship's Provision, and may properly appertain to and be judged necessary for every Man of the Ship's Crew, or for each Passenger, shall be deemed Ammunition of War; and if any such be there found, they may seize and confiscate the same according to Law: But neither the Vessels, Passengers or the rest of the Goods shall be detained for that Reason, or hindered from pursuing their Voyage.

ARTICLE XIII.

One Year allowed to Subjects on both Sides, in case of a War.

In case of a Rupture between the contracting Parties (which God forbid) the Persons, Effects or Vessels of the Subjects of either Party, shall not be detained or confiscated, but there shall be the Space of one Year at least allowed them, wherein they may sell, dispose, carry off, or send away their Effects and transport their Persons.

ARTICLE XIV.

Men or Ships not to be detained or forced.

The Merchants, Mariners, Vessels or Effects of either Party, shall not be arrested or forced into
Service

Service without their own Consent, under any Pretence whatsoever; and if any Domestick Servant or Mariner desert his Service or Vessel, he shall be delivered up: But nothing contained in this Article is to be so understood, as to tend to the Hindrance or Obstruction of the ordinary Course of Justice on either Side.

Deserters to be given up.

ARTICLE XXVIII.

The Subjects of both Parties shall be respected and treated in their respective Dominions in like manner as the most favoured Nation, and the Subjects of *Russia* which shall come into *England* in order to learn Arts and Commerce there, shall be protected, favoured and instructed: Likewise if any *Russian* Vessels shall be met with out at Sea by any *English* Vessels, they shall in no wise be hindered or molested by them, provided they comport themselves in the *British* Seas in the accustomed manner; but on the contrary, they shall be favoured by them, and have all possible Assistance given them, and that in the very Ports or Havens belonging to the Dominions of *Great-Britain*.

Mutual good Offices.

Russians to be protected and favoured in England.

ARTICLE XXIX.

Peace, Amity, and good Understanding shall continue for ever between the contracting Parties; and as it is usual to limit Treaties of Commerce for a certain Space of Time, it is agreed between the contracting Parties, that this shall continue for the Space of fifteen Years, to be computed from the Day of signing this present Treaty; and that before the Expiration of the said Term, they shall come to a further mutual Agreement for renewing and prolonging the same.

Peace and Amity for fifteen Years.

Treaty of Peace, Amity and Commerce between Great-Britain *aud* Ruſſia; *concluded a* Weſtminſter, June 16, 1623.

ARTICLE I.

1623.
Perpetual Amity and Alliance.

THIS Alliance ſhall remain ſincere, firm and perfect, and be for ever inviolably obſerved and kept between the King of *Great-Britain* and the Emperor, and Great Duke of *Ruſſia*, and their Heirs and Succeſſors, Crowns, Kingdoms and People and their Subjects and People, as well as the renowned Princes themſelves, ſhall love like Brethren and be as one Nation, wiſhing the good Honour and Reputation one of another both by Word and Deed.

ARTICLE III.

Neither Party to aſſiſt the Enemy of the other.

Neither of the ſaid Princes ſhall aid or aſſiſt any Enemy of the other, either preſent or future, with Ships of War, Ammunition, Victuals, or other Materials, or Proviſions for War, nor ſuffer any Soldiers of other Princes to paſs through his Kingdoms or Dominions againſt the other Confederate; but on the contrary, ſhall endeavour to divert and defeat any Attempt or Purpoſe of ſuch Enemies, and avoid and oppoſe all hurtful Practices againſt the ſaid Confederate.

ARTICLE X.

Free Trade and Commerce.

All ſuch Privileges and Grants for Freedom of Trade and Commerce, as by Treaties have been given and granted to the *Engliſh* Merchants by his Majeſty of *Ruſſia* and his noble Progenitors, ſhall remain and ſtand in their full Force and Strength; and by Virtue of this Alliance, the Subjects of both Princes may freely and peaceably, without any Hindrance or Moleſtation, both by Land and Sea, and with-

within the fresh Water Rivers of each other's Countries, use all Kind of Traffick and Merchanize whatsoever; and may buy up and freely export all Manner of Jewels, Precious Stones, and all other Things fitting for the Treasury of the said Princes, with the same Freedom and Liberty, as if they were Natives; provided that this Freedom of Trade and Commerce be understood, with regard to the Subjects of *Great-Britain*, to extend to all such Merchants only, and none other, as are allowed to trade in the Dominions of *Russia* by the Licence of the King of *Great-Britain*, and according to the gracious Letters and Privileges granted to the *English* Merchants by his Majesty of all *Russia*, and by the Holy Patriarch of *Moscow* and of all *Russia*, or which shall be hereafter granted or enlarged to them : And with regard to the Subjects of *Russia*, to all such Merchants, and none other, shall be allowed to trade into the Dominions of *Great-Britain* by the Licence of his Majesty of all *Russia*, and according to the gracious Privileges and Grants of both their renowned Majesties.

ARTICLE XVI.

The Ambassadors, Messengers, or Posts of both the said Princes, which shall be sent unto the Country of either upon any princely Affairs, shall freely pass without Lett or Interruption, together with their People, and all Goods whatsoever, according to the genuine Sense of this Treaty.

<small>Free Passage for Ministers and Messengers.</small>

ARTICLE XVII.

If either of the said Princes shall have occasion to send their Ambassadors, Messengers or Posts through the Countries and Dominions of the other, into and from *Germany, Spain, France, Denmark, Sveathland,* and *Netherland,* or unto and from *Persia, Turkey,* and other Parts of the *East,* not in open Hostility with either of their Majesties; or if they

<small>Free Passage for Ministers and Messengers to other Countries.</small>

they shall happen by any Casualty, by Land or [Water], either in their going or returning, to r[e]ceive any Damage in either of their Countries, th[ey] shall be suffered freely and peaceably to pass wi[th] all their Goods and People whatsoever, to su[ch] Place as their Prince's Pass shall direct them, a[nd] with meet Convoys shall be safely conducted, bo[th] by Land and Water through either of their Dom[i]nions, without the least forceable detaining or Hi[n]drance whatsoever.

Treaty of Alliance and Commerce betwe[en] Great-Britain and Sweden; concluded [at] Whitehall, October the 21st, 1661.

ARTICLE I.

1661.
Perpetual Peace and Amity.

THAT there be and continue from hencefo[r]wards, a good, true, firm and perpetual Peac[e,] Friendship, good Will and Correspondence betwe[en] the Kings of *Great-Britain* and *Sweden*, and all a[nd] singular their Kingdoms, Countries, Dominion[s,] Provinces, Lands, Islands, Colonies, Cities, Town[s,] People, Citizens, and all their Subjects and Inh[a]bitants whatsoever, so as both Parties shall beha[ve] towards each other with true Amity and Affectio[n.]

ARTICLE II.

Mutual Friendship and Aid against all Enemies.

The said Confederates, and their Dominions, Su[b]jects, People and Inhabitants, shall take Care [of] and promote each other's Advantage; and sha[ll] also certify one another of any Dangers threatene[d] and Conspiracies and Machinations formed by t[he] Enemies of either, and shall oppose and hind[er] them, as far as lies in their Power: Nor shall it [be] lawful for either of the Confederates, by himsel[f] or by any other Persons whomsoever, to negocia[te] or attempt any thing to the Hurt or Disadvantag[e]

the other's Lands or Dominions whatsoever, any
here, either by Land or Sea; nor shall he by any
eans protect any Enemies or Rebels, to the Pre-
dice of the other Confederate, nor receive nor ad-
it into his Dominions any Rebel or Traitor, who
all make any Attempt against the Estate of the
her; much less shall he afford them any Advice,
id or Countenance, or suffer any Advice, Assis-
nce or Favour to be given them by his Subjects,
eople and Inhabitants.

ARTICLE III.

The said Kings and Kingdoms shall, with all andour and Diligence, take all possible Care, that e Impediments which have hitherto interrupted e Freedom of Navigation and Commerce, not ily between both Nations, but also with other eople and Nations through the Dominions, Coun- ies, Seas and Rivers of both Confederates, be re- oved; and they shall sincerely endeavour to assert, tablish, defend and promote the aforesaid Free- om of Navigation and Commerce on both Sides, gainst all Disturbers thereof, by the Methods greed on in this Treaty, or by such as may here- ter be agreed on; and shall not suffer any thing be done or committed contrary to this Treaty, ei- er by themselves, or by their Subjects and People. *Free Navigation and Commerce.*

ARTICLE IV.

It shall be free for either of the said Confederates, d their Inhabitants and Subjects, to enter by and or Sea into the Kingdoms, Countries, Pro- nces, Territories, Islands, Cities, Villages, Towns alled or unwalled, fortified or unfortified, Har- urs, Dominions or Jurisdictions whatsoever of the her, freely and securely, without any Licence or fe Conduct, general or special; and there to pass d repass, to reside therein, or to travel through e same, and in the mean time to buy Provisions *Free Passage and all Priveleges of Trade.*

and

and all Neceſſaries; and they ſhall be treated wi
all manner of Civility; it ſhall be lawful alſo f
both the Confederates and their Subjects, Citize
and Inhabitants, to trade, traffick, and carry
Commerce in all Places where Commerce has be
at any time hitherto uſed, and in whatſoever Goo
and Merchandize they pleaſe; provided they a
not contraband; and they ſhall have Liberty
import and export them at Diſcretion, the d
Cuſtoms being always paid, and the Laws and O
dinances of both Kingdoms, whether relating
Merchandize, or to any other Right, always o
ſerved : Which Things being pre-ſuppoſed, tl
People, Subjects and Inhabitants of one Confed
rate ſhall have and hold in the Countries, Land
Dominions and Kingdoms of the other, ſuch fu
and ample Privileges, Exemptions, Liberties an
Immunities, as any Foreigner whatſoever doth
ſhall enjoy in the ſaid Dominions and Kingdon
on both Sides.

ARTICLE V.

Merchants, Mariners, Ships, or Goods not to be unduly arreſted or detained.

Neither the Merchants, Captains of Ships, Ma
ters, Mariners, or other Perſons whatſoever, nor th
Ships, Goods or Merchandize of either of the Cor
federates, or of his Subjects or Inhabitants, ſhall i
any publick or private Name, by Virtue of an
general or ſpecial Edict, be ſeized or detained b
Arreſts, in any of the Countries, Harbours, Road
Shores or Dominions whatſoever of the other Cor
federate for the publick Uſe, military Expedition
or for any other Cauſe, much leſs for the privat
Uſe of any one; nor be compelled by any manne
of Violence, or be in any wiſe moleſted or injurec
Provided only that ſuch Arreſts as are agreeable t
Law and Equity be not prohibited, if they ar
made according to the ordinary Forms of Law
and not for the Sake of gratifying any one's privat
Wil

Vill, and are indispensably necessary for the Administration of Right and Justice.

ARTICLE VI.

But if one or more Ships of either of the Confederates, whether Ships of War or private Merchant Ships, shall be drove by Storms, Pirates, Enemies, or other urgent Necessity, into the Ports, Havens, or upon any of the Coasts of the other Confederate, they shall be received courteously, and with all Civility, and enjoy friendly Protection, without being in any respect hinder'd from the Means of refitting, or from purchasing whatever they want for their Provision, Repairs and Conveniency, at the Market-Price: Nor shall they on any account be prohibited to depart in like manner from such Port and Haven when they please, without paying any Duties or Customs, so long as nothing be done or committed contrary to the Statutes and Ordinances of that Place, which such Ships shall so arrive and abide at.

Ships forced in to be harboured and assisted.

ARTICLE VII.

For the like Reason, if any one or more Ships, publick or private, of either of the Confederates, or of their Subjects or Inhabitants, run ashore, are cast away, or suffer Shipwreck, or any other Damage, the Sufferers shall be kindly and amicably protected, and have such Assistance in Consideration of a due Premium, that all Remains of such Wreck or other Loss may be preserved, and restored to the Owners and Proprietors; provided they, their Attorneys or Procurators, lay Claim to such Ships and Goods, within twelve Months after the Wreck happened; saving always the Laws and Customs of both Nations.

Mutual Protection and Assistance, in case of Wrecks and other Losses at Sea.

ARTICLE IX.

Free Export of Arms, and Ingress and Egress for all Ships.

It shall be lawful for the said Confederates, a the People and Subjects of both, to buy and expo out of the respective Countries, Dominions a Kingdoms of either, all manner of Arms and mi tary Equipage, and safely and freely to carry th Ships to any Ports, Havens and Shores of eith there to stay, and thence to depart, provided th behave modestly, peaceably, and agreeably to t Laws and Customs of each Place, and do not

Ships of War to enter into Ports on Conditions.

any respect hinder the Freedom of Commerce: like manner, Ships of War and Guardships sh have free Access to the Ports, Havens or Rivers the other Confederate; and it shall be free for the to cast Anchor, and abide there, and to depart fro thence without any Injury or Molestation, provid the following Conditions are observed.

Not to exceed five or six Ships.

N°. I. That the Squadron shall not exceed t Number of five or six Ships, which shall allowed to come into the Port of the oth Confederate without any previous Notice.

To exhibit Letters of safe Conduct.

N°. II. That the Commander of such Squadr and Ships shall, without Delay, exhibit l Letters of safe Conduct to the Governor Magistrate of the Castle, Fort, City or Pr vince, where he shall so arrive, and give N tice of the Reasons of his coming, and f what End, and how long he designs to stay that Port or Haven.

Not to come too near the Forts.

N°. III. That such Ships shall not approach abide nearer to the Forts or Castles than convenient.

N°. IV. Th

Nº. IV. That the Mariners, Ships Companies and Soldiers, shall not go ashore in Bodies above forty at a Time, nor in any Number that may give Suspicion. *Not more than forty to go ashore together.*

Nº. V. That while they are there, they shall not do any Damage to any Person, not even to their Enemies; and above all, shall not stop or obstruct the Passage of any Merchant Ship whatsoever, into or out of the Harbour. *Not to do any Hurt or Hindrance to any.*

Nº. VI. That they shall not go out from thence like as out of their own Harbour, and return again, in order to annoy the Navigation of any Nation whatsoever. *Not to go in and out, as in their own Ports.*

Nº. VII. That they shall in all respects, live and behave modestly, and conformably to the Laws and Customs of each Place, and have special regard to the reciprocal Friendship between the Confederates: But if either of the Confederates shall think it advantageous or necessary to enter the Ports of the other Confederate with a greater Number of Ships, and to enjoy the Conveniences thereof, he shall signify the same to his Confederate two Months before hand; during which time they shall agree upon proper Regulations for admitting the same; but if the Ships of either are drove into the Ports of the other, for avoiding Tempests or Enemies; in such case, the Reason of their coming shall be notified to the Governor or chief Magistrate of the Place, and their Abode there must not be longer than the time allowed by the Governor or chief Magistrate; a Regard being always had to the Laws and Conditions in this Article before comprized. *A greater Number of Ships not to come in without special Leave.*

ARTICLE

ARTICLE X.

Free Passage and Commerce. It shall be lawful for any of the Subjects and habitants of *Sweden* to travel in *England*, and all Dominions thereof, and to pass through the f[ame] by Land or Sea at Pleasure, to any other Nat[ion] whatsoever, and to renew Commerce with th[em] and freely to traffick in all Kinds of Merchand[ize] and the same to carry thither and export f[rom] thence: And the Subjects of the King of *Gr[eat] Britain* shall enjoy the same Liberties in the Ki[ng]doms, Dominions, and Territories of the Kin[g of] *Sweden*; on Condition that the Laws, Ordina[nces] and peculiar Rights of each Nation, relating [to] Commerce and Merchandize, be observed on b[oth] Sides.

ARTICLE XI.

Although the foregoing Articles of this Tre[aty] and the Laws of Friendship do forbid, that eit[her] of the Confederates shall furnish any Aid or S[up]plies to the Enemies of the other; yet it is by [no] means to be understood that either Confeder[ate] with his Subjects and Inhabitants, who is no [a] Party in a War, shall be restrained the Liberty [of] Trade and Navigation with the Enemies of [the] other Confederate, who is involved in such W[ar:] Provided only, that no Goods called Contraba[nd,] and especially Money, Provisions, Arms, [Bom]with their Fuzees, and other Appurtenances, F[ire] Balls, Gunpowder, Matches, Cannon Ball, Spe[ars,] **Free Trade for one Party with an Enemy of the other; contraband Goods excepted.** Swords, Lances, Pikes, Halberts, Guns, Mort[ars,] Petards, Grenadoes, Musket rests, Bandeliers, S[alt]petre, Muskets, Musket Bullets, Helmets, He[ad] Pieces, Breast-Plates, Coats of Mails, commo[nly] called Cuirasses, and the like Kind of Arms; S[ol]diers, Horses with the Furniture, nor Pistols, Be[lts,] or any other Instruments of War; nor Ships [of] War and Guardships, be carried to the Enemie[s] other Confederate, on the Penalty of being made Prize without Hopes of Redemption, if they are seized by the other Confederate; nor shall either Confederate permit that the Rebels or Enemies of the other be assisted by any of his Subjects, or that any Ships be sold or lent to, or in any manner made use of by the Enemies or Rebels of the other to his Disadvantage or Detriment: But it shall be lawful for either of the Confederates, and his People or Subjects, to trade with the Enemies of the other, and to carry them any Merchandize whatsoever, not above excepted, without any Impediment; provided they are not carried to those Ports or Places which are besieged by the other; in which Case they shall have free Leave either to sell their Goods to the Besiegers, or to repair with them to any other Port which is not besieged.

ARTICLE XII.

But least such Freedom of Navigation and Passage of the one Confederate might be of Detriment to the other, while engaged in War, by Sea or Land, with other Nations, by concealing and conveying the Goods and Merchandizes of the Enemies of the Confederate so engaged in War, under the Name of a Friend and Ally; for the avoiding of all Suspicion and Fraud of such Sort, it is agreed, that all Ships, Carriages, Wares and Men belonging to the other Confederate, shall be furnished in their Journeys and Voyages with safe Conducts, commonly called Passports and Certificates, such as are underwritten verbatim, signed and subscribed by the chief Magistrate of that Province and City, or by the chief Commissioners of the Customs and Duties, and specifying the true Names of the Ships, Carriages, Goods, and Masters of the Vessels, as also the exact Dates, without any Fraud or Collusion, together with such other Descriptions of that Sort, as are expressed in

Either Party carrying on Trade with an Enemy to have Passports and Certificates.

the

the following Form of a safe Conduct and Certi-
cate. Wherefore, if any Person shall affirm up(
the Oath, by which he is bound to his King, Sta
or City, that he has given in true Accounts, a
be afterwards convicted, on sufficient Proof of a
wilful Fraud therein, he shall be severely punished
and incur the Penalties of Perjury.

English Form of the Passport.

WE *N. N.* Governor or chief Magistrate,
the Commissioners of the Duties and Cu
toms of the City or Province of *N.* (the Title
Office of the respective Government of that Pla,
being added) do make known and certify, that
the   of the Month of   in the Year of
N. N. N. Citizens and Inhabitants of *N.* and Su
jects of his Sacred Royal Majesty of *Sweden*, pe
sonally appeared before us in the City or Town
N. in the Dominions of his Sacred Royal Majes
of *Sweden*, and declared to us upon the Oath, I.
which they are bound to our Most Gracious S
vereign, his Sacred Royal Majesty of *Sweden*, a
to our City, that the Ship or Vessel called *N.*
about   Lasts or Tons, belongs to the Po
City or Town of *N.* in the Dominions of *N.* a,
that the said Ship does rightfully belong to him
other Subjects of his Sacred Royal Majesty
Sweden; that she is bound directly from the Port
N. to the Port of *N.* laden with the followin
Merchandize, *viz.* [here shall be specified the Goo
with their Quantity and Quality, for Examp
about so many Chests or Bales, about so ma
Hogsheads, *&c.* according to the Quantity a
Condition of the Goods] and likewise affirmed
the Oath aforesaid, that so much only of the sa
Goods and Merchandize belong to the Subjects
his Sacred Royal Majesty of *Sweden*, or so much
such Goods belong to *N. N. N.* [specifying wh
Nation the Proprietors are of] and that they c
cla

lared upon their said Oath, that the said Goods bove specified and no others, are put on board, r are to be put on board the above named Ship)r the said Voyage, and that no Part of those ;oods belong to any other Person whatsoever but iose above mentioned, and that no Goods are isguised or concealed therein under any fictitious fame whatsoever, but that the Wares above menoned are truly and really put on board for the fe of the said Owners, and no others; and that ie Captain of the said Ship named *N.* is a Cizen of the City of *N.* Therefore, since it fully)pears to us [the Governor or chief Magistrate, Commissioners of the Duties and Customs of e City aforesaid] after strict Examination, that e said Ship or Vessel and the Goods on board e same are free, and do truly and really belong the Subjects of his Sacred Royal Majesty of *weden,* or to the Inhabitants of other Nations as oresaid, we do most humbly and earnestly require all and singular Powers by Land and Sea, Kings, inces, Republicks, and free Cities; also of all enerals, Admirals, Commanders, Officers and overnors of Ports, and all others guarding any arbour or Sea, which may happen to meet this iip in her Voyage, or if she chance to fall in iong or pass through their Squadrons, or to stay their Harbours, that, for the Sake of the Alnce and Friendship which subsist respectively been them, or their Superiors and his Sacred)yal Majesty our Most Gracious Sovereign the ng of *Sweden,* they will not only permit the said iptain with the said Ship *N.* and the Men, Goods d Merchandizes belonging to the same to proute his Voyage freely, without Lett or Molestan, but also if he think fit to depart out of the d Harbour elsewhere, that they will shew all d Offices to him and his Ship, as a Subject of Sacred Royal Majesty of *Sweden,* as they shall

in like manner experience the same from his S
cred Royal Majesty of *Sweden*, and from all h
Ministers and Subjects in the like or any oth
Case. In Witness whereof we have taken ca
that the said Presents signed by our own Hands
sealed with the Seal of our City. Given, &c.

Therefore when the Goods, Ships, or Men
either Confederate, or his Subjects and Inhabitan
shall meet in the open Sea, or in any Ports, H
vens, Countries or Places whatsoever, with a
Ships of War or Privateers, or any Subjects a
Inhabitants of the other Confederate, after pr
ducing their Letters of safe Conduct and Certi
cates aforesaid, nothing farther shall be demand

All Ships to pass free on producing such Passport.
of them, nor any Inquiry whatsoever made wi
respect to the Goods, Ships or Men, much l
shall they be injured, damaged or molested, but th
shall be suffered freely to prosecute their Voyage a
Purpose. But in case that the said solemn and stat
Form of a Certificate be not produced, or there

Not to be searched, unless wanting Passports or on just Suspicion.
any other just and strong Cause of Suspicion, wl
a Ship ought to be searched, which shall only
deemed justifiable in such Case, and not otherwis
if the Goods of an Enemy are then found in su
Ship of the Confederate, that Part only which b
longs to the Enemy shall be made Prize, and wh

Enemies Goods only to be confiscated, wherever found.
belongs to the Confederate shall be immediate
restored: The same Rule shall likewise be observe
if the Goods of the other Confederate are fou
on board a Ship of an Enemy: If any thing
done by either Party contrary to the genuine Ser
of this Article, both Confederates shall take Ca
that the severest Punishments, due for the m
heinous Crimes, be inflicted on such of their Su
jects and Inhabitants as shall offend herein, for th
Contempt and Transgression of the Royal Cor
mands, and that full and immediate Satisfaction
made to the injured Party for all Damage and E
penc

ences (of which the moſt ſummary Proof ſhall be
admitted) by the other Confederate, or his Subjects
and Inhabitants, without any intricate Niceties of
the Law.

ARTICLE XIII.

Neither of the Confederates ſhall ſuffer the Ships, Neither Party to harbour the Enemies of the other, or their Captures.
Veſſels, Goods or Merchandize of the other, or
of his People and Subjects taken at Sea or elſewhere
by Enemies or Rebels to be brought into his Ports
or Dominions, but ſhall publickly forbid any thing
of that Kind to be done; and if any Ships, Veſſels,
Goods or Merchandize of either, or of his People
or Subjects, taken at Sea, or elſewhere, ſhall be
carried into the Ports or Countries of the other by
any Enemy or Rebel of the Confederates, or of
either of them, ſuch Confederate ſhall not ſuffer
the ſame, or any Part thereof to be ſold in that
Port, or any other Place in his Dominion; but
ſhall take care that the Maſter of the Ship or Veſſel
ſo taken, as alſo the Mariners and Paſſengers, ſhall,
as ſoon as they arrive, be immediately ſet at Liberty; together with as many of the Priſoners,
being Subjects of either Kingdom, as ſhall be
brought thither; nor ſhall he permit the ſaid Ship
or Veſſel to ſtay in that Harbour, but ſhall oblige
her, with her Goods, Merchandize and Lading,
immediately to leave the Port; provided neverthe-
leſs, that nothing in this Article be prejudicial to except in Alliance with either of the Confederates.
the Alliances formerly entered into by either of
the Confederates with other Nations; but when
they do not interfere, the above Article ſhall remain in full force.

ARTICLE XIV.

If it ſhall happen hereafter, while this Friendſhip This Peace not to be diſſolved by private Injuries.
and Alliance ſubſiſts, that any of the People and
Subjects of either of the Confederates ſhall do, or
endeavour any thing contrary to this Treaty, or any

any Part thereof, by Land, Sea, or in any Water: this Friendship, Treaty and Alliance between th said Confederates, shall not on that Account be ir terrupted or diffolved, but shall neverthelefs cor tinue and remain entire; and thofe particular Per fons only shall fuffer Punifhment, who shall violat this Treaty; and they who shall receive any Injury shall have Right and Juftice done, and Satisfactio made to them for all their Lofs and Injury fuftaine within twelve Months after the Demand of fuc

Reftitution to be made to Subjects for all Loffes; and Offenders to be punifhed.

Reftitution: But in cafe fuch Delinquents and Per fons guilty of fuch Violence, shall refufe to appea and fubmit to Juftice, or to make Satisfaction with in the Term aforefaid, whoever they are, they fha be renounced as Enemies of both States, and thei Subftance, Goods and Poffeffions, what and hov great foever, shall be confifcated and fold toward making full and juft Satisfaction for the Injuries b them committed; and the Offenders themfelves when they come into the Jurifdiction of either State shall moreover fuffer condign Punifhment accord ing to the Nature of the Crime.

ARTICLE XV.

All former Rights at Sea faved to both Parties.

The prefent Treaty and Confederacy shall dero gate nothing from any Pre-eminence, Right an Dominion whatfoever of either of the Confederate in any of their Seas, Streights and Waters whatfo ever, but they shall have and hold the fame, in a ample Manner as they have hitherto enjoyed them and as to them of Right appertains.

ARTICLE XVI.

Freedom of Navigation and Commerce to be mutually fupported in all Places.

Whereas it is the principal End of this Treaty that fuch a Freedom of Navigation and Com merce, as is ftipulated by the foregoing Articles may be and remain on both Sides, to both the Con federates, their Subjects and Inhabitants, in th *Baltick*, the *Sound*, the *Northern*, *Weftern*, *Britif* and *Mediterranean Seas*, and the *Channel*, and all the other Seas of *Europe*; it is agreed, that both Sides shall sincerely contribute their joint Advice, Aid and Assistance, that the said mutual Freedom of Navigation and Commerce may be established and promoted in all the said Seas and Streights and (if there there be occasion) that it be defended against all Disturbers who shall offer to interrupt, prohibit, hinder or constrain it for their own Pleasure, and to the Detriment of the Confederates: And both Confederates shall in the most courteous Manner shew their good Will and Readiness for promoting the Advantage, and removing any Inconveniencies of the other Confederate: Saving nevertheless those Treaties heretofore entered into by both Nations, with other Kingdoms, Republicks and States, which shall subsist in full force; but hereafter, neither of the Confederates shall by any means enter into any Treaty, or make any Compact with other foreign Nations or People whatsoever, to the Prejudice of the present Treaty in any respect, without the previous knowledge and Consent of the other Confederate; and if any thing be otherwise stipulated hereafter with any other, it shall be reckoned null and void, and shall entirely give Place to what is mutually agreed to by this present Treaty.

No Treaty to be made with any foreign Nation without the previous Consent of the other Confederate.

Treaty between Great-Britain *and* Sweden; *concluded at* London *in the Year* 1656, *whereby the Treaty of* Upsal *of* 1654, *is confirmed and explained.*

THE 2d, 3d, 4th, 5th, and 6th Articles of this Treaty are comprehended in the 9th, 11th, 12th, and 13th Articles of the above recited Treaty of 1661.

1656.

ARTICLE X.

Swedes to have Liberty of fishing on the British Coasts. It shall be free for the Subjects of the King of Sweden to fish and catch Herrings and other Fish throughout the Seas and Coasts belonging to the Dominion of *Great-Britain*, so as they do not exceed the Number of one thousand Vessels employed in such Fishery; nor shall they be any ways hindered or disturbed in such their fishing; nor shall any Charges or Duties be exacted from them on Pretence or Account of such their fishing, by any publick Guard Ships of *Great-Britain*, or their Privateers acting under Commissions or Letters of Marque, or by any fishing Vessels on the Northern Coasts of *Britain*; but on the contrary, they shall be treated in the most courteous and friendly Manner, and even be permitted to dry their Nets on the Shores, and to furnish themselves with all necessary Provisions at reasonable Rates from the Inhabitants.

Treaty of Peace between Great-Britain *and* Sweden; *concluded at* Upsal, *April the* 5*th*, 1654.

1654. THE 1st, 2d, 3d, 4th, 5th, 6th, 7th, 9th, 10th, 11th, 12th, 13th, 14th, and 15th Articles of this Treaty, are comprehended in, and are almost verbatim the same with the following Articles of the above recited Treaty of 1661, *viz.* 1st, 2d, 3d, 4th, 5th, 6th, 7th, 9th, 10th, 11th, 12th, 14th, 15th, and 16th Articles.

Articles and Clauses of several Treaties made between Great-Britain *and* Sweden, *concerning the Continuance, Revival, or Confirmation of former Treaties.*

Treaty of Alliance between Great-Britain *and* Sweden; *concluded at* Stockholm, January 21, 1720.

THIS Treaty refers to two former Treaties made between the said two Crowns in the years 1700, and 1665, as its Basis and Foundation, and confirms the said two Treaties, and amongst others, contains the following Stipulations.

1720.

ARTICLE I.
For a mutual Friendship and good Correspondence in all their Dominions by Sea and Land.

ARTICLE XII.
For a reciprocal and unlimited Freedom of Navigation and Commerce in *Europe*.

ARTICLE XIV.
For a reciprocal Restraint as to harbouring the Ships of an Enemy of the other, or assisting or supplying such Enemy in any Respect.

ARTICLE XV.
For a Salvo to the special Regalities, Rights and Dominion of the Crown of *Sweden* in the *Baltick*, and of the Crown of *Great-Britain* in the *British* Seas.

A Salvo to each to be allowed.

ARTICLE

ARTICLE XVIII.

Freedom of Trade with an Enemy allowed.
For a Freedom of Trade to either Party with Enemy of the other Ally, but with an Except: as to Contraband Goods.

This Treaty expired, and
But by the 20th Article, this Treaty is continue in force for the Term of eighte Years only, fo that unlefs it has been cc tinued or revived by a fubfequent Treaty, t Treaty of 1720, is at prefent expired and c termined.

Treaty of Alliance between Great-Britain *a* Sweden; *concluded at the* Hague, Janua 13, 1700.

this alfo.
THIS Treaty confirms all former Treaties a Alliances between the two Crowns for th feveral Terms of Duration; but by the 18th A ticle it was to have Continuance only for eighte Years, fo that it is now expired with that of 172

Treaty of Alliance and Commerce between Grea Britain *and* Sweden; *concluded at* Wei minfter, Sept. 30, 1674.

THIS Treaty refers to a Treaty of Allian and Commerce made between the two Crow on the 1ft of *March*, 1664-5, to continue in for for ten Years, with an Article therein for the fu rher Continuance and Prolongation of the fame l a fubfequent Treaty, if the contracting Powe fhould think fit; wherefore the faid Treaty 1664-5, is by this Treaty continued for the furth
Ter

Term of two Years, from and after the Expiration of the firſt Term of ten Years: but it does not appear that the ſaid Treaty has been further continued or revived by any ſubſequent Treaty, until it was confirmed by the Treaty of 1720, which laſt being made for eighteen Years only, and the ſaid Term ſince expired, both Treaties muſt be determined together.

There is another Treaty ſet forth in the Books, entitled,

A Treaty of Commerce between Great-Britain *and* Sweden; *made at* Stockholm, February 16, 1666.

BUT this appears to be no more than an Extract made *ex Parte* by *Charles* II. King of Sweden, of ſeveral Marine Articles out of the two Treaties of 1664-5, and 1661, between him and Great-Britain, together with his Edict for the due Obſervance of the ſame by his own Subjects.

Proviſional Treaty of Navigation and Commerce between Great-Britain *and* Denmark; *concluded at* Copenhagen, June 20, 1691.

ARTICLE VI.

IF any *Daniſh* Veſſels ſhall happen to meet with any *Engliſh* Ships of War or Privateers, either on the Coaſt or in the open Sea, in ſuch Caſe the 20th Article of the Marine Treaty concluded at *Nimeguen* in 1679, between the Crown of *Sweden* and the States General ſhall be obſerved between them, and they ſhall regulate themſelves in all Points agreeably thereto.

The

The 20th Article of the Marine Treaty 1679, between *Sweden* and the States Genera[l] referred to in the above recited Treaty 1691.

Ships of War only to send their Boat on board Merchant Ships to inspect their Passports and Certificates.

If any *Swedish* Ships shall, either upon the Coas[t] or in the open Sea, meet with any Ships of W[ar] or Privateers belonging to the States General, [or] their Subjects; in such Case the said Ships of W[ar] shall, for the avoiding of all Inconvenience, ke[ep] without Canon Shot, and send their Boat to su[ch] Ship belonging to *Swedish* Subjects and Inhabitant[s] and board her with two or three Men only, to who[m] the Master or Owner of such *Swedish* Ship shall she[w] his Passport, as likewise his Sea Letters, the one [to] certify concerning the Lading, and the other of t[he] Place of Habitation in the *Swedish* Dominions; [as] likewise the Name of the Master or Owner, a[nd] also of the Ship, whereby it may be known wheth[er] there be any Contraband Goods on board, and t[he] Quality of the Ship and of the Master or Owner m[ay] sufficiently appear: To which Passports and S[ea] Letters entire Faith and Credit shall be given.

Treaty of Alliance and Commerce betwe[en] *Great-Britain and Denmark; concluded* [at] *Westminster, November 29, 1669.*

ARTICLE I.

Perpetual Peace and Amity in all Places.

THERE shall be from hence forward a tru[e] sincere and perfect Amity, Peace and A[l]liance between both the most Serene Kings, the[ir] Heirs and Successors, and likewise between the[ir] Kingdoms, States, Provinces, Dominions, Cou[n]tries, Islands, Cities, Subjects, Vassals, of whats[o]ever Condition, Dignity or Degree, by Land a[nd]

y Sea, in Rivers and fresh Waters, and in all Places
s well within *Europe* as without, so that the one
1all no ways hurt, injure or incommode the King-
oms, Countries, Provinces and Dominions, People
r Subjects of the other, nor as far as in them lies
iffer them to be injured by any other; but they
1all rather shew true Friendship and Affection to-
'ards each other, and upon all Occasions promote
1e Welfare and Utility of each other, and of their
ubjects mutually, as they would their own, and to
1e utmost of their Power, by Deed and by Counsel,
revent and avert all Injuries and Wrongs whatever.

ARTICLE V.

It shall be free for the Subjects of both Kings to _{Free Intercourse and Commerce.}
to the Kingdoms, Provinces, Marts, Ports and
ivers of the other, with their Merchandizes, by
and and by Sea, in Time of Peace, without any
icence or Passport, general or special, and there
abide, and traffick, so as they pay the usual
ustoms: Saving always the Sovereignty and Right
both Kings in their own Kingdoms, Provinces,
ountries and Territories respectively.

This Stipulation for a general Liberty of
Navigation and Commerce is restrained by an
Exception in the next Article, as to such *Da-* _{Exceptions to the above Article.}
nish Ports as had been prohibited by former
Treaties for *English* Subjects to enter into or
trade in; and as to the *British* Colonies, which
are prohibited to the *Danish* Subjects, without
special Licence from the Sovereigns of such
Ports and Colonies respectively.

ARTICLE X.

The Subjects of both Crowns, carrying on their _{Trading Ships not to be forced out of their Course, or to un-liver their Cargo.}
rade by Sea, and sailing near the Coasts of either
ingdom, shall not be obliged to enter into any
rt whatsoever out of their direct Course, but
all be at Liberty to pursue their intended Voyage,

with-

without being any ways hindred or detained; a[nd] when forced into Port by Strefs of Weather, a[nd] there lying at Anchor, they shall not be compell[ed] to unliver, barter or sell their Goods, but it sha[ll] be lawful for them to dispose of the same at the Pleasure, and do whatever else they shall jud[ge] most conducive to their Affairs; provided nothin[g] be done whereby either Prince may be defrauded [or] prejudiced in his Rights and Customs.

ARTICLE XVI.

<small>Either Party may trade with an Enemy of the other in all Goods except Contraband.</small>   It shall be lawful for either Confederate, h[is] People or Subjects, to carry on Trade with the En[e]mies of the other, and to carry and supply the[m] with all Manner of Goods (Contraband Goo[ds] only excepted) without any Molestation, unless be in Ports and Places actually besieged by the [o]ther Ally; in which Case they shall be at Libert[y] either to dispose of their Goods to the Besiegers, [or] to convey them to some other Port or Place whic[h] is not besieged.

ARTICLE XX.

<small>All Ships to carry Passports and Certificates, during a War with either Confederate.</small>   But least this Liberty of Navigation and Passa[ge] for one Ally, his Subjects and Inhabitants, migh[t] during a War, which the other may be engaged i[n] by Sea or by Land with any other State, be [of] Prejudice to such other Ally; and the Goods an[d] Merchandize belonging to the Enemy be fraudu[tu]lently concealed under the colourable Pretence [of] their being in Amity together; wherefore, in orde[r] to prevent all Frauds of that Sort, and to remov[e] all Suspicion, it is thought proper, that the Ship[s,] Merchandizes and Ships Crew belonging to th[e] other Ally, be furnished upon their Voyages wit[h] Passports and Certificates according to the Form an[d] Tenor following, viz.

For.

Form of the Danish *Passport and Certificate.*

Christian the Fifth, by the Grace of God, King of *Denmark* and *Norway, &c.*

BE it known to all and singular Persons who shall see these our Letters of Passport, that our Subject and Citizen of our City of   hath humbly represented to us, that the   ship called the   of the Port of   of   e Burthen of   Tons, doth appertain to him d certain other of our Subjects, and that they e the sole Proprietors of the same, and that the   id Ship is laden with certain Goods, a Particular hereof is contained in a Cocket, which has been ade out by the Officers of our Customs, and is w on board the said Ship; and that the same be- ngs to our Subjects, or others having an Interest erein, who are the Subjects of neutral Powers; d that she is ready to depart from the Port of   in order to proceed to some other Place or   laces, where she may commodiously traffick with   e said Goods, which are not Contraband, nor ap- rtaining to either of the Parties now engaged in ᵀar; or in order fairly to earn her Freight; all hich having been attested by our said Subject, by a   ᵀriting duly signed by him, and affirmed by Vir- e of his Oath to be true, upon Pain of Confisca- ɔn of the said Goods, we have thought proper to ·ant him these our Letters of Passport; and there- re we desire and request all Governors of Coun- ¡es, and Commanders at Sea, all Kings, Princes, ates, and free Towns, and particularly the Parties ɔw engaged in War, and their Commanders, Ad- irals, Generals, Officers, Governors of Ports, ɔmmanders of Ships, Captains, Owners, and all ·hers having any Command at Sea, or the Guard ₍ any Port, whom the said Ship shall happen to   eet with, or to fall in with any of their Fleets or   iips at Sea, or to arrive at any of their Ports;

that

that in Virtue of the Alliance and Amity wh
subsist between us and the King or State, they
only suffer the said Master with the Ship
Men, Goods, and all Merchandizes which are
board her, to pursue his Voyage towards any Pl
whatsoever with full Liberty, without being
ways molested, hindred or detained, but that t
likewise shew him all kind Offices of Civility,
unto our Subject, if any Occasion should off
which we and our Subjects shall be ready to
knowledge on the like or any other Occasion. Giv
this   Day of   in the Year

We the President, Consuls, and Senators of t
Town of   do attest and certify, that *N.*
Citizen and Inhabitant of the City or Town
         on the   Day of   in the Year
came and appeared personally before us, and
clared to us by Virtue of the Oath, by which he
bound to our Sovereign Lord the King, that
Ship or Vessel named   of the Port of
of the Burthen of   Tons, belongs to the Po
City or Town of   in the Province of
and that the said Ship does really and truly app
tain to him, and is now ready to depart direct
from the Port of   laden with the Goods sp
cified in the Cocket which he hath received fro
the Officers of the Customs, and that he hath
firmed upon his said Oath, that the above me
tioned Ship, together with the Goods and Me
chandizes with which she is laden, belongs to
said Majesty's Subjects only, and that she does n
carry any Prohibited Goods appertaining to eith
of the Parties now engaged in War.

In Witness whereof, we have caused the prese
Certificate to be signed by the Syndick of our Tow
and have thereunto put our Seal. Given, &c.

(161)

The original Paſſport ſhould be in *Latin*, as the Treaty was made originally in that Language; but the Form of the Paſſport is no where publiſhed with the *Latin* Treaty.

Whenever therefore any Merchandizes, Goods, Ships and Men of either Confederate, his Subjects or Inhabitants ſhall be met with in the open Sea, Freights, Ports, Roads, Lands, or in any Places whatſoever, by any publick Ships of War or Privateers, or by the Men, Subjects or Inhabitants of the other Confederate, upon exhibiting the ſaid Letters of Paſſport only, nothing further ſhall be required of them, nor ſhall any further Search or Inquiry be made in relation to the Goods, Ships or Men; much leſs ſhall they be any ways injured or moleſted, but they ſhall be moſt freely diſmiſſed, in order to purſue their intended Courſe and Voyage: but in caſe this ſolemn and ſtated Form of the Paſſport and Certificate be not exhibited, or there appear other juſt and ſtrong Cauſe of Suſpicion, then ſuch Ship ought to be viſited; which however is to be underſtood to be allowed of in ſuch Caſe only and not otherwiſe: If any thing ſhall be done by either Party againſt the other Confederate, contrary to the true and genuine Senſe of this Article, both Confederates ſhall take care that their Subjects and Inhabitants reſpectively, who ſhall tranſgreſs therein, be ſeverely puniſhed, and that ample and immediate Satisfaction be made to the other Confederate, his Subjects and Inhabitants, for all Loſſes, Injuries and Charges ſo ſuſtained or incurred.

All Ships to be diſmiſſed on exhibiting their Paſſports, unleſs upon ſtrong Suſpicion.

ARTICLE XXII.

No Veſſels or Ships, nor any Goods or Merchandize whatever, which ſhall be laden on board any Ships of any Sort, Kind or Quality whatſoever, how-

No Ship or Goods of either to be made Prize, but upon legal Proceeding.

M

howsoever taken, and belonging to any Subjects of either King, shall be adjudged as Prize under any Colour or Pretence whatsoever, but upon judicial Examination and legal Proceeding in due Form of Law, in a Court of Admiralty lawfully constitute for that Purpose, in order to judge of such Maritime Captures.

ARTICLE XXIII.

Ships or Goods not to be arrested or detained unless for publick Defence or by legal Arrest.

Captains of Ships or their Pilots, Soldiers or Mariners belonging to them, or the Ships themselv and the Goods and Merchandizes with which the shall be laden, may not be detained by any Seizu or Arrest by Virtue of any general or special Ord of any Person, or for any Cause, unless it be for the Defence and Preservation of the Kingdoms; b this shall not be understood to intend such legal A rests as shall be made by the Authority of the Law by reason of any Contract with any other, or f other just Cause, in which Cases it shall be free proceed in all Things according to the due Cou of Law and Justice.

ARTICLE XXVIII.

Ships of War of one Party to protect all Ships of the other.

Any Guard Ships, or Ships of War of eith Party, which shall happen to meet or come up wi any Merchant Ships, or other Ships whatsoever b longing to the other Confederate or his Subject either within *Europe* or without, holding the sa Course, shall be obliged to guard and protect th as long as they shall continue to hold the sa Course.

ARTICLE XXIX.

Pirates not to be harboured or assisted.

For the greater Security of Commerce and Fr dom of Navigation, it is agreed and conclud that neither Party, as far as may be and in th lies, shall suffer any publick Pirates, or such l Robbers, to harbour in any of their Ports, or to shelte

sheltered or supplied with Provisions by any of their Subjects or Inhabitants, or assisted in any way; but on the contrary, they shall use their Endeavours, that all such Pirates and Robbers, and their Accomplices and Abettors, be apprehended and brought to condign Judgment, and that all Ships and Merchandizes, as much as can be found of them, be restored to the true and legal Owners or their Attorneys, provided their Right in them be made out by due and legal Proofs in the Court of Admiralty for Maritime Causes.

Ships and Goods piratically taken to be restored.

ARTICLE XXX.

The Subjects and People of both Parties shall always have free Access to the Ports and Coasts of the other Confederate, and it shall be lawful for them to abide there, and to depart from thence, and to pass through all the Seas and Territories of both Kings respectively (so as they do no Injury or Damage) not only with Merchant Ships and Vessels of Burthen, but likewise with Ships of War, whether they be publick Ships, or Privateers acting under special Commissions; and whether they be drove in by Stress of Weather, or for avoiding the Danger of the Sea, or to repair their Ships, or buy Provisions; provided they do not exceed the Number of six Ships of War when they come in voluntarily, nor stay in or near such Ports any longer than shall be needful for repairing their Ships, or buying Provisions and other Necessaries: And if upon Occasion they should be desirous of entering into such Ports with any greater Number of Ships of War, it shall not be lawful for them so to do, without timely Notice of their Arrival being first given by Letter, and previous Leave obtained from those to whom such Ports shall appertain; but if they shall be compelled by Storm or other urgent Necessity to put into any Harbour, in such Case, notwithstanding the Want of such previous Notice, the Ships shall

All Ships of either Party forced in, to be harboured and assisted.

Number of Ships of War coming in voluntarily, limited,

except previous Notice and Leave for more.

shall not be limited to any certain Number, on Condition neverthelefs that the Commander of such Ships do immediately upon their Arrival, certify to the chief Magistrate or Governor of that Place, Port or Coast where they shall happen to arrive, the Cause of his Arrival; and they must not continue there any longer than the Time allowed by such chief Magistrate or Governor, nor do or attempt any Act of Hostility in such Ports, nor any thing prejudicial to the Confederate to whom such Ports belong.

Their Time of stay limited.

ARTICLE XXXI.

Subjects of either Party not to accept or act under any Commissions against the other.

It shall not be lawful for the Subjects of the said Kings, or the Inhabitants of the Kingdoms and Countries under their Obedience, to procure any Commissions or Letters of Reprizals from any Prince or State, with whom either Confederate shall be at Variance or open War: much lefs shall they any ways injure or molest the Subjects of either by Virtue of such Letters; and both the said Kings shall strictly enjoin their own Subjects respectively, that they do not procure or accept of any such Commissions from any Princes or States whatsoever, but shall, as much as in them lies, absolutely prohibit and prevent any Depredations to be committed by Virtue of such Commission.

ARTICLE XXXII.

Ships of either Party taken in any Port of the other, to be pursued and restored.

If any Ship or Ships belonging to the Subjects of either Kingdom be taken in the Ports of either by any third Party, they in whose Port or Dominion whatsoever such Ships shall be taken, shall be obliged to use their utmost Endeavours in Conjunction with the other Party, to pursue and recover such Ship or Ships, and to restore them to the proper Owners; which however must be done at the proper Costs and Charges of such Owners, or of those who have an Interest therein.

ARTICLE

ARTICLE XXXIII.

In cafe there fhall be found in any Ships taken by the Subjects of either Confederate, and brought into any Port belonging to the other, any Mariners or other Perfons being Subjects of that Confederate into whofe Port or Rivers fuch Prize fhall be brought, they fhall be civilly treated by the Captors, and immediately fet at Liberty without any Ranfom.

Subjects of either taken in a Prize and brought into their own Port, to be fet at Liberty.

ARTICLE XXXIV.

If any Ship of War of either Crown fhall happen to take a Ship belonging to the other, laden with Prohibited Goods, it fhall not be lawful for the Commander of fuch Captor to open or break up any Chefts, Cafks or Packs found therein, nor to remove or any ways alienate any of the Goods, until they are firft brought on Shore, and an Inventory be made of them in the Prefence of the Judges of Maritime Caufes.

Prohibited Goods on board Ships of either Party, not to be meddled with, 'till brought on Shore and duly inventoried.

ARTICLE XXXV.

For the greater Security of the Subjects of both Kings, and that the greater Care may be taken that no Violence be done or offered to any of them by the faid Ships of War, his *Britannick* Majefty's Captains of his Ships of War, and all other his Subjects, fhall be ftrictly ordered and enjoined that they no ways injure or moleft his *Danifh* Majefty's Subjects; and if they tranfgrefs herein, their Perfons and all their Goods fhall be bounden and liable, until juft and ample Satisfaction and Compenfation be made for all Damage fo done by them, and for all Advantages which may have arifen or fhall arife to them therefrom: In like manner, all Commanders of Ships of War belonging to his *Danifh* Majefty, and all other his Subjects whatfoever, fhall be ftrictly enjoined under the like Penalties, not to in-

Subjects of both Parties to be enjoined not to injure the other, on Pain of full Reftitution.

injure or moleſt any of his *Britannick* Majeſty's Subjects: Provided nevertheleſs that all Actions in ſuch Caſes ſhall be tried and determined by due and legal Proceſs in the Court of Admiralty of the ſaid Kings reſpectively; or if either Party, being an Alien in that Place where the Matter in queſtion is to be tried and ſettled, ſhall rather chuſe it before certain ſpecial Commiſſaries to be immediately appointed by either King to whom it ſhall belong, upon the Requeſt of ſuch Party; ſo as all Proceedings of this Sort ſhall not only be carried on in the moſt eaſy and moderate way in Point of Expence, but ſhall likewiſe be finally determined within the Space of three Months at fartheſt.

<small>All Actions to be tried in the Court of Admiralty, or by ſpecial Commiſſaries, if either Party be an Alien.</small>

The Books make mention of another Treaty made in the following Year, under Title of

Articles of Alliance and Commerce between Great-Britain *and* Denmark; *concluded at* Copenhagen, *the* 11*th of* July, 1670.

BUT this ſeems to be no more than a *French* Tranſlation, or rather an Extract (it being not quite ſo full and compleat as the other) of the original Treaty made in *Latin* in 1669; or it may poſſibly be a Renewal of the Treaty made the foregoing Year, but contains no further Articles or new Matter.

Treaty

Treaty of League and Alliance between Great-Britain *and* Denmark; *concluded in the Year* 1661.

THE 1st, 6th, 19th, 20th, and 21st Articles of this Treaty are comprehended in the 1st, th, 29th and 30th Articles of the above recited Treaty of 1669.

1661.

Treaty of League and Alliance between Great-Britan *and* Denmark; *concluded at* Westminster, September 15, 1654.

THE 1st, 2d, 13th and 14th Articles of this Treaty are comprehended in the 1st, 5th, 9th and 30th Articles of the Treaty of 1669.

1654.

Treaty of Peace and Amity between Great-Britain *and* Denmark; *concluded at* London, April 19, 1621.

THE 1st, 13th and 14th Articles of this Treaty are comprehended in the 1st, 5th and th Articles of the Treaty of 1669.

1621.

Articles and Clauses of Treaties between Great-Britain *and* Denmark, *ratifying or renewing former Treaties.*

Treaty of 1669.

ARTICLE XLI.

THE former Treaties which have been made at any time heretofore between the said Allies or the Kings their Predecessors, as well for the Kingdoms of *Great-Britain,* &c. as for the hereditary Kingdoms of *Denmark* and *Norway,* &c. respectively, shall not be deemed to be infringed or abrogated in any the least Point, by any Agreement or Article contained in this present Treaty but they shall remain in their full Force, Effect and Virtue, in so far as they are not contrary or repugnant to this present Treaty, or any Article thereof

The 12th Article of the Treaty of 1661 and the 20th Article of the several Treaties of 1639, and 1621, are almost verbatim the same with the said 41st Article of 1669 and entirely so in Effect, as to the ratifying former Treaties.

Treaty of Amity and Commerce between Great-Britain *and the Duke of* Savoy *(now King of* Sardinia*) concluded at* Florence, September *the* 19*th,* 1669.

ARTICLE I.

THAT Peace which has not been interrupted for many Years, is by thefe Prefents ratified nd confirmed between the King of *Great-Britain* nd the Duke of *Savoy,* &c. and their Subjects fhall : obliged on all Occafions to fhew all kind of Cility and reciprocal Affection towards each other.

1669.
Former Peace renewed.

ARTICLE II.

It fhall be lawful and free for all Kind of Ships nd Veffels belonging to his *Britannick* Majefty or s Subjects, to carry and bring into the Ports of *illa Francha, Nice,* or *Saint Hofpice,* all Things hatfoever, and all Kind of Merchandize of what ature foever and wherever produced, and they ay freely land and lodge all fuch Goods and Merandizes in any Places within fuch Ports for the ecurity and Prefervation of the fame, without any onfifcation, or the Exaction of any Impoft or)uty whatfoever, in cafe that fuch Goods or any art of them be not fold in fuch Ports.

Free Liberty for *Britifh* Subjects to import and land all Goods in certain Ports.

ARTICLE V.

All Kind of Ships and Veffels belonging to his *ritannick* Majefty or his Subjects, which fhall fail om *England,* or from any other Port under his Iajefty's Obedience, or belonging to his Dominons, which fhall not be infected with the Plague, nd fhall arrive at the Ports of *Nice, Villa Francha,* · *Saint Hofpice,* with Certificates and Atteftations · their good Health, and not having traded on their

Britifh Ships coming from any *Englifh* Ports with Certificates of Health, not to perform Quarantine.

their Voyage in any Place, or with any Perſo
ſuſpected to be infected, ſhall be free from pe
forming any Quarantine, or obſerving any Days
Purgation whatever; and all Perſons on board ſu
Ships ſhall be at Liberty to trade immediately
ſuch Ports.

ARTICLE XIII.

Britiſh Ships of War to be well received, ſupplied and protected in the three Ports of Savoy.

Whenever any Ships of War belonging to I
Britannick Majeſty ſhall enter into any of the ſa
Ports, they ſhall be received there with the ſan
Honours in all Points as any other Ships or Veſſ
belonging to any other Prince whatſoever; and d
ring the Time of the Continuance of any ſu
Ships in the ſaid Ports, they ſhall not be refuſ
any thing which ſhall be neceſſary or convenient f
them, they paying a reaſonable Price for the ſam
and with regard to Proviſions, it ſhall be lawf
for all Perſons employed, to provide and furni
Proviſions for ſuch Ships, to contract for the Pu
chaſe of all Things neceſſary and convenient f
their Suſtenance throughout his Royal Highneſ
Dominions, and to bring all Things ſo purchaſ
into the ſaid Ports, without paying any Dut
Cuſtom or Impoſt whatſoever, but only payi
the prime Coſt for the ſame: And his Majeſty
ſaid Ships of War ſhall, during their Continuan
in the ſaid Ports, be protected and defended agai
any Perſon whatſoever, who ſhall offer to do the
any Violence, or to commit Hoſtilities agair
them.

Tre

Treaty of Commerce between Great-Britain *and the* Sultan *of the* Turks: *Wherein the antient Conventions made in the Reigns of Queen* Elizabeth, *King* James, *and* Charles I. *are recited and confirmed; concluded at* Adrianople, *in* September 1675.

Or rather,

A Grant and Confirmation of Privileges then made by the Sultan *to the* English *Nation.*

ARTICLE I.

THAT the *English* Nation and the *English* Merchants, and all other Nations or Merants that do or shall arrive under the Colours and otection of *England*, with their Ships, great and all, Merchandize, Effects, and all their other ods, shall at all Times sail securely in our Seas, d go and come with all manner of Safety and eedom, in all Places within the Limits of our Imrial Dominions, in such manner that no Person atsoever of that Nation, nor his Goods or Efts, shall receive any Molestation or Impediment m any Person whatsoever. {Free Navigation for all *English* Ships and Goods.}

ARTICLE IV.

All *English* Ships or Vessels, great or small, may all Times come and enter into any Port or Harur whatsoever of our Dominions, and depart m thence when they please, without being de'd or hinder'd by any Person whatsoever. {Free Ingress and Egress for all *English* Ships.}

ARTICLE V.

That if any Accident happen to any *English* ip, great or small, from the Danger of the Sea, or {*English* Ships in Distress to be succour'd and supplied.}

or any other Neceffity, all Ships, as well Impe
as thofe belonging to private Perfons, which f
happen to be near fuch Ship in Diftrefs, and
other Ships which fhall be failing upon the Seas
be near enough to fuccour them, fhall be oblige
give them Aid and Affiftance ; and when they f
be entered into our Ports or Harbours, they 1
ftay there as long as they pleafe, buy all mar
of Provifions and other Neceffaries for their N
ney, and take in frefh Water, without any Trou
or Hindrance from any Perfon whatfoever.

ARTICLE XVII.

Englifh Ships not to be molefted, but kindly treated out at Sea.

Our Galleys, Ships, or other Veffels of our E
pire, which fhall meet with any *Englifh* Ships
Sea, fhall not do, or give, nor fuffer the leaft
jury or Moleftation to be done or given to the
nor ftop them, or take or demand any thing fr
them, but fhall falute them, and they fhall fhev
reciprocal Kindnefs to one another, without of
ing any Affront.

ARTICLE XVIII.

The *Englifh* to enjoy all Privileges granted to any other Chriftian Nation.

All the particular Privileges and Stipulatio
which have in time paft been granted to the *Fren*
the *Venetians*, or any other Chriftian Nation wh
ever, whofe King was in Peace and Friendfhip w
the *Porte*, are hereby given and granted in
fame Manner to the *Englifh* Nation, to the E
that the Tenor of our prefent Imperial Treaty n
at all Times hereafter be obferved by all manner
Perfons, and that nobody may in any manner p
tend, under any Colour whatfoever, to contrav
or violate the fame.

ARTICLE XXII.

The *Englifh* to trade freely in *Turky*, and to export all Goods, excepting Arms and Ammunition.

The *Englifh* Nation, and all that come under
Colours of *England*, with their Ships, great or fm
may fail, traffick, buy, fell, and live in all Place

r Dominions, and, excepting Fire-Arms, Gun-
wder, and other such like Merchandize, may
t on board and carry away in their Ships any
ods of our Dominions as they please, without
 Trouble or Hindrance of any Person whatever;
l their Ships and Vessels may freely come into
l securely cast Anchor, and trade at all Times in
 Places of our Dominions, and there buy Provi-
ns, and all other Things for their Money, with-
: any Contradiction or Hindrance of any Per-
ı whatsoever.

ARTICLE XXXVI.

The *English* Merchants, and all others who shall *Free Trade to and from Muscovy and Persia, paying the ordinary Duties only.*
under the Colours of *England*, may with all
nner of Security, trade, sell, and buy, through-
: all our Dominions, all Sorts of Merchandize,
ose only excepted which are prohibited;) and they
y likewise go and trade to *Muscovy* by Sea or
nd, or by the way of the River *Tanais*, or *Don*,
through *Russia*, and may bring their Merchan-
:e from thence into our Empire: And in like
nner they may go to trade in *Persia*, and return
ough any Part thereof which we have conquer'd
l the Confines of the same, without any Hin-
ınce or Molestation from our Officers, and they
ıll pay the Customs and other Duties of that
untry, and nothing more.

ARTICLE XXXVII.

The *English* Merchants, and all others who shall *Free Trade to A-leppo, &c. on pay-ing the antient Custom.*
under the Colours of *England*, may freely and
ely traffick and trade in *Aleppo*, *Cairo*, *Scio*, *Smyr-*
:, and in all Places of our Dominions, paying ac-
:ding to antient Custom *Three per Cent.* for all
ir Merchandizes, and no more.

ARTICLE

ARTICLE XLVIII.

Pirates of Tunis and Algiers not to moleſt or injure the Engliſh in their Perſons or Goods.

For as much as it is notorious, that certain rates of *Tunis* and *Algiers*, in Breach of our Imperial Capitulations, and contrary to our Will and Intention, do take and carry off by Sea, the Ships, Merchandize, and Men who are the Subjects of the King of *England*, and of other Kings and States in Alliance with our Supreme *Porte*, to the great Damage and Prejudice of the ſaid *Engliſh* Nation; for theſe Cauſes we command, and do by theſe Preſents enjoin, that Mandates be iſſued and diſpatched for the entire and perfect Reſtitution of all Goods and Merchandize ſo taken from the *Engliſh* Nation, and that all the *Engliſh* who have been taken and made Slaves, or impriſoned by the ſaid Pirates, be forthwith ſet at Liberty; and if after the Day of the Date of our preſent Imperial Capitulations, the ſaid Pirates of *Tunis* and *Algiers* ſhall continue to commit any Robberies or other Outrages upon them, and will not reſtore their Goods and Men, we forbid the ſaid Pirates to be received into any Port of our Dominions, and particularly into the Harbours of *Tunis*, *Algiers*, *Modon*, or *Coron*; and we do expreſsly forbid our Beglerbeys and other Miniſters to permit them to enter therein, or to ſuffer them to be there received or entertained; but on the contrary, we command the ſaid Beglerbeys, Cadys, and other Miniſters, to proſecute, baniſh, and puniſh them.

ARTICLE LIV.

Free Importation of all Goods into Turky and Exportation of all but Goods prohibited.

The *Engliſh* Merchants may freely come to all the Ports of our Dominions to trade, and to import woollen Cloth, Kerſeys, Spices, Pewter, Lead, and all other Merchandize, and nobody ſhall give them any Trouble or Hindrance: They may alſo buy and export all Sorts of Merchandize, except what is prohibited, without Hindrance or Moleſtation on; and after they have paid the Customs conformably to the present Imperial Capitulation and antient Usage, the Commissioners of the Customs and other Officers shall demand nothing more.

ARTICLE LIX.

The Galleys and other Ships of the Imperial Navy, sailing from the Dominions of the Grand Signior, and meeting any *English* Ships at Sea, shall not molest or retard them in their Voyage, nor take any thing whatsoever from them, but they shall always shew right good Friendship towards each other, without doing each other the least Damage; and this being accordingly declared in the Imperial Capitulations, the Beys and Captains sailing upon the High Seas, and those of *Algiers*, *Tunis*, and *Tripoli*, meeting with *English* Ships sailing from one Port to another, shall not take away any of their Money or Goods, on Pretence that they have Goods of the Enemy on board, nor search them on that Account, nor molest or retard them in their Voyage; so that their Goods shall only be examined at the Entrance of Forts, and in the Harbours where the Searchers belonging to the Customs are used to go on board; and when they are out at Sea, they shall not be liable to any farther Search or Inquiry

Turkish Ships of War, or those of *Algiers*, &c. not to molest or search any *English* Ships at Sea.

Articles of Peace and Commerce between Gre
Britain *and the Emperor of* Fez *and* M
rocco; *concluded at* Mequinez, January
14*th*, 1727-8.

ARTICLE I.

1727-8. THAT all *Moors* and *Jews*, Subjects to
Emperor of *Morocco*, shall be allowed a f
Traffick, *viz.* to buy or sell for thirty Days in
City of *Gibraltar*, or Island of *Minorca*, and
to reside in either Place, but to depart with th
Effects, without Lett or Molestation, to any P
of the said Emperor of *Morocco's* Dominions.

ARTICLE IV.

All *British* Sub-
jects taken by any
Cruizers, to be set
at Liberty.
That all his *Britannick* Majesty's Subjects,
well Passengers as others, taken by any of the E
peror of *Fez* and *Morocco's* Cruizers, on board a
foreign Ship or Vessel whatever, shall immediat
be set at Liberty, and sent to the City of *Gibr*
tar.

ARTICLE V.

Free Liberty to
buy all Necessa-
ries for the *Bri-*
tish Fleet, or for
the City of *Gib-*
raltar.
That there be Permission for buying of Prov
sions and all other Necessaries for his *Britann*
Majesty's Fleet, or for the City of *Gibraltar*,
any of the Emperor of *Fez* and *Morocco's* S
Ports at the Market Prices, and the same to
shipped off without paying Customs, as has be
extorted lately, contrary to the Treaty of Pea
subsisting.

Artic

Articles of Peace and Commerce between Great-Britain *and* Algiers; *ratified, confirmed, and renewed at* Algiers, October *the* 29th, 1716.

ARTICLE I.

THAT the Ships and other Veſſels, and the Subjects and People of either Side, ſhall not henceforth do to each other any Harm, Offence or Injury, either in Word or Deed, but ſhall treat each other with all poſſible Reſpect and Friendſhip.

1716. Mutual Amity and Forbearance from Injuries.

ARTICLE II.

That from this Time forward for ever, the Iſland of *Minorca* and City of *Gibraltar* ſhall be eſteemed in every Reſpect by the Government and People of *Algiers*, to be Part of his *Britannick* Majeſty's Dominions, and the Inhabitants thereof to be looked upon as his Majeſty's natural Subjects, in the ſame manner as if they had been born in any other Part of *Great-Britain*, and they with their Ships and Veſſels wearing *Britiſh* Colours, and being furniſhed with proper Paſſes, ſhall be permitted freely to trade and traffick in any Part of the Dominions of *Algiers*, and ſhall paſs without any Moleſtation whatſoever, and ſhall have the ſame Liberties and Privileges that are ſtipulated in this, and have been made in all other Treaties in the behalf of the *Britiſh* Nation and Subjects, and therefore none of the Cruizers of *Algiers*, ſhall at any Time cruize within Sight of the Ports of the ſaid Iſland of *Minorca* and City of *Gibraltar*.

Minorca and Gibraltar to be reputed in all Reſpects Part of the Britiſh Dominions; and the Inhabitants entitled to the ſame Privileges.

Algerines not to cruize within Sight of either.

ARTICLE III.

That if an *Engliſh* Ship ſhall receive on board any Paſſengers and Goods belonging to the Kingdom of *Algiers*, they ſhall defend them and their Goods

The Engliſh to defend the Perſons and Goods of Algerines on board their Veſſels.

Goods so far as lieth in their Power, and not deliver them to their Enemies; and the better to prevent any unjust Demands being made upon th Crown of *Great-Britain*, and to avoid Disputes an Differences that may arise, all Goods and Merchandizes that shall from henceforward be shipped b the Subjects of *Algiers* on board the Ships c

Such Goods to be registred with the Consul before they are shipped. Vessels of *Great-Britain* upon Freight, shall be fir registred in the Office of *Cancellaria* before th *British* Consul residing in the Port, where the are so shipped, and the Quantity, Quality, an Value thereof shall be expressed; and the Cons is to manifest the same in the Clearance given to th Ship or Vessel before she shall depart; to the En that if any Cause of Complaint should happe hereafter, there may be no greater Claim made o the *British* Nation, than what by this Method ma be proved just and equitable.

ARTICLE IV.

English Ships to go free with proper Passes. That if any of the *Algerine* Cruizers shall mee with any *British* Ships provided with Scollop Passe of either Ships or Settees, that shall fit with thos delivered to them by the *British* Consul, the shall pass free and unmolested.

Articles of Peace and Commerce between Great Britain *and* Algiers, *concluded at* Algiers October 28, 1703.

ARTICLE III.

1703.
All Prizes and American Ships belonging to England to go free with Certificates only.
ALL Prizes taken by any of her Majesty o *Great-Britain*'s Subjects, and all Ships anc Vessels built and fitted out in any of her Majesty' Plantations in *America*, that have not been in *Eng*land, shall not be molested in Case of no Pass, bu a Certificate in Writing, under the Hand of th

ommanding Officer that shall so take Prizes, and a Certificate under the Hands of the Governor or Chief of any of her Majesty's Plantations in *America*, or where any Ship shall be built or fitted, shall be a sufficient Pass for either of them; and our Faith shall be our Faith, and our Word our Word.

Peace confirmed and additional Articles made with the Government of Algiers, *on the 17th of* August, 1700.

ARTICLE I.

WE the Dey, Bashaw and Aga, Governors of the City and Kingdom of *Algiers*, do by these Presents renew and confirm the Peace we so happily enjoy with the King of *Great-Britain* and his Subjects, made in the Year 1682, in every Part and Article, more particularly that of the 8th, wherein it is expressed, no Ship or Vessel belonging to our Government of *Algiers* shall cruize near or in Sight of any of the Roads, Havens or Ports, Towns or Places belonging to the said King of *Great-Britain*, or any ways disturb the Peace and Commerce of the same: And in Compliance with the 8th Article of that Treaty, we do sincerely promise and declare, that such Orders shall for the future be given to all our Commanders, that under a severe Penalty, and our utmost Displeasure, they shall not enter into the Channel of *England*, nor come or cruize in Sight of any Part of his Majesty of *Great-Britain*'s Dominions, any more for the Time to come.

1700.

Treaty of 1682 confirmed.

Algerines not to cruize near any Places belonging to *Great-Britain*, or in the *English* Channel.

ARTICLE II.

English Ships without a Pafs, lawful Prize, with a Saving as to Men, Ships, and Freight.

After the laſt Day of *September*, 1701, if ar Ship of *England* be ſeized, not having a Paſs, tl Goods in that Ship ſhall be Prize, but the Maſte Men, and Ships ſhall be reſtored, and the Freig immediately paid to the ſaid Maſter, to the utmc Value, as he ſhould have had if he had gone ſa. to the Port whither he was bound.

ARTICLE III.

A ſpecial Officer to protect all *English* Ships of War in the Mould of *Algiers*.

That whereas Captain *John Munden* has given good Aſſurance, that he received a great Affro ſome Years paſt from ſome of our rude Sailors our Mould; we do hereby promiſe, that at Times whenever any of the King of *Great-Britain* Ships of War come to this Place, Order ſhall l given to an Officer of the Government immediatel who ſhall attend at the Mould all the Day time d ring their ſtay here, to prevent any ſuch Diſord for the future, that no Miſunderſtanding may ha pen between us; and if any ſuch Diſorder ſhou happen, the Officer of the Mould ſhall ſecure t Perſon or Perſons, and they ſhall be puniſhed wi the utmoſt Severity.

Articles of Peace and Commerce between Grea Britain *and* Algiers; *ratified and confirm on the 5th of* April, 1686.

ARTICLE I.

Mutual Amity and Friendſhip.

THAT the Ships and other Veſſels, Subjeᶜ and People on both Sides, ſhall not fro henceforth do to each other any Harm, Offence, Injury, either in Word or Deed; but they ſh treat each other with all poſſible Reſpect and Frier hip, and that all Demands and Pretenfions whatoever to this Day between both Parties fhall ceafe and be void.

ARTICLE II.

That any of the Ships or other Veffels belonging to the faid King of *Great-Britain*, or to any of his Majefty's Subjects, may fafely come to the Port of *Algiers*, or to any other Port or Place of that Kingdom, there freely to buy and fell, paying the fual Cuftoms of *Ten per Cent.* as in former Times, for fuch Goods as they fell, and the Goods they fell not, they fhall freely carry on board without paying any Duties for the fame; and that they fhall freely depart from thence whenfoever they pleafe without any Stop or Hindrance whatfoever: As to Contraand Merchandize, as Powder, Brimftone, Iron, Plank, and all Sorts of Timber fit for building of Ships, Ropes, Pitch, Tar, Fufils, and other Habiliments of War, his faid Majefty's Subjects fhall pay no Duty for the fame to thofe of *Algiers*.

Free Navigation and Trade for all the Englifh in Algiers, paying the ufual Cuftoms.

ARTICLE III.

That all Ships and other Veffels, as well thofe belonging to the King of *Great-Britain*, or to any of his Majefty's Subjects, as thofe belonging to the Kingdom or People of *Algiers*, fhall freely pafs the Seas, and traffick without any Search, Hindrance or Moleftation from each other; and that all Perfons or Paffengers, of what Country foever, and all Monies, Goods, Merchandizes and Moveables, to whatfoever People or Nation belonging, being on board any of the faid Ships or Veffels, fhall be wholly free, and fhall not be ftopped, taken or plundered, nor receive any Harm or Damage whatfoever from either Party.

Free Paffage and Commerce for all Ships of both Nations; and all Perfons and Goods on board either to be fafe,

ARTICLE IV.

That the *Algiers* Ships of War, or other
meeting with any Merchant Ships or Veſſels
ſaid Majeſty's Subjects, not being in any
Seas appertaining to his Majeſty's Dominio[n]
ſend on board one ſingle Boat with two Sitte[rs]
beſides the ordinary Crew of Rowers; and
more ſhall enter ſuch Merchant Ship or Veſſ[el]
out expreſs Leave from the Commander [of]
but the two Sitters alone; and that upon pr[o]

All Ships on both Sides to paſs freely on producing Paſſes and Certificates.

a Paſs under the Hand and Seal of his Maj[eſty]
whomſoever he ſhall appoint to be Lord Hi[gh Ad-]
miral, or to execute the Office of Lord Hi[gh Ad-]
miral for *England* and *Ireland*, or of the Lor[d High]
Admiral for *Scotland*, for the ſaid Kingdom[s reſpec-]
tively, that the ſaid Boat ſhall preſently
and the Merchant Ship or Veſſel ſhall proce[ed quiet-]
ly on her Voyage; and any of the Ships
or other Veſſels of his ſaid Majeſty meetin[g with]
any Ships or other Veſſels of *Algiers*, if th[e Com-]
mander of any ſuch *Algier* Ship or Veſſel ſ[hall pro-]
duce a Paſs firmed by the chief Governo[r of Al-]
giers, and a Certificate from the *Engliſh* C[onſul re-]
ſiding there, the ſaid *Algier* Ship or Ve[ſſel ſhall]
proceed freely.

ARTICLE V.

Algerines not to force away or uſe any Violence to any Perſons on board an *Engliſh* Ship.

That no Commander or other Perſo[n of any]
Ship or Veſſel of *Algiers*, ſhall take out of [any Ship]
or Veſſel of his ſaid Majeſty's Subjects an[y Perſon]
or Perſons whatſoever, to carry them any[where to]
be examined, or upon any other Prete[nce; nor]
ſhall they uſe any Torture or Violence to [any Per-]
ſon of what Nature or Quality ſoever, [being on]
board any Ship or Veſſel of his Majeſty's [Subjects,]
upon any Pretence whatſoever.

ARTICLE VII.

That no Ship nor any other Vessel of *Algiers* shall have Permission to be delivered up to the Men of *Sallee*, or to go to *Sallee*, or to any other Place at Enmity with the King of *Great-Britain*, to be made use of as Corsairs or Sea Rovers against his said Majesty's Subjects.

Algerine Ships not to be carried to *Sallee*, or elsewhere to be used against *Great-Britain*.

ARTICLE VIII.

That none of the Ships, or other smaller Vessels of *Algiers*, shall remain cruizing near or in Sight of any of his Majesty's Roads, Havens or Ports, Towns and Places, nor any way disturb the Peace and Commerce of the same.

Algerines not to cruize near any *British* Ports, &c.

ARTICLE IX.

That if any Ship or Vessel of *Tunis*, *Tripoli*, or *Sallee*, or of any other Place dependant on them, bring any Ships, Vessels, Men or Goods, belonging to any of his said Majesty's Subjects to *Algiers* or to any other Port or Place in that Kingdom, the Governors there shall not permit them to be sold within the Territories of *Algiers*.

English Ships, Men or Goods, brought into *Algiers* shall not be sold there.

ARTICLE X.

That if any of the Ships of War of the said King of *Great-Britain* do come to *Algiers*, or to any other Port or Place of that Kingdom with any Prize, they may freely sell it, or otherwise dispose of it at their own Pleasure, without being molested by any, and that his Majesty's said Ships of War shall not be obliged to pay Customs in any Port, and that if they shall want Provisions, Victuals, or any other Things, they may freely buy them at the Rates in the Market.

English Ships of War may dispose of any Prizes in *Algiers*, and buy all Necessaries; and to pay no Customs.

ARTICLE XI.

Christian Captives escaping on board English Ships of War, after Notice of their Arrival, not to be remanded.

That when any of his said Majesty's Ships of War shall appear before *Algiers*, upon Notice there of given by the *English* Consul, or by the Commander of the said Ships to the chief Governor of *Algiers*, publick Proclamation shall be immediately made to secure the Christian Captives; and if after that any Christians whatsoever make their Escape on board any of the said Ships of War, they shall not be required back again, nor shall the said Consul or Commander, or any other of his Majesty's Subjects, be obliged to pay any thing for the said Christians.

ARTICLE XII.

No British Subjects to be made Slaves or sold in Algiers.

That henceforward no Subjects of his Majesty of *Great-Britain*, &c. shall be bought or sold, or made Slaves in any Part of the Kingdom of *Algiers*, upon any Pretence whatsoever.

ARTICLE XIX.

Passengers being Subjects to either Party, not to be molested in Persons or Goods on board Enemies Ships.

That no Subject of his said Majesty, being Passenger, and coming or going with his Baggage from or to any Port, shall be any way molested or meddled with, although he be on board any Ship or Vessel in Enmity with *Algiers:* And in like manner no *Algerine* Passenger being on board any Ship or Vessel in Enmity with the said King of *Great Britain*, shall be in any way molested, whether in his Person or in his Goods which he may have laden on board the said Ship or Vessel.

ARTICLE XX.

Mutual Salutes on English Ships of War coming into Algiers.

That at all Times when any Ship of War of the King of *Great-Britain*'s carrying his said Majesty's Flag at the Maintop-mast-head, shall appear before *Algiers*, and come to an Anchor in the Road: That immediately after Notice thereof given by his said

[...]ajesty's Consul, or Officer from the Ship, unto [th]e Dey and Government of *Algiers*, they shall, in [h]onour to his Majesty, cause a Salute of one and [tw]enty Cannon to be shot from the Castles and [P]orts of the City, and that the said Ship shall re[tu]rn the Salute by firing off the same Number of [Ca]non.

ARTICLE XXI.

This Peace shall be in full Force and Virtue, and [co]ntinue for ever.

This Peace perpetual.

ARTICLE XXII.

That in case it shall happen hereafter that any [th]ing is done or committed contrary to this Treaty, [w]hether by the Subjects of the one or the other [P]arty, the Treaty notwithstanding shall subsist in [fu]ll Force, and such Contraventions shall not oc[ca]sion the Breach of this Peace, Friendship and [g]ood Correspondence; but the Party injured shall [am]icably demand immediate Satisfaction for the [sa]id Contraventions, before it be lawful to break [th]e Peace; and if the Fault was committed by any [p]rivate Subjects of either Party, they alone shall [b]e punished as Breakers of the Peace, and Di[st]urbers of the publick Quiet: And our Faith [sh]all be our Faith, and our Word our Word.

Violations and Contraventions by the Subjects of either, shall not make a Breach of the Peace; but Satisfaction to be made, and Offenders punished.

Articles of Peace and Commerce between Great-Britain *and* Algiers; *concluded the* 5th *of* March, 1682.

THIS Treaty is in Substance and almost verbatim the same with the above recited Treaty of 1686, excepting that the Words dependant on them, in the 19th Article of the Treaty of 1686, are

1682.

are not inserted or contained in the correspond*
Article of the Treaty of 1682.

---

*The Form of the Passport referred to in
4th Article of both Treaties of 1686,
1682, and which is subjoined to the Treat*
1682.

The Form of the Passport.

PERMIT the Ship   to pass w
her Crew, Passengers, Goods and Merch.
dizes, without any Lett, Hindrance, Seizure
Molestation, the said Ship appearing to us
good Testimony to belong to our Subjects (or
the Subjects of the King our Sovereign Lord) a
not to a Stranger.

Given under my Seal (or our Seals) a
the Seal of the Office of High A
miral (or of our Office of Admiral
this   Day of   in the Y(
of our Lord

To all Persons to whom these Presents may cc
cern.

By the Command of

1672.
1664.
1662.

The Treaty of Peace, concluded with the *Alg*
rines in 1672, as likewise the Articles of Pea
and Commerce settled and concluded with them l
Admiral Allen, on the 30th of *October* 1664, a
those concluded by Sir *John Lawson* in 1662, a
terwards ratified by the *Grand Signior*, are all con
prehended in the above recited Treaty of 1686.

Artic

'rticles and Clauses of Treaties between Great-Britain *and* Algiers, *reviving or confirming former Treaties.*

Articles of Peace and Commerce between Great-Britain *and* Algiers, *agreed on in* October 1716.

ARTICLE I.

[I]T is agreed and concluded, that from this Day and for ever forwards, the Peace made by Ar[thu]r *Herbert*, Esq; then Admiral of his Majesty's [Fle]et, and Sir *William Soams*, Bart. Ambassador to [the] Grand Signior in the Year 1686, with the additional Articles agreed to with Captain *Munden* and [Co]nsul *Cole*, in the Year 1700.
And likewise the further additional Articles a[gre]ed to with *George Byng*, Esq; then Rear Admiral [of] the Red Squadron of her Majesty's Fleet, in [the] Year 1703, be renewed and confirmed: And [to]gether with the additional Articles agreed to in [thi]s Treaty with Captain *Norbury*, Captain *Eaton*, [an]d *Thomas Thompson*, Esq; his Majesty's Consul at [Al]giers, be kept inviolably between the King of [Gr]eat-Britain and the Dey and Governor of *Algiers* [in] the West, the Aga, Kahya, and the rest of the [Se]niors of the Divan, and between all the Dominions and Subjects of either Side.

Treaties and Articles agreed on 1686, 1700, and 1703, confirmed.

Articles

Articles of Peace and Commerce between Great Britain *and* Algiers, *made in the Year* 1703

ACTICLE I.

Treaties and Articles agreed on in 1682, 1686, and 1700, confirmed.

IT is agreed and concluded, that from this D and for ever forwards, the Peace made by *thur Herbert*, Esq; then Admiral of his Majest Fleet in the *Mediterranean* in the Year 1682, a since confirmed by Sir *William Soams*, Bart. A bassador to the Grand Seignior in the Year 168 with the additional Articles agreed to with Capt. *Munden*, and Consul *Cole*, in the Year 1700, renewed and confirmed (with the further Additi of the Articles agreed to in this Treaty with *Geo: Byng*, Esq; Rear Admiral of the Red Squadron her Majesty's Fleet) be kept inviolably between t Queen of *Great-Britain*, and the Dey, Bashaw, ga, and Governors of the City and Kingdom *Algiers*, and between all the Dominions and St jects of either Side.

Articles of Peace between Great-Britain *a* Tripoly; *concluded* July *the* 19th, 1716

ARTICLE I.

1716. *Perpetual Peace and Amity.*

IN the first Place, it is agreed and conclude that from this Time forward for ever, there sh be a true and inviolable Peace between the M Serene King of *Great-Britain*, and the Most Illu trious Lords and Governors of the City and Kin dom of *Tripoly* in *Barbary*, and between all the D minions and Subjects of either Side; and if t Ships and Subjects of either Party shall happen meet upon the Seas or elsewhere, they shall r mol

\]olest each other, but shall shew all possible respect and Friendship.

ARTICLE III.

That all Ships and other Vessels, as well those belonging to the said King of *Great-Britain*, or to any of his Majesty's Subjects, as those belonging to the Kingdom or People of *Tripoly*, shall freely pass the Seas and traffick where they please, without any Search, Hindrance or Molestation from each other, and that all Persons or Passengers, of what Country soever, and all Monies, Goods, Merchandizes and Moveables, to whatsoever People or Nation belonging, being on board any of the said Ships or Vessels, shall be wholly free, and shall not be stopped, taken or plundered, or receive any Harm or Damage whatsoever from either Party.

All Ships on both Sides to pass freely with all Persons and Goods.

ARTICLE IV.

That the *Tripoly* Ships of War, or any other Vessels thereunto belonging, meeting with any Merchant Ships or other Vessels of the King of *Great-Britain*'s Subjects (not being in any of the Seas appertaining to any of his Majesty's Dominions) may send on board one single Boat with two Sitters, besides the ordinary Crew of Rowers; and no more but the two Sitters to enter any of the said Merchant Ships, or any other Vessels, without the express Leave of the Commander of every such Ship or Vessel, and then, upon producing to them a Pass under the Hand and Seal of the Lord High Admiral of *England*, the said Boat shall presently depart, and the Merchant Ship or Ships, Vessel or Vessels, shall proceed freely on her or their Voyage; and altho' the Commander or Commanders of the said Merchant Ship or Ships, Vessel or Vessels, produce no Pass from the Lord High Admiral of *England*, yet if the major Part of the Ship or Vessel's Company be Subjects to the said King of *Great-Britain,*

All Ships on both Sides to pass freely on producing Passes, or the major Part of the Crew being Subjects.

Britain, the said Boat shall presently depart, a[nd] the Merchant Ship or Ships, Vessel or Vessels sh[all] proceed freely on her or their Voyage: And any [of] the said Ships of War, or other Vessels of his sa[id] Majesty, meeting with any Ship or Ships, Vessel [or] Vessels belonging to *Tripoly*, if the Commander [or] Commanders of any such Ship or Ships, Vessel [or] Vessels, shall produce a Pass signed by the ch[ief] Governors of *Tripoly*, and a Certificate from t[he] *English* Consul residing there; or if they have [no] such Pass or Certificate, yet if the major Part [of] their Ship's Company be *Turks*, *Moors*, or Slav[es] belonging to *Tripoly*, then the said *Tripoly* Ship [or] Ships, Vessel or Vessels, shall proceed freely.

ARTICLE V.

Ships of *Tripoly* shall not force away or use Violence to any Person on board any *English* Ships.

That no Commander or other Person of an[y] Ship or Vessel of *Tripoly* shall take out of any Shi[p] or Vessel of his said Majesty's Subjects, any Pers[on] or Persons whatsoever, to carry them any where t[o] be examined, or upon any other Pretence; no[r] shall use any Torture or Violence unto any Perso[n] of what Nation or Quality soever, being on boar[d] any Ship or Vessel of his Majesty's Subjects upo[n] any Pretence whatsoever.

ARTICLE VII.

No Ships of *Tripoly* to be carried to any Enemy of Great-Britain.

That no Ship or any other Vessel of *Tripoly* sha[ll] have Permission to be delivered up, or to go to an[y] other Place at Enmity with the said King of *Great Britain*, to be made use of as Corsairs against hi[s] said Majesty's Subjects.

ARTICLE VIII.

British Ships, Men or Goods taken by an Enemy, not to be sold in *Tripoly*.

That if any Ship or Vessel of *Tunis*, *Algiers*, *Te*tuan or *Sallee*, or any other Place being at Wa[r] with the said King of *Great-Britain*, bring an[y] Ships or Vessels, Men or Goods belonging to hi[s] said Majesty's Subjects to *Tripoly*, or to any Por[t]

o

Place in that Kingdom, the Governors there will not permit them to be sold within the Territories of *Tripoly*.

ARTICLE XV.

That no Subject of his said Majesty being a Passenger from or to any Port, shall be any way molested or meddled with, although he be on board any Ship or Vessel in Enmity with *Tripoly*.

British Subjects not to be molested even on board an Enemy.

ARTICLE XVI.

That if any of the Ships of War of the said King of *Great-Britain* come to *Tripoly*, or to any other Port or Place of that Kingdom with any Prize, they may freely sell it, or otherwise dispose of it at their own Pleasure, without being molested by any; and that his Majesty's said Ships of War shall not be obliged to pay Customs in any Sort; and that if they shall want Provisions, Victuals, or any other Things, they may freely buy them at the current Price.

British Ships of War may sell their Prizes and buy Provisions, &c. in Tripoly, and to pay no Customs.

ARTICLE XVII.

That when any of his Majesty's Ships of War shall appear before *Tripoly*, upon Notice thereof given to the *English* Consul, or by the Commander of the said Ships to the chief Governor of *Tripoly*, Publick Proclamation shall be immediately made to restore the Christian Captives; and if after that any Christians whatsoever make their Escape on board of the said Ships of War, they shall not be remanded back again, nor shall the said Consul or Commander, or any other his Majesty's Subjects, be obliged to pay any thing for the said Christians.

Christian Captives escaping on board English Ships of War, after Notice of their Arrival, not to be remanded.

ARTICLE XIX.

That at all Times, when any Ship of War of the King of *Great-Britain*, &c. carrying his said Majesty's Flag, appears before the said City of *Tripoly*

Mutual Salutes on English Ships of War coming into Tripoly.

Tripoly, and comes to anchor in the Road, imme diately after Notice thereof given by his said M jesty's Consul, or Officer from the Ship, unto t Dey and Government of *Tripoly*, they shall, Honour to his Majesty, cause a Salute of twent seven Cannon to be fired from the Castle and Fo of the City, and that the said Ship shall return t Salute by firing the same Number of Cannon.

ARTICLE XX.

British Merchant Ships not to be detained in *Tripoly* longer than three Days.

That no Merchant Ship belonging to *Great-B tain*, or any other Nation under the Protection the *British* Consul, being in the Port of *Trip* shall be detained from proceeding to Sea on h Voyage longer than threee Days, under the Pr tence of arming out the Ships of War of t Government, or any other whatsoever.

ARTICLE XXIII.

Minorca and *Gibraltar* to be reported Part of the *British* Dominions, and the People entitled to the same Privileges.

That whereas the Island of *Minorca* in the *Me* terranean Sea, and the City of *Gibraltar* in *Spa* have been yieled up and annexed to the Crown *Great-Britain*, as well by the King of *Spain* as all the several Powers of *Europe* engaged in the l War; now it is hereby agreed and fully conclude that from this Time forward for ever, the s Island of *Minorca* and City of *Gibraltar* shall esteemed in every respect by the Governors of *T poly* to be Part of his *Britannick* Majesty's own D minions, and the Inhabitants thereof to be look upon as his Majesty's natural Subjects, in the sa manner as if they had been born in any other P of *Great-Britain*, and they with their Ships a Vessels, wearing *British* Colours, shall be permitt freely to trade and traffick in any Part of the Kir dom of *Tripoly*, and shall pass without any M lestation whatsoever, either on the Seas, or el where, in the same manner, and with the sa

Fr

Freedom and Privileges as have been stipulated in this and all former Treaties in behalf of the *British* Nation and Subjects.

ARTICLE XXIV.

None of the Ships or Vessels belonging to *Tripoly*, shall cruize or look for Prizes before or in Sight of the Ports of the Island of *Minorca*, and the City of *Gibraltar*, to disturb or molest the Trade thereof in any manner whatsoever.

Ships of Tripoly not to cruize before Minorca or Gibraltar.

ARTICLE XXV.

All and every the Articles in this Treaty shall be inviolably kept and observed between *Great-Britain* and *Tripoly*, and all other Matters not particularly expressed in this Treaty, and provided for in any former, shall still remain in full force, and shall be esteemed the same as if inserted here.

Former Treaties confirmed.

The Treaty of Peace and Commerce between *Great-Britain* and *Tripoly*, concluded *May* the 1st 1676, which was ratified by another Treaty, made on the 7th of *February*, 1686; as likewise the Treaty of Peace and Commerce between the said Parties, concluded *October* the 18th, 1662, are comprehended in the above recited Treaty of 1716.

1676.
1686.
1662.

Articles of Peace between Great-Britain *and* Tunis; *concluded* August *the* 30th, 1716.

ARTICLE I.

THAT from henceforward a firm Peace for ever, free Trade and Commerce, shall be and continue between the Subjects of *Great-Britain*, and the People of the Kingdom of *Tunis*, and the Dominions thereunto belonging.

1716.
Perpetual Peace and free Trade.

ARTICLE

(194)

ARTICLE II.

Freedom of Trade for all Ships of both Parties, paying the ancient Duties.

That the Ships of either Party f
Liberty to enter into any Port or R
to the Dominions of either Party, pa
only for what they shall sell, transp
without any Trouble or Molestation
joy any other Privileges accustomed
Exaction that hath been upon the l
lading of Goods at *Goletta* and the
be reduced to the ancient Customs i

ARTICLE I

All Ships on both Sides to go unmolested.

That there shall be no Seizure of
either Party at Sea or in Port, but
quietly pass without any Molestatio
tion, they displaying their Colours;
vention of all Inconveniences that m
Ships of *Tunis* are to have a Certific
Hand and Seal of the *British* Consul
long to *Tunis*; which being produce

All Passengers and Goods in English Ships to be free.

Ship shall admit two Men to come c
peaceably, to satisfy them they are *l*
though they have Passengers of otl
board, they shall be free both they a

ARTICLE IV

English Ships having Men or Goods on board belonging to Tunis, to defend them.

That if an *English* Ship shall rec
any Goods or Passengers belonging
dom of *Tunis*, they shall be bound t
and their Goods so far as lieth in the
not deliver them unto the Enemies;
to prevent any unjust Demands bein
the Crown of *Great-Britain*, and to
and Differences which may arise,

Goods of Subjects of Tunis shipped on board English Ships to be entered before the Consul, and certified by him.

Merchandizes that shall from he
shipped by the Subjects of this Gov
in this Port, or any other whatsoever
Ships or Vessels belonging to *Great-B*

first entered in the Office of *Chancellaria*, before the *British* Conful refiding at the refpective Port, expreffing the Quantity, Quality and Value of the Goods fo fhipped, which the faid Conful is to certify in the Clearance given to the faid Ship or Veffel before fhe departs; to the end that if any Caufe of Complaint fhould happen hereafter, there may be no greater Claim made on the *British* Nation, than by this Method fhall be proved to be juft and equitable.

ARTICLE X.

That as the Ifland of *Minorca* in the *Mediterranean Sea*, and the City of *Gibraltar* in *Spain*, have been yielded and annexed to the Crown of *Great-Britain*, as well by the King of *Spain*, as by all the feveral Powers of *Europe* engaged in the late War; now it is hereby agreed and fully concluded, that from this Time forward for ever, the faid Ifland of *Minorca* and City of *Gibraltar* fhall be efteemed in every refpect by the Government of *Tunis* to be Part of his *Britannick* Majefty's own Dominions, and the Inhabitants thereof to be looked upon as his Majefty's natural Subjects, in the fame manner as if they had been born in any other Part of *Great-Britain*; and they with their Ships and Veffels wearing the *British* Colours, fhall be permitted freely to trade or traffick in any Part of the Kingdom of *Tunis*, and fhall pafs without any Moleftation whatfoever, either on the Seas or elfewhere, in the fame manner, and with the fame Freedom and Privileges as have been ftipulated in this and all former Treaties in behalf of the *British* Nation and Subjects.

Minorca and *Gibraltar* to be reputed Part of the *British* Dominions; and the Inhabitants to be entitled to the fame Privileges.

ARTICLE XI.

And the better and more firmly to maintain the good Correfpondence and Friendfhip that hath been long and happily eftablifhed between the Crown of of *Great-Britain* and the Government of *Tunis*, is hereby agreed and concluded by the Parties be forementioned, that none of the Ships or Vesse belonging to *Tunis*, or the Dominions thereof, sha be permitted to cruize or look for Prizes of an Nation whatsoever, before or in Sight of the afore

Ships of Tunis not to cruize before or near Minorca or Gibraltar. said City of *Gibraltar*, or any of the Ports of th Island of *Minorca*, to hinder or molest any Vesse bringing Provisions and Refreshments for his Br tannick Majesty's Troops and Garrisons in tho Places, or give any Disturbance to the Trade c Commerce thereof; and if any Prize shall be take by the Ships or Vessels of *Tunis* within the Spac of ten Miles of the aforesaid Places, she shall b restored without any Dispute.

ARTICLE XII.

Liberty of repairing, &c. all Ships of War on both Sides in all Ports. That all the Ships of War belonging to eithe Party's Dominions, shall have free Liberty to us each other's Ports, for washing, cleaning, and re pairing any of their Defects; and to buy and t ship off any Sort of Victuals, alive or dead, o any other Necessaries, at the Price the Natives bu at in the Market, without paying Custom to an Officer: And whereas his *Britannick* Majesty's Ship of War do frequently assemble and harbour in th Port of *Mahon* in the Island of *Minorca*; if at an

British Ships of War or Troops at Port Mahon to send and buy Provisions at Tunis, when they please. time they, or his Majesty's Troops in Garrison there, should be in want of Provisions, and shoul send from thence to purchase Supplies in any Par of the Dominions belonging to *Tunis*, they shall b permitted to buy Cattle, alive or dead, and all o ther Kind of Provision, at the Prices it is sold i the Market, and shall be suffered to carry it of without paying Duty to any Officer, in the sam manner as if his Majesty's Ships were themselve in the Port.

ARTICLE

ARTICLE XIII.

That in cafe any Ships of War belonging to the Kingdom of *Tunis* fhall take in any of their Enemies Ships any *Englifhmen* ferving for Wages, they are to be made Slaves; but if Merchants or Paffengers, they are to enjoy their Liberty and Goods free.

Englifhmen taken in Service on board an Enemy of Tunis, may be made Slaves, but not Merchants or Paffengers.

ARTICLE XV.

And the better to prevent any Difpute that may hereafter arife between the two Parties, about Salutes and publick Ceremonies, it is hereby agreed and concluded, that whenever any Flag Officer of *Great-Britain* fhall arrive in the Bay of *Tunis*, in any of his Majefty's Ships of War, immediately upon Notice given thereof, there fhall be five and twenty Cannon fired from the Caftles of *Goletta*, or other the neareft Fortification belonging to *Tunis*, according to Cuftom, as a Royal Salute to his *Britannick* Majefty's Colours, and the fame Number fhall be returned in Anfwer thereto by his Majefty's Ships: And it is hereby ftipulated and agreed, that all Ceremonies of Honour fhall be allowed to the *Britifh* Conful, who refides here, to reprefent in every refpect his Majefty's Perfon, equal to any other Nation whatfoever; and no other Conful in the Kingdom to be admitted before him in Precedency.

Proper Salutes to be paid and returned on the Arrival of a Britifh Flag Officer.

Due Honour to the Britifh Conful.

ARTICLE XVIII.

It is moreover agreed, concluded and eftablifhed, that in cafe any *Britifh* Ship or Ships, or any of the Subjects of his Majefty of *Great-Britain*, fhall import at the Port of *Tunis*, or any other Port of this Kingdom, any warlike Stores, as Cannons, Mufkets, Piftols, Cannon, Powder or fine Powder, Bullets, Mafts, Anchors, Cables, Pitch, Tar, or the like; as alfo Provifions, *viz.* Wheat, Barley, Beans, Oats, Oil, or the like; for the faid Kind of

No Duty to be paid by Britifh Ships importing Stores or Provifions to Tunis.

Mer-

Merchandize they shall not pay any Sort, of Duty or Custom whatever.

1686.
1674.
1662.

The several Treaties of Peace and Commerce between *Great-Britain* and *Tunis*, concluded and ratified in the Years 1686, 1674, and 1662, are comprehended in the above recited Treaty of 1716.

A PLACARD of AMPLIATION.

WE the Sates General of the *United Netherlands*, to all thofe that fhall fee thefe Prefents or hear the fame read, fend Greeting, and do make known, that whereas feveral Requifitions have been made to us by, and in the Name of feveral trading Inhabitants of this Country, to have an Elucidation or Interpretation in relation to fome Articles contained in our Placard of the 7th of *July* aft paft, touching and concerning the Prohibition of the Exportation of fome Goods and Merchandizes out of thefe Countries for abroad:

Therefore, we, in order to fatisfy them, have found good by thefe Prefents to declare;

Firft, That under the Word of Mafts, Yards, Tops, and all Sorts of round Timber, and other fit for the building of Ships, faw'd and unfaw'd, the Exportation whereof is prohibited by us, in our faid Placard, are contained and to be underftood green Firr and *Norway* and other Mafts, Stumps for Bowfprits, Yards, Tops and all other round Timber; there are likewife contained among it Milrods for Oars, and fix or eight-fquare cut Timber, ufed or fit to be made ufeful for any of the faid Articles; Knee Timber, crooked Timber, of what Quality of Wood foever, without any Diftinction of Length, Thicknefs and Breadth, *Silefia*, *Hamburgher*, *Weefelifh*, or *Rhenifh* Timber, Wood Blocks of Oak or Beach Wood, either whole or faw'd; as alfo green Firr and *Norway* Balks, either intire or cut, above twenty Feet long, and above one Inch and a half thick; all oaken Planks, be it *Dantzig* Plank, or the

the so called Upper or Low-Land, of what Dimension or Thickness soever; likewise all green Firr, or *Norway* Deal Boards, saw'd either abroad or in these Provinces, longer than twenty Feet, and thicker than $1\frac{1}{2}$ Inch without any further.

Secondly, That under the Word of Ropes and Cordage prohibited to be exported by the Placard, are also comprehended bending Ropes, as also Cable Yarn, Rope Yarn, Leach Yarn, Sail Twine and the like.

Thirdly, That under the Word of Iron, prohibited likewise to be exported therein, shall not be comprehended, but be permitted to be exported whole Cast Iron Pots, Kettles, and Hearth Plates (the broken and split ones remain under the Prohibition as well as old Iron) further, it shall be permitted to export Iron Chests, made up Locks, Padlocks; as also small Locks, Snuffers and the like Iron Trifles ready made up; likewise Iron Wire, which is not comprehended under the issued Prohibition.

Fourthly, That under the Copper, which by the said Placard is forbidden to be exported, is not comprehended the small made up Copper-Work of small Kettles, Chaffing Dishes, Cascrols, Candlesticks, Snuffers, and such like other minute Furniniture, nor Copper-Wire.

Fifthly, That among the prohibited Metal is not comprehended Tutenage.

Further, that the said Placard shall be thus modified and altered so as it is by these Presents modified and altered, that without receding from the Treaties which have been made between this State and other Powers, and which by the Inhabitants of these Provinces

inces or State, shall be punctually observed and obeyed, all Exportation by Sea of the prohibited Wares and Goods to the Lands and Dominions of the Allies of this State; as also to those, which in relation to this State are neuter, shall be free and open, provided however that the Shippers of such Goods to be sent abroad, shall previously declare to the College of Admiralty of the District from whence the Exportation is to be made, the exact Quantity and Value of those Goods; as also for what Place they are designed, and then and there give due and sufficient Security to the Satisfaction of the said College of Admiralty, and to the Amount of treble the Value of the said Goods, to bring in Certificates, and to prove within a certain Time to be limited by the said College, that the Goods are arrived at the intended Place, and have been delivered there under Penalty of treble the Value as aforesaid, so that the Security they have given shall not be cleared nor discharged, till after the Exhibition and Acceptation that the Proof has been satisfactory; and that the said Proof shall not be deemed as such, if they should pretend or prove that the Ship, in which the Goods are laden was taken by any other Nation, or that the Goods were taken from aboard of the Ship wherein they were laden, unless it is proved at the same Time that the same Ship sailed and continued and was still, at the Time of such Disaster, actually under the Convoy of one or more Ships of War of this State; or in case there was no Opportunity to take the Benefit of such a Convoy, that then at least the Original Orders shall be exhibited whereby it appears that such Goods were ordered from the Place declared, to be sent thither, and this, if thought necessary upon an Affirmation upon Oath that the said Orders are sincere, and the only ones which have relation to the said Goods, and upon which the same Goods were sent, and that the said

Ship

Ship and Goods, or the Goods alone, and by itſel
were taken without any Colluſion or Concurrenc
or Deſign; that beſides, a Sentence of Confiſcatic
ſhall be produced and proved that the ſaid Gooc
were laden here in the Country, on board of
known and unſuſpected Veſſel, ſo that it in ever
reſpect ſhall appear that the Shippers, and th
Maſters of the Ships have been upon their *Bon*
Fide: And to the End that no Abuſe may be mad
of this Conceſſion, nor attempted to elude the goo
Intention of their High Mightineſſes by any ſ
niſter Arts, the Shippers and the Maſters of Ship
that ſhall be found to have made their Machina
tions to ſend the prohibited Goods to *France*, ſhal
alſo be corporally puniſhed, beſides and above th
Forfeit and Penalty of treble the Value, and of th
Forfeiture of the Ship, if, and as far as the ſamı
doth belong to the Shipper or Maſter.

In the like manner, under the ſame Precaution
as far as applicable, it ſhall likewiſe be permittec
ſo as it is permitted hereby to export the Goods by
Land and by the Rivers, if the Colleges of Ad
miralty judge that there is no fear, that the ſaic
Ships may be intercepted by the way, and thus
fall into the Hands of the Enemies, in which caſt
they ſhall be at Liberty to refuſe the Exportation,
or unleſs therein for the bettter Precaution that the
Goods ſhall remain at the Place where they are
ſaid to be deſigned for, and not to be ſent to other
Places where it ſhould not be adviſeable, other
Cautions and Additions ſhould be required, which
the ſaid Colleges of Admiralty ſhall have Power
to cauſe to be inſerted in the Inſtructions, which
they ſhall paſs in relation thereunto, ſo as they likewiſe ſhall have Liberty to take other Precautions in
the return and calling back of the like Goods,
which were to be exported when they find that this
Country ſhall have Occaſion for them.

And to the End that nobody may pretend any
Igno-

...norance hereof, we do require and desire the ...rds the States, Statholder, commissioned Coun-...lors and Deputy States of the respective Pro-...ices, and all other Justiciaries and Officers of the ...d Country, to cause this our Placard forthwith ...d every where to be publickly read, published ...d affixed, where it is needful, and where the like ...iblications and Affixions are usually made: And ... do further charge and command the Counsellors ...the Admiralty, Attornies and Commissaries Ge-...ral, as also all Admirals, Vice Admirals, Cap-...ns, Officers and Commanders, to obey this our ...acard, and cause the same to be obeyed, to pro-...:d and cause to be proceeded against the Contra-...ners thereof, without Connivance, Favour, Dis-...iulation or Composition; for we have judged this ... be thus necessary for the Service of the Country. ...Thus done and resolved in the Assembly of the ...igh mentioned Lords the States General at the ...*igue*, under the Seal of the State and Signature ...the Lord President of our Assembly, and of one ...our *Griffiers* on the 31st of *August* 1747, was ...;ned *E. Tamminga*. Underneath stood, by the ...:dinance of the High mentioned Lords the States ...:neral, signed *Jan de la Bassecour*. Upon the empty ...ace the Seal of their High Mightinesses is stampt ... a red Wafer, covered with a Paper cut square;

St. Gravenhague:

By *Jacobus Scheltus*, Printer to their High Mightinesses the States General of the *United Netherlands*, in the Year 1747.

With Privilege.

PLA-

PLACART.

THE States General of the *United Netherla*[nds] to all thofe that fhall fee thefe Prefents [or] hear the fame read, fend greeting, and do ma[ke] known and certify, that whereas, we in the prefe[nt] Conjuncture of Times, for the Service of th[efe] Countries, we have occafion for many Sorts of A[m]munition and warlike Materials, as alfo Provific[ns] for Beafts; and having underftood that confideral[le] Quantities thereof are daily carrying out of t[his] Country, whereby we ourfelves may happen to [be] in want of them; therefore it is, in order to provi[de] againft the fame, we have thought it proper to o[r]dain and command, fo as we by thefe Prefents [do] ordain and command, that from this Time fo[r]ward, until our further Refolution and Order, [it] fhall not be permitted to export out of this Cou[n]try abroad the following Sorts of Arms, Ammun[i]tion, and other warlike Stores, as alfo Fodder ar[d] Provifions, to wit, Salt-petre, Sulphur, refined [or] unrefined, Gunpowder, Matches, Cannon, Swiv[el] Guns, Mortars, Carriages, Balls, Bombs, Cu[i]raffes, Grenadoes, Muskets, Forkets, Fufils, Pi[f]tols, Petards, Salfages, Pitch, Crantzes, Helmet[s] Cafkets, Curaffes, Bandeliers, Pouches, whole an[d] half Pikes, Halberts, Swords; and further, a[ll] Sorts of Weapons, ferving for the Hand, or f[i]ring Inftruments, where amongft are compre[e]hended Gun-Barrels and Locks, and what fu[r]ther may be requifite to mount the fame; Boot[s,] Saddles, Piftol-Cafes, and all what is neceffary fo[r] the dreffing of Horfes. *Item*, Mafts, and all Sort[s] of round Timber, Timber for building of Ship[s] faw'd or unfaw'd, Sail-Cloth, Hemp, Rope[s,] Anchors, Pitch, Tar, Lead, Pewter, Iron and Stee[l]

(205)

lings, all Sorts of Copper and Metal, Sea-Coal, alſo Hay, Oats, Straw and Horſe Beans, all un- r the Penalty of forfeiting the ſaid Species which ıll be endeavoured to be exported and found out; d moreover, of twice the Value thereof, one ird Part for the Informer, one third Part for the ficer that ſhall ſeize them, and one third Part the Publick: Provided however that hereunder : not comprehended nor underſtood, ſuch of the d Articles, that may happen to be exported for : Uſe of the Camps and Armies of this State or r Allies, nor ſuch Articles thereof which are ex- rted in their own or hired Ships of the *Eaſt* and *eſt-India* Companies of this Country, or to the o- ːr Colonies of this State, nor in the licens'd Ships particular Perſons for the Service of the ſaid ɩlonies or of the Inhabitants of the ſame, pro- led they have previouſly deſired and obtained Per- ɩſſion for ſo doing, from the reſpective College Admiralty, under whoſe Diſtrict the Exportation to be made, and have given there ſufficient Se- rity, for treble the Value of the Goods, to verify d to prove ſatisfactory, within a certain Time, cording and in Proportion to the Diſtance of the ace, to be limited by the College, that the ſaid oods are arrived and delivered at the intended ace of their Deſtination.

And to the End that nobody may pretend Igno- nce hereof, we do require and deſire the Lords e States, Stadholder, commiſſioned Counſellors, e deputed States of the reſpective Provinces, and l other Juſticiaries and Officers of the ſaid Coun- y forthwith and without delay, to cauſe this our lacart to be publickly read, publiſhed and affixed ery where it is required, and in ſuch Places where is uſual to make ſuch Publication and Affixion: nd we do further charge and command the Coun- llors of the reſpective Admiralties, Attornies **eneral and Commiſſaries,** as alſo all Generals, Admirals,

mirals, Vice-Admirals, Captains, Officers, and Comanders, to obey and cause to be obeyed this or Placart, to proceed and cause to be proceeded against them that shall act contrary thereunto without Connivance, Favour, Dissimulation or Composition, for we have found it to be necessary for the Service of the Country and State.

Thus done and resolved in the Assembly of the said and High mentioned Lords the States General in the *Hague*, under the Seal of the State and the Signature of the Lord President of our Assembly, and one of our Griffiers on the 7th Day of *July* 174 Was signed *C. Bentinck*. Underneath was written by the Ordinance of the High mentioned Lord the States General, signed *Jan de la Baffecour*; and underneath was stampt the Seal of their High Mightinesses on a red Wafer, covered with a Paper square cut;

In St. Gravenhague:

By *Jacobus Scheltus*, Printer in Ordinary to the High and Mighty Lords the States General of the *United Netherlands* 1747.

With Privilege.

A Copy of a Certificate for a private Ship to annoy the Enemy in Time of War.

GEORGE the Second, by the Grace of God, King of *Great-Britain*, *France*, and *Ireland*, to [all] People to whom these Presents shall come [gr]eeting: Whereas we by our Declaration of the [nin]eteenth Day of *October*, in the Year of our [L]ord one thousand seven hundred and thirty-nine, [fo]r the Reasons therein contained have declared War [ag]ainst *Spain*, and whereas we by our Declaration [of] the twenty-ninth Day of *March*, in the Year of [ou]r Lord one thousand seven hundred and forty-[fo]ur, for the Reasons therein contained have de[cl]ared War against *France*. And whereas we by [ou]r Commission, under our Great Seal of *Great-[Br]itain*, bearing Date the eighteenth Day of *June* [fo]llowing, have willed, required, and authorized [ou]r High Admiral of *Great-Britain* and *Ireland*, &c. [fo]r the Time being, and our Commissioners for ex[ec]uting the Office of our High Admiral of *Great-[Br]itain* and *Ireland*, &c. and the Commissioners for [ex]ecuting the said Office for the Time being, or [an]y three or more of them, to issue forth, and grant [C]ommissions to any of our loving Subjects or o[th]ers, whom our High Admiral aforesaid, or our [sai]d Commissioners for executing the said Office, [an]d the Commissioners for executing the same for [th]e Time being, shall deem fitly qualified in that [be]half for the apprehending, seizing and taking [th]e Ships, Vessels and Goods belonging to *France* [an]d *Spain*, or the Vassals and Subjects of the *French* [Ki]ng, or the King of *Spain*, or either of them or [ot]hers, inhabiting within any of their or either of

their

their Countries, Territories and
such other Ships, Vessels and Goo
be liable to Confiscation pursuant
Treaties between us and other Pri
Potentates, and to bring the same
our High Court of Admiralty of
other Court of Admiralty as shall
thorized in that behalf, for Procee
dication and Condemnation to be
according to the Course of Adm
of Nations, and with such Clause
serted, and in such manner as b
mission more at large appeareth.
said Commissioners for executing
High Admiral aforesaid, have
Hutton fitly qualified, who hath
nished and victualled a Ship called
of the Burthen of about five hundre
whereof he the said *William Hutton*
and whereas he the said *William H*
sufficient Bail, with Sureties to us
Court of Admiralty, according to
Form set down in our Instructions
eighteenth Day of *June*, one tho
dred and forty-four, and in the ei
our Reign, a Copy whereof is g
Captain *William Hutton*. Know
we do by these Presents grant Con
do licence and authorize the said
to set forth in warlike manner the
the *Cumberland*, under his own
therewith by Force of Arms to
and take the Ships, Vessels and C
to *France* and *Spain*, or the Vassals
the *French* King, or King of *Sp*
them, or others inhabiting within
either of their Countries, Territc
nions, and such other Ships, Vess
are or shall be liable to Confiscat

the respective Treaties between us and other Princes, States and Potentates, and to bring the same to such Port as shall be most convenient, in order to have them legally adjudged in our said High Court of Admiralty of *England*, or before the Judges of such other Admiralty Court as shall be lawfully authorized within our Dominions, which being condemned, it shall and may be lawful for the said *William Hutton* to sell and dispose of such Ships, Vessels and Goods so adjudged and condemned, in such sort and manner as by the Course of Admiralty hath been accustomed, except in such Cases where it is otherwise directed by our said Instructions: Provided always that the said *William Hutton* keep an exact Journal of his Proceedings, and therein particularly take Notice of all Prizes which shall be taken by him, the Nature of such Prizes, the Times and Places of their being taken, and the Values of them as near as he can judge, as also of the Station, Motion and Strength of the Enemies, as well as he or his Mariners can discover by the best Intelligence he can get, and also of whatsoever else shall occur unto him or any of his Officers or Mariners, or be discovered or declared unto him or them, or found out by Examination or Conference with any Mariners or Passengers of or in any the Ships or Vessels taken, or by any other Person or Persons, or by any other ways and means whatsoever, touching or concerning the Designs of the Enemies, or any of their Fleets, Vessels or Parties, and of their Stations, Ports and Places, and of their Intents therein, and of what Merchant Ships or Vessels of the Enemies bound out or home, or any other Place as he or his Officers or Mariners shall hear of, and of what else material in these Cases may arrive to his or their Knowledge; of all which, he shall from Time to Time, as he shall or may have Opportunity, transmit an Account to our High Admiral of *Great-Britain* for the Time being,

P

being, or our said Commissioners for executing the Office of our High Admiral aforesaid, or the Commissioners for executing that Office for the Time being or their Secretary, and to keep a Correspondence with him or them by all Opportunity that shall present. And further, provided that nothing be done by the said *William Hutton*, or any of his Officers, Mariners and Company, contrary to the true Meaning of our aforesaid Instructions but that the said Instructions shall be by them, and each, and every of them, as far as they, or any of them are therein concerned in all Particulars well and duly performed and observed. And we pray and desire all Kings, Princes, Potentates, State and Republicks, being our Friends, all Allies and all others to whom it shall appertain to give the said *William Hutton* all Aid, Assistance and Succour in their Ports with his said Ship, Company and Prizes, without doing or suffering to be done to him any Wrong, Trouble, or Hindrance, we offering to do the like when we shall be by them thereunto desired: And we will and require all our Officers whatsoever to give him Succour and Assistance, as Occasion shall require. In Witness whereof, we have have caused the Great Seal of our High Court of Admiralty of *England* to be hereunto affixed. Given at *London* the twentieth Day of November in the Year of our Lord one thousand seven hundred and forty-seven, and in the twenty-first Year of our Reign.

SAMUEL HILL, Register

George R.

(L.S.)

Instructions for the Commanders of such Merchant Ships and Vessels as may have Letters of Marque, or Commissions for private Men of War against the French King, *his Vassals and Subjects, or others inhabiting within any of his Countries, Territories or Dominions, by Virtue of our Commission granted under the Great Seal of* Great-Britain, *bearing Date the twenty-ninth Day of* March 1744. *Given at our Court at* St. James's *the twenty-ninth Day of* March 1744, *in the seventeenth Year of our Reign.*

I.

THAT it shall be lawful for the said Commanders of Merchant Ships and Vessels authorized by Letters of Marque, or Commissions for private Men of War, to set upon by Force of Arms, and subdue and take the Men of War, Ships, and other Vessels whatsoever; as also the Goods, Monies, and Merchandizes, belonging to the *French* King, his Vassals and Subjects, and others inhabiting within any of his Countries, Territories or Dominions, and such other Ships, Vessels, and Goods, as are, or shall be liable to Confiscation,

tion, purfuant to the Treaties between us, and other Princes, States, and Potentates: But fo as that no Hoftility be committed nor Prizes attacked feized, or taken, within the Harbours of Princes and States in Amity with us, or in their Rivers or Roads within Shot of their Cannon.

II. That all Ships of what Nation foever carrying any Soldiers, Arms, Powder, Ammunition, or any other Contraband Goods, to any of the Territories Lands, Plantations, or Countries of the *French* King, fhall be feized as Prizes.

III. That the faid Commanders of fuch Merchan Ships and Veffels fhall bring fuch Ships and Goods as they have feized, or fhall fo feize and take, to fuch Port of this our Realm of *England*, or fome other Port of our Dominions as fhall be moft con venient for them, in order to have the fame legally adjudged in our High Court of Admiralty of *Eng land*, or before the Judges of fuch other Admiralty Court, as fhall be lawfully authorized within our Dominions: But if fuch Prize be taken in the *Medi terranean*, or within the Streights of *Gibraltar*, then the Captor may, if he doth not think fit to bring the fame to fome Port of *England*, or other our Dominions, carry fuch Ship and Goods into the Ports of fuch Princes or States as are in Alliance or Amity with us.

IV. That after fuch Ship fhall be taken and brough into any Port, the Taker or one of his chief Of ficers, or fome other Perfon prefent at the Capture fhall be obliged to bring or fend, as foon as poffible may be, three or four of the principal of the Com pany (whereof the Mafter and the Pilot to be al ways two) of every Ship fo brought into Port, be fore the Judge of the Admiralty of *England*, or hi Surrogate, or before the Judge of fuch other Ad miralty Court, within our Dominions, as fhall b lawfully authorized as aforefaid, or fuch as fhall b
law

lawfully commiffioned in that behalf, to be fworn and examined upon fuch Interrogatories as fhall tend to the Difcovery of the Truth, touching the Intereft or Property of fuch Ship or Ships, and of the Goods and Merchandizes found therein : And the Taker fhall be further obliged at the Time he produceth the Company to be examined, to bring and deliver into the Hands of the Judge of the Admiralty of *England*, his Surrogate, or the Judge of fuch other Admiralty Courts within our Dominions, as fhall be lawfully authorized, or others commiffioned as aforefaid, all fuch Paffes, Sea-Briefs, Charter-Parties, Bills of Lading, Cockets, Letters, and other Documents and Writings as fhall be delivered up, or found on board any fuch Ship; the faid Taker, or one of his chief Officers, or fome other Perfon who was prefent at the Capture, and faw the faid Papers and Writings delivered up or otherwife found on board at the Time of the Capture, making Oath, that the faid Papers and Writings are brought and delivered in, as they were received or taken, without any Fraud, Addition, Subduction or Embezzlement.

That fuch Ships, Goods, and Merchandizes, taken by Virtue of Letters of Marque or Commiffions for private Men of War, fhall be kept and preferved, and no Part of them fhall be fold, fpoiled, wafted or diminifhed, and that the Bulk thereof fhall not be broken before Judgment be given in the High Court of Admiralty of *England*, or fome other Court of Admiralty lawfully authorized in that behalf, that the Ships, Goods and Merchandizes are lawful Prize; and that no Perfon or Perfons taken, or furprized in any Ship or Veffel, as aforefaid, though known to be of the Enemy's Party, fhall be in cold Blood killed, maimed, or by Torture or Cruelty inhumanly treated, contrary to the common Ufage and juft Permiffion of War;

and

and whoever shall offend in any of the Premisse shall be severely punished.

VI. That the said Commanders of such Merchai[n]t Ships or Vessels, who shall obtain the said Lette[r] of Marque or Commissions as aforesaid, for priva[te] Men of War, shall not do or attempt any thin[g] against the true Meaning of any Article or A[r]ticles, Treaty or Treaties depending between [us] and any of our Allies, touching the Freedom [of] Commerce in the Time of War, and the Autho[-]rity of the Passports, or Certificates under a ce[r]tain Form in some one of the Articles or Treati[es] so depending between us and our Allies, as afor[e]said, when produced and shewed by any of th[e] Subjects of our said Allies, and shall not do [or] attempt any thing against our loving Subjects [or] the Subjects of any Prince or State in Amity wit[h] us, nor against their Ships, Vessels or Goods, bu[t] only against the *French* King, his Vassals and Sub[-]jects, and others inhabiting within his Countrie[s,] Territories or Dominions, their Ships, Vessels an[d] Goods, except as before excepted; and against suc[h] other Ships, Vessels and Goods, as are or shall b[e] liable to Confiscation.

VII. That all Captains and Commanders of Ship[s] who have, or shall have Letters of Marque, o[r] Commissions for private Men of War, are hereb[y] required and enjoined to observe carefully and re[-]ligiously the Terms of the Treaty Marine, betwee[n] his late Majesty King *Charles* the Second, and thei[r] High Mightinesses the States General of the *Unite[d] Netherlands*, concluded at *London* the first Day o[f] *December* 1674, Old Style, and confirmed by sub[-]sequent Treaties: And they are hereby required t[o] give Security pursuant to the tenth Article of th[e] aforesaid Treaty Marine, for their due Performanc[e] thereof.

VIII. That after Condemnation of any Prize, it shal[l] or may be lawful for the Commanders of such Mer[-] chant Ships or Veffels, or the Owners of the fame, to keep fuch and fo many Ships, Veffels, Goods and Merchandizes, as fhall be condemned to them, for lawful Prize, in their own Poffeffion, to make Sale or difpofe thereof in open Market, or otherwife, to their beft Advantage, in as ample manner as at any time heretofore has been accuftomed in Cafes of Letters of Marque, or of juft Prizes in Time of War; other than wrought Silks, Bengals and Stuffs mix'd with Silk or Herba, of the Manufacture of *Perfia, China*, or *Eaft-India*, or Callicoes painted, dyed, printed or ftained there, which are to be depofited for Exportation, according to the Directions of an Act made in the eleventh Year of the Reign of the late King *William* the Third, entitled, *An Act for the more effectual employing the Poor by encouraging the Manufactures of this Kingdom*; and that it fhall be lawful for all manner of Perfons, as well our Subjects as others, according to Law, to buy the faid Ships, Veffels, Goods and Merchandizes, fo taken and condemned for lawful Prize, without any Damage or Moleftation to enfue thereupon to the faid Buyers, or any of them, by reafon of the contracting or dealing for the fame.

IX. That if any Ship or Veffel, belonging to us or our Subjects, or to our Allies or their Subjects, fhall be found in Diftrefs, by being in Fight, fet upon, or taken by the Enemy, or by reafon of any other Accident, the Captain, Officers, and Company, who fhall have fuch Letters of Marque or Commiffions as aforefaid, fhall ufe their beft Endeavours to give Aid and Succour to all fuch Ship or Ships, and fhall, to the utmoft of their Power, labour to free the fame from the Enemy, or any other Diftrefs.

X. That our Subjects, and all other Perfons whatfoever, who fhall either in their own Perfons ferve, or bear any Charge or Adventure, or in any fort fur-

further or set forward the said Adventure, according to these Articles, shall stand and be freed by Virtue of the said Commission; and that no Person be in any wise reputed or challenged for an Offender against our Laws, but shall be freed, under our Protection, of and from all Trouble and Vexation that might in any wise grow thereby, in the same manner as any other our Subjects ought to be by Law, in their aiding and assisting us, either in their own Persons or otherwise, in a lawful War against our declared Enemies.

XI. That the said Commanders of such Merchant Ships and Vessels, or their Owners or Agents, before the taking out Commissions, shall give Notice in writing, subscribed with their Hands, to our High Admiral of *Great-Britain*, for the Time being, or our Commissioners for executing the Office of our High Admiral, or the Commissioners for executing that Office for the time being, or the Lieutenant or Judge of the said High Court of Admiralty, or his Surrogate, of the Name of their Ship, and of the Tonage and Burthen, and the Names of the Captain, Owners or Setters out of the said Ship, with the Number of Men, and the Names of the Officers in her, and for what Time they are victualled, and also of their Ordnance, Furniture and Ammunition; to the End the same may be registred in the said Court of Admiralty.

XII. That those Commanders of such Merchant Ships and Vessels, who shall have such Letters of Marque, or Commissions as aforesaid, shall hold and keep, and are hereby enjoined to hold and keep a Correspondence, by all Conveniences, and upon all Occasions, from Time to Time, with our High Admiral of *Great-Britain* for the Time being, or our Commissioners for executing the Office of our High Admiral, or the Commissioners for executing that Office for the Time being, or their Secretary, so as from Time to Time to render and give unto him or them, not only an Account or Intelligence of their Captures or Proceedings, by Virtue of such their said Letters of Marque, or Commissions as aforesaid; but also, of whatsoever else shall occur into them, or be discovered and declared unto them, or found out by them, by Examination of, or Conference with any Mariners, or Passengers of or in the Ships or Vessels taken, or by any other ways and means whatsoever, touching or concerning the Designs of the Enemy, or any of their Fleets, Ships, Vessels or Parties; and of the Stations, Seas, Ports and Places, and of their Intents therein; and of what Merchant Ships or Vessels of the Enemy, bound out or home, as they shall hear of; and of what else material in these Cases may arrive to their Knowledge, to the End such Course may be thereupon taken, and such Orders given, as may be requisite.

XIII. That no Commander of a Merchant Ship, or Vessel who shall have a Letter of Marque or Commission as aforesaid, shall presume (as they will answer it at their Peril) to wear any Jack, Pennant, or any other Ensign or Colour usually borne by our Ships, but that, besides the Colours borne usually by Merchant Ships, they do wear a red Jack, with the Union Jack, described in the Canton, at the upper Corner thereof near the Staff; and that one third Part of the whole Company of every such Ship or Vessel so fitted out as aforesaid, shall be Landmen.

XIV. That such Commanders of Merchant Ships, and Vessels who shall obtain such Letters of Marque or Commissions as aforesaid, shall also from Time to Time, upon due Notice being given them, observe all such other Instructions and Orders, as we shall think fit to direct, for the better carrying on of this Service.

XV. That all Persons who shall violate these Instructions, shall be severely punished, and also required
to

to make full Reparation to Persons injured, contrary to these Instructions, for all Damages the shall sustain by any Capture, Embezzlement, Demurrage or otherwise.

That before any such Letters of Marque, or Commissions, issue under Seal, Bail with Sureties shall be given before the Lieutenant and Judge of our High Court of Admiralty of *England*, or his Surrogate, in the Sum of three thousand Pound Sterling, if the Ship carries above one hundred and fifty Men; and if a lesser Number, in the Sum of fifteen hundred Pounds Sterling: Which Bail shall be to the Effect, and in the Form following.

Which Day, Time and Place personally appeare

who submitting themselves to the Jurisdiction of the High Court of Admiralty of *England*, obliged themselves, their Heirs, Executors and Administrators, to our Sovereign Lord the King, in the Sum of   Pounds of lawful Money of *Great-Britain*, to this Effect; that is to say, that whereas
is authorized by Letters of Marque, or a Commission for a private Man of War, to arm, equip, and set forth to Sea the Ship called the   of the Burthen of about   Tons; whereof he the said   goeth Captain, with   Men, Ordnance, Ammunition and Victuals, to set upon by Force of Arms, and to subdue, seize and take the Men of War, Ships and other Vessels whatsoever, together with the Goods, Monies and Merchandizes, belonging to the *French* King, or to any of his Vassals and Subjects, or others inhabiting within any of his Countries, Territories or Dominions whatsover, and such other Ships, Vessels and Goods, as are, or shall be liable to Confiscation, excepting only within the Harbours or Roads within Shot of the Cannon of Princes and States in Amity

with his Majesty. And whereas he the said ⸺⸺ has a Copy of certain Instructions approved of, and passed by his Majesty in Council, delivered to him to govern himself therein, as by the Tenor of the said Commission and of the Instructions thereto relating, more at large appeareth. If therefore nothing be done by the said ⸺⸺ or any of his Officers, Mariners or Company, contrary to the true Meaning of the said Instructions, but that the Commission aforesaid, and the said Instructions, shall in all Particulars, be well and duly performed and observed as far as they shall the said Ship, Captain and Company, any way concern: And if they or any of them, shall give full Satisfaction for any Damage or Injury which shall be done by them, or any of them, to any of his Majesty's Subjects or Allies, or Neuters, or their Subjects; and also shall duly and truly pay or cause to be paid to his Majesty, or the Customers or Officers appointed to receive the same for his Majesty, the usual Customs due to his Majesty, of and for all Ships and Goods so as aforesaid taken and adjudged for Prize: And moreover, if the said ⸺⸺ shall not take any Ship or Vessel, or any Goods or Merchandizes belonging to the Enemy, or otherwise liable to Confiscation, through Consent, or clandestinely, or by Collusion, by Virtue, Colour or Pretence of his said Commission; that then this Bail shall be void, and of none Effect; and unless they shall so do, they do all hereby severally consent, that Execution shall issue forth against them, their Heirs, Executors and Administrators, Goods and Chattels, wheresoever the same shall be found, to the Value of the said Sum of ⸺⸺ Pounds, before mentioned. And, in Testimony of the Truth thereof, they have hereunto subscribed their Names.

By his Majesty's Command,

HOLLES NEWCASTLE.

Ex-

Extracted from the Registry of the High Court of Admiralty of *England*.

George R.

(L.S.)

Instructions for the Commanders of such Merchant Ships and Vessels as may have Letters of Marque or Commissions for private Men of War against France *and* Spain, *their Vassals and Subjects, or others inhabiting within any of their Countries, Territories, or Dominions, by Virtue of our Commission granted under the Great Seal of* Great-Britain, *bearing Date the eighteenth Day of* June 1744. *Given at* Kensington *the eighteenth Day of* June 1744, *in the eighteenth Year of our Reign.*

I.

THAT it shall be lawful for the said Commanders of Merchant Ships and Vessels authorized by Letters of Marque or Commissions for private Men of War, to set upon by Force of Arms, and subdue and take the Men of War, Ships, and other Vessels whatsoever; as also the Goods, Monies and Merchandizes, belonging to *France* and *Spain,* their Vassals and Subjects, and others inhabiting within any of their Countries, Territories or Dominions, and such other Ships,
Vessels

Vessels and Goods, as are, or shall be liable to Confiscation, pursuant to the Treaties between us and other Princes, States and Potentates; but so as that no Hostility be committed, nor Prize attacked, seized, or taken, within the Harbours of Princes and States in Amity with us, or in their Rivers or Roads, within Shot of their Cannon.

II.

That all Ships carrying any Contraband Goods to *France* and *Spain*, shall be seized as Prize to his Majesty.

III.

That no Goods laden in *Dutch* Ships shall be deemed Contraband, other than such as are declared so to be, by the Treaty Marine, concluded between *England* and *Holland* in the Year 1674.

IV.

That all Captains and Commanders of Ships, who have, or shall have Letters of Marque, or Commissions for private Men of War, are hereby required and enjoined to observe carefully and religiously the Terms of the Treaty Marine, between his late Majesty King *Charles* the Second, and their High Mightinesses the States General of the *United Netherlands*, concluded at *London* the first Day of *December* 1674, Old Style, and confirmed by subsequent Treaties: And they are hereby required to give Security pursuant to the tenth Article of the aforesaid Treaty Marine, for their due Performance thereof.

V.

That all Sorts of Fireworks, and Things thereto belonging, as Cannon, Muskets, Mortars, Petards, Bombs, Grenadoes, Saucisses, Peckransen, Carriages, Rests, Bandaliers, Powder, Match, Saltpetre, Bullets, Pikes, Swords, Head-Pieces, Curiasses, Halberds, Horses, Saddles, Holsters, Belts,

Sail-

Sailwork, Rigging, Cables, Cordage, Masts, Lead, Pitch, Tar, Hemp, together with all other Equipage that serves for Sea or Land, laden in *Danish* or *Swedish* Ships, or Ships belonging to neutral Countries, and bound to the Enemies Country, are accounted Contraband Goods.

VI.

That the said Commanders of such Merchant Ships and Vessels shall bring such Ships and Goods as they have seized, or shall so seize and take, to such Port of this our Realm of *England*, or some other Port of our Dominions as shall be most convenient for them, in order to have the same legally adjudged in our High Court of Admiralty of *England*, or before the Judges of such other Admiralty Court, as shall be lawfully authorized within our Dominions: But if such Prize be taken in the *Mediterranean*, or within the Streights of *Gibraltar*, then the Captor may, if he doth not think fit to bring the same to some Port of *England*, or other our Dominions, carry such Ship and Goods into the Ports of such Princes or States as are in Alliance or Amity with us.

VII.

That after such Ship shall be taken and brought into any Port, the Taker or one of his chief Officers, or some other Person present at the Capture, shall be obliged to bring or send, as soon as possible may be, three or four of the principal of the Company (whereof the Master and the Pilot to be always two) of every Ship so brought into Port, before the Judge of the Admiralty of *England*, or his Surrogate, or before the Judge of such other Admiralty Court, within our Dominions as shall be lawfully authorized as aforesaid, or such as shall be lawfully commissioned in that behalf, to be sworn and examined upon such Interrogatories as shall tend to the Discovery of the Truth, touching the Interest of Property of such Ship or Ships, and of the Goods and Merchandizes found therein: And the Taker shall be further obliged at the Time he produceth the Company to be examined, to bring and deliver into the Hands of the Judge of the Admiralty of *England*, his Surrogate, or the Judge of such other Admiralty Courts within our Dominions, as shall be lawfully authorized, or others commissioned as aforesaid, all such Passes, Sea-Briefs, Charter Parties, Bills of Lading, Cockets, Letters, and other Documents and Writings as shall be delivered up, or found on board any such Ship; the said Taker, or one of his chief Officers, or some other Person who was present at the Capture, and saw the said Papers and Writings delivered up, or otherwise found on board at the Time of the Capture, making Oath, that the said Papers and Writings are brought and delivered in, as they were received or taken, without any Fraud, Addition, Subduction, or Embezzlement.

VIII.

That all such Ships, Goods and Merchandizes, taken by Virtue of Letters of Marque or Commissions for private Men of War, shall be kept and preserved, and no Part of them shall be sold, spoiled, wasted, or diminished, and that the Bulk thereof shall not be broken before Judgment be given in the High Court of Admiralty of *England*, or some other Court of Admiralty lawfully authorized in that behalf, that the Ships, Goods and Merchandizes are lawful Prize, or otherwise liable to Confiscation; and that no Person or Persons taken, or surprized in any Ship, or Vessel as aforesaid, though known to be of the Enemy's Party, shall be in cold Blood killed, maimed, or by Torture or Cruelty inhumanly treated, contrary to the common Usage and just Permission of War: And whosoever shall offend

fend in any of the Premisses, shall be severely punished.

IX.

That the said Commanders of such Merchant Ships or Vessels, who shall obtain the said Letters of Marque or Commissions as aforesaid, for private Men of War, shall not do or attempt any thing against the true Meaning of any Article or Articles, Treaty or Treaties, depending between us and any of our Allies, touching the Freedom of Commerce in the Time of War, and the Authority of the Passports, or Certificates under a certain Form in some one of the Articles or Treaties so depending between us and our Allies as aforesaid, when produced and shewed by any of the Subjects of our said Allies, and shall not do or attempt any thing against our loving Subjects, or the Subject of any Prince or State in Amity with us, nor against their Ships, Vessels or Goods, but only against *France* and *Spain*, their Vassals and Subjects, and others inhabiting within their Countries, Territories or Dominions, their Ships, Vessels and Goods, except as before excepted, and against such other Ships, Vessels and Goods, as are or shall be liable to Confiscation.

X.

That after Condemnation of any Prize, taken from *France* or *Spain* as aforesaid, it shall or may be lawful for the Commanders of such Merchant Ships or Vessels, or the Owners of the same, to keep such and so many Ships, Vessels, Goods and Merchandizes, as shall be condemned to them for lawful Prize, in their own Possession, to make Sale or dispose thereof in open Market, or otherwise, to their best Advantage, in as ample manner as at any time heretofore has been accustomed in Cases of Letters of Marque, or of just Prizes in Time of War; other than wrought Silks, *Bengals*, and Stuffs

Stuffs mixed with Silk or Herba, of the Manufacture of *Perſia, China*, or *Eaſt-India*, or Callicoes painted, dyed, printed or ſtained there, which are to be depoſited for Exportation, according to the Directions of an Act made in the eleventh Year of the Reign of the late King *William* the Third, entitled, *An Act for the more effectually employing the Poor, by encouraging the Manufactures of this Kingdom:* And that it ſhall be lawful for all manner of Perſons, as well our Subjects as others, according to Law, to buy the ſaid Ships, Veſſels, Goods and Merchandizes, ſo taken and condemned for lawful Prize, without any Damage or Moleſtation to enſue thereupon to the ſaid Buyers, or any of them, by reaſon of the contracting or dealing for the ſame.

XI.

That if any Ship or Veſſel belonging to us, or our Subjects, or to our Allies or their Subjects, ſhall be found in Diſtreſs, by being in Fight, ſet upon, or taken by the Enemy, or by reaſon of any other Accident, the Commander, Officers and Company, who ſhall have ſuch Letters of Marque or Commiſſions as aforeſaid, ſhall uſe their beſt Endeavours to give Aid and Succour to all ſuch Ship or Ships, and ſhall to the utmoſt of their Power, labour to free the ſame from the Enemy, or any other Diſtreſs.

XII.

That our Subjects, and all other Perſons whatſoever, who ſhall either in their own Perſons ſerve, or bear any Charge or Adventure, or in any Sort further or ſet forward the ſaid Adventure, according to theſe Articles, ſhall ſtand and be freed by Virtue of the ſaid Commiſſion; and that no Perſon be in any wiſe reputed or challenged for an Offender againſt our Laws, but ſhall be freed under our Protection,

tection, of and from all Trouble and Vexation that might, in any wife grow thereby, in the fame manner as any other our Subjects ought to be by Law, in their aiding and affifting us, either in their own Perfons, or otherwife in a lawful War againft our declared Enemies.

XIII.

That the faid Commanders of fuch Merchant Ships and Veffels, or their Owners or Agents, before the taking out Commiffions, fhall give Notice in writing, fubfcribed with their Hands, to our High Admiral of *Great-Britain* for the Time being, or our Commiffioners for executing the Office of our High Admiral, or the Commiffioners for executing that Office for the Time being, or the Lieutenant or Judge of the faid High Court of Admiralty, or his Surrogate, of the Name of their Ship, and of the Tonnage and Burthen, and the Names of the Captains, Owners or Setters out of the faid Ship, with the Number of Men, and the Names of the Officers in her, and for what Time they are victualled, and alfo of their Ordnance, Furniture and Ammunition; to the End the fame may be regiftred in the faid Court of Admiralty.

XIV.

That thofe Commanders of fuch Merchant Ships and Veffels, who fhall have fuch Letters of Marque or Commiffions as aforefaid, fhall hold and keep and are hereby enjoined to hold and keep a Correfpondence by all Conveniences, and upon all Occafions, from Time to Time, with our High Admiral of *Great-Britain* for the Time being, or our Commiffioners for executing the Office of our High Admiral, or the Commiffioners for executing tha Office for the Time being, or their Secretary, fo a from Time to Time to render and give unto him o them, not only an Account or Intelligence of thei

Cap

aptures or Proceedings, by Virtue of such their Letters of Marque or Commissions as aforesaid, but also, of whatsoever else shall occur unto them, or be discovered and declared unto them, or found out by them, by Examination of, or Conference with any Mariners, or Passengers of or in the Ships or Vessels taken, or by any other ways and means whatsoever, touching or concerning the Designs of the Enemies, or any of their Fleets, Ships, Vessels or Parties, and of the Stations, Seas, Ports and Places, and of their Intents therein, and of what Merchant Ships or Vessels of the Enemies bound out or home, as they shall hear of; and of what else material in these Cases may arrive to their Knowledge, to the End such Course may be thereupon taken, and such Orders given as may be requisite.

XV.

That no Commander of a Merchant Ship, or Vessel, who shall have a Letter of Marque or Commission as aforesaid, shall presume, as they will answer it at their Peril, to wear any Jack, Pendant, or any other Ensign or Colour usually born by our Ships, but that, besides the Colours born usually by Merchant Ships, they do wear a red Jack with the Union Jack, described in the Canton at the upper Corner thereof near the Staff; and that one third Part of the whole Company of every such Ship or Vessel so fitted out as aforesaid, shall be Landmen.

XVI.

That such Commanders of Merchants Ships and Vessels, who shall obtain such Letters of Marque or Commissions as aforesaid, shall also from Time to Time, upon due Notice being given them, observe all such other Instructions and Orders as we shall think fit to direct for the better carrying on of this Service.

Q 2   XVII.

XVII.

That all Perfons who fhall violate thefe Inftructions, fhall be feverely punifhed, and alfo required to make full Reparation to Perfons injured, contrary to thefe Inftructions, for all Damages they fhall fuftain by any Capture, Embezzlement, Demurrage or otherwife.

XVIII.

That before any fuch Letter of Marque or Commiffion iffue under Seal, Bail with Sureties fhall be given before the Lieutenant and Judge of our High Court of Admiralty of *England*, or his Surrogate, in the Sum of three thoufand Pounds Sterling, if the Ship carries above one hundred and fifty Men, and if a leffer Number, in the Sum of fifteen hundred Pounds Sterling: Which Bail fhall be to the Effect, and in the Form following.

Which Day, Time and Place, perfonally appeared

who fubmitting themfelves to the Jurifdiction of the High Court of Admiralty of *England*, obliged themfelves, their Heirs, Executors and Adminiftrators, to our Sovereign Lord the King, in the Sum of   Pounds, of lawful Money of *Great-Britain*, to this Effect; that is to fay, that whereas   is authorized by Letters of Marque, or a Commiffion for a private Man of War, to arm, equip, and fet forth to Sea, the Ship called the   of the Burthen of about   Tons; whereof he the faid   goeth Captain, with   Men, Ordnance, Ammunition and Victuals, to fet upon by Force of Arms, and to fubdue, feize and take the Men of War, Ships and other Veffels whatfoever, together with the Goods, Monies and Merchan-chandizes, belonging to *France* and *Spain*, or to any of their Vaſſals and Subjects, or others inhabiting within any of their Countries, Territories or Dominions whatſoever, and ſuch other Ships, Veſſels and Goods, as are or ſhall be liable to Confiſcation, excepting only within the Harbours or Roads, within Shot of the Cannon of Princes and States in Amity with his Majeſty. And whereas, he the ſaid   has a Copy of certain Inſtructions, approved of, and paſſed by his Majeſty in Council, delivered to him to govern himſelf therein, as by the Tenor of the ſaid Commiſſion, and of the Inſtructions thereto relating, more at large appeareth. If therefore, nothing be done by the ſaid   or any of his Officers, Mariners or Company, contrary to the true Meaning of the ſaid Inſtructions, but that the Commiſſion aforeſaid, and the ſaid Inſtructions ſhall, in all Particulars, be well and duly performed and obſerved, as far as they ſhall the ſaid Ship, Captain and Company any way concern: And if they or any of them, ſhall give full Satisfaction for any Damage or Injury which ſhall be done by them, or any one of them, to any of his Majeſty's Subjects or Allies, or Neuters, or their Subjects; and alſo ſhall duly and truly pay or cauſe to be paid to his Majeſty, or the Cuſtomers or Officers appointed to receive the ſame for his Majeſty, the uſual Cuſtoms due to his Majeſty, of and for all Ships and Goods, ſo as aforeſaid taken and adjudged for Prize: And moreover, the ſaid   ſhall not take any Ship or Veſſel, or any Goods or Merchandizes, belonging to the Enemies, or otherwiſe liable to Confiſcation, through Conſent or clandeſtinely, or by Colluſion, by Virtue, Colour or Pretence of his ſaid Commiſſion; that then this Bail ſhall be void and of none Effect; and unleſs they ſhall

shall so do, they do all hereby severally consent that Execution shall issue forth against them, their Heirs, Executors and Administrators, Goods and Chattels, wheresoever the same shall be found, to the Value of the said Sum of
Pounds before mentioned. And in Testimony of the Truth thereof, they have hereunto subscribed their Names.

By His Majesty's Command,

HOLLES NEWCASTLE

George R.

(L.S.)

Additional Instructions to such Merchant Ships and Vessels as have, or may have Letters of Marque, or Commissions for private Men of War, against France *and* Spain, *their Vassals and Subjects, or others inhabiting within any of their Countries, Territories, or Dominions, by Virtue of our Commission granted under the Great Seal of* Great-Britain, *bearing Date the eighteenth Day of* June 1744. *Given at our Court at* St. James's *the 27th Day of* December 1744, *in the eighteenth Year of our Reign.*

I.

THAT all Captains or commanding Officers of Privateers, do send an Account of, and deliver over what Prisoners shall be taken on board any Prizes, to the Commissioners appointed for the Exchange of Prisoners of War, or the Persons appointed in the Sea Port Towns, to take Charge of Prisoners; and that such Prisoners be subject only to the Orders, Regulations and Directions of the said Commissioners; and that no Commander or other Officer of any Man of War, or private Ship of War, do presume upon any Pretence whatsoever to ransom any *French* or *Spanish* Prisoners.

II.

That no Commander of any Man of War, or Privateer, shall ransom any Ship taken as Prize, when such

such Ship may conveniently be brought into some Port of his Majesty's Dominions; and in case any Ship, taken as Prize, shall be ransomed, the Reasons for so doing, and the Condition of such Ransom shall be transmitted to the Judge of the Admiralty, and preparatory Examinations upon the standing Interrogatories shall be taken as in all Cases of Prize, and a Condemnation of such Ransom shall be had, according to the antient Course and Practice of the Admiralty; and in case any Commander of any Privateer or Merchant Ship, having a Letter of Marque, shall act contrary to their several Instructions, such Commander shall forfeit his Commission to all Intents and Purposes, and shall, together with his Bail, be proceeded against according to Law, and be condemned in Costs and Damages.

III.

That all Commanders of Privateers or Merchant Ships, that shall have Letters of Marque, shall by every Opportunity send exact Copies of their Journals to the Secretary of the Admiralty, and proceed to the Condemnation of their Prizes as soon as may be, and without any Delay.

By His Majesty's Command,

HARRINGTON.

George R.

(L.S.)

An additional Instruction to all Ships of War and Privateers, that have, or may have Letters of Marque against France *and* Spain, *their Vassals or Subjects, or others inhabiting within any of their Countries, Territories or Dominions. Given at our Court at* St. James's, *the* 30th *Day of* March 1747, *in the twentieth Year of our Reign.*

WHEREAS by all our Instructions to our Men of War, and to the Commanders of such Merchant Ships and Vessels as have obtained Letters of Marque, or Commissions for private Men of War, against *France* and *Spain*; it has been our Royal Will and Pleasure to command, and we have strictly commanded and enjoined the several Commanders of Men of War and Privateers, not to attempt any thing against the Subjects of any Prince or State in Amity with us, nor against their Ships, Vessels, Goods or Merchandize, but only to take, seize, or destroy the Ships, Vessels, Goods or Merchandize belonging to *France* and *Spain*, their Vassals and Subjects: And whereas we have had proper Informations, by which it appears that our aforesaid Instructions and Commands have not been duly obeyed; and that, notwithstanding the same, great Irregularities and unjustifiable Violences have been committed by our Privateers, particularly upon the Subjects of the *Sultan* of the *Ottoman* Empire, by seizing in a hostile and violent Manner

their

their Goods and Effects, and mifufing their Perfons. For the avoiding for the future fuch Violations of our Inftructions and Commands, we ftrictly charge and enjoin all Ships of War, that they do not, upon any Pretence, moleft, detain, or imprifon the Perfons of any of the Subjects of the *Ottoman* Empire, nor feize, or detain as Prize, their Ships or Effects in the *Levant* Seas, or any other Part of the Ocean, where a proper, regular, and free Trade fhall be carried on, under Pain of our higheft Difpleafure, and fuch Punifhment as by Law may be inflicted. And for the more exact and regular proceeding in the Premiffes, we hereby order and direct, that no Effects or Merchandizes, taken on board any Enemy's Ship, which fhall be claimed by any Subjects of the Grand Signior's, as being their Property, fhall be proceeded againft for Condemnation in any other Court but the High Court of Admiralty of *England*, nor in that Court until Notice be firft given of the faid Proceeding to the *Turkey* Company, to the End that Care may be taken that a proper and legal Defence may be made on behalf of the Claimants, Subjects of the Grand Signior.

SAMUEL HILL, Regifter.

FORM

FORM of a PROTEST from the Capture of a Ship as Prize.

BY this public Inftrument of Proteft, be it known and manifeft to all People, That on the   Day of   in the Year of our Lord   before me *A. B.* Notary Publick, refiding in the Town and Borough of   in the County of   in the Kingdom of *Great-Britain*, by lawful Authority, admitted and fworn perfonally, appeared *C. D.* Mafter and Commander of the Good Ship or Veffel called the   of   in the Kingdom of   of the Burthen of   Tons or thereabouts, now riding in the *Downs*, or lying at Anchor in the Port of   who upon his Faith and Honefty folemnly declared, and for Truth affirmed, and witneffed as followeth (that is to fay) that the faid Ship did on the   Day of   Inftant, N. S. fet fail from *Hamburgh*, bound to   in   laden with, (fpecifying the Cargo) for   *E. F.* a neutral Account; and Yefterday being arrived between *Dover* and *Dungenefs* on the *Englifh* Coaft, and being under fail for her intended Port, fhe fell in with an *Englifh* Privateer, called   *G. H.* Commander, who having taken from this Atteftant his Documents and Papers of all Kinds, feized the faid Ship, and brought her this Day into the *Downs*, or into the Port of   where he ftill detains her, and hath caufed this Atteftant, *his Mate and Boatfwain* to be brought on Shore and examined before Commiffioners there: And the faid Atteftant alfo declared that the faid Ship was at the Time of the faid Capture in good State and Condition, well fitted and provided for the Peformance of her intended

tended Voyage, and was, and is prevented proceeding therein, only by the Capture and Detention of her, by the said Privateer as aforesaid, and by no other Cause whatsoever. By reason of all which Premises, the said Master doth by these Presents make and enter his Protest in due Form against the said Privateer the   her Owners, Captain and Mariners, and all others whom it doth or may concern, of and for all Losses, Costs, Charges, Damages and Delays whatsoever to the said Ship or Lading, her Owners or Freighters, already suffered and sustained, or hereafter to be suffered and sustained by means of her being seized and detained by the said Privateer as aforesaid: To be all allowed and recovered in Time and Place convenient, and these Presents to serve and avail for that Purpose as Occasion shall be or required. Thus was this done and protested in   aforesaid, in the Presence of *I. K.* and *L. M.* Witnesses thereto requested. In Testimony of the Truth whereof, he the said Attestant, and they the said Witnesses have subscribed their Names in the Registry, or Office of me the said Notary; and I the said Notary have hereunto set my Hand and affixed my Seal of Office of a Notary, the Day and Year first above written.

A. B. Notary Publick, at   (S.)

INTERROGATORIES, concerning whose Right or Property (Prizes taken from the Enemy in Time of War belong) to be first administred before any Distribution can be made.

Standing Interrogatories to be administred on behalf of our Sovereign Lord George *the Second, by the Grace of God of* Great-Britain, France *and* Ireland, *King Defender of the Faith in his Office of Admiralty to the respective Masters and some of the Mariners and others of the Crew, of all and singular the Ships and Vessels, Goods and Merchandizes seized, or which shall hereafter be seized in the   or the Districts thereof, or taken or seized, or which shall hereafter be taken and seized, by any private Man of War, by Virtue of Letters of Marque or Commission of War, or without any Commission; and also of all and singular Ships and Vessels whatsoever recovered from the Enemies of our said Sovereign Lord the King, by any of his Majesty's Ships of War or otherwise, and brought into any Port of the aforesaid Isle or the Districts thereof, or such other Person or Persons from whom the Truth may properly be discovered, relating to the Property of such Ships and Vessels, Goods and Merchandizes seized, or which shall hereafter be seized as aforesaid, follow; to wit,*

First, LET the Witnesses be asked, Where was you born, and where have you lived for these seven Years last past? and where do you now live?

live? and how long have you lived in the Place where you now dwell? Are you a Subject to the Crown of *Great-Britain*, or to what Prince or State are you a Subject? and let the Witnesses be asked jointly and severally, and as above.

II.

Item, Let the Witnesses be asked, when and by whom was the Ship and Lading, Goods and Merchandizes, concerning which you are now examined taken and seized, and into what Port were the same carried? Was there any Resistance made or Guns fired against Ship or Persons who seized and took the same? and what, or how many, and by whom? And let the Witnesses be asked jointly and severally, and as above.

III.

Item, Let the Witnesses be asked, was you present at the Time of the taking and seizing the Ship and her Lading, or any Goods and Merchandizes, concerning which you are now examined? or how, and when was you first made acquainted therewith? was the said Ship and Goods taken by a Man of War or a private Man of War? and to whom did such Man of War or private Man of War belong? had they any Commission to act as such, and from whom? and by whom and what particular Ship, or by whom was or were the said Ship, Goods and Merchandizes, seized and taken? and let the Witnesses be asked jointly and severally, and as above.

IV.

Item, Let the Witnesses be asked, upon what Pretence was the said Ship and Lading seized and taken? to what Port or Place was she afterwards carried? has she ever been condemned? upon what Account or for what Reason has she been condemned? and by whom and by what Authority was she so condemned? and let the Witnesses be asked jointly and severally, and as above.

Item,

(239)

V.

Item, Let the Witnesses be asked, who by Name was the Master of the Ship or Vessel, concerning which you are now examined, at the Time she was taken and seized? how long have you known the said Master? who first appointed him to be Master of the said Ship, and where did he take Possession thereof, and who by Name delivered the same to him? where is the said Master's fixed Place of Habitation, with his Wife and Family, and how long has he lived there? what Countryman is he by Birth, and to what Prince or State subject? and let the Witnesses be asked jointly and severally, and as above.

VI.

Item, Let the Witnesses be asked, what Number of Mariners belonged to the Ship or Vessel at the Time she was taken and seized? what Countrymen are they, and where did they all come on board? had you the Witness, or any of the Officers or Company of Mariners belonging to the said Ship or Vessel, any Part, Share or Interest in the said Ship or her Lading, or in any of the Goods, concerning which you are now examined? and what in particular, and the Value thereof at the Time the said Ship was so taken, or the said Goods so seized? and let the Witnesses be asked jointly and severally, and as above.

VII.

Item, Let the Witnesses be asked, did you belong to the Ship or Vessel, concerning which you are now examined at the Time she was taken and seized? how long had you known her; when and where did you first see her? of what Burthen is she, and of what Country building? what was her Name, and how long had she been so called? do you know of any other Names she was called by, and what were such Names as you know or have heard? and

let

let the Witnesses be asked jointly and severally, and as above.

VIII.

Item, Let the Witnesses be asked, to what Ports and Places was the said Ship or Vessel, concerning which you are now examined, bound or intended to proceed the Voyage wherein she was taken and seized? To and from what Ports and Places did she sail the said Voyage before she was taken and seized? Where did the Voyage begin, and where was the Voyage to have ended? What Sort of Lading did she carry at the Time of her first setting out on the said Voyage? And what particular Sort of Lading and Goods had she on board at the Time she was so taken and seized? Was the said Ship or Vessel at the Time she was so taken and seized proceeding or intended to proceed upon a lawful, and what particular Trade? Had she at that Time any and what Prohibited Goods on board her? And let the Witnesses be asked jointly and severally, and as above.

IX.

Item, Let the Witnesses be asked, who were the Owners of the Ship or Vessel, concerning which you are now examined, at the Time she was taken and seized? How do you know that they were Owners of the said Ship at that Time? What Nation are they by birth, and where do they live with their Wives and Families? To what Prince or State are they subject? And let the Witnesses be asked jointly and severally, and as above.

X.

Item, Let the Witnesses be asked, was there any Bill of Sale made to the Owners of the said Ship? In what Month or Year, and where, and before what Witnesses was the same made? And when did you the Witness last see it, and what is become there-

thereof? And let the Witnesses be asked jointly and severally, and as above.

XI.

Item, Let the Witnesses be asked, in what Port or Place was the Lading which was on board the Ship, at the Time she was taken and seized, first put on board the said Ship? in what Month and Year, and Quantities, and Particulars thereof? Were the same laden and put on board the said Ship, in one Port and at one Time, or in several Ports and Places, and how many by Name, and at how many several Times, and what Particulars, and what Quantity at each Port? Who by Name were the several Laders or Owners thereof, and what Countrymen are they? where do they now live and carry on their Trade or Business, and of what Religion are they? Where were the said Goods to be delivered, and for whose Account, and to whom by name did they then really belong, and for whom designed, and for what particular Purposes? And let the Witnesses be asked jointly and severally, and as above.

XII.

Item, Let the Witnesses be asked, how many Bills of Lading were signed for the Goods seized on board the said Ship? Were the same colourable, and were any Bills of Lading signed which were of a different Tenor with those which were on board the said Ship at the Time she was taken and seized, and what were the Contents of such other Bills of Lading, and what are become thereof? And let the Witnesses be asked jointly and severally, and as above.

XIII.

Item, Let the Witnesses be asked, what Bills of Lading, Invoices, Letters, or any Instruments, or Writing, or Papers, have you to prove the Property in the Ship and Goods, concerning which you are now

now examined? Produce the same, and set forth the particular Times when, and in what Manner, and upon what Account, and for what Consideration, you became possessed thereof? And let the Witnesses be asked jointly and severally, and as above.

XIV.

Item, Let the Witnesses be asked, in what particular Port or Place, and what Degree of Latitude, was or were the Ship and Goods, concerning which you are now examined, taken and seized? At what Time, and upon what Day of the Month, and in what Year, was or were the said Ship and Goods so taken and seized? And let the Witnesses be asked jointly and severally, and as above.

XV.

Item, Let the Witnesses be asked, was there any and what particular Charter-Party signed for the Voyage or intended Voyage, wherein the Ship, concerning which you are now examined, was taken and seized? What is become thereof? When and between whom were the same made? What were the Contents thereof? And let the Witnesses be asked jointly and severally, and as above.

XVI.

Item, Let the Witnesses be asked, what particular Papers, Bills of Lading, Letters, or other Writings, were on board the said Ship at the Time of the seizing of the said Ship, and what is become thereof? And let the Witnesses be asked jointly and severally, and as above.

XVII.

Item, Let the Witnesses be asked, what Loss or Damage have you sustained, by reason of the seizing and taking of the said Ship, Goods, and Merchandizes, concerning which you are now examined?

To what Value does such Loſs or Damage amount? And how, and after what Manner, do you compute ſuch your Loſs and Damage? Have you received or do you expect to receive any, and what Satisfaction, for ſuch Loſs and Damage which you have ſuſtained? And when and from whom did you receive, or do you expect to receive, the ſame? And let the Witneſſes be aſked jointly and ſeverally, and as above.

SUPPLEMENT.

FRANCE.

IN the Treaty of Navigation and Commerce concluded at *Utrecht*, *March* 31, O. S. 1713, p. 1, & feqq. add the following Articles: *Queen Anne. Lewis XIV.*

ARTICLE II.

That the Commerce and Friendship between the Subjects of the abovesaid Parties may be hereafter secure, and free from all Trouble and Molestation, it is agreed and concluded, that if at any Time any ill Understanding, and Breach of Friendship, or Rupture, should happen between their said Majesties (which God forbid); in such case, the Term of Six Months shall be allowed, after the said Rupture, to the Subjects and Inhabitants, on each Part, residing in the Dominions of the other; in which Term, they themselves may retire, together with their Families, Goods, Merchandizes, and Effects, and carry them whithersoever they shall please: As likewise at the same Time, the selling and disposing of their Goods, both moveable and immoveable, shall be allowed freely, and without any Disturbance; and during the said Term, they shall not be detained by any Arrests, of their Persons, Effects, Goods, or Merchandizes. And further, the Subjects on each Side shall have and enjoy good and speedy Justice, so that they may avail themselves of it, in order to withdraw, within the said Space of Six Months, their Goods and Effects, intrusted as well to the Publick, as to private Persons. *Six Months allowed to the Subjects of both their Majesties, to withdraw their Persons and Effects after a Rupture.*

ARTICLE VIII.

Subjects of either Party to enjoy all the Privileges of the moſt favoured Nations, in the Dominions of the other.

It is eſtabliſhed as a general Rule, that all and ſingular the Subjects of their ſaid Majeſties, ſhall uſe and enjoy reſpectively, in all Countries and Places ſubject to their Power, the ſame Privileges, Liberties, and Immunities, without any Exception, as fully as the moſt favoured Nation now doth, or hereafter ſhall, uſe and enjoy, in reſpect to any Rights, Duties, or Impoſitions, relating to Perſons, Merchandiſe, Effects, Ships, Freight, Seamen, Navigation, and Trade; and that they ſhall have the ſame Degree of Favour in all Affairs, as well in thoſe tranſacted in Courts of Juſtice, as in thoſe which concern Commerce, or any other Rights.

ARTICLE XXXIII.

The Remains of Shipwrecks, and their Lading, ſhall be reſtored to the Proprietors.

In Caſe that either Ships of War, or Merchant-Ships, forced by Storms, or other Misfortunes, on Rocks or Shelves, on the Coaſts of the one or the other Party, ſhould there be broken to Pieces and ſhipwrecked; whatſoever is ſaved of ſuch Ships, their Apparel, Effects, Merchandiſe, or the Produce thereof if ſold, ſhall be faithfully reſtored to the Proprietors, Reclaimers, or their Factors, paying only the Expences of preſerving the ſame, as it ſhall have been ſettled on both Sides, in reſpect to the Rights of Salvage, ſaving alſo the

Severe Puniſhment to be inflicted on thoſe who are guilty of Inhumanity.

Rights and Cuſtoms of each Nation; and both their Majeſties ſhall interpoſe their Authority, that ſuch of the Subjects may be ſeverely puniſhed, who in the like Accidents ſhall be found guilty of Inhumanity.

N. B. This Treaty of Commerce does not appear to have been renewed by the Treaty of *Aix la Chapelle* in 1748.

IN

IN the Forms of the Paſſports, &c. here only in *Engliſh*, as well as the Form of the Act containing the Oath, and the Form of the Certificates, from p. 12. to p. 15. add the *French* and *Latin*, from the original, as follows.

Formulaire des Paſſeports et Lettres, qui ſe doivent donner dans l'amirauté de France *aux navires & barques qui en ſortiront, ſuivant l'article* 21. *du preſent traité.*

*L*OUIS Comte de *Thouloufe* Amiral de *France*, à tous ceux qui ces preſentes lettres verront, ſalut. Sçavoir faiſons, que nous avons donné congé & permiſſion à maitre & conducteur du navire nommé de la ville de du port de tonneux ou environ, étant de preſent au port & havre de de s'en aller à chargé de après que viſitation aura été faite de ſon navire, avant que de partir, fera ſerment devant les officiers, qui exercent la juriſdiction des cauſes maritimes, comme le dit vaiſſeau appartient à un ou pluſieurs des ſujets de ſa majeſté, dont il ſera mis acte au bas des preſentes; comme auſſi de garder & faire garder, par ceux de ſon equipage, les ordonnances & reglemens de la marine, & mettre au greffe le rôle, ſigné & verifié, contenant les noms & ſurnoms, la naiſſance & demeure des hommes de ſon equipage, & de tous ceux qui s'embarqueront, lequel il ne pourra embarquer ſans le ſçû & permiſſion des officiers de la marine ; & en chacun port ou havre ou il entrera avec ſon navire, fera apparoir aux officiers & juges de la marine du preſent congé, & leur fera fidele rapport de ce, qui fera fait & paſſé durant ſon voyage, & portera les pavillons, armes & enſeignes du Roy, & les nôtres, durant ſon voyage. En temoin de quoi nous avons fait appoſer nôtre ſeing,

& le féel de nos armes à ces préfentes, & icelles fait contrefigner par nôtre fecretaire de la marine à jour de   mille fept cent
Signé *Louis* Comte de *Tholoufe*——& plus bas
                       par

Formulaire de l'Acte contenant le Serment.

Nous   de l'amirauté de
maitre du navire, nommé an paſſeport cideſſus, a prêté le ferment mentionné en icelui. Faite à   le   jour de   mille fept cens·

Formula literarum certificatoriarum petendarum dandarumque à magiſtratu aut officialibus vectigalium & teloniorum burgi & portus, in burgis & portubus ſuis reſpectivis, navibus & navigiis inde vela facientibus, ſecundum articuli vigeſimi primi hujus tractatus diſpoſitionem.

Nos *A. B.* magiſtratus aut officiales vectigalium (aut) teloniorum burgi & portus *C.* certificamus & atteſtamur, quod die   menſis   ·   anno Dom. 17   . perſonaliter coram nobis comparuit *D. E.* de *F.* & ſolenni jurejurando declaravit, Quod navis ſive navigium vocat' *G.* menſurarum, quas tuns vocant   capax, cujus *H. I.* de *K.* ſolitæ habitationis loco eſt magiſter ſive præfectus, ei & aliis etiam ſereniſſimæ regiæ majeſtatis dominæ noſtræ clementiſſimæ ſubditis, iiſque ſolis, juſto titulo propria ſit: jam vero de portu *L.* iter deſtinaſſe ad portum *M.* onuſtam mercibus & mercimoniis hinc infra ſpeciatim deſcriptis & enumeratis, ſcilicet & prout ſequitur viz. . . . .

In quorum fidem has certificatorias literas signavimus, & figillo noftri officii figillavimus. Dabantur die   menfis   A. D. 17 .

IN the *American* Treaty of Peace, &c. concluded at *London* November 16, 1686, from p. 15. to p. 21, inclufive, after article XVI. (here printed by Miftake XVII.) in p. 20. add : — Between *James* II. and *Lewis* XIV.

ARTICLE XVII.

If any Differences or Difputes fhould arife between the Subjects of either King, in the faid Iflands, Colonies, Forts, Cities, and Governments, under the Dominion of either refpectively, whether at Sea or Land, this Peace and good Correfpondence fhall not thereby be interrupted or infringed; but the faid Differences which may happen between the Subjects of the faid Kings, fhall be adjudged and determined by the Governors of each Jurifdiction refpectively, where they fhall have arifen, or by them whom they fhall depute: and if the faid Differences cannot within the Space of one year be determined by the faid Governors, they fhall tranfmit the Proceedings with the firft Opportunity to the one or the other of the faid Kings, that fuch Differences may be determined according to Juftice, in the Manner which fhall be agreed upon between their Majefties *. — All Differences between the Subjects of either King to be decided where they have arifen: But if not determined within a Year, the Proceedings muft be tranfmitted to the one or other of their Majefties.

IN the Treaty of Peace at *Utrecht*, March 31, 1713, p. 21. to p. 23. inclufive, add :

ARTICLE X. †

The Moft Chriftian King fhall reftore to the Kingdom and Queen of *Great Britain*, to be poffeffed in full Right for ever, the Bay and Streights — *Hudfon's* Bay reftored to the *Englifh*.

---

* Article XIX. is in p. 41.
† See Article VII. in p. 40.

of *Hudson*, together with all Lands, Seas, Sea-Coasts, Rivers, and Places, situated in the said Bay and Streights, and which belong thereunto, no Tracts of Land or of Sea being excepted, which are at present possessed by the Subjects of *France*.

ARTICLE XIX.

But if (which God forbid) the Dissensions which have been composed, should at any Time be renewed, between their said Majesties or their Successors, and break out into open War, the Ships, Merchandizes, and all the Effects both moveable and immoveable, on both Sides, which shall be found to be and remain in the Ports and Dominions of the adverse Party, shall not be confiscated or any way detained or damaged, but the entire Space of Six Months, to be reckoned from the Day of the Rupture, shall be allowed to the said Subjects of each of their Majesties, in which Term they may sell the aforesaid Things, or any other Part of their Effects, or carry and remove them from thence, wherever they please, without any Molestation, and retire from thence themselves.

In the Marine Treaty of *St Germains*, 24 *Feb.* 1676-7, p. 23. the Preamble to Article I. omitted there, is inserted in p. 41.

In the Marine Treaty at *St Germains*, *March* 29, 1632, all the Articles relating to the Marine are in p. 34 to p. 36. except the VIIIth, which is in p. 43.

In the Treaty of Alliance at *London*, *August* 29, 1610, all the Articles concerning the Marine are in p. 36. except Article I. which is in p. 44.

In the Treaty of Peace between *Ardres* and *Guines*, *June* 7th, 1546, in Article III. p. 37 and 38.

to the Memorandum ending, *and* 1478. add, and 1483, *and in the subsequent Treaties* 1549-50, 1559, and 1564.

IN the Treaty of Peace at *Ryswick*, September 10, 1697, p. 40. to Article V. add the two following:

ARTICLE X.

To cut off all Manner of Dispute and Contention which may arise concerning the Restitution of Ships, Merchandises, and other moveable Goods, which either Party may complain to have been taken and detained by the other, in Countries and on Coasts far distant, after the Peace is concluded, and before it is there notified; all Ships, Merchandizes, and other movable Goods, which shall be taken on either Side after the Signing and Publication of the present Treaty, within the Space of Twelve Days, in the *British* and *Northern* Seas; within the Space of Six Weeks, from the said *British* and *Northern* Seas, as far as Cape *St Vincent*; within the Space of Ten Weeks, beyond the said Cape, and on this Side the Equinoctial Line or Equator, as well in the Ocean and *Mediterranean* Sea as elsewhere; lastly, within the Space of Six Months, beyond the Boundaries of the said Line, throughout the whole World; shall belong and remain to the Possessors, without any Exception, or farther Distinction of Time or Place, or any Consideration to be had of Restitution or Compensation.

Times and Distances settled with regard to Ships taken after Peace is concluded, and before it is notified.

ARTICLE XII.

But if (which God forbid) the Differences now composed between the said Kings, should at any Time be renewed, and break out into open War, the Ships, Merchandises, and all kind of moveable Goods of either Party, which shall be found to be and remain in the Ports and Dominions of the adverse

Six Months allowed for the Removal of Effects in case of a Rupture.

verſe Party ſhall not be confiſcated, or in any Manner detained or damaged; but the whole Space of Six Months ſhall be allowed to the Subjects of both the ſaid Kings, that they may carry away and tranſport the aforeſaid Goods, and any Thing elſe which is theirs, whitherſoever they ſhall think fit, without any Moleſtation.

AFTER the Treaty of Peace at *Bredah*, *July* 21, 1667, in p. 41, 42. containing the Articles II. and IV. add:

The XVIIIth Article makes the ſame Stipulation, which is expreſſed too, almoſt verbatim, in the ſame Words, with the XIIth Article of the Treaty of *Ryſwick*, in 1697.

TO the Act of the Oath taken by the King of *France*, and the Queen-Regent his Mother, &c. dated at *Ruel*, *July* 3, 1644, after the Words *in any Manner*, at the Bottom of p. 42. add,

Moreover, we promiſe to repeat the preſent Oath, when we ſhall have attained the Age of Majority, and ſhall be duly required ſo to do.

Likewiſe after the Words, *contravened in any ſort*, in p. 43. add:

And we will cauſe the aforeſaid Oath, which the King takes at preſent, to be by him taken again in due Form, when he ſhall attain to the Age of Majority.

IN the Treaty of Peace and Alliance at *Suſa*, *April* 24, 1629, in p. 43. after Article I. add:

ARTICLE V.

Ancient Alliances to remain in Force.

All the antient Alliances, as well of the one as of the other Crown, ſhall remain in Force, without any Alteration made by the preſent Treaty.

IN the Treaty of Commerce at Paris, *May* 26, 1606, (misprinted in p. 45. *February* 24, 1605-6) after Article I. add:

ARTICLE XIV.

It is agreed, that the Liberty of Commerce shall be maintained in the State in which it is at present on both Sides, as well of Goods manufactured as not manufactured, according to the present and preceding Treaties; nor shall it be lawful on either Side to make any Prohibitions against Trade, excepting always contraband Goods, the Transportation of which has been in all Times, and is to this Day, prohibited and forbidden by the Laws of both Kingdoms.

Commerce to be maintained in it's present State.

AFTER the Treaty of Peace and Commerce, *April* 5, 1515, in p. 47. add:

Treaty of Peace and Commerce between England *and* France, *concluded at* Troyes *in* Champagne, May 21, 1420.

ARTICLE XXVIII.

It is concluded and agreed, that henceforward all Dissensions, Hatred, Rancour, Enmities, and Wars, shall entirely cease between *England* and *France*, and the People of those Kingdoms; and that from this Time and for ever, Peace, Tranquillity, Concord, mutual Affection, and firm Friendship, shall subsist and flourish between the said Kingdoms and their Subjects; and the said Kingdoms shall be assisting to each other in Counsel and mutual Aid against any Persons whatsoever, who shall do, or attempt to do, any Violence, Injury, or Damage, to either of the said Kingdoms; and the Subjects of each Kingdom shall have mutual Intercourse and Trade together, freely and securely,

Peace and Amity agreed to.

The Subjects of each Kingdom to have a mutual Intercourse and free Trade.

curely, on Condition that they pay the usual Duties and Customs.

N. B. This is the first perpetual Treaty made with *France*, after the Conquest of that Kingdom by *Henry* V. of *England*.

IN the Definitive Treaty of Peace at *Aix la Chapelle*, in *October* 1748, antecedent to Art: XVI. in p. 47. insert the two following:

ARTICLE I.

Universal and perpetual Peace between the contracting Powers.

There shall be a Christian, universal, and perpetual Peace, as well by Sea as Land, and a sincere and lasting Friendship between the contracting Powers, their Heirs and Successors, Kingdoms, States, Provinces, Countries. Subjects, and Vassals, of what Rank or Condition soever they may be, without Exception of Places or Persons.

ARTICLE III.

The Treaties of *Westphalia* of 1648; those of *Madrid*, between the Crowns of *England* and *Spain*, of 1667 and 1670; the Treaties of Peace of *Nimeguen*, of 1678 and 1679; of *Ryswick*, of 1697; of *Utrecht*, of 1713; of *Baden*, of 1714; the Treaty of the Triple Alliance of the *Hague*, of 1717; that of the Quadruple Alliance of *London*, of 1718; and the Treaty of Peace of *Vienna*, of 1738; serve as a Basis and Foundation to the general Peace, and to the present Treaty; and for this Purpose, they are renewed and confirmed in the best Form, and as if they were here inserted Word for Word; so that they shall be punctually observed for the Future in all their Tenor, and religiously executed on the one Side and the other; such Points however excepted, as have been derogated from in the present Treaty.

SPAIN.

SPAIN.

IN the Treaty of Peace between *Great Britain* and *Spain* at *Utrecht*, *July* 2, 1713, in p. 49. after Article VIII. add:

ARTICLE IX.

It is farther agreed and concluded, as a general Rule, that all and singular the Subjects of each Kingdom shall, in all Countries and Places on both Sides, have and enjoy at least the same Privileges, Liberties, and Immunities, as to all Duties, Impositions, or Customs, whatsoever, relating to Persons, Goods, or Merchandises, Ships, Freight, Seamen, Navigation, and Commerce; and shall have the like Favour in all Things, as the Subjects of *France*, or any other foreign Nation the most favoured, have, possess, or enjoy, or at any Time hereafter may have, possess, or enjoy *.

Subjects of both Parties to have the same Immunities as the Subjects of France, or the most favoured Nation.

* See Article XV. in p. 81 and p. 67.

IN the Treaty of Navigation and Commerce at *Utrecht*, November 28, 1713, from p. 49, to p. 61, inclusive, to the *English* Form of the certificatory Letters, in p. 59, add the *Latin* Form, as follows:

Formula literarum certificatoriarum, quibus urbes & portus maritimi naves & navigia inde solventia dimittant.

Omnibus & singulis ad quos præsentes literæ pervenerint, Nos præfecti consules, aut supremus magistratus, aut teloniorum aut custumarum commissarii urbis vel provinciæ *N*. notum testatumque facimus, quod *NN*. magister navis *N*. coram nobis, mediante

mediante folenni juramento, declaravit, navem *N.* dictam tonnarum aut eo circiter capacem, cujus ipfe eft magifter, ad urbis *NN*, incolas in dominiis fereniffimi regis *Hifpaniorum* jure proprietatis & dominii pertinere: quoniam autem in juftis fuis negotiis & itineribus benigne acceptum & accommodatum vellemus, omnes & fingulas perfonas, quibus dictum magiftrum vel obviam fieri, vel apud quos illum cum navi fua & mercibus fuis appellere aut fubfiftere contigerit, ut eum benigne admittant, humaniter tractent, eumque ad, in, & per portus, oras, ftationes navium, fluvios & dominia, navigare, meare, remeare, & negotiari, prout ipfi vifum fuerit, (illo interim vectigalia, aliaque tributa, quæ debebuntur exfolvente) permittant, rogamus; quod nos grato & benevolo animo, prout officiorum vices fe obtulerint, agnofcemus. In cujus rei teftimonium præfentes literas manu fignavimus, & urbis noftræ figillo muniri fecimus.

IN the fame Treaty, after the Words, *between the two Crowns,* in Article VI. p. 61. add:

<small>Six Months allowed to the Subjects of each Party to withdraw their Effects, after a Declaration of War.</small> And it is further agreed, that if it fhould happen (which God prevent) that War fhould arife and be declared between their Majefties and their Kingdoms, then after the Declaration of fuch a Rupture, the Space of Six Months fhall be allowed to the Subjects of each Party, refiding in the Dominions of the other, in which they fhall be permitted to withdraw with their Families, Goods, Merchandifes, Effects, and Ships, and to tranfport them, after having paid the due and accuftomed Impofts, either by Sea or Land, to whatever place they pleafe; and they fhall alfo be fuffered to fell and alien their moveable and immoveable Goods, and freely and without any Difturbance to carry away the Price of them; nor fhall their Goods, Wealth, Merchandifes, or Effects, much lefs their Perfons, be in the mean

mean Time detained or molested, by any Seizure or Arrest. Moreover, the Subjects on each Side shall, in the mean Time, enjoy and obtain quick and impartial Justice, by means of which they may, before the Expiration of the Six Months, recover the Goods and Effects which they have intrusted, as well to the Publick, as to private Persons.

Subjects on each Side to obtain speedy Justice for the Recovery of their Effects, before the Expiration of Six Months.

TO the Treaty of *Munster* in 1648, after Article VI. in p. 62. add:

ARTICLE XI.

Society, Conversation, and Commerce, among the respective Subjects, shall not be hindered; and if any Hinderances or Impediments happen, they shall be really and effectually removed.

Commerce not to be interrupted.

ARTICLE XX.

The Merchants, Masters of Ships, Pilots, Seamen; their Ships, Merchandises, Commodities, and other Goods belonging to them, shall not be seized and arrested, either by virtue of any general or particular Commission, or for any other Cause whatsoever; nor upon the Account of War, or otherwise; nor even under Pretext of employing them for the Preservation and Defence of the Country. It is not hereby, however, intended to comprehend the Seizures and Arrests of Justice in the ordinary Methods, upon Account of the Debts, proper Obligations, and valid Contracts, of those upon whom such Seizures shall have been made; in which Case Actions and Suits shall be carried on, according to Right and Reason.

Ships, Mariners, Merchandises, &c. of one Party, not to be arrested by the other, except for the Sake of Justice.

IN the Treaty of Peace and Alliance [Commerce] *November* 15, 1630, from p. 67, to 69, inclusive, Article XVI, XX, and XXIV. are respectively

spectively in p. 125, 82, and 83. but the following is omitted, *viz.*

ARTICLE XVIII.

Subjects of the one Party not to assist the Enemies of the other, with Money, Provisions, Arms, &c.

And whereas the said Kings solemnly promise, never to give any warlike Assistance to the Enemies of each other; so it is likewise provided, that their Subjects or Inhabitants, of whatever Nation or Quality, shall not, on Pretence of Trade and Commerce, or under any other Colour, assist the Enemies of either Prince, in any Manner; nor furnish them with Money, Provisions, Arms, Engines, Guns, or Instruments, fit for War, or any other warlike Furniture: and they who shall act contrary hereunto, shall be liable to the severest Punishments, and be proceeded against as Covenant-Breakers and seditious Persons.

IN the Treaty of Peace and Alliance [Commerce] at *London, August* 18, 1604, Article XV. is the same, Word for Word, with Article XXIV. in that of 1630, inserted in p. 83. after which add:

ARTICLE XVI.

Six Months allowed to the Subjects of either Party, to withdraw their Effects in case of a Rupture.

If it should happen hereafter (which God forbid) that Differences should arise between the said Kings, whereby the Intercourse of Commerce may be in Danger of being interrupted, then the Subjects on both Sides shall be informed of that Matter, and shall be allowed Six Months, from the Time of such Information, to transport their Merchandises; and no Arrest, Interruption, or Damage, of their Persons or Goods, in the mean Time, shall be made or given.

IN the Treaty of Peace and Alliance [Commerce] *February* 11, 1542, from p. 73 to 76. inclusive, where it is said in the *N. B.* in p. 76. that the Treaty of *Cambray* in 1524 does not now appear

pear to be any where subsisting; the Meaning is, that the Articles I, II, III, V, VI, and XII. of that Treaty, are the same, Word for Word, with the Articles II, III, IV, X, XI, and XIII. of the Treaty in 1542, except an immaterial Difference in Article XII. of the Treaty of 1529; in which the Treaty of 1520 is declared to be and remain in the same State in which it was before the Commencement of the War, and continue in Force as if War had not been declared.

This Treaty of 1529, is the first perpetual Treaty between *England* and *Spain*, after the Union of the Kingdoms of *Castile* and *Arragon*, in the Person of *Charles* I. of *Spain*, afterwards Emperor, under the Title of *Charles* V.

IN the Treaty of Commerce at *Madrid*, *December* 14, 1715, before Article V. in p. 80. insert:

ARTICLE III.

His Catholick Majesty allows the Subjects of Great-Britain to gather Salt in the Island of *Tortudos*, they having enjoyed that Permission in the Time of King *Charles* II. without Interruption. *British Subjects to take Salt at Tortudos.*

N. B. In the Treaty of *Aix la Chapelle* in 1748, Article III. recited in the Conclusion of the Treaties between *Great Britain* and *France*, in this Supplement, p. 254. relates also to *Spain*.

TO the Treaties with *Spain*, ending in p. 83. add:

Treaty between Great Britain *and* Spain, *concluded at* Madrid, October 5, 1750. George II. Ferdinand VI.

Article V. is the same with the above recited Article III. of the Treaty in 1715.

(260)

ARTICLE VII.

British Subjects to enjoy the same Privileges which they enjoyed before the last War, by royal Cedulas, and by the Treaty of 1667.

The *British* Subjects shall enjoy all the Rights, Privileges, Franchises, Exemptions, and Immunities, whatever, which they enjoyed before the last War; by Virtue of Cedulas or royal Ordinances, and by the Articles of the Treaty of Peace and Commerce made at *Madrid* in 1667; and the said Subjects shall be treated in *Spain* in the same Manner as the most favoured Nation, and consequently no Nation shall pay less Duties upon Wool, and other Merchandises, which they shall bring into or carry out of *Spain* by Land, than the said Subjects shall pay upon the same Merchandises, which they shall bring in or carry out by Sea. And all the Rights, Privileges, Franchises, Exemptions, and Immunities, which shall be granted and permitted to any Nation whatever, shall also be granted and permitted to the said Subjects; and his *Britannick* Majesty consents, that the same be granted to the Subjects of *Spain* in his *Britannick* Majesty's Kingdoms.

ARTICLE IX.

Treaty of Aix la Chapelle, and the Treaty of Commerce at Utrecht, confirmed.

Their *Britannick* and *Catholick* Majesties confirm, by the present Treaty, the Treaty of *Aix la Chapelle*, and all the other Treaties therein confirmed, in all their Articles and Clauses, excepting those which have been derogated from by the present Treaty; as likewise the Treaty of Commerce concluded at *Utrecht* in 1713, those Articles excepted which are contrary to the present Treaty.

The

The UNITED PROVINCES.

IN the marine Treaty of *London*, *December* 1, 1674, after Article IX. in p. 91, 92, add:

ARTICLE XII.

And whenever the Ambassadors of the said Lords the States, or any other publick Ministers, resident at the Court of His most Serene Majesty of *Great Britain*, shall complain of the Unjustness of Sentences, which may have been given, his Majesty will cause the same to be reviewed and examined in his Council, that it may appear whether the Orders and Precautions prescribed in this Treaty, have been observed, and have had their due Effect; and will also take Care, that the same be fully provided for, and that Right be done to the Party complaining within the Space of Three Months. And likewise when the Ambassadors, or other publick Ministers of his Majesty, resident with the States General, shall complain of the Unjustness of Sentences, the said States will cause a Review and Examination thereof to be made in the Assembly of the *States General*, that it may appear whether the Orders and Precautions prescribed in this Treaty have been observed, and have had their due Effect; and they will likewise take Care, that the same be fully provided for, and that Right be done to the Party complaining, within the Space of Three Months: Nevertheless, it shall not any ways be lawful to sell or unlade the Goods in Controversy, either before the Sentence given or after it, during the Review thereof on either Side, unless it be with the Consent of the Parties interested.

Revisions.

TO the *English* Form of the Passport, in p. 93, 94. add the *Latin*, as follows:

Formula literarum commeatus (vulgo literarum maritimarum) petendarum dandarumque a consulibus civitatum & portuum Uniti Belgii, *omnibus navibus navigiisve inde vela facientibus secundum articuli quinti hujus tractatus dispositionem.*

SERENISSIMIS, illustrissimis, potentissimis, nobilissimis, spectatissimis, prudentissimis dominis imperatoribus, regibus, rerum publicarum moderatoribus, principibus, ducibus, comitibus, baronibus, dominis consulibus, scabinis, senatoribus, judicibus, officialibus justitiaris & rectoribus omnium civitatum & locorum, tam ecclesiasticorum quam secularium, quibus hæ exhibebuntur, Nos consules & rectores civitatis notum facimus, magistrum seu præpositum navis se nobis stitisse, & solenni jurejurando affirmasse, dictam navem, cui nomen est menfurarum, quas vulgo *lastas* vocant, plus minus cujus ille hoc tempore magister five præpositus est, pertinere ad incolas provinciarum Uniti Belgii. *Ita eum Deus adjuvet.* Cum autem acceptissimum nobis foret, prædictum magistrum seu præpositum navis in iis, quæ probe justeque ab eo agenda erunt, adjuvari, rogamus vos universos & singulos, ubicunque dictus magister seu præpositus, navem mercesque in ea invectas & illatas appellet, velitis, jubeatis, eum benigne recipi, humaniter tractari, sub legitimorum consuetorumque vectigalium, ac aliarum rerum, solutione admitti, ingredi, manere, egredi portus, flumina, & dominia vestra; & omni modo navigationis, mercatus, commerciorum ac promercalium jure specieque uti, omnibus in locis, quibus hoc ei melius, rectius, visum fuerit; grato animo id rependere vobis paratissimi semper, promptissimique. In
quorum

quorum majorem fidem & teſtimonium has civitatis noſtræ ſigillo ſignari curavimus; datas in   die   anno domini   .

N. B. The Treaty at *Bredah*, $\frac{21}{31}$ *July*, 1667, in p. 100. though proviſional, has been renewed and confirmed by ſubſequent Treaties.

IN the Treaty of Peace and Alliance at *Bredah*, of the ſame Date, after Article XXIX. in p. 105, 106. add:

ARTICLE XXXII.

If it ſhall happen at any Time (which God of his Mercy forbid), that the Differences now compoſed between his ſaid Majeſty, and the ſaid States General, ſhould break out again into open War, it is agreed, that thoſe Ships, Merchandiſes, or any Kind of Moveables of either Party, which ſhall be found to be and remain in the Ports, and under the Power, of the adverſe Party on either Side, ſhall not upon that Account be confiſcated or detained, but the full Space of Six Months ſhall be allowed to the Subjects and Inhabitants on both Sides, that they may tranſport from thence the aforementioned Things, and any Thing elſe which belongs to them, whither they ſhall think fit, without any Kind of Moleſtation.

Six Months allowed for the Removal of Effects, in caſe of War.

Articles XVIII, XIX, XX, XXIV, XXV, XXVI, XXVII, XXVIII, XXIX, and XXXIV, of this Treaty, are Word for Word the ſame with Articles XII, XIII, XIV, XVII, XVIII, XIX, XX, XXII, and XXVI. which are all that are relative to the Marine, in the Treaty of Peace and Commerce between the Republick of *England* and the States General, concluded at *Weſtminſter, April* 5, 1654; the firſt Treaty between *England* and the States General after 1648, when *Philip* IV.

King of *Spain*, by the Treaty of *Munster*, declared the Seven United Provinces of the Low Countries to be free and sovereign States. In which Treaty of 1654, made when *Oliver Cromwell* was Protector, Article I. is as follows:

Peace and Friendship.

It is agreed and concluded, that from this Day forward, there be a true, firm, and inviolable Peace; a sincere, intimate, and close Friendship, Affinity, Confederacy, and Union, between the Republick of *England*, and the States General of the United Provinces of the *Netherlands*, and the Lands, Countries, Cities, and Towns, under the Dominion of each, without Distinction of Places, together with their People and Inhabitants, of what Degree soever.

IN the Treaty of Peace and Alliance at *Whitehall*, $\frac{4}{14}$ *September*, 1667, in p. 107. add:

ARTICLE XIV.

This Peace not to be interrupted by the Subjects of either Party.

If it shall happen during this Friendship, Confederacy, and Alliance, that any Thing shall be done or attempted by any of the Subjects or Inhabitants of either Party, against this Treaty, or any Part thereof, by Land, Sea, or fresh Waters; nevertheless, this Amity and Alliance between the said Nations shall not thereby be broken or interrupted, but shall remain and continue in full Force; and

The Particular Persons offending, and no others, to be punished, and make satisfaction.

only those particular Persons shall be punished, who have committed any Thing against this Treaty, and none else; and Justice shall be rendered, and Satisfaction given, to all Persons concerned, by all those who have committed any Thing contrary to this Treaty by Land or by Sea, or other Waters in any Part of *Europe*, or any Places within the Streights of *Gibraltar*, or in *America*, or upon the Coasts of *Africa*, or in any Lands, Islands, Seas, Creeks, Bays, Rivers; or in any Places on this Side

Side the *Cape of Good Hope*, within the Space of a Year after Juſtice ſhall be demanded, as aforesaid. But in caſe the Offenders againſt this Treaty do not appear and ſubmit themſelves to Judgment, and give Satisfaction within the reſpective Times above expreſſed, according to the Diſtance of the Places, they ſhall be declared Enemies of both Parties; and their Eſtates, Goods, and Revenues, whatever, ſhall be confiſcated for due and full Satisfaction of the Injuries and Wrongs by them offered; and their Perſons alſo, when they come within the Dominions of either Party, ſhall be liable to ſuch Puniſhments as every one ſhall deſerve for his reſpective Offences. *Offenders not appearing to be declared Enemies, and forfeit their Effects.*

AFTER the Treaty of *Bredah*, Article IX. ending with the Words, *The Concluſion of the Treaty of* 1662, inſert:

Treaty of Friendſhip and Concord between Great Britain *and the* States General, *for the Renewal and Confirmation of former Treaties,* concluded at Weſtminſter, May 27, 1728.

ARTICLE II.

That this Friendſhip and Concord may be better preſerved, it is agreed and concluded, between the King of *Great Britain* and the *States General*, that all and ſingular the Treaties of Peace, Friendſhip, Alliance, Navigation, and Commerce, here under named, ſhall be approved and confirmed.

HERE follows in the Original, an Enumeration of Treaties, which (except a Confirmation of the Treaty of 1716, and of two more Treaties ſubſequent to 1716, but not relative to the Marine) is Word for Word the ſame as the Liſt inſerted in the Treaty of 1716, in p. 109, 110.

PORTUGAL.

PORTUGAL.

TO the Treaty of Peace and Alliance, in 1654, after Article IX. p. 116, 117. add:

ARTICLE X.

Subjects of England to trade freely to and from the Territories of the King of Portugal.

That the People of the Republick of *England* may freely transport in their Ships all Things, Goods, and Merchandises, of what Kind soever they may be, even Arms, Provisions, and other the like Things [*etiam arma, annonem, aliave similia*], from the Ports and Dominions of the said Republick, or from any other Ports and Dominions whatever, provided that they are not exported immediately from the Ports and Dominions of *Portugal*, to any Ports or Territories whatever of the King of *Castile*; and that neither the most serene King of *Portugal* or his Subjects, shall hinder the said Ships, Goods, or Men, by Seizures, Reprisals, or any other Cause whatever, from navigating securely to the Ports and Territories of the said King of *Castile*, and from having Commerce therein; and that the People of this Republick may freely import, as well Arms, Corn, Fish, as all other Kinds of Merchandises, into the Kingdoms, Ports, and Territories, of the King of *Portugal*, and sell the same at Pleasure, either in Parcels or in Bulk, to whatever Persons, or for whatever Price, they can obtain; and they shall not be forbidden, circumscribed, or inhibited, by his said royal Majesty, or his Ministers, Governors, Farmers of the Customs, or Monopolists, or by any Chamber or Jurisdiction whatever, private or publick: and that the Goods or Merchandises which have paid the Customs or Imposts, in any of his Majesty's Ports, shall be freely transported into any other Ports or Places whatever of his said Majesty, without

out paying any other or farther Cuſtom, Duty, or Sum of Money, beſides that which the *Portugueſe* Merchants ſhould pay, if the Goods and Merchandiſes had belonged to them.

IN the Treaty of Peace and Commerce at *London*, *January* 29, 1641-2, after Article XI. p. 122, 123. inſert:

ARTICLE XVIII.

If it ſhould happen hereafter (which God forbid) that any Difficulties or Doubts ſhould ariſe between the ſaid Kings, which might give Occaſion to apprehend the Interruption of Commerce and Correſpondence between their Subjects; publick Advice thereof ſhall be given to the Subjects of both Sides, in all and every the Kingdoms, States, and Provinces, of both Kings; and after that Notice given, they ſhall be allowed Two Years on both Sides, to tranſport their Merchandiſes and Goods; and in the mean Time, there ſhall be no Injury or Prejudice done to any Perſons or Goods on either Side.

Two Years allowed, after Notice given, to remove Effects.

N. B. This is the firſt Treaty with *Portugal*, after that Kingdom, by throwing off it's Subjection to *Spain*, had recovered it's Independency under the Duke of *Braganza*, ſtiled *John* IV.

EMPEROR, or the AUSTRIAN NETHERLANDS.

IN the Treaty of Peace and Alliance at *Madrid*, *November* 15, 1630, in p. 125, 126, add:

See other general Articles of this Treaty, in p. 68, & ſeq.

TREATY

TREATY of Peace and Commerce, *August* 18, 1604. To the *N. B.* in p. 128. prefix these Words:

The Substance of the XIIth Article of this Treaty is fully comprehended in the XVIth, XVIIIth, and XXth Articles of the Treaty of 1630; and the other Articles, making no particular Mention of the *Netherlands*, is referred to under *Spain*, p. 70, & seqq.

IN the Treaty at *London*, of 24 *February*, 1495, after Article XV. in p. 130. insert:

ARTICLE XIX.

Ships taken in the Ports of either Prince to be sued for.
That if any Ship shall be taken in any Port, or within the Liberties of either of the aforesaid Princes, by any Person not subject to the aforesaid Princes; that Prince, in whose Port or Liberties such Ship is taken, shall be obliged, together with the other Prince, to sue for the Restitution of the said Ship, but at the Cost and Expence of the Party injured.

RUSSIA.

IN the treaty of *Petersborough*, *December* 2, 1734, after Article XIV. p. 134, 135. insert:

ARTICLE XV.

Persons wrecked to be assisted, and the Wrecks preserved.
In case of Wreck on any Part of the Dominions of the contracting Parties, all Sorts of Assistance shall be given to the Unfortunate; no Violence shall be done them, nor shall their Effects saved either by themselves or others, or driven on Shore, be hidden or detained from them; neither shall they be hurt under any Pretext whatever, but they shall

shall be preserved, and the Persons wrecked shall pay what is reasonable for the Assistance given to them, their Ships, and Effects.

IN the Treaty at *Westminster, June* 16, 1623, from p. 136 to 138. inclusive, add:

ARTICLE VII.

If anie of the Subjectes of either of theis renowned Princes, their Merchaunts, or voluntarie Souldiers, tradinge and serveinge in other Countries, without the Prince's Leave, shall be founde, under Colour of Commerce, or anie Pretexte whatsoever, to carry any Manner of warlike Munition to the Enemie, or receave Entertainment with the Enemie, and so happen to be taken in the Warres, that shall not be imputed to the renowned Princes, or held for anie Breach of Contracte, but that the Partie offending shall take the Perill upon his owne Head. *Misbehaviour of Subjects not to be imputed to either Prince.*

ARTICLE XIX.

And if it happen that the Merchauntes or Subjectes of the said renouned Princes shall suffer Wracke uppon the Coastes or within the Rivers of the Domynions of either, whether by Casualtie, Tempest, or other Misfortune whatsoever, in such Case the Goods saved shall be freely restored to the Owners, only allowinge a reasonable Consideration to the People of the Countrie, which shall be aydinge and helpinge in the Recovery thereof *. *Wrecks to be taken Care of and restored to the Owners.*

TO the Treaties with this Power, ending in p. 138. add the following:

* The Term of this Treaty has been prolonged by the subsequent Treaties.

George II.
Elizabeth,
Emprefs.
1742.

Treaty *of Alliance between his* Britannick *Majefty and her Imperial Majefty of all the* Ruffias, *figned at* Mofcow, Decemb. 11, 1742.

ARTICLE I.

Perpetual Friendfhip and Alliance.
There fhall be for ever between his Majefty the King of *Great Britain*, and her Imperial Majefty of all the *Ruffias*, their Heirs and Succeffors, as alfo between their Kingdoms, Countries, States, People, and Subjects, every where, as well by Sea as by Land, a faithful, firm, and perpetual Friendfhip, Alliance, and Union; and they fhall on the one Side and on the other, be fo far from doing any Injury or Damage to each other, that they fhall exert themfelves in promoting their mutual Interefts, and in maintaining each other reciprocally, in all the Kingdoms, Provinces, States, Rights, Commerce, Immunities, and Prerogatives, whatfoever, which they were poffeffed of before the Year 1741, or which they may acquire by Treaties.

ARTICLE XXI.

This Treaty to continue in Force 15 Years.
Peace, Friendfhip, and good Underftanding, fhall laft for ever between the high contracting Parties; but as it is ufual to fix a certain Time for Treaties of formal Alliance, the faid high contracting Parties have agreed, that this fhall continue in Force for the Space of Fifteen Years, to be reckoned from the Day of the figning of this Treaty.

Separate ARTICLE I.

Treaty of 1734 to continue in Force as long as the prefent Treaty.
It is agreed by this Separate Article, that the Treaty of Commerce and Navigation, which was concluded on the 4th of *December*, 1734, between his *Britannick* Majefty, and her Imperial Majefty of the *Ruffia*;, fhall be confirmed in all it's Points and

and Articles, by the present Alliance; and it is now agreed, that it shall remain in Force, and shall be reciprocally observed for the same Time as this Alliance shall last, to be reckoned from the Day of the signing of the Treaty of this Day.

Treaty between his Britannick *Majesty, and her Imperial Majesty of all the* Russias, *signed at* St Petersburg, *September* $\frac{19}{30}$, 1755.

George II. *Elizabeth,* Empress. 1755.

ARTICLE II.
The high contracting Parties renew expresly, by this Convention, the Treaty of defensive Alliance concluded between them on the 11th of *December*, 1742, at *Moscow*, in all it's Articles.

The Treaty of 1742 renewed.

ARTICLE XIII.
This Convention shall subsist for the Space of Four Years, to be reckoned from the Day when the Ratifications of it shall be exchanged.

This Treaty to continue in Force Four Years.

SWEDEN.

IN the Treaty at *Whitehall*, *October* 21, 1661, to the *English* Form of the Passport, in p. 146 to 148. add the *Latin*, as follows:

Formula Literarum Certificatoriarum.

NOS *NN*. gubernator, aut supremus magistratus, aut teloniorum & custumarum commissarii civitatis vel provinciæ *N*. [*apposito titulo aut officio respective gubernamenti istius loci*] notum testatumque facimus, quod   die   mensis   anni   personaliter coram nobis comparuerint, in civitate aut oppido *N*. dictionis sacræ regiæ majestatis Sueciæ, *N.N.N.* cives & habitantes in *N.*, ac subditi

subditi sacrae regiae majestatis Sueciae, atque sub fide illius juramenti, quo S.R.M. Sueciae, domino nostro clementissimo, & civitati nostrae attinentur & obstricti sunt, nobis declaraverint, quod navis aut navigium N. dictum,——lastarum aut tonnarum capax, pertineat ad portum civitatem, aut oppidum N. dictionis N. quodque dicta navis ejus aut subditorum S.R.M. Sueciae justo titulo propria sit; jam vero de portu N. iter vel itinera directe destinasse ad N. sequentibus onustam mercibus, viz. [*hic specificentur bona cum quantitate & qualitate eorum e. g. tot circiter plaustra vel involucra, tot circiter dolia, &c. quemadmodum quantitas & conditio mercium fuerit.*] Iidemque asseveraverint sub juramento praedicto tantum N. ex dictis bonis mercibusque ad subditos S.R.M. Sueciae vel tantum N. ad N.N.N. [*cujuscunque nationis possessores fuerint, exprimatur*] pertinere; quodque N.N.N. sub fide dicti juramenti affirmaverint dicta bona superius specificata, & non alia, esse imposita aut imponenda in praenominatam navem pro dicto itinere; & quod nulla pars eorum bonorum ad alium quenquam pertineat, quam hosce supradictas, neque in illa sub quocunque fictitio nomine alia bona colorata aut celata sint, sed vere & realiter praenominatas merces in usum praedictorum proprietariorum impositas esse, & non aliorum: quodque dictae navis Navarchus nominatus N. civis sit civitatis N.——Idcirco cum post exactam examinationem nobis supradictis [*gubernatori aut supremo magistratui aut teloniorium aut custumarum commissariis civitatis praedictae*] sufficienter constet, dictam navem aut navigium bonaque imposita libera esse, ac vere & realiter pertinere ad subditos S.R.M. Sueciae, vel aliarum nationum incolas supradictos, ab omnibus proinde ac singulis terrarum, mariumque, potestatibus, regibus, principibus, rebuspublicis ac liberis civitatibus, nec non bellorum ducibus, thalassiarchis, generalibus, officialibus, portuumque praefectis, aliisque

omnibus

omnibus quibus cuſtodia aliqua portus aut maris commiſſa eſt, quibuſcunque navim hanc navigando obviam venire, quorumcunque in claſſes forte incidere & tranſire, aut in portubus morari, contigerit, humillime & officioſe requirimus, ut ratione fœderum & amicitiæ, quæ reſpective unicuique aut ſuperioribus, cujuſcunque eſt, ac cum *S.RM. Sueciæ* rege ac domino noſtro clementiſſimo intercedit, dictum Navarchum cum navi *N.* & perſonis, rebus, ac mercimoniis ad eandem ſpectantibus, non modo ſine impedimento ac moleſtiis iter ſuum libere proſequi permittant, ſed etiam ſi ex dicto portu alio quovis tendere commodum duxerit, ei tanquam *S.RM.* ſubdito, cum navi ſua omnia humanitatis officia exhibeant, eadem viciſſim a *S.RM. Sueciæ* omnibuſque ejus miniſtris & ſubditis in pari vel alio caſu experturi.

In cujus rei fidem præſentes manu ſubſcriptas civitatis noſtræ ſigillo muniri curavimus. Dabantur, &c.

N. B. This is the lateſt Treaty of Commerce ſubſiſting between the Crowns of *England* and *Sweden*; for, although ſeveral Treaties have been concluded ſince the Year 1661, they were all temporary, and are now expired.

IN the Treaty at *London* in 1656, before Article X. in p. 152. inſert: *Oliver Cromwell*, Protector. *Chriſtina.*

ARTICLE VIII.

The Subjects of the Moſt Serene Lord Protector and the Republick, ſhall hereafter enjoy all the Prerogatives in the ſeveral Branches of Trade, which they uſed to carry on in *Ruſſia* and *Poland*, or elſewhere in the Dominions of the Moſt Serene King of *Sweden*, which they enjoyed heretofore in Preference to other Nations; and if at any Time they deſire further Privileges, their Deſires ſhall be gratified

Subjects of *England* to enjoy all their uſual Prerogatives.

gratified by all the Means possible: and if the Most Serene King of *Sweden* shall grant greater and more ample Privileges than the abovementioned in *Poland* and *Prussia*, to any Nation besides, or People not subject to him; or shall suffer any Nation or People to enjoy such larger Privileges there; then the People and Citizens of this Republick shall enjoy the same Privileges in all Respects, after they have desired it of his Most Serene Majesty. And moreover, if any Edicts which have been published since 1650, happen to be burdensome to the *English* and *Scots*, dwelling or trading in *Poland* or *Prussia*, the same shall after this Time be of no Force, as far as it shall be in the Power of the King of *Sweden* to prohibit it; but the Subjects of the said Lord Protector shall hereafter be entirely free from those Burdens.

DENMARK.

IN the Treaty of Alliance and Commerce at *Westminster, November* 29, 1669, after Article I. p. 157. insert:

ARTICLE III.

Neither Party to aid the Enemies of the other, with Soldiers, Arms, &c.

The aforesaid Kings, for themselves, their Heirs and Successors, mutually do undertake and promise, that they will not aid or furnish the Enemies of either Party, which shall be Aggressors, with any Provisions of War, as Soldiers, Arms, Engines, Guns, Ships, or other Necessaries, for the Use of War; or suffer any to be furnished by their Subjects. But if the Subjects of either Prince shall presume to act contrary thereunto, then that King whose Subjects shall have so done, shall be obliged to proceed against them with the highest Severity, as against seditious Persons and Breakers of the League.

(275)

TO the Form of the *Danish* Paſſport and Certificate in *Engliſh*, inſerted in Article XX. in p. 159, 160. add the ſame in *French*, as follows:

Chriſtian *Cinquieme, par la Grace de Dieu Roi de* Dennemarc *& de* Norwege, *&c.*

SOIT notoire à tous & chacuns, qui nos preſentes lettres de paſſeport verront, que notre ſujet & citoien de notre cité de   nous a humblement repreſenté, que le navire nommé   du port de   tonneaux, lui appartient & à quelques autres de nos ſujets, & qu'ils en ſont les ſeuls proprietaires, & qu'il eſt de preſent chargé de denrées, qui ſont contenuës en un billet des officiers de nos douanes, que le navire a à bord; & qu'il appartient à nos ſujets ou à d'autres intereſſez, qui ſont en neutralité: & eſt prêt à partir du port de   pour aller en tel autre-lieu ou lieux, ou il pourra commodement trafiquer avec les dites merchandiſes, qui ne ſont pas deffenduës, ni appartenantes à l'un ou à l'autre des parties en guerre, ou bien trover ſon fret; ce que noſtre dit ſujet ayant atteſté par eſcrit ſigné de ſon ſeing, & affirmé par ferment, être veritable ſous peine de confiſcation deſdites denrées, nous avons jugé à propos de lui accorder nos preſentes lettres des paſſeport; & partant nous prions & requerons tous gouverneurs de pays, & commandans par mer, rois, princes, republiques, & villes libres, & particulierement les parties, qui ſont preſentement en guerre, & leur commandans, admiraux, generaux, officiers, maitres de ports, commandans de navires, capitaines, fretteurs, & tous autres, qui ont quelque juriſdiction par mer, ou la garde d'aucun port, qu'il lui arrivera de rencontrer, ou parmi la flotte, ou navires, deſquels il lui arrivera de tomber ou demeurer dans leur ports, qu'en vertu de l'alliance & amitie,

amitié, que nous avons avec aucun roy ou eſtat, ils ſouffrent le dit maitre avec le navire perſonnes, biens, & toutes les merchandiſes, qui ſont ſur ſon bord, pour ſuivre ſon voyage vers quelque lieu que ce ſoit, non ſeulement avec liberté & ſans aucune moleſtation, detention, ou empéchement, mais encore qu'ils lui rendent tous offices de civilité, comme à noſtre ſujet, s'il y a occaſion ; ceque nous & les noſtres ſerons prêts à reconnoitre en pareille ou autre occaſion. Donné le   jour de
de l'année

Nous le preſident, conſuls & ſenateurs de la ville de   atteſtons & certifions, que le   jour de de l'année   eſt venu & comparu en perſonne devant nous *N.N.* citoyen & habitant de la cité ou ville de   & ſous le ſerment, qu'il eſt obligé envers le roy noſtre ſouverain ſeigneur, nous a declaré, que le navire ou vaiſſeau, nommé   du port de tonneaux, appartient au port, cité au ville de en la province de   & qui le dit navire lui appartient juſtement, & eſt de preſent prêt à partir directement du port de   chargé des denrées mentionnées au billet, qu'il a receu des officiers des douanes, & qu'il a affirmé per le ſerment ſufdit, que le vaiſſeau ci deſſus nommé avec les denrées & merchandiſes, dont il eſt chargé, appartient ſeulement a ſujets de ſa majeſté, & ne port point de merchandiſes deffenduës, qui appartient à l'une ou à l'autre des parties, que ſont a preſent enguere.

En temoignage de quoi, nous avons fait ſigner le preſent certificat par le ſyndic de noſtre ville, & y avons fait appoſer noſtre ſceau. Donné, &c.

AFTER Article XX. ending in p. 161. add the following:

ARTICLE XXI.

Britiſh Ships paſſing by *Gluckſtadt*

That all Ships of Subjects and People of the Kingdom of *Great Britain*, together with their lading

lading and Merchandise, passing by the Port of *Gluckstadt*, or other Places and Towns under the Dominions of the King of *Denmark*, situated upon the River *Elbe*, shall, both going and returning, be free and exempt from all Customs, Imposts, Search, Seizure, and Molestation, except only the Case of Search in the Time of War, when the King of *Denmark* shall be at War with any other King or State. *and other Places upon the Elbe, to be free from all Customs and Search.*

ARTICLE XXV.

If the Ships of either of the Allies, and their Subjects and People, whether they are Merchant-Ships or Ships of War, shall happen to run on Ground, or fall upon Rocks, or are forced to lighten themselves, or shall otherwise suffer Shipwreck (which God forbid), upon the Coasts of either King; the aforesaid Ships, with their Tackle, Goods, and Merchandise, or whatever shall be remaining of them, shall be restored to their Owners and Proprietors, provided they or their Agents claim the said Ships and Goods, within the Space of a Year and a Day after such Shipwreck suffered; saving always the Rights and Customs of both Nations. The Subjects also and Inhabitants, dwelling upon the said Coasts and Shores, shall be obliged to come to their Aid in Case of Danger, and as much as in them lies to give their Assistance; and shall do their utmost Endeavour, either for freeing the Ship, or saving the Goods, Merchandise, and Apparel, of the said Ship, and what else of the same they shall be able, and for the conveying the same into some safe Place, in order to be restored to the Owners; they paying Salvage, and giving such Recompence to the Persons, by whose Assistance and Diligence the said Merchandise and Goods shall have been recovered and preserved, as they shall deserve; and finally, both Parties, in Case of such Misfortune, shall cause to be observed on *The Remains of a Shipwreck to be preserved and restored to the Owners.*

their Side, what they would defire to be obferved and done on the other Side.

ARTICLE XXVI.

Ships, Commanders of Ships, Mariners, &c. not to be arrefted, unlefs for the Prefervation of the Kingdom, or the Sake of Juftice.

The Commanders of Ships, or their Pilots, Soldiers, Mariners, and Seamen, as alfo the Ships themfelves, and the Goods and Merchandife on board them, fhall not be feized or arrefted by any Warrant, either general or fpecial, or for any Caufe, unlefs for the Defence and Prefervation of the Kingdom; which yet fhall not be underftood to be meant of Seizures and Arrefts made by Authority of Law, for Debts contracted, or any other legal Caufe whatever; in which Cafe it fhall be lawful to proceed according to the Rules of Juftice and Law.

ARTICLE XXXVI.

Sentences concerning Prizes to be given according to Juftice.

Both Kings fhall take great Care, that Judgment and Sentence concerning Prizes taken at Sea, may be given according to the Rules of Juftice and Equity, by Perfons not fufpected or interefted; and being once given by fuch Judges as aforefaid, they fhall ftrictly charge and require their Officers, and whom it fhall concern, to fee the fame put in due Execution, according to the Form and Tenor thereof.

ARTICLE XXXVII.

Sentences, if complained of, to be examined in Council.

If the Ambaffadors of either King, or any other publick Minifters, refiding with the other King, fhall happen to make Complaint of any fuch Sentence, that King to whom Complaint fhall be made, fhall caufe the faid Judgment and Sentence to be reheard and examined in his Council, that it may appear whether all Things requifite and neceffary have been performed according to the Rules of this Treaty, and with due Caution; and if the contrary hath happened it fhall be redreffed, which

is

is do be done at the fartheſt within three Months Time: neither ſhall it be lawful, either before giv-ing the firſt Sentence, or afterwards, during the Time of rehearing, to unlade or ſell, and alien the Goods in Controverſy, unleſs it is done by Conſent of Parties, and to prevent the periſhing of the ſaid Goods and Merchandiſe.

No Goods to be ſold 'till the final Sentence is given, unleſs by Conſent, or to prevent Loſs.

ARTICLE XL.

Alſo it is agreed, that if the *Hollanders*, or any other Nation whatſoever (the *Swediſh* Nation only excepted), hath obtained already, or ſhall hereafter obtain, any better Articles, Agreements, Exemptions, or Privileges, than what are contained in this Treaty, from the King of *Denmark*, the ſame ſhall be likewiſe granted to the King of *Great Britain* and his Subjects, effectually and fully, to all Intents and Purpoſes. And on the other Side, if the *Hollanders*, or any other Nation whatever, hath or ſhall obtain from his Majeſty of *Great Britain*, any better Articles, Agreements, Exemptions, or Privileges, than what are contained in this Treaty, the ſame and like Privileges ſhall be granted to the King of *Denmark* and his Subjects alſo, in moſt full and effectual Manner *.

The *Engliſh* to enjoy the ſame Privileges as any other Nation, except the *Swedes*.

The *Danes* to enjoy the ſame Privileges as the *Hollanders*, or any other Nation.

Note, This Treaty was ſucceeded by that at *Copenhagen*, in *July* 11, 1670; which, Article for Article, is the ſame in Subſtance, and is the lateſt ſubſiſting Treaty of Commerce between *England* and *Denmark*; for, although another Treaty was made in 1691, it appears to be only proviſional, and to have been intended to laſt no longer than the War ſhould continue between *England* and *France*. *Vid. Corps Dipl. Tom. VII. Part ii. p. 293.*

* See Article XLI. in p. 168.

SAVOY.

IN the Treaty at *Florence*, September 19, 1669, in p. 169 and 170. insert the following Articles:

ARTICLE XII.

British Mariners deserting, and entering on Board other Ships, to be returned to their Captain.

All Mariners, Subjects of his Majesty, who, without Leave of their Captain and Master, shall retire and enter on Board of any other Ship or Vessel, on Complaint being made thereof, to the Officer of his Royal Highness, at *Nice*, *Villa Francha*, or *St Sulpice*, shall be taken out of the Ship which shall have received them, and they shall be returned to their first Captain or Master. If any Mariner leaves his Captain or Master, and retires to any publick or private House in the said Ports, and shall be hid by the Inhabitants thereof, he shall be taken out of the same by Force, and the Master of the House shall be condemned in the Penalty of Twenty Dollars for every the like Offence. If any Mariner lies on Shore, in any private or publick House, without a Permission in writing signed by his Officer, the Master of the House who harboured him shall be fined Ten Dollars. If any Mariner contracts a Debt with an Inhabitant of the said Ports, or runs in Debt to him farther than for One Dollar, without Permission in writing of the Captain or Master, the Creditor shall lose his Right; but if any Mariner gets any Person who is not a Mariner to answer for his Debt, the Mariner shall go free, but he who answered for him may be detained for the Debt.

Penalties for concealing *British* Mariners.

Concerning the Debts of the Mariners.

ARTICLE XV.

All Privileges granted in the

It is finally agreed, that all Immunities, Priviledges, and Concessions, contained in the general Publication,

Publication, which has been made a free Port by his Royal Highnefs, and which are not mentioned or fpecified in the preceding Articles, fhall be underftood, as exprefsly mentioned and contained in this prefent Inftrument, for the full and perfect Advantage of his *Britannick* Majefty's Subjects, in all Difpofitions and Intentions: and all Immunities, Privileges, or Advantages, which hereafter fhall be granted to any other Kingdom or State whatever, all and every one of thofe Privileges, Immunities, and Advantages, are and fhall be as fully, and in all their Circumftances, allowed to the Subjects of his Majefty, as if they had been exprefsly granted by this Inftrument.

general Publication of free Ports, to be enjoyed by the Britifh Subjects.

Alfo all Immunities, which hereafter fhall be granted to any other State.

T U R K Y.

IN the Treaty at *Adrianople*, September 1675, after Article XXXVII. p. 173. infert:

ARTICLE XXXVIII.

In cafe that the *Englifh* Ships, which come to our City of *Conftantinople*, are forced by Dangers at Sea, or by bad Weather, to put in at *Caffa*, or fuch other Port; fo long as the *Englifh* continue on Board, without felling the Commodities and Merchandife, no Perfon fhall do them any Violence, nor give them any Trouble or Hinderance; but in all Places where there is Danger, the *Cadees*, and our other Minifters, fhall always defend and protect the faid *Englifh* Ships, their Men and Goods, left they receive any Damage.

Englifh Ships forced into Caffa, and fuch Ports, to be protected.

F E Z

FEZ and MOROCCO.

TO the Treaty of Peace and Commerce at *Mequinez*, *January* 14, 1727-8, in p. 176. add the following Treaties.

1721. *Treaty of Peace between* George I. *King of Great Britain, and* Muli Ismael, *Emperor of Morocco, concluded at* Fez, January 23, 1721.

ARTICLE I.

English to be well used and respected.

In order to establish Peace between the Two Powers, both by Land and Sea, and all their respective Dominions, it is agreed, that the *English* may now, and always hereafter, be well used and respected by our Subjects.

ARTICLE II.

English Ships to have free Ingress and Egress to and from the Emperor's Ports.

That all *English* Ships of War and Merchant-Ships, which shall come to any Port of the Emperor's Dominions, to trade or otherwise, and shall have on Board a Cargo, not proper for vending in the Place where they shall come, may depart with the same to any other Port of the Emperor's Dominions, and shall pay Duty but once for the same;

No Duties to be paid for Implements of War.

and that no Duty at all shall be paid for any Implements of War, such as Fire-Arms, Swords, and any Thing belonging to the Army; as also for Materials of all Kinds for Ship-building: And if any *English* Ship shall arrive at any of the Emperor's Ports, with any Merchandise destined for any other Part of the World, that no Duty shall be paid for such Merchandise, but such Ships shall depart with the same, without any Manner of Molestation. If any *English* Ships shall be thrown upon the

the Emperor's Coasts by Stress of Weather, or otherwise, the same shall be protected, and may safely depart without any ill Usage or Interruption: In like Manner shall be treated the Emperor's Ships, happening to be thus thrown on the Coast of *Great Britain*, or the Dominions thereto belonging.

Ships of either Party in Distress to be protected.

ARTICLE III.

That all the *English* Ships and Emperor's Ships, may pass and repass the Seas, without Hinderance, Interruption, or Molestation, from each other; nor shall any Money, Merchandise, or any Demand, be made or taken by the Ships of either Power from each other; and if any Subjects of any other Nation shall be on Board either of the *English* or the Emperor's Ships, they shall be safely protected by both Sides.

Ships of one Party to give no Interruption to the Ships of the other.

ARTICLE IV.

If the Emperor's Ships of War meet with any *English* Ships, and shall want to see their Passports, they are to send a Boat with Two Men of Fidelity, to peruse the said Passports, who are to return without any farther Trouble, and then both Sides are to proceed quietly on their respective Voyages; the same Usage shall be received by the Emperor's Merchant-Ships from the *English* Ships of War, who shall allow the Passports made out by the *English* Consul; and if the Consul shall not be present to make them, then the Passports made out by the *English* Merchants shall be good and valid.

Passports to be inspected by Two Persons of Fidelity.

What Passports shall be valid.

ARTICLE V.

If the *English* Ships of War, Privateers, or Letter of Marque Ships, shall take Prizes from any Nation with whom they shall be at War, they shall have Liberty to bring and dispose of the same in any

English allowed to sell their Prizes in the Emperor's Dominions.

any of the Emperor's Dominions, without any Duty or Charge whatever.

ARTICLE VI.

English Ships, driven by Storm or an Enemy, to be protected on the Emperor's Coasts.

If any *English* Ship shall, by Storm, or in flying from her Enemy, come upon the Emperor's Coasts, the same shall be safely protected, and nothing touched or taken away, but shall be under the Direction of the *English* Consul, who shall send the Goods and People where he shall think fit.

ARTICLE VIII.

English Subjects not to be compelled to sell their Goods under Value, or to carry Goods for others.

That no *English* Merchants, Captains of Ships, or other Person or Persons whatever, who are *English* Subjects, shall be forced to sell any of their Goods for less than their real Value; and that no Captain, Master, or Commander, of any *English* Ship, shall be compelled to carry any Goods or Merchandises for any Person or Persons whatever; nor shall any Sailor be forced away from any *English* Ship.

ARTICLE X.

Six Months for removal, in case of War.

If it shall happen that this Peace by any Means shall be broken, the Consul, and all other *English* Subjects, shall have Six Months Time to remove themselves, with their Families and Effects, to any Place they please, without Interruption; and all Debts owing to them shall be justly paid to them.

ARTICLE XIII.

Spaniards of *Gibraltar* and *Port-Mahon* to sail freely under *English* Colours.

That not any of the *Spanish*, whether Captains, Sailors, or other Persons, under the *English* Government, in *Gibraltar* or *Port-Mahon*, shall be taken or molested, sailing under *English* Colours, with Passports.

ARTICLE XV.

If any Ships of War shall be on the Emperor's Coasts, which are Enemies to the *English*, and any *English* Ship of War, or other *English* Ships, shall happen to be or arrive there also, they shall not in any Manner be hurt or engaged by their Enemy: And when such *English* Ships shall sail, their Enemy's Ships shall not sail under Forty Hours afterwards.

English Ships meeting the Ships of War of an Enemy on the *Morocco* Coasts, such Ships shall not sail 'till Forty Hours after the *English*.

Treaty of Peace between George II. *King of* Great Britain, *and the Emperor of* Morocco, *concluded* December 15, 1734.

1734.

ARTICLE II.

If any of the Emperor's Subjects shall be made Slaves, and escape to an *English* Ship of War, or to *Gibraltar*, *Port Mahon*, or any of the *English* Dominions, they shall be protected, and with all convenient Speed sent to their respective Homes: The like Treatment is to be given to the *English*, who shall be Slaves, and escape to any Part of the Emperor's Dominions.

Subjects of either Party to be protected by the other.

Treaty of Peace and Friendship between George II. *King of* Great Britain, *and the Emperor of* Morocco, *concluded at* Fez, January 15, 1750-51.

1750 51.

ARTICLE I.

For establishing Peace and Friendship, it is agreed and concluded, for firm and valid, both by Land and Sea, in all the Dominions of both Powers, that the *English* in general shall and may, now and all Times hereafter, enjoy and continue in Peace and Friendship with the Emperor and his Subjects, and

Peace and Friendship.

(286)

and be well used and respected by the Emperor's Subjects, agreeably to the Order and Commands of the Emperor.

ARTICLE II.

Rules concerning Passports.

That such a Number or Quantity of Passports as may be necessary, be transmitted to the Emperor, indented in such a Manner, as shall tally with the Passports which shall be received by the *English* Merchants in *England*; and if an *English* Ship of War meets with any Merchant-Ships belonging to the Emperor, such Merchant-Ships shall be obliged to produce and shew their Passports, given to them by the *English* Consul.

Passports to be shewed.

ARTICLE V.

Treaty of 1721 confirmed.

The Fifteen Articles of Peace made and concluded between King *George* the First and *Muli Ismael*, are hereby agreed to and confirmed by his Majesty King *George* the Second, as good and valid, and shall be faithfully kept and observed.

ALGIERS.

TO the End of p. 186. concluding with the Words, Treaty of 1686, add:

Which also, as well as the Treaties confirmed therein, and those of 1682 and 1691, are all comprehended in the Treaty entituled, *Articles of Peace and Commerce between* Great Britain *and* Algiers, concluded at Algiers, June 28, 1698; which is the same, Article for Article, with that of 1686: but, as the VIth Article is here, p. 183. omitted, we shall supply it, as follows, from the correspondent one of 1698.

ARTICLE VI.

That no Shipwreck belonging to the said King of *Great Britain*, or to any of his Majesty's Subjects, upon any of the Coasts belonging to *Algiers*, shall be made or become Prize; and that neither the Goods thereof shall be seized, nor the Men made Slaves; but that all the Subjects of *Algiers* shall do their best Endeavours to save the said Men and their Goods.

Subjects of Great Britain to be assisted in case of Shipwreck.

IN the Treaty of Peace, &c. 17th of *August*, 1700, After Article I. p. 179. insert the following Note.

The VIIIth Article of the Treaty of 1682, here referred to, is Word for Word the same as the VIIIth Article of the Treaty of 1686.

IN the Articles of Peace, &c. in *October* [20], 1716, after Article I. in p. 177 and 187. insert:

In the Years 1718 and 1723-4, two other Treaties were made with *Algiers*, but as they contain nothing more than general Confirmations of Peace, it is not thought necessary to insert them.

AFTER the Treaty in 1703, p. 188. insert the following

Treaty between Great Britain *and* Algiers, *concluded at* Algiers, March 18, 1729.

It is agreed and concluded, that from this Day and for ever forward, the Peace made by *Arthur Herbert*, Esq; [in 1682], then Admiral of his Majesty's Fleet, and Sir *William Soames*, Bart. Ambassador to the Grand Seignior in 1686; with the additional Articles agreed to with Capt. *Munden*

Former Treaties of Peace confirmed.

and

and Conful *Cole*, in 1700; and likewife the farther additional Articles agreed to with *George Byng*, Efq; Rear-Admiral of the Red Squadron of his Majefty's Fleet, in 1703; together with the additional Articles agreed to with Captain *Norbury*, Captain *Eaton*, and *Thomas Thomfon*, Efq; his Majefty's Conful, in 1716, be renewed and confirmed in this Treaty with *Philip Cavendifh*, Efq; Rear Admiral of the Red Squadron of his Majefty's Fleet, and be kept inviolable, between the Moft Serene King of *Great Britain*, and the Moft Illuftrious Lord the Dey, Bafhaw, and Governor, of the City and Kingdom of *Algiers*, and between all the Dominions and Subjects on either Side; and that the Ships and other Veffels, and Subjects and People of either Side, fhall not henceforth do to each other any Harm, Offence, or Injury, either in Word or Deed, but fhall treat one another with all poffible Refpect and Friendfhip.

Additional Article to the Treaties fubfifting between Great Britain *and* Algiers, *agreed to at* Algiers, June 3, 1751, *by the* Dey Mahomet *and His* Britannick *Majefty's Plenipotentiaries, the Hon.* Auguftus Keppel *and* Ambrofe Stannyford, *Efq;*

Packets and Exprefs-Boats bearing his *Britannick* Majefty's Commiffion, to be treated with the fame Refpect as Ships of War.

That all Packets or Exprefs-Boats, bearing his *Britannick* Majefty's Commiffion, which fhall be met by any of the Cruizers of *Algiers*, fhall be treated with the fame Refpect as his Majefty's Ships of War, and all due Refpect fhall be paid to his Majefty's Commiffion, and both at meeting and parting they fhall be treated as Friends. And if any of the Algerine Cruizers commit the leaft Fault or Violence againft them, the Captains or Raizes fo offending fhall, on their Arrival at Algiers, and proper complaint being made of them, be moft

feverely

severely punished, without admitting their Excuses.

TRIPOLI.

THE Treaty of Peace, &c. in 1716, is confirmed and comprehended in a subsequent Treaty of Peace and Commerce, concluded at *Tripoli*, September 19, 1751.

And the Articles I, III, IV, V, VII, VIII, XV, XVI, XVII, XIX, XX, XXIII, XXIV, and XXV, here inserted in p. 188 to p. 193. inclusive, from the former Treaty of 1716, are the same, almost Word for Word, with the Articles I, III, IV, V, VII, VIII, XV, XXII, XVI, XVIII, XXVIII, XXI, and XXX, in the latter Treaty of 1751, except in the following Places: *viz.*

In Article VIII. at the End, are added these Words,

Like as it is at *Algiers*.

Also in Article XV. to the End, are added these Words,

And the same is to be regarded in Favour of the Subjects of *Tripoli*.

Lastly, in Article XXV. instead of the Words, *And all other Matters*, &c. to the End of the Article, are inserted these Words,

And between the Dominions and Subjects of either Side: And our Faith shall be our Faith, and our Word our Word.

BESIDES these, there are in the Treaty of 1751, the following Articles relative to the Marine.

ARTICLE VI.

Shipswrecked on the Coasts of *Tripoli* not to become Prize, or be plundered, but to be assisted.

That no Shipwreck belonging to the said King of *Great Britain*, or to any of his Majesty's Subjects, upon any Part of the Coasts belonging to *Tripoli*, shall be made or become Prize; and that neither the Goods thereof shall be seized, nor the Men made Slaves; but that all the Subjects of *Tripoli* shall do their best Endeavours to save the said Men and their Goods.

ARTICLE XXIV.

British Subjects to enjoy all Privileges granted to the most favoured Nation.

That his *Britannick* Majesty's Subjects, over and above the Stipulations contained in this and all former Treaties, shall enjoy all the Privileges and Advantages which now are, or which hereafter may be, granted to any of the Subjects of the most favoured Nation.

ARTICLE XXV.

No Duty to be paid on the Importation of warlike Stores or Provisions into the Dominions of *Tripoli*.

That in case any of his said Majesty's Subjects, shall import into the said Kingdom of *Tripoli*, or into any of the Ports and Dominions thereunto belonging, any warlike Stores, as Cannon, Muskets, Pistols, Cannon Powder, 'or fine Powder, Brimstone, Bullets, Iron, Planks, and all Sorts of Timber fit for building Ships; Pitch, Tar, Rosin, Ropes, Cables, Masts, Blocks, Anchors, Sails, and

and all other Habiliments of War, as well by Sea as by Land; as alſo Proviſions, *viz.* Wheat, Barley, Beans, Oats, or the like, they ſhall not pay any Sort of Duty or Cuſtom whatever.

ARTICLE XXVI.

That new *Mediterranean* Paſſes ſhall be iſſued out, and given to his ſaid Majeſty's trading Subjects, with all convenient Speed; and that the Time for the Continuance of the old Paſſes for the Ships in the *Indies*, and remote Parts, ſhall be three Years; and for all other Ships and Veſſels one Year, to commence from the Delivery of the Counter-Tops of the new Paſſes at *Algiers*; of which his Majeſty's Conſul here ſhall give the earlieſt Notice to the Baſhaw and Government. And it is hereby expreſsly agreed and declared, that the ſaid new Paſſes ſhall, during the abovementioned Spaces of Time, of three Years and one Year, be of full and ſufficient Force and Effect, to protect all Ships and Veſſels of his ſaid Majeſty's Subjects, who ſhall be provided with the ſame. <small>Rules concerning Paſſes.</small>

ARTICLE XXVIII.

That if at any Time the Garriſons of *Gibraltar* or *Port-Mahon* ſhall be in Want of Proviſion, and ſhould ſend for the ſame to *Tripoli*, or any Part of the Dominions thereof, they ſhall, if it is to be had, be ſupplied with it at the Market Price. <small>*Gibraltar* and *Port Mahon* to be ſupplied with Proviſions at Market Price.</small>

ARTICLE XXIX.

Packets having Commissions from his Britannick Majesty, to be treated with the same Respect as Ships of War.

That all Packets, bearing his *Britannick* Majesty's Commission, which shall be met by any of the Cruizers of *Tripoli*, shall be treated with the same Respect as his Majesty's Ships of War, and all due Respect shall be paid to his Majesty's Commission; and both at meeting and parting they shall be treated as Friends; and if any of the *Tripoli* Cruizers commit the least Fault or Violence against them, the Captains or Raizes so offending, shall, on their Arrival at *Tripoli*, and on proper complaint being made of them, be most severely punished, without admitting their Excuses.

TUNIS.

THE Treaty of Peace at *Tunis*, *August* 30, 1716, is confirmed and comprehended in a subsequent Treaty at *Tunis*, *October* 19, 1751; and the Articles I, II, III, IV, X, XI, XII, XIII, XV, and XVIII, of the former, are the same in Substance with the correspondent Articles in the latter, except in the following Particulars, viz.

TO the beginning of Article I. prefix these Words;

That all former Grivances and Losses, and other Pretences, between both Parties, shall be void and of no Effect.

IN Article XV. inſtead of what follows the Words, *in any of his Majeſty's Ships of War*, inſert theſe Words:

There ſhall be ſhot off from the Caſtles of the *Goletta*, or other the neareſt Fortifications belonging to *Tunis*, a Number of Guns, according to Cuſtom, as a royal Salute to his *Britiſh* Majeſty's Colours; and the ſame Number ſhall be returned, in Anſwer thereto, by his Majeſty's Ships.

MOREOVER, beſides the Articles here inſerted from the Treaty of 1716, there are, in that of 1751, the following Articles relative to the Marine:

ARTICLE V.

That if any of the Ships of either Party ſhall, by Accident of foul Weather, or otherwiſe, be caſt away upon any of the Coaſts belonging to the other, the Perſons ſhall be free, and the Goods ſaved and delivered to the Proprietors thereof.

Ships of either Party being wrecked, the Men to be free, and the Goods reſtored.

ARTICLE VI.

That the *Engliſh* who do at preſent, or ſhall at any Time hereafter, inhabit in the City or Kingdom of *Tunis*, ſhall have free Liberty, when they pleaſe, to tranſport themſelves, with their Families and Children, although born in the Country.

The Engliſh at Tunis to have Liberty to remove themſelves and Families.

ARTICLE

ARTICLE XIV.

Slaves of Tunis, escaping on Board an English Man of War, to be free.

That if any Slave of *Tunis* should make his Escape from thence, and get on Board an *English* Man of War, the said Slave shall be free; and neither the *English*, nor any of his Nation, shall in any Manner be questioned about the same.

ARTICLE XIX.

Ships of Tunis not to assist the Enemies of Great Britain.

That in case a War should happen between his *Britannick* Majesty, and any other State or Nation whatever, the Ships of *Tunis* shall not in any Sort afford Assistance to the Enemies of his Majesty, or his Subjects.

ARTICLE XXII.

Ships of Gibraltar or Minorca, having proper Passes, and being properly manned, to be treated as English.

That whereas *Gibraltar* and the Island of *Minorca* do belong to his *Britannick* Majesty *, if it any Time any of the Cruizers of *Tunis* should meet with any Vessels of the said Places under *English* Colours, furnished with proper Passports, they shall be treated in all Respects like other *English* Ships, provided there is no more than one third Part of the Ship's Company, who are not Subjects of his said Majesty; for in such Case they the said Strangers shall be deemed as Prisoners: But it is allowed to embarque as many Merchants or Passengers as they see good, be they of what Nation soever: And if at any Time a *Tunis* Man of War shall take a Ship from their Enemies, on Board of which may happen to be any *English* Subjects, they shall be

* *Minorca* has been taken from us by the *French*, since the making of this Treaty, and is still in their Possession.

immediately

immediately released with all their Goods and Merchandise; provided always, that they are furnished with proper Passports: and this Article is to be observed reciprocally on the Parts of the *English*.

ARTICLE XXIII.

That if any *British* Ships or Vessels meet with any of the Ships or Vessels belonging to the State of *Tunis*, and there should be any Injury or Offence given by either Side, Justice being properly demanded, shall be immediately done, and the Aggressor be severely punished, without occasioning any Breach or War. Private Injuries to be redressed, without occasioning a War.

The Articles XXV. and XXVI. relate also to the Marine; but these being the same, *verbatim*, as the Articles XXVI. and XXIX. of the preceding Treaty with *Tripoli*, only changing the Word *Tripoli* for *Tunis*, we shall not swell the Book with a needless Repetition of them.

FINIS.

ERRATA.

IN the Contents, page ix. line 28. instead of *These not*, &c. read, *These two last Articles not*. P. 18. l. 3. *in Article VII. f.* stick upon the Sands, *r*. be cast on Shore. P. 34. l. 17. *instead of* for the, *r*. in. P. 38. l. *penult. from the Bottom, f.* three *r.* four. Ibid. to l. ult. add, 1483, and in the subsequent Treaties, 1549-50, 1559, and 1564. P. 57. l. 11. *In Article XXIV. dele the Word* Pots. P. 70. l. 1. f. Alliance *r.* Commerce. *And at the Head of the Article, insert* Article VII. P. 113. after l. 3. *insert at the Head of the Treaty the Word* Preamble. P. 137. l. 15. *after the Words* and by, *insert* his Father. Ibid. l. 17. *after the Words* enlarged to them, *insert*, by his Majestie of all Russia, and the Holy Patriarch. P. 180. l. 14. *f.* three *r.* eight. P. 298. *after* 1716, *add*, which also, together with the former, is comprehended in the Treaty of 1751.

Just Published,

In One Volume Octavo, Price 5 s.

The Third Edition of

A SURVEY of TRADE.

By *WILLIAM WOOD*, Esq;

Secretary to the Honble the Commissioners of His Majesty's Customs.

APPENDIX.

The Definitive Treaty between his Britannick Majesty, the Most Christian King, and the King of Spain, *concluded at* Paris 10 February 1763, *to which the King of* Portugal *acceded on the same Day.*

ARTICLE II.

THE treaties of *Westphalia* of 1648; those of *Madrid* between the crowns of *Great Britain* and *Spain* of 1667, and 1670; the treaties of peace of *Nimeguen* of 1678, and 1679; of *Ryswick* of 1697; those of peace and of commerce of *Utrecht* of 1713; that of *Bladen* of 1714; the treaty of the triple alliance of the *Hague* of 1717; that of the quadruple alliance of *London* of 1718; the treaty of peace of *Vienna* of 1738; the definitive treaty of *Aix la Chapelle* of 1748; and that of *Madrid*, between the crowns of *Great Britain* and *Spain*, of 1750; as well as the treaties between the crowns of *Spain* and *Portugal*, of the 13th of *February* 1668; of the 6th of *February* 1715; and of the 12th of *February* 1761; and that of the 11th of *April* 1713; between *France* and *Portugal*, with the guaranties of *Great Britain*; serve as a basis and foundation to the peace, and to the present treaty; and for this purpose they are all renewed and confirmed in the best form, as well as all the treaties in general, which subsisted between the high contracting parties before the war, as if they were inserted here word for word, so that they are to be exactly observed for the future in their whole tenor, and religiously executed on all sides, in all their points, which shall not be derogated from by the present treaty, notwithstanding all that may have been stipulated to the contrary by any of the high contracting parties: and all the said parties declare, that they will not suffer any privilege, favour, or indulgence, to subsist, contrary to the treaties above confirmed, except what shall have been agreed and stipulated by the present treaty.

ARTICLE IV.

His most Christian majesty renounces all pretensions which he has heretofore formed, or might form to *Nova Scotia*, or *Acadia*, in all its parts; and guaranties the whole of it, and with all its dependencies to the king of *Great Britain*. Moreover, his most Christian majesty cedes, and guaranties to his said *Britannick* majesty, in full right, *Canada*, with all its dependencies, as well as the island of *Cape Breton*, and all the other islands and coasts in the gulph and river of St. *Laurence*, and in general every thing that depends on the said countries, lands, islands, coasts, with the sovereignty, property, possession, and all rights acquired by treaty or otherwise, which the most Christian king, and the crown of *France*, have had, till now, over the said countries, islands, lands, places, coasts, and their inhabitants; so that the most Christian king cedes and makes over the whole to the said king, and to the crown of *Great Britain*, and that in the most ample manner and form, without restriction, and without any liberty to depart from the said cession and guaranty, under any pretence, or to disturb *Great Britain* in the possessions above-mentioned.

ARTICLE V.

The subjects of *France* shall have the liberty of fishing and drying on a part of the coasts of the island of *Newfoundland*, such as is specified in the 13th article of the treaty of *Utrecht*; which article is renewed and confirmed by the present treaty, (except what relates to the island of *Cape Breton*, as well as to the other islands and coasts in the mouth and in the gulph of St. *Laurence*) and his *Britannick* majesty consents to leave the subjects of the most Christian king, the liberty of fishing in the gulph of St. *Laurence*, on condition that the subjects of *France* do not exercise the said fishery, but at the distance of three leagues from all the coasts belonging to *Great Britain*, as well those of the continent, as those of

the

the iflands fituated in the faid gulph of St. *Laurence.* And as to what relates to the fifhery on the coaft of the ifland of *Cape Breton* out of the faid gulph, the fubjects of the moft Chriftian king fhall not be permitted to exercife the faid fifhery, but at the diftance of 15 leagues from the coafts of the ifland of *Cape Breton*; and the fifhery on the coafts of *Nova Scotia* or *Acadia*, and every where elfe out of the faid gulph, fhall remain on the foot of former treaties.

ARTICLE VI.

The king of *Great Britain* cedes the iflands of *St. Pierre* and *Miquelon*, in full right, to his moft Chriftian majefty, to ferve as a fhelter to the *French* fifhermen; and his faid Chriftian majefty engages not to fortify the faid iflands, to erect no building upon them, but merely for the convenience of the fifhery, and to keep upon them a guard of 50 men only for the police.

ARTICLE VII.

In order to re-eftablifh peace on folid and durable foundations, and to remove for ever all fubjects of difpute with regard to the limits of the *Britifh* and *French* territories on the continent of *America*, that for the future, the confines between the dominions of his *Britannick* majefty, and thofe of his moft Chriftian majefty in that part of the world, fhall be fixed irrevocably by a line drawn along the middle of the river *Miffifippi*, from its fource to the river *Iberville*, and from thence, by a line drawn along the middle of this river, and the lake *Maurepas* and *Ponchartrain*, to the fea; and for this purpofe, the moft Chriftian king cedes, in full right, and guaranties to his *Britannick* majefty, the river and port of the *Mobile*, and every thing which he poffeffes, or ought to poffefs, on the left fide the river *Miffifippi*, except the town of *New Orleans*, and the ifland in which it is fituated, fhall remain to *France*; provided that the river *Miffifippi* fhall be equally free, as well to the fubjects of *Great Britain*, as to thofe of *France*, in its whole breadth and length, from its fource to the fea, and exprefsly that part which is between the faid ifland of *New Orleans*,

Orleans, and the right bank of that river, as well as the passages both in and out of its mouth. It is further stipulated, that the vessels belonging to the subjects of either nation, shall not be stopped, visited or subjected to the payment of any duty whatsoever.

ARTICLE IX.

The most Christian king cedes and guaranties to his *Britannick* majesty, in full right, the islands of *Grenada* and of the *Grenadines*. And the partition of the islands called Neutral, is agreed and fixed, so that those of St. *Vincent*, *Dominica*, and *Tobago*, shall remain, in full right to *Great Britain*; and that that of St. *Lucia* shall be delivered to *France*, to enjoy the same likewise in full right; and the high contracting parties guaranty the partition so stipulated.

ARTICLE X.

His most Christian majesty cedes in full right, and guaranties to the king of *Great Britain* the river *Senegal*, with the forts and factories of St. *Lewis*, *Podor*, and *Galam*; and with all the rights and dependencies of the said river *Senegal*.

ARTICLE XVI.

The decision of the prizes made, in the time of peace, by the subjects of *Great Britain*, on the *Spaniards*, shall be referred to the courts of justice of the admiralty of *Great Britain*, conformably to the rules established among all nations, so that the validity of the said prizes, between the *British* and *Spanish* nations, shall be decided and judged according to the law of nations, and according to the treaties, in the courts of justice of the nation who shall have made the capture.

ARTICLE XVII.

His *Britannick* majesty shall cause to be demolished all the fortifications which his subjects shall have erected in the bay of *Honduras*, and other places of the territory of *Spain* in that part of the world, four months after the ratification of the present treaty: and his Catholic majesty

majesty shall not permit his *Britannick* majesty's subjects, or their workmen, to be disturbed or molested under any pretence whatsoever, in the said places, in their occupation of cutting, loading, and carrying away logwood: and for this purpose, they may build without hindrance, and occupy without interruption, the houses and magazines which are necessary for them, for their families, and for their effects: and his Catholic majesty assures to them, by this article, the full enjoyment of those advantages and powers on the *Spanish* coasts and territories, as above stipulated, immediately after the ratifications of the present treaty.

ARTICLE XVIII.

His Catholic majesty desists, as well for himself as for his successors, from all pretensions which he may have formed in favour of the *Guipuscoans*, and other his subjects, to the right of fishing in the neighbourhood of the island of *Newfoundland*.

ARTICLE XX.

His Catholic majesty cedes and guaranties, in full right, to his *Britannick* majesty, *Florida*, with Fort St. *Augustin*, and the bay of *Pensacola*, as well as all that *Spain* possesses on the continent of *North America*, to the east, or to the south-east of the river *Missisippi*; and in general, every thing that depends on the said countries and lands, with the sovereignty, property, possession, and all rights acquired by treaties and otherwise, which the Catholic king and the crown of *Spain* have had, till now, over the said countries, lands, places, and their inhabitants; so that the Catholic king cedes and makes over the whole to the said king, and to the crown of *Great Britain*, and that in the most ample manner and form.

Treaty of Commerce and Navigation between Great Britain *and* Ruffia, *concluded at St.* Petersburgh *the* 20*th day of* June 1766.

ARTICLE I.

THE peace, friendſhip, and good underſtanding, which have hitherto happily ſubſiſted between their majeſties of *Great Britain* and of all the *Ruſſias*, ſhall be ratified and confirmed by this treaty; ſo that from this time forward, and in all time coming, there ſhall be, between the crown of *Great Britain* on the one hand, and the crown of all the *Ruſſias* on the other, as alſo between the ſtates, countries, kingdoms, dominions, and territories, that are ſubject to them, a true, ſincere, firm, and perfect peace, friendſhip, and good underſtanding, which ſhall laſt for ever, and ſhall be inviolably obſerved, as well by ſea as by land, and on the freſh waters; and the ſubjects, people, and inhabitants on the one part and on the other, of what ſtate or condition ſoever they be, ſhall perform to each other all acts of kindneſs and aſſiſtance poſſible, and ſhall not do to one another any hurt or injury whatever.

ARTICLE II.

The ſubjects of the two high contracting powers ſhall have full liberty of navigation and commerce in all the ſtates ſituated in *Europe*, where navigation and commerce are permitted at preſent, or ſhall be permitted hereafter, by the high contracting parties, to any other nation.

ARTICLE III.

It is agreed, that the ſubjects of the two high contracting parties ſhall have leave to enter, trade, and remain with their ſhips, boats, and carriages, loaded or unloaded, in all the ports, places, and towns, where ſuch leave is granted to the ſubjects of any other nation; and the ſailors, paſſengers, and ſhips, as well *Britiſh* as *Ruſſian*, (though there ſhould be among their crews ſubjects of ſome other foreign nation) ſhall be received

and

and treated as the most favoured nation; and neither the sailors nor passengers shall be forced to enter, against their will, into the service of either of the two contracting powers, excepting, however, such of their subjects, as they may want for their own proper service; and if a domestic or sailor desert his service or his ship, he shall be restored. It is likewise agreed, that the subjects of the high contracting parties shall have leave to purchase, at the current price, all sorts of commodities of which they may stand in need, to repair and refit their ships, boats and carriages; to purchase all kinds of provisions for their present subsistence or their voyage; and to remain or depart at their pleasure, without lett or impediment, provided they conform to the laws and ordinances of the respective states of the high contracting parties where they may happen to be. In like manner the *Russian* ships that are navigating the sea, and are met by *English* ships, shall not be impeded in the course of their voyage, provided, in the *British* sea, they conform to the established practice; but, on the contrary, shall receive from them all kind of assistance, as well in the ports of the dominion of *Great Britain*, as in the open sea.

ARTICLE IV.

It is agreed, that the subjects of *Great Britain* shall be at liberty to bring, by water or by land, into all, or into such provinces of *Russia*, where freedom of trade is permitted to the subjects of any other nation, all sorts of merchandize or effects, the traffic or entry of which is not prohibited: and in like manner the subjects of *Russia* shall be at liberty to bring, buy, and sell freely, in all, or in such states of *Great Britain* where freedom of trade is permitted to the subjects of any other nation, all sorts of merchandize and effects, the traffic and entry of which is not prohibited; which is also to be equally understood of the manufactures and products of the *Asiatic* provinces, provided this is not actually forbid by some law at present in force in *Great Britain*; comprehending all sorts of merchandize and effects, which subjects of any other nation may buy there, and transport into other countries, particularly wrought gold and silver, excepting the current coin of *Great Britain*. And in order to preserve a just equality between the *Russian* and *British* merchants, with regard to the exportation of provisions and other commodities, it is further stipulated, that the subjects of *Russia* shall pay the same duties on exportation, that are paid by the *British* merchants on exporting the same effects from the ports of *Russia*; but then each of the high contracting parties shall reserve to itself the liberty of making, in the interior parts of its dominions, such particular arrangement as it shall find expedient for encouraging and extending its own navigation. The *Russian* merchants shall enjoy the same liberties and privileges as the *British* merchants of the *Russian* company enjoy; and, as the design of the two high contracting parties, and the intention of this treaty, is to facilitate the reciprocal commerce of their subjects, and to extend its limits and mutual advantages, it is agreed, that the *British* merchants, trading in the dominions of *Russia*, shall have liberty, in case of death, a pressing exigency, or absolute necessity, when there are no other means of procuring money, or in case of a bankruptcy, to dispose of their effects, whether of *Russian* or foreign merchandize, in such manner as the persons concerned shall find most advantageous. The same thing shall be observed with regard to the *Russian* merchants in the dominions of *Great Britain*. All which, however, is to be understood with this restriction, that every sort of permission, on the one side and on the other, specified in this article, shall not be in any thing contrary to the laws of the country; and the *British*, as well as the *Russian* merchants, and their factors, shall punctually conform to the rights, statutes, and ordinances of the country where they trade, in order to prevent all kind of fraud and imposition. It is for this reason, that the decision of such events, happening to the *British* compting-houses in *Russia*, shall be submitted at *Petersburgh*, to the college of commerce, and in other towns where there

there is no college of commerce, to the tribunals that have the cognizance of commercial affairs.

ARTICLE V.

It is agreed, that the subjects of *Great Britain*, if they have no rixdollars to pay the customs or other duties for the merchandize which they import or export, shall be allowed to pay them in other foreign coin of a known name and established value, equal to that of the rixdollar, or in the current coin of *Russia*, the rixdollar valued at a hundred and twenty-five copecks (or pennies.)

ARTICLE VI.

All possible assistance and dispatch shall be given to the loading and unloading of ships, as well for the importation as the exportation of commodities, according to the regulations on that head established; and they shall not be in any manner detained, under the penalties denounced in the said regulations. In like manner, if the subjects of *Great Britain* make contracts with any chancery or college whatever, to deliver certain commodities or effects, upon notifying that such commodities are ready to be delivered, and after they shall have been actually delivered at the time specified in these contracts, they shall be received, and immediately thereupon the accounts shall be settled and cleared between the said college or chancery, and the *British* merchants; at the time fixed in the said contracts. The same conduct shall be observed towards the *Russian* merchants in the dominions of *Great Britain*.

ARTICLE VII.

It is agreed, that the subjects of *Great Britain* may, in all the towns and places of *Russia*, where freedom of trade is permitted to any other nation, pay for the commodities they purchase in the same current coin of *Russia*, which they take for the commodities they sell, unless in their contracts they have stipulated the contrary; and this ought to be equally understood of *Russian* commodities in the dominions of *Great Britain*.

ARTICLE VIII.

In the places where embarkations are ordinarily made, permission shall be granted to the subjects of the high contracting parties to load their ships and carriages with, and transport by water or by land all such sorts of commodities as they shall have purchased, (with an exception, however, of those whose exportation is prohibited) upon paying the customs, provided these ships and carriages conform to the laws.

ARTICLE IX.

The subjects of the high contracting parties shall pay no greater duty for the importation or exportation of their commodities, than is paid by the subjects of other nations. Nevertheless, to prevent on both sides the defrauding of the customs, if it should be discovered that commodities have been entered clandestinely, and without paying the customs, they shall be confiscated; but, besides that, no other punishment shall be inflicted upon the merchants on either side.

ARTICLE X.

Permission shall be granted to the subjects of the two contracting parties to go, come, and trade freely with those states with which one or other of the parties shall at that time, or at any future period, be engaged in war, provided they do not carry military stores to the enemy. From this permission, however, are excepted places actually blocked up, or besieged, as well by sea as by land; but, at all other times, and with the single exception of military stores, the abovesaid subjects may transport to these places all sorts of commodities, as well as passengers, without the least impediment. With regard to the searching of merchant ships, men of war and privateers shall behave as favourably as the reason of the war, at that time existing, can possibly permit towards the most friendly powers that shall remain neuter; observing, as far as may be, the principles and maxims of the law of nations, that are generally acknowledged.

ARTICLE XI.

All cannon, mortars, muſkets, piſtols, bombs, grenades, bullets, balls, fuſees, flint-ſtones, matches, powder, ſaltpetre, ſulphur, breaſt-plates, pikes, ſwords, belts, cartouch-bags, ſaddles and bridles, beyond the quantity that may be neceſſary for the uſe of the ſhip, or beyond what every man ſerving on board the ſhip, and every paſſenger ought to have, ſhall be accounted ammunition or military ſtores; and, if found, ſhall be confiſcated, according to law, as contraband goods, or prohibited commodities; but neither the ſhips nor paſſengers, nor the other commodities found at the ſame time, ſhall be detained, or hindered to proſecute their voyage.

ARTICLE XII.

If, what God forbid! the peace ſhould come to be broke between the two high contracting parties, the perſons, ſhips, and commodities, ſhall not be detained or confiſcated; but they ſhall be allowed, at leaſt, the ſpace of one year, to ſell, diſpoſe, or carry off their effects, and to retire wherever they pleaſe; a ſtipulation that is to be equally underſtood of all thoſe who ſhall be in the ſea or land ſervice: and they ſhall farther be permitted, either at or before their departure, to conſign the effects which they ſhall not as yet have diſpoſed of, as well as the debts that ſhall be due to them, to ſuch perſons as they ſhall think proper, in order to diſpoſe of them according to their deſire, and for their benefit; which debts the debtors ſhall be obliged to pay in the ſame manner as if no ſuch rupture had happened.

ARTICLE XIII.

In caſe of a ſhipwreck happening in any place belonging to one or other of the high contracting parties, not only ſhall all kind of aſſiſtance be given to the unhappy ſufferers, and no ſort of violence ſhall be offered to them; but even the effects which they ſhall have ſaved themſelves, or which they ſhall have thrown overboard into the ſea, ſhall not be concealed, with-held,

or

or damaged, under any pretext whatfoever: on the contrary, the abovefaid effects and commodities fhall be preferved and reftored to them, upon their giving a moderate recompence to thofe who fhall have affifted them in faving their lives, their fhips, and their commodities.

ARTICLE XIV.

Permiffion fhall be granted to *Britifh* merchants to build, buy, fell, and hire houfes in all the territories and towns of *Ruffia*, excepting, however, with regard to the permiffion of building and buying houfes in thofe towns of *Ruffia*, which have particular rights of burgherfhip and privileges inconfiftent with fuch indulgence; and it is exprefsly fpecified, that at St. *Peterfburg, Mofcow*, and *Archangel*, the houfes which the *Britifh* merchants fhall buy, or caufe to be built, fhall be exempt from all quartering of foldiers, as long as they fhall belong to them, and fhall be inhabited by them; but, with regard to the houfes which they fhall hire or let, thefe fhall be fubject to all the ufual charges of the town; the tenant and landlord fettling that matter between them. As to every other town of *Ruffia*, the houfes which they fhall purchafe, or caufe to be built, in the fame manner as thofe which they fhall hire or let, fhall not be exempted from the quartering of foldiers. Permiffion fhall likewife be granted to *Ruffian* merchants to build, buy, fell, and let houfes in *Great Britain* and *Ireland*, in the fame manner as is done by the fubjects of the moft favoured nations. They fhall enjoy the free exercife of the *Greek* religion in their houfes, or in fuch places as are deftined for that purpofe; and in like manner the *Britifh* merchants fhall enjoy the free exercife of the proteftant religion. The fubjects of either power, eftablifhed in *Ruffia* or in *Great Britain*, fhall have power to difpofe of their eftates, and to leave them by will to whomfoever they think proper, following the cuftom and laws of their own proper country.

ARTICLE XV.

Paſſports ſhall be granted to all *Britiſh* ſubjects, who deſire to quit the dominions of *Ruſſia*, two months after they ſhall have ſignified their deſign of departing, without obliging them to give ſecurity; and if, in that time, there appear no juſt cauſe for detaining them, they ſhall be allowed to go; nor ſhall they be obliged to apply for that purpoſe, to any other quarter than to the college of commerce, or to that which may hereafter be eſtabliſhed in its place. The ſame eaſy methods of departing ſhall, upon like occaſions, and agreeable to the cuſtom of the country, be granted to *Ruſſian* merchants, who want to quit the dominions of *Great Britain*.

ARTICLE XVI.

Britiſh merchants, who ſhall hire or employ domeſtics, ſhall, in this particular, be obliged to conform themſelves to the laws of this empire. And *Ruſſian* merchants ſhall be equally obliged to do the ſame in *Great Britain*.

ARTICLE XVII.

In all law-ſuits and other proceedings, the *Britiſh* merchants ſhall be amenable only to the college of commerce, or to that which ſhall hereafter be eſtabliſhed for the adminiſtration of juſtice between merchants. But, if it ſhould happen that the *Britiſh* merchants ſhould have law-ſuits in any place at a diſtance from the above-mentioned college of commerce, both they and the adverſe party ſhall prefer their complaints to the magiſtrate of the ſaid towns, with this proviſo, however, that the *Britiſh* merchants ſhall have the right to appeal from the ſentence of the magiſtrate, and to demand that of the college of commerce, if they find themſelves aggrieved. The *Ruſſian* merchants in the dominions of *Great Britain*, ſhall, in their turn, have the ſame protection and juſtice, which, according to the laws of that kingdom, are granted to other foreign merchants, and ſhall be treated as the ſubjects of the moſt favoured nation.

ARTICLE XVIII.

The *British* merchants in *Russia*, and the *Russian* merchants in *Great Britain*, shall not be obliged to shew their books or papers to any person whatever, unless it be to make proof in the course of justice; still less shall the said books or papers be taken or detained from them. If, however, the case should happen, that any *British* merchant becomes bankrupt, he shall be amenable at St. *Petersburgh* to the college of commerce, or to that which shall hereafter be established for the administration of justice in mercantile affairs, and in other remote towns, to the magistrate of the place; and he shall be proceeded against according to the laws that are or shall be made for this purpose. Nevertheless, if the *British* merchants, without becoming bankrupts, refuse to pay their debts, whether to the treasury of her Imperial majesty, or to individuals, it shall be lawful to lay an arrest upon part of their effects equivalent to their debts; and in case these effects should not be sufficient for discharging such debts, they may themselves be arrested and detained in custody, until such time as the greater part of their creditors, as well with respect to number, as to the value of their respective demands, have consented to their enlargement. With regard to their effects laid under arrest, they shall remain as a deposit in the hands of those who shall be named and duly authorised for that purpose, by the greater part of their creditors, as is above specified: which delegates shall be obliged to appraise the effects as soon as possible, and to make a just and fair distribution of them to all the creditors, in proportion to their respective demands. The same procedure shall, in the like cases, be observed towards the *Russian* merchants in the dominions of *Great Britain*, and they shall be there protected agreeably to the regulations made in the preceding article.

ARTICLE XIX.

In case of complaints and law-suits, three persons of fair and unblemished character among the foreign merchants, shall, with a proper regard to circumstances, be
named

named by the college of commerce, and where there is no such college, by the magistrate, to examine the books and papers of the parties; and the report they shall make to the college of commerce, or to the magistrate, of what they shall find in the said books or papers, shall be held a good proof.

ARTICLE XX.

The commissioners of the customs shall have the charge of examining the servants or clerks of the *Russian* merchants, when they cause their goods to be entered, whether they have, for that effect, the orders or full powers of the masters; and if they have not such, they shall not be credited. The same conduct shall be observed towards the servants of the *British* merchants. And when the said servants, having the orders or full powers of their masters, shall cause their goods to be entered on account of their masters, these last shall be as responsible as if they themselves had caused them to be entered. All the *Russian* servants employed in the shops shall likewise be registered, and their masters shall answer for them in the affairs of trade, and in the bargains which they make in their name.

ARTICLE XXI.

In case the *Russian* merchants, who are indebted to the *British* merchants, withdraw from the places of their abode to other parts or districts, the college of commerce, after complaints shall have been made to them on the subject, and proofs of the debts have been adduced, shall cite them three times, allowing them a sufficient space to appear in person; and if they do not appear within the term prescribed, the said college shall condemn them, and send, at the expence of the plaintiff, an express to the governors and waywodes, with orders to put the sentence in execution, and thus shall oblige the debtors to pay the sums specified.

ARTICLE XXII.

The brokerage shall be settled with justice; and the brokers shall be responsible for the quality of the goods and fraudulent package, and shall be obliged, after sufficient proofs, produced against them, to make up the losses to which they have given occasion.

ARTICLE XXIII.

A regulation shall be made to prevent the abuses that may be committed in the package of leather, hemp and flax; and if any dispute happen between the buyer and the seller, concerning the weight or the tare, the commissioners of the customs shall determine it according to equity.

ARTICLE XXIV.

In order the more effectually to encourage and promote the trade of *Great Britain*, it is agreed, that for the future, the *English* woollen cloths, hereafter specified, shall not pay any greater duties on entry, than are settled in this article, viz. *English* cloth, for the use of the soldiery, shall pay (in rixdollars) only two copecs (or pennies) for every arsheen, (or $71\frac{1}{4}$ yards) as a duty on entry; coarse cloth of the county of *York*, known in the *Russian* tariff by the name of Costrogy, shall only pay two copecs for every arsheen; broad flannel shall only pay one copec per arsheen; narrow flannel shall only pay three-fourths of a copec per arsheen, all as duties on entry. And in every thing that regards the imposts and duties payable on the importation or exportation of commodities in general, the subjects of *Great Britain* shall be always considered and treated as the most favoured nation.

ARTICLE XXV.

The peace, friendship, and good understanding, shall continue for ever between the high contracting parties; and as it is customary to fix a certain term to the duration of treaties of commerce, the above-mentioned high contracting parties have agreed, that this treaty shall continue for twenty years, counting from the day of signing; and after the expiration of that term, they may agree upon the means to renew and prolong it.

www.ingramcontent.com/pod-product-compliance
Lightning Source LLC
Chambersburg PA
CBHW051248300426
44114CB00011B/932